The Encyclopedia of
JAPANESE
POP
CULTURE

The Encyclopedia of
JAPANESE
POP
CULTURE

By Mark Schilling

Earlier versions of the articles on Rie Miyazawa, Doraemon, Hayao Miyazaki, Tora-san, *yakuza* movies, and Hayao Miyazaki appeared in *The Japan Quarterly*; on *pachinko*, Tetsuya Komoro, and Seiko Matsuda in *The Japan Times*; on karaoke and Downtown in *Mangajin*. Credits and sources for illustrations appearing on the cover and title page are provided on page 6; all others appear on pages 341–43.

Weatherhill
an imprint of Shambhala Publications, Inc.
Horticultural Hall
300 Massachusetts Avenue
Boston, Massachusetts 02115
www.shambhala.com

First edition, 1997
Fifth printing, 2005

Printed in U.S.A.
⊗ This edition is printed on acid-free paper that meets the American National Standards Institute Z39.48 Standard.
Distributed in the United States by Random House, Inc.,
and in Canada by Random House of Canada Ltd

Library of Congress Cataloging-in-Publication Data
   Schilling, Mark, 1949–
      The encyclopedia of Japanese pop culture / Mark Schilling. —1st ed.
        p.   cm.
      Includes bibliographical references and index.
      ISBN 0-8348-0380-1 (pbk. : alk. paper)
      1. Popular culture—Japan. 2. Japan—Civilization—1945–
   I. Title.
      DS822.5.S3 1997
      952.04—dc21
                                                97-3728
                                                    CIP

To Bob Huston and Mike Druckenmiller,
for giving me reasons to write.

CONTENTS

INTRODUCTION

Japan, the Japanese are fond of lamenting, has a strong presence in the global economy, but no international face. Westerners, they know, would find it far easier to identify three Japanese cars in a parking lot than three former Japanese prime ministers in a crowded room.

Even Western Japanophiles are forever paying homage to the same few cultural icons. Movie folk visiting Japan from Europe or Hollywood are often effusive in their praise of Japanese films, but their pantheon of Japanese directors rarely includes anyone but the eternal triumvirate of Kurosawa, Ozu, and Mizoguchi.

In the case of pop culture, the fog is even thicker. Few Westerners could name a single Japanese rock singer, comedian, or cartoonist. Many have seen Japanese TV programs while never realizing they originally came from Tokyo, not Hollywood. The Power Rangers, as any five-year-old in Cleveland can tell you, are All-American heroes. The show's Japanese brand of chop-socky action remains, but its original Japanese face has been carefully excised.

And yet postwar Japanese pop culture has been extraordinarily fertile, vibrant, and commercially successful, despite the well-known Japanese eagerness to embrace things Western. In the aftermath of the war, with their traditional culture devastated and often actively suppressed, Japanese adopted as much of their conqueror's popular culture as they could find or afford. When Japanese films or TV programs look back at the chaotic early postwar days, the music on the soundtrack is often Glenn Miller swing tunes, the movies in the theater posters are often from Hollywood.

But while yearning after the symbols of the American lifestyle—from Coca Cola and Mickey Mouse to American-sized refrigerators and automobiles—Japanese also began creating their own postwar pop culture that, while evidencing American and other foreign influences, was definitely different from its models. Cartoonist Osamu Tezuka was a fervent admirer of Walt Disney, but he took his own work in new, more serious direction and, in the process, made it possible for *manga,* Japan's unique contribution to comic art, to escape the kiddy ghetto and become a major force in the nation's cultural life.

While Tezuka was first winning fame for his *manga* in the late forties, a child singer named Hibari Misora was lifting spirits with an uptempo jazz tune titled "Kappa Boogie-Woogie." But as she matured into the country's most popular female pop singer, Hibari became known as the foremost interpreter of *enka,* ballads about loneliness and loss that, though based on Western music, are regarded as quintessentially Japanese.

This pattern of initial Western influence followed by the development of "purely" Japanese forms has been repeated again and again, not only in individual careers but throughout the culture. After the start of television broadcasts in 1953, many of the programs were modified versions of American originals. Public broadcaster NHK repackaged *I've Got a Secret* and *What's My Line* as *Watashi no Himitsu* (My Secret). Producers, however, were soon creating their own game shows that not only beat the foreign imitations in the ratings but added distinctly Japanese twists to the format.

Also, the growth in the number of nationwide networks from the original two to the current six as television ownership soared in the late fifties and early sixties generated a huge new demand for programming that local producers could not fill, a demand mainly satisfied by U.S. imports. Shows like *Laramie, Ben Casey, Combat,* and *Bewitched* found large, appreciative audiences. Today

middle-aged Japanese still hum the theme to *Rawhide* and watch Vic Morrow refight World War II on rented video cassettes.

But as the networks began seducing big-name talent away from the movies, producing better shows, and creating their own stars, the imports lost their ratings luster. By the 1970s imported programs, other than movies, had largely vanished from prime time. Japan was, notoriously, the only major television market in the world where *Dallas* failed to become a hit. Japanese viewers wanted Japanese programs—and little else.

The Japanese pop-music industry has also successfully absorbed the Western influences, including the mid-fifties fad for rock 'n' roll. Though preferences soon shifted from raucous rockabilly to the softer, sweeter sounds of American and European pop balladeers, rock proved to be a hardy transplant. Following the 1965 Japan tour of the Ventures, hundreds of bands formed and began playing *ereki* (electric) music.

But as earnestly as some Japanese musicians tried to imitate the Ventures, Beatles, and other foreign rock groups, other bands, both amateur and professional, began melding Japanese lyrics with Western sounds to create a domestic brand of rock that may not have pleased purists but won millions of fans during what came to be known as the Group Sounds era.

Though many Western pop acts, from

the Bay City Rollers to Michael Jackson, mounted successful assaults on the Japanese music market over the next three decades, local artists continued to dominate the charts. Of the all-time top fifty singles in Japan, as complied by *Oricon* magazine to May 1994, only one is by a foreigner: not Mick Jagger or Madonna, but Daniel Boone with "Beautiful Sunday," which was used as the theme song for a 1976 TBS morning show. That domination has continued through the middle of the decade. Of the 566.5 billion yen in recorded music sales in 1995, Japanese music accounted for 72.2 percent, and all of the year's top ten singles and albums were by Japanese artists.

The Japanese movie industry has had by far the hardest time fending off the foreign, or more specifically, Hollywood, competition. Since its all-time peak in 1958, when admissions reached 1.1 billion, the industry has steadily declined, battered by the rise of television in 1960s, the emergence of computer games in the 1970s, and the steady growth in the popularity of Hollywood films throughout the period. By 1995 the market share of Japanese films had shrunk to thirty-seven percent and only three of the year's top-ten grossing films were Japanese—both postwar lows.

But compared with its counterparts in Europe, which have been decimated by Hollywood, the Japanese film industry is still holding its own quite well. One indication is the success of Hayao Miyazaki and Isao Takahata, whose animated films had gone head-to-head with Disney rivals at the local box office five straight times by 1995 and beaten them every time. But though a growing number of foreign fans praise them for the beauty of their animation and the psychological realism of their characters, the products of Miyazaki and Takahata's Studio Ghibli are created for the domestic audience.

Despite its domination of the local market, Japanese pop culture often gets no respect, for good reason. It is frequently banal, vulgar, derivative, and utterly commercialized. Television, with its legions of untalented talents mugging on lowest-common-denominator quiz and variety shows, is perhaps the worst offender, but the music, movie, and *manga* industries are little better. Often the only aim is to extract the maximum amount of yen from the product while paying minimal attention to the quality of the content, aesthetic or moral.

Sex and violence sells, so rack after rack of *manga* in the neighborhood convenience stores depict rapes, beatings, and killings in graphic detail. Bathroom humor gets laughs, so comics appear on prime-time shows in stained undershorts or wearing giant foam-rubber turds on their heads. Charm is considered more marketable than talent, so cute teenagers who can barely carry a tune find themselves singing on network television and recording CDs.

Having said that, this critic must also admit that the same comics who clown boorishly on one show can surprise with their improvisational agility on another, that some *manga* are amusing and enlightening, and that many Japanese pop musicians are technically accomplished. A few can even rock.

Many writers for the English-language media in Japan would rather not admit it, however. Assuming that pop-culture phenomena appealing to the mass audience are beneath contempt and can therefore be safely ignored, they prefer to discover and promote artists on the commercial fringe, be they traditionalists, avant-gardists, or simple self-publicists. Their readers, consequently, learn a great deal about Butoh dancers and *taiko* drummers whose audiences number in the hundreds, and virtually nothing about pop singers and groups who fill stadiums. It is as though Japanese in living in Los Angeles were, after years of reading nothing but music reviews in the local Japanese-language paper, to be thoroughly acquainted with the oeuvre of Patti Smith and Henry Rollins, but have only a fleeting acquaintance with the Grateful Dead, Madonna, and Michael Jackson.

This is not to argue against writing about *taiko* drummers, only to propose that an examination of the most successful and representative of Japan's postwar pop-culture phenomena might yield insights into the character of modern Japan.

That, in brief, is the aim this book. It is an encyclopedia rather than a survey, with more articles about people than products, because I wanted to bring the individual faces of Japanese pop culture into sharper focus. At the same time, I tried to describe why these faces were important and place them in their cultural context, to give my sketches background as well as foreground. Otherwise, they would have little more meaning for the foreign reader than the faces in junk-shop postcards.

In choosing subjects, I used objective criteria—most sales, longest run, highest ratings—but often the choice to include one subject and not another came down to my own feeling (or prejudice, if you will) about what was important and what was not. The book could have easily contained twice as many articles, but I tried to put more emphasis on depth than breadth of coverage, both to avoid boring the specialist with the obvious and confusing the nonspecialist with a welter of unfamiliar names.

The result, I realized as I went along, was not only a super Web site in print, with the cross references serving as links, but a graphic illustration of the intertwined nature of Japanese pop culture in the late twentieth century. *Manga* become TV shows, which in turn become movies. Songs become hits by being used as themes on TV dramas. TV talents boost their muscial careers by pitching products on TV commercials.

And everyone who is anyone in Japan's tight-knit pop-culture world seems to know everyone else. The anchor of the highest-rated news program was once the co-host on a music show with the woman who wrote the biggest-ever bestseller. The biggest young male movie star of the 1950s appeared in a 1970s TV cop show that launched the career of the biggest young male movie star of the 1980s. And all of the biggest names in pop music sing on the same TV musical extravaganza every New Year's Eve, just as they've been doing for more than four decades.

The composite portrait that emerges from these sketches also illustrates the closeness of the links between Japanese pop culture and its Western, particularly American, equivalents. In addition to the individuals influenced by Western models and the fads imported wholesale from abroad, from 1950s biker fashions to 1990s rap, are the many musicians, actors, and other pop-culture figures who made the journey to the West themselves. The founder of the most successful talent agency of the past three decades studied at a Los Angeles high school and claims that his show-business strategy was inspired by Alice Cooper. The most suc-

cessful record producer of the 1990s, whose songs have dominated the decade's top ten, spent a mid-career year in London studying at the source of 1980s Britpop.

The links between Japanese and Western pop cultures run the other way as well. Although many of the attempts to make an impression on Western audiences have been brief (Kyu Sakamoto's one-shot hit with "Sukiyaki"; Yusaku Matsuda's Hollywood career) or out-and-out failures (Seiko Matsuda's English-language records, Haruki Kadokawa's "international" movies), others have succeeded, sometimes spectacularly. One has only to look at the international popularity of the Power Rangers, the enormous overseas sales of Katsuhiro Otomo's *manga* series *Akira*, or the vogue among American teenagers for Sanrio's cutesy character goods. Though not all of these links will continue to thrive, the evidence of the past few years suggests that the traditional Western resistance to the face of Japanese pop culture is weakening.

My hope is that this book makes the main features of that face more recognizable and distinct. When this composite portrait is done, it will look in many ways distinctly, even exotically, Japanese, but in many other ways, quite familiar. Popular culture everywhere speaks to much the same desires and needs. Despite its claims to uniqueness, Japan's is no exception.

Much of this book is a critical memoir of movies seen, music heard, and TV programs watched over the past twenty-two years, since I arrived in Tokyo. Also, thanks to the Japanese love of revisiting their own postwar popular culture, I have been able to catch most of what I missed the first time around. I have seen rockabilly singers from the 1950s on TV, heard the early *enka* of Hibari Misora at *karaoke* clubs and watched the Waka Daisho films of Yuzo Kayama on video.

But writing this book required far more than downloading personal memories and opinions onto the computer screen. Some of the information came from my work as a writer on film for *Screen International,* on television for *Television Business International,* and on popular culture for a variety of publications. Some of it came from digging in the used book stores in Jimbocho, the attic of the nation. Some of it came from the flood of nostalgic books and magazines published to mark the fiftieth anniversary since the end of World War II. Some of it even came from academic sources, though not many scholars have plumbed the mysteries of Seiko Matsuda's appeal.

Without the help of many people I could not have made my deadline, while preserving a few fragments of health and sanity. I would especially like to thank the staff at the library of the Foreign Correspondents' Club of Japan, who tirelessly answered my queries and cheerfully dug out dusty clip files. I would also like to express my appreciation to Mark Schreiber, Bill Marsh, and Clyde Newton for critiquing several of the articles and catching egregious errors and omissions.

Among others who helped along the way with illustrations and advice were Yoshie Yamaguchi, Andy Adams, Toru Okuyama, Steve McClure, Miyoko Ogawa, and the members of JAK. Although several editors brought their own brands of polish to the articles, including Pam Noda, Ron Rhodes, Mark Thompson, and Virginia Murray, the one who shepherded this project from beginning to end, with unfailing energy, enthusiasm, and perspicacity, was Jeffrey Hunter of Weatherhill. *Arigato* and *otsukaresan.*

Finally, I would like to thank my wife Yuko for putting up with this project over the past two years, as well as helping me with more name readings than either of us would care to remember, and to my two children, Ray and Lisa, for introducing me to the delights of Doraemon, Ultraman, Downtown, and Namie Amuro, to name only a few. It may be an authorial cliché to say that I couldn't have written the book without their support, but it happens to be the truth.

NOTES ON NOMENCLATURE

The business of making and selling pop culture is much the same in Japan as it is in the West. There are, however, differences that may be confusing to readers who assume that Japanese and Americans calculate ratings or box-office figures the same way or wonder why there are no articles about wacky late-night infomercials on cable TV.

First, ratings. During the period covered by this book, Japanese ratings agencies have used a household, not an individual, ratings system. For more than two decades, however, two- and even three-set households have been the norm in Japan and the rest of the developed world, making a household rating system, which monitors only whether a set is on, not who is watching it, increasingly meaningless. Accordingly, ratings agencies in the West long ago switched to individual systems.

Although Japanese advertising agencies and sponsors have been agitating for the introduction of a similar system for years, television networks, afraid of a drop in ratings and consequent loss of revenues, have resisted. This resistance is now eroding, but for the programs mentioned in this book, household ratings are the measure of success.

Another difference is that, since the founding of TV Tokyo—the youngest of the major networks—in 1964, television in Japan has essentially meant the five commercial networks and public broadcaster NHK. The other four commercial nets are Asahi National Broadcasting Co., Ltd. (TV Asahi), The Fuji Television Network (Fuji TV), Nippon Television Network (NTV), and Tokyo Broadcasting System Inc. (TBS). The official English name of NHK is Japan Broadcasting Corporation, though its initials stand for Nippon Hoso Kyokai.

Although cable and satellite channels have proliferated in the 1990s, their viewership has remained small—by 1996 only three million of the nation's forty-two million TV households subscribed to multichannel cable—and cable's impact on the market share of the big six has been tiny. The two leading ratings services do not even bother to measure the ratings of cable and satellite shows. This will soon change—by the end of the decade Japan may have as many as four hundred digital satellite channels on the air—but in the period covered by this book, cable and satellite programs have not even been a blip on the pop culture radar screen.

What all this means in practice is that the top ten Japanese programs of 1996 will have more impressive rating numbers than the top ten U.S. shows of the same year. As a general rule of thumb, a Japanese show whose ratings are in the twenties is considered a hit, and in the thirties and above, a superhit.

Movie box-office figures are another potential source of confusion. In the United States, the common measure of a hit or flop is box-office gross: i.e, the total amount paid by the public to an exhibitor for tickets to a given movie. In Japan, however, the preferred measure is distributor revenues, or the cut of the box office receipts owed by the exhibitor to the film's distributor.

A rough rule of thumb is that distributor revenues are one-half of gross. In Japan a film with distributor revenues of one billion yen or more is considered a hit, five billion yen or more a blockbuster. At an exchange rate of one hundred yen to one dollar, these figures may not sound like much—ten million dollars would not even pay for the ad campaign of a big-budget Hollywood movie and fifty million dollars is now the average production budget for a major studio release—but converted to gross, they are more impressive. With a population of one hundred twenty-five million and the highest ticket prices anywhere—1,800 yen for an adult ticket in 1996—Japan has long been the world's second-largest movie market, after the United States.

In describing record sales, the text makes occasional references to *Oricon*. This is the Japanese equivalent to *Billboard,* a weekly music-industry magazine that, since January 1968, has been publishing hit charts.

In rendering the titles of Japanese films, television shows, and pop songs into English, I have aimed to be reader friendly by leaving the many English words sprinkled about in them in English spelling; hence "drama" instead of *"dorama,"* "exciting" instead of *"ekusaitingu,"* and Yumi Matsutoya's hit album is *Cobalt Hour* instead of *Kobaruto Awaa.* Translations of titles are given in parentheses. When there is an "official" English title, I have used it, even if it doesn't reflect the Japanese very accurately; otherwise, the title is translated literally. Japanese words that may not be known to most English readers are set in italic. Japanese names are written in Western order, given name followed by family name, consistent with the convention adopted by *The New York Times* and other publications for educated but nonspecialist readers.

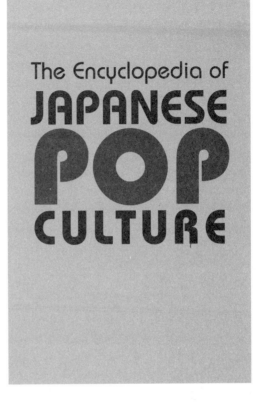

The Encyclopedia of
JAPANESE
POP
CULTURE

ANIMAL FRIENDS

If Japan is the country of the cute, with adorable characters and logos frolicking across a myriad of surfaces, from toys for tots to posters for politicians, it is also the land of the boom, or *buumu*, where the new, the different, or the simply bizarre suddenly becomes a universal obsession and just as quickly falls from favor, yet another victim of media overkill.

These strands of the national psyche come together in the Japanese attitude toward the animals—including elephants, pandas, koalas, cats, and frilled lizards—that have become the objects of postwar booms for being so gosh-darned cute. Foreign visitors who have arrived at the height of one of these fads may be excused for believing the Japanese to be the most animal-loving nation on the face of the earth. Where else would thousands of people line up for long hours, and even days, for a brief glimpse of a bored panda chewing bamboo shoots behind a thick plate of glass? Or buy millions of postcards, pencil boxes, and other goods decorated with kittens dressed as punk bikers?

But the Japanese have also been less than loving in their dealings with the animal world, hunting and trapping many native mammals to the point of extinction, while extirpating the occasional four- or eight-legged foreign escapee with the relentlessness and determination of an army battling an alien invasion. If nature caged (or abstracted into cuddly stuffed animals) is often *kawaii* (cute) to the Japanese, nature in the raw is often *kowai* (frightening).

Japan's postwar animal obsession began in tragedy. In August 1943, when food supplies, especially in cities, were running critically low, authorities ordered the disposal of all large mammals in Tokyo's Ueno Park, including two elephants. Their keepers starved them to death.

After the war, only three elephants remained in the entire country, two in Nagoya and one in Kyoto. In 1949 Tokyo children who wanted their own elephant began a letter-writing campaign, and in response Indian prime minister Jawaharlal Nehru announced that he would find the "best elephant in India" for them. In July of that year Nehru made good on his promise by sending a fifteen-year-old female elephant, named Indira after his daughter, from Mysore to Tokyo.

Meanwhile, another elephant search was under way by the Kodansha publishing house. Eager to change its image from that of a wartime publisher of jingo literature to one more international and peace-loving, Kodansha brought a baby elephant from Thailand to Kobe in September 1949. Named Hanako, the elephant was transported to Ueno Zoo by train and installed in the refurbished Elephant House.

More spectacular was the arrival three weeks later of Indira, who walked the nine kilometers from the Shiodome Pier to her new home in Ueno. As the two-meter-tall elephant loped down Showa Avenue, which runs through the center of Tokyo, thousands of kids gaped in amazement; they had never seen anything so big. Admissions to the zoo soared, as did sales of tin elephants and elephant-shaped badges. Postwar Japan had its first animal star.

Indira was so popular that she went on tour in 1950, traveling in a specially built car to seventeen cities in eastern Japan. In 1952, "Zosan" (The Elephant)—a song that was to become a children's classic—received its premiere performance in front of her cage.

Put in the shade by her larger rival, Hanako was transferred in 1954 to a small zoo in the western Tokyo suburb of Kichijoji,

where she became a nervous wreck, pacing restlessly in her tiny pen and, on two separate occasions, crushing drunks who wandered into it. The more fortunate Indira lived to the ripe old age of forty-nine at Ueno, renowned to the end as "Mr. Nehru's present to the children of Japan."

Japan's biggest-ever animal boom was also occasioned by a diplomatic gesture. During Prime Minister Kakuei Tanaka's 1972 visit to Beijing, the Chinese government presented him with an unusual gift: two giant pandas. Called Ran Ran and Kan Kan, they were flown to Tokyo on a special Japan Airlines plane in October 1972.

Public excitement over the arrival of these cute balls of black and white fur soon approached fever pitch. Prior to the pandas' debut at Ueno Zoo, seventeen Tokyo coffee shops changed their name to Panda. When the zoo unveiled the pandas' enclosure—a refurbished tiger's cage—to the press on November 4, more than one thousand cameramen and reporters turned out—far more than greeted the arrival of most foreign dignitaries and celebrities.

When the pandas were put on public display for the first time the following day, more than five thousand people were waiting at the gates, forty of whom had camped there overnight. At 9:00 A.M. the gates opened and the crowd sprinted to the panda cage in a mad rush. Unable to control this frenzied mob, local authorities called out riot police, but the cops could not stop panda fans from pouring into the park. At 2:00 P.M., with the line stretching to Ueno Station, zoo officials closed the panda show for the day. Of the fifty-six thousand people who had hoped to catch a glimpse of Ran Ran and Kan Kan, only eighteen thousand succeeded.

Six months after their arrival, the pandas were moved into a spacious new panda house with 153 square meters of floor space enclosed by thick glass and complete with special air-conditioning and air-cleaning units. The pandas also had a 234-square-meter exercise area, installed with an artificial hill and swimming pool. Built at a cost of twenty-five million yen, this "Panda Castle," as it was dubbed by the media, was more spacious and well-appointed than the rabbit-hutch dwellings of many park visitors. Not that they minded: Ran Ran and Kan Kan were furry royalty.

The park attracted so many panda fans—nine million in the first year, a number greater than the population of Tokyo proper—that government officials seriously considered building a new zoo to accommodate them all. A third of the park visitors who wanted to see the pandas never got a chance because of the crowds.

Gradually, however, panda fever abated. Ran Ran died in 1979, followed by Kan Kan in 1980. A new male and female arrived to take their place and, in 1986, Japan's first panda cub, Ton Ton, was born. Although these events stirred new interest in the pandas, by 1995 annual park admissions had fallen to four million, less than half the 1970s peak. Today visitors to the Panda Castle can usually walk right in and stay as long as they like. The pandas are still there, but the lines are gone.

In the 1980s, the pandas were joined by a succession of animals who captured the public's affection. This was the decade that Japan's animal mania peaked and became thoroughly commercialized, with adorable four-legged images appearing everywhere, from school lunch boxes to movie screens.

The buyers, more often than not young and female, were also worshipers at the altar of the cute in music, *manga*, fashion, and even calligraphy. By mid-decade the round, childish hand favored by grade-school students and certain *manga* artists had become a fad among young women, including OLs ("office ladies" or female clerical workers) who used it in company correspondence to the consternation of their straitlaced bosses. For their private letters, these same OLs preferred stationery decorated with—what else?—cutesy-cute animals, often from SAN-RIO's hugely successful menagerie.

The first of the decade's animal icons, however, presented cute with a wryly humorous twist. In 1981 photographer Satoru Tsuda began producing wallet-sized laminated cards and wall posters with cute kittens made to look like Japanese bikers with attitude, emblazoned with the caption *Namennayo!*, a tough-guy epithet that literally translates as "Don't lick me!" but actually means something like "I'm not going to take any of that crap!"

At the time the media was full of stories about gangs of bikers, called *boso-zoku*, rampaging through the night streets and gangs of teenaged punks, or *tsuppari* groups, raising hell in schools (see **ZOKU**). Tsuda's kittenish bikers, dressed raffishly in school uniforms with jackets defiantly unbuttoned and gang armbands over their sleeves, mildly satirized the gangs; but more importantly they transformed an often-scary reality into cute, cool, affordable images that soon became enormously popular among schoolgirls.

Working with a small army of assistants, Tsuda began to crank out more *Namennayo!* photos, including shots of kittenish students sneaking off to the john for a smoke or a cat cop slapping the cuffs on a meowing *yakuza* gangster. By June, at the peak of the boom, nearly one hundred thousand retail outlets nationwide were peddling a wide array of *Namennayo!* goods. The selection eventually included ashtrays, key holders, combs, postcards, stationery sets, and those indispensable punk accessories, cigarette lighters.

The joke soon wore thin, however, and the cats began disappearing from shelves. Today, though the concept of the punk-as-cute survives—felt dolls of bikers and other socially marginal types were popular mid-nineties arcade-game prizes—*Namennayo!* cats can usually only be found at flea markets and in junk shops, looking more woebegone than defiant.

The next animal boom was not a comment on any social phenomenon at all, save the Japanese obsession with the cute in the most unlikely forms and the skill of Japanese marketers in converting that obsession into yen with amazing rapidity. In March 1984 Mitsubishi Motor Corporation launched an ad campaign for its Mirage line of cars that featured the Australian frilled lizard, a beast whose two-legged scamper across the desert sands had a goofy abandon and grim determination that struck TV viewers as hilarious. The frilled lizard ads became a hit and the lizard itself became a national phenomenon.

By May, Japanese toy makers were displaying an array of frilled lizard goods at the annual Tokyo Toy Show, including a plastic frilled lizard whose legs churned like the real thing when pushed by a stick attached to its body. Cute! One of the stranger sights of 1984 was OLs wheeling these gizmos down the corridors of corporate Japan, to the amusement of their colleagues.

A *Namennayo!* cat with attitude, in *tsuppari* school uniform.

In June six live lizards imported from Australia made their debut at Tokyo's Odakyu Department Store. The crowds came to gape, even though the lizards didn't have enough space to run. But if lizard fans had encountered the real thing in the Australian outback, their first reaction would probably have been not delight but fear. When approached by intruders, the one-meter-long adult lizard extends its neck frill, which usually rest on its shoulders, with the suddenness of a scaly umbrella popping up, opens its mouth wide to display a razor-sharp set of teeth, and hisses threateningly. Then, if the intruder does not make tracks for the nearest Land Rover, the lizard performs its own disappearing act by running at top speed on its hind legs.

In October the lines started forming for another, more traditionally cuddly visitor from Australia, the koala. Like the pandas twelve years earlier, the six koalas who arrived at Narita Airport aboard a special charter flight were intended as governmental goodwill ambassadors. Two went to Nagoya, two to Kagoshima, and two to Tama Zoo in a suburb of Tokyo. The Tama Zoo Koala House, which was even more luxurious than the Ueno Panda Castle, cost five hundred fifty million yen to build, including a small eucalyptus forest to make the koalas feel right at home.

Like the pandas, the koalas became media celebrities and star zoo attractions. On November 11, the first national holiday after the opening of the Tama Zoo Koala House, twenty-six thousand visitors came to see Tom Tom and Tam Tam—continuing the panda tradition, they were given cutesy names consisting of two alliterative syllables—but only ten thousand could pass through the Koala House's portals.

Though not as rare as the pandas, the koalas proved to be even more fragile when suddenly transferred to a new environment. In the first three years after the arrival of the initial shipment of six, five of the twenty koalas in Japanese zoos died. Critics in Australia argued that the shipments of koalas abroad ought to be halted. In May 1987 a zookeeper at a Yokohama nature park, unable to handle the stress of keeping the koalas under his care alive and healthy, hung himself from a park tree. A year later, distressed by the continuing deaths of koalas in foreign countries, including Japan, the Australian state of New South Wales banned the export of the marsupial. The cult of cute, Japan was discovering, had its downside.

But though real animals did not always easily adapt to becoming zoo attractions, their images flourished on big and small screens during the decade. Debuting in April 1983, a Tokyo Broadcasting System nature quiz show called *Waku Waku Dobutsu Land* (Exciting Animal Land) became a long-running hit by introducing viewers to strange, exotic, and irresistibly cute animals from all over the world. An early segment of the show on the Australian frilled lizard proved particularly popular and inspired the Mitsubishi Motor Company ad campaign that generated the frilled lizard boom. TBS sold the format for the show to broadcasters in nearly forty countries, including the United States, where it appeared as *Animal Crack-ups*.

That same year the Fuji TV network and Shogakkan publishing house released *Antarctica*, a film about the struggle of two dogs abandoned by a Japanese research expedition to survive the brutal Antarctic winter. Based on a true story, *Antarctica* drew tears from millions and became the biggest hit in the history of Japanese cinema, earning a total of 5.9 billion yen in distributor revenues, or 80 million dollars at then current exchange rates.

The success of *Antarctica* inspired a spate of hit movies with animal heroes. One was the 1986 *Koneko Monogatari* (known in English as *The Adventures of Chatran*). This film about the journey of a kitten and puppy through the Hokkaido wilderness pulled in 5.4 billion yen (65 million dollars) for distributor Toho, the second-ever highest total for a domestic film, outstripped only by *Antarctica*. Scripted by nature writer Masanori Hata and directed by Hata and Kon Ichikawa, *Koneko Monogatari* was later released in the United States with a new title, *The Adventures of Milo and Otis*, and English-language narration by Dudley Moore.

Still another hit animal movie was the 1987 *Hachiko Monogatari* (The Story of Hachiko), a drama based on a true story. Loyal Hachiko went to greet his master, a college teacher, at Tokyo's Shibuya Station every day on his return from classes, and continued to do so for years after the teacher's death. Hardhearted critics turned thumbs down on this weepily sentimental tale, but animal-loving audiences made it a box-office smash.

In the 1990s, however, animal surfeit set in. Having long since seen every species on the planet, with the possible exception of a few fast-mutating microbes, Japanese audiences became jaded and the popularity of animal movies and TV shows slumped. *Waku Waku Dobutsu Land* went off the air in March 1992 and *Kuruta* (Napoleon), a 1995 Japan-Australian coproduction about the journey of a puppy through the Australian outback, died at the box office. Although NHK and the commercial networks continue to produce programming featuring cute animals, the days when Japanese prime-time television seemed like one long trip to the zoo are gone—at least, until the next generation of animal lovers comes along.

ASHITA NO JOE

The Japanese college kids of the late 1960s looked, sounded, and acted a lot like their American counterparts: they wore jeans, let their hair grow, protested the war in Vietnam, and battled cops in the streets (though Americans usually didn't show up for demonstrations wearing helmets, carrying staves, and marching in conga lines).

But the student demonstrators and other members of Japan's Baby Boom generation were also different. Instead of growing up in middle-class affluence, with a car in the garage and a TV set in the living room, a lot

of them had as children experienced the poverty of Japan's early postwar years, and as teenagers the explosive growth of the 1960s that may have put a television in every house but ravaged the environment around it. They had been educated by teachers whose textbooks, under Occupation dictates, extolled democracy, but who were still in their heart-of-hearts devoted to prewar values, including the character-building value of suffering and the glory of sacrificing your all for a higher cause.

During the height of student unrest, a *manga* appeared that perfectly reflected the passions and struggles of the period, while expressing quite traditional sentiments. Called *Ashita no Joe* (Tomorrow's Joe), it told the story of a young boxer named Joe Yabuki from a Tokyo working-class neighborhood who battles his way to the top. On the way, however, he does a stretch in reform school, has a fateful encounter with the daughter of a rich industrialist, and kills his archrival, Toru Rikiishi, in the ring. Devastated by this death, Joe vows to never punch another opponent in the head. Despite this self-imposed handicap, he beats his new rival, Carlos Rivera, to become the Asian bantamweight champion.

Finally, after many vicissitudes, Joe faces the world champion, Jose Mendoza. Punch drunk from his years in the ring, Joe stands little chance of winning. During the bout,

The eponymous hero of *Ashita no Joe*, captured in a contemplative moment.

Joe finds himself totally outmatched. His manager wants to throw in the towel, but Joe refuses. "Let me fight until I'm white ashes," he says. Rousing himself to a superhuman effort, Joe manages to down the champion before losing by a decision. At the end of the bout, and the *manga*, he is spent but satisfied.

Drawn by Tetsu Chiba and written by Asao Takamori, *Ashita no Joe* debuted in *Shonen Magajin* (Youth Magazine) in January 1968 and ran for six years. An animated version of the *manga* appeared on TV in 1970. The *manga*, especially, became an enormous hit, followed breathlessly by everyone from kids to salarymen.

Two years into the story, shortly after Rikiishi's death in his epic battle with Joe, six hundred fans gathered at headquarters of *Shonen Magajin*'s publisher to hold a mock funeral; Rikiishi's gutsy determination to win—which included starving himself so he could make his weight for his bout with Joe—had inspired the sympathy of the *manga*'s fans. Members of Tenjo Sajiki (Ceiling Gallery), a theatrical troupe led by avant-garde playwright and poet Shuji Terayama, mounted a real boxing ring and performed songs from Terayama's musical, *Rikiishi Toru ga Shinda* (Toru Rikiishi Has Died) to the accompaniment of electric guitars. Terayama also wrote an essay on Rikiishi that appeared in a national newspaper.

The most viscerally affected by the *manga*'s heroics, however, were the students who were then fighting their own passionate struggles against Japan's power structures and found in Joe an inspiration for battling on. In a popular phrase from the period, they fought at the barricades "clutching [*Shonen*] *Magajin* in one hand and the [*Asahi*] *Journal* in the other." The *Asahi Journal* was a weekly magazine of news and opinion known for its left-leaning editorial policy.

Nearly three decades later, *Ashita no Joe* still maintains its hold on Baby Boomers and later generations of *manga* fans. A 1995 ad campaign by a major Japanese life-insurance company that featured Joe spurred a flood of interest, including hundreds of requests for posters and videos. The company, a spokesman said, had to order a first-ever extra printing of ad-campaign posters. "We were surprised by the intensity of the reaction," he commented.

Less surprised was Tokyo Metropolitan University professor Hiroshi Takayama, who is a Baby Boomer and the co-author of a book about *Shonen Magajin*. "The beginning and end of Joe coincided exactly with my college days," he wrote. "'Joe became a part of me. Even now, when I read it I become excited and emotional. . . .When I read the scene in which Rikiishi goes through the ropes, I feel myself moving with him."

BLOOD TYPES

The Japanese, the Japanese themselves are fond of saying, are a homogeneous people who share the same language, culture, and history. Not a few preface statements about that language, culture, and history with "We Japanese" (*Ware-ware Nihonjin*), which seems to imply that, simply by virtue of their own Japaneseness, they can speak for 125 million of their compatriots. This phrase annoys many non-homogeneous types, who point out that Japan is home to minorities—Ainus, Okinawans, ethnic Koreans, and the traditionally despised *burakumin* caste—who do not fit into the "We Japanese" mold.

But even members of the homogeneous majority are fond of making at least one distinction that separates them from millions of their fellows: their blood type. While in the West the only time most people think about whether they are A, B, O, or AB is when they are about to give blood, in Japan many believe that blood type is a determiner of character. Know the blood type, in other words, and you will know the person. Asking new acquaintances or even job applicants their blood type is as common a conversational gambit as the question "What's your sign?" is among American New Agers.

Like astrology, blood typology has long been derided as nonsense and worse. And like the faithful readers of astrology columns in U.S. newspapers, many Japanese have a sneaking feeling that there may be something to it. That feeling has created a lucrative market for blood-type experts, who have churned out hundreds of books on the subject, some of which have become bestsellers. Companies have launched a wide and wacky array of blood-type products, from soft drinks to condoms. Match-making agencies commonly use blood types as a factor in choosing partners for their clients. And

Condoms differentiated by blood type were among the unusual manifestations of marketing genius spurred by this fad.

though they are often loath to admit it, even major corporations have made personnel decisions on the basis of blood types.

The start of this only-in-Japan phenomenon was the publication in 1927 of a study by Professor Takeji Furukawa of the Tokyo Women's Teachers School titled "Personalities According to Blood Types." Furukawa's theories found favor among military leaders, who began organizing army and navy units according to blood types, and educators, who studied the relationship between blood types and academic performance.

But when World World II ended, Japan's interest in blood types evaporated. Much of that interest had been a nationalistic reaction to the racist theories of certain Western researchers, who had ranked Asians lower than Caucasians on the racial scale because of the preponderance of "animalistic" type B blood in their population. In the postwar world, classifying people by blood type seemed about as appropriate as the Nazis' grading them by nationality and race, and Furukawa's theories fell out of favor as outdated and just plain wrong.

The revival came in 1971 with the publication of *Ketsuekigata de Wakaru Aisho* (Understanding Compatibility from Blood Types) by Masahiko Nomi. The fruit of twenty-five years of research, the book gave a veneer of scientific credibility to Nomi's assertions about the influence of blood type on work, friendship, romance, and family life. The book sold 1.2 million copies and launched Nomi and his son, Toshitaka, on successful careers as gurus of blood typology, whose ideas have had an impact far beyond Japan's New Age fringe. One indication of that impact was the response to a blood-type questionnaire Toshitaka sent to Diet members: ninety-eight percent. The lawmakers probably wouldn't have been so obliging if they had thought the whole idea screwy.

According to the Nomis and the crowd of blood-type experts who have come after them, type A folks—the largest blood group in Japan, accounting for thirty-nine percent of the population—tend to be soft-spoken, cautious, orderly, conformist, and perfectionist. In other words, they resemble the stereotype of the average Japanese.

The next largest group, at twenty-nine percent, are type Os, who are enthusiastic, self-confident, domineering, and goal-oriented. They tend to make good business managers and political leaders. (Most Diet members, according to Nomi's survey, are type Os.) Type Bs, the third largest group at twenty-two percent, are impulsive, passionate, creative, and bold. They have a reputation for flakiness. The smallest group, the ABs at only four percent, are strong at generating original ideas and planning.

In 1990 Mitsubishi Electric Corporation—Japan's third-largest electric machinery maker—took these classifications seriously enough to launch a work team called the Fantastic Idea Project (Kiso Tengai Project), whose five members were all ABs. Instructed to bring at least ten ideas about new products to a training session, they came with a total of one hundred eighty. Telecommunications Machinery Department manager Enko Ito, who had recruited this creative Dream Team, knew that he was on the right track. "I'm sure we'll develop eye-opening products by making the most of [the team members'] blood-type characteristics," Ito told a reporter for the Asahi Shimbun. But when the media reported that Mitsubishi was using blood-type theory—still regarded as New Age mumbo-jumbo in some conservative business circles—to guide personnel decisions, the company decided to disband the team and later denied that it had ever existed.

About the same time condom maker Jex came up with its own original idea for cashing in on the blood-type craze: condoms specially made for each blood-type group. Determining from survey results that type As had a rather unimaginative attitude toward sex, Jex developed a condom for them in one standard shape, color (pink), and thickness (.03 mm). This and other blood-typed condoms proved to be a hit, despite the rather insulting implications.

In 1991 soft-drink maker Pokka Corporation launched sodas with punning names for each blood type, including Considerate Soda (Ki o Tsukaisoda) for type As and Emotional Soda (Jo ni Atsusoda) for type Os. "The idea was to make our carbonated soda stand out from the pack," explains Pokka spokesman Yoshiaki Inoue. "There was a lot of interest in blood types at the time, so we thought that blood-type drinks would be a fun way to appeal to customers. The aim was entertainment."

Pokka sold the sodas for two years, discontinuing them in 1993 when the blood-type fad started to wane. Interestingly, the company had better luck with Omikuji Soda, a brand that featured a fortune on each can, like the omikuji (written oracles) sold at Shinto shrines. "It was popular with customers who bought soda from vending machines," Inoue commented.

But though books on blood types have disappeared from the bestseller lists, the idea that blood types matter remains firmly entrenched in the Japanese mind. In a society whose members are so often pushed into the same "We Japanese" mold, an interest in blood types is a small way of staking a claim to being special. But it can also have its downside: if this type O writer had listened to the Nomis, he never would have married his type O wife and had his two type O children—and oh what a loss that would have been.

CHIBI MARUKO-CHAN

In Japan TV cartoons, or *terebi anime*, are not a Saturday morning treat (Japanese kids go to school on Saturdays) but a daily fixture on the tube, filling the early evening hours on most of the five commercial networks. Although some shows become long-running hits, the turnover is rapid, the casualty rate high.

Also, with the exception of the occasional family show that tries to appeal to everyone from preschoolers to adults, most shows are clearly targeted at the school-age set, though more than a few of the "kids" tuning in are college students or young office workers. Given that many of those same young adult viewers read the *manga* on which these shows are based, this shouldn't be surprising.

But it wasn't until 1990 that animation studio Nippon Animation got around to making a cartoon show aimed specifically at the women in that young adult audience:

Chibi Maruko-chan (Little Miss Maruko). Originally a *manga* by Momoko Sakura that debuted in the girls' comic *Ribbon* in 1986, *Chibi Maruko-chan* depicted the misadventures of a third-grade schoolgirl in Shizuoka Prefecture in the early 1970s. Located in Mount Fuji country—a tea-growing area that is the Japanese equivalent of the U.S. Midwestern heartland—Shizuoka was Sakura's home prefecture. Also, Chibi Maruko's middle-class milieu closely resembled her own as a child, and the *manga's* characters and stories were drawn from her personal experiences.

The TV show, which debuted in January 1990 on the Fuji TV network, was like the *manga* in being loosely autobiographical and frankly nostalgic, with close attention to period detail. But more than the 1970s trivia, viewers were attracted to the character of the heroine. Though she may have looked like a third grader as drawn by a third grader, with hair like an inverted soup bowl, and sounded cutesy cute, with a sweet, lisping voice, Chibi Maruko-chan was not just another bland figure of whimsy designed to sell chocolates and pencil boxes to schoolgirls.

Instead she was Bart Simpson's Japanese cousin. She hated to do homework, loved to sleep late, and was forever scheming, not always successfully, to get the better of her older sister or get her way with her weak-willed father and indulgent grandfather. But

Chibi Maruko-chan demonstrates her exuberant and mischievous charm.

rather than *The Simpsons* brand of topical black humor, the show's creators presented Chibi Maruko-chan as a warmly humorous character living in a time and place when human relations were more important than exam scores or the corporate bottom line.

To really understand the show, in other words, it helped to be a twentysomething woman who had known that time and place personally. As it turned out, millions of women fell into that category (or felt they did) and tuned in. But the show also appealed to viewers who were the same age as the heroine, or even as old as her parents. It became an immediate hit, scoring high ratings and stirring up a nationwide sensation.

Comparisons were made with **SAZAE-SAN**, another popular animated family show that debuted in 1969. Sazae-san's family represented bedrock values and attitudes that had a strong appeal to cultural traditionalists. The children got into mischief, but spoke to their parents and teachers politely, with deference to their adult authority. The father may have been a bumbler, but he was still a respected figure, given an honored place at the table next to his kimonoed father-in-law.

In the world of Chibi Maruko-chan, however, this traditional family structure had begun to disintegrate, with the father and grandfather behaving more like Chibi Maruko-chan's buddies than authority figures. Also, rather than the ideally childlike paragons of *Sazae-san*, the show's kids spoke to adults as (sometimes sassy) equals and were more interested in classroom one-upmanship than innocent schoolyard games.

Even so, the show's world was still a far cry from that of 1990, with its media horror stories of teachers beating children to death for minor infractions of school rules or children bullying unpopular classmates to the point of suicide. To a generation of Japanese young adults, as well as their even younger brothers and sisters, the *Chibi Maruko-chan* show was a friendly, familiar place that had both the ring of a lived reality and a happy ending for each episode.

Inevitably, the show became big business as well. As the ratings climbed, reaching an all-time high for a half-hour animated show of 39.9 percent in October 1990, so did the sales of hundreds of Chibi Maruko-chan character goods. Little girls could outfit themselves from head to toe with logo merchandise and even sprinkle Chibi Maruko-chan flavoring *(furi-kake)* on their rice. Eventually, sales of spin-offs reached the one billion dollar mark. The show's theme song, a maddenly infectious ditty titled "Odoru Ponpokorin," sold more than two million copies and became the biggest hit single in more than a decade. There was also a movie, released for the 1990–91 New Year holiday season, that earned twelve million dollars for distributor Toho and finished the year in the domestic box office top ten.

Finally, after three years, Sakura had had enough; she told the producers that she was running out of fresh ideas and wanted to end the show. So, even though it was still pulling down high ratings, Chibi Maruko-chan left the air. After a one-year sabbatical, however, Sakura decided to please her millions of fans and revive her best-known character. Chibi Maruko-chan reappeared on Fuji TV in January of 1995 and promptly resumed her place near the top of the animated heap. Though no longer the ratings monster of 1990, she was still a formidable young lady to her TV competition—and she seemed likely to remain in the third grade forever.

CONSUMER CULTURE

In 1955, after a decade of recovery from the devastation of war, Japanese began to think less about survival and more about American-style affluence. As a play on the Three Sacred Treasures—the mirror, sword, and jewel—that had been handed down as tokens of imperial rule since ancient times, the local media described a new Three Sacred Treasures for Japan's burgeoning consumer society: the washing machine, refrigerator, and television set.

But though the government issued an economic white paper the following year proclaiming the end of the postwar period, with its economic hardships and social chaos, ordinary Japanese were still far from ready to buy these treasures and join their American counterparts in consumer paradise. In the early 1950s a young salaryman fresh out of college was getting an average monthly paycheck of 10,000 yen, while a ninety-five-liter refrigerator cost 85,000 yen and a fourteen-inch black-and-white television, 140,000 yen.

Rather than spend two year's pay to chill a few beers and watch a pro-wrestling match on the tube, most Japanese lived much the way they had before the war. Dad drank his after-work bottle of Kirin at a bar and watched pro-wrestling star **RIKIDOZAN** bash big, hairy foreigners in a showroom window

The Three Sacred Treasures of early postwar consumerism.

or at one of the outdoor televisions scattered around the central city. (The television, of course, was a postwar novelty: broadcasts did not begin until 1953.)

Meanwhile, back home, Mom washed the clothes with a scrub board and basin, listened to her favorite soap opera on the radio, and if she needed to cool the occasional watermelon, bought a block of ice for her wooden ice box. The chilling and freezing of vegetables and other perishables was still an idea whose time had not yet come.

The kids—Japan's Baby Boomers—spent much of their free time outdoors, amusing themselves in ways that had not changed in generations. Scratch a middle-aged salaryman today and you will often find an expert marble shooter, top spinner, or flipper of the colored trading cards called *menko*, which featured pictures of popular fictional heroes and villains. The last skill required the hurling of one's own *menko* at the right velocity and angle to flip over a friend's lying on the ground. The successful flipper then got to keep the flipped card and, if he hung onto his collection over the years, is today materially wealthier from the nostalgia boom that has propelled the prices of the rarer cards into the stratosphere.

In the mid-fifties, however, Japanese wanted more than the simple, traditional pleasures they now look back on so fondly. After a decade of watching Hollywood

movies, they yearned for the fabulously rich lifestyles they saw on the screen. Big houses! Big cars! Big fridges! The American dream!

Gradually, as incomes rose in Japan's postwar economic boom, doubling from 1950 to 1958, they began to grasp bits and pieces of that dream. The washing machine was among the first. Debuting in 1946, the early models were noisy monsters whose vibrations made the entire house shake, but makers continued to refine the technology and lower the prices. In 1953 Sanyo debuted a machine that used a rotary stream of water to wash clothes quickly and thoroughly. The price of 28,500 yen was right and sales were explosive. In 1953 total production of washing machines was only 100,000 units. Five years later, this number had grown to 980,000 units, a jump of nearly ten times. By the end of the decade, forty percent of all

Japanese households had installed washing machines and retired the scrub board.

The refrigerator took longer to gain acceptance: by 1958, only 3.2 percent of all households had one. In addition to being overpriced, Japanese fridges could store little more than the night's beer supply and a few ice cubes. Also, though every housewife could understand the advantage of a machine that washed and wrung out the clothes, fewer could see the point of an electric box that chilled food. Housewives usually bought the ingredients for the day's dinner from the local butcher, fishmonger, or greengrocer the same afternoon. Long onions, white radishes, and other vegetables were often stored outside. Frozen foods for the home were unheard of.

By the 1964 Tokyo Olympics, however, as prices came down and attitudes changed, the refrigerator had become part of the middle-class lifestyle, with nearly half of all homes owning one. But for much of the decade, people used fridges mainly as glorified picnic coolers during the hot months and unplugged them in the winter. It was not until the 1970s and the debut of models with separate freezer compartments that consumers began to use them all year round. Frozen foods became consumer staples as more young housewives came to appreciate their convenience and live separately from their more traditionally minded in-laws, for whom real cooking meant fresh ingredients, not frozen Chinese eggrolls.

The third treasure, television, was the most prized by young and old alike. When television broadcasting began in 1953, first on pubcaster NHK, then on commercial network NTV, few Japanese could watch at home: NHK beamed its first broadcast, on February 1, to 866 households. Thousands, however, gathered around the televisions manufacturers had displayed in showrooms and on raised platforms in public places. These early sets were usually tuned to pro wrestling, boxing, or sumo matches, all of which could be easily watched and enjoyed by a crowd of viewers, even with a fuzzy picture and blurry sound.

The first person in the neighborhood to buy a set, usually on installment with years to pay, found his house nightly inundated by neighbors eager for a chance to stare at the bright, flickering screen. Among a people starving for entertainment after years of privation, the tube quickly become a national addiction.

As mass production began and prices fell in the late 1950s more average consumers could satisfy that addiction. Total production rose from 310,000 units in 1956 to 2.87 million in 1959—an increase of 9.3 times. But the one event that transformed Japan from a TV-wanting to TV-owning nation was the wedding of Crown Prince Akihito and

commoner Michiko Shoda on April 10, 1959 (see **ROYAL WEDDINGS**). In the weeks prior to this big event, consumers rushed to buy black-and-white TVs, even if they had to break the family budget. By the big day, fifteen million Japanese were tuned in—the biggest TV audience in the history of the medium. By 1960, 29.1 percent of all households owned televisions, compared with 13.7 percent the year before.

The 1964 Tokyo Olympics—Japan and Asia's first ever—not only offered brilliant proof that Japan had arrived as a modern nation but gave another big boost to TV sales. By 1965, ninety percent of homes had bought sets and Japan's age of mass home entertainment had truly begun.

In the early days of broadcasting, the mere thought of turning on the set was enough to set pulses racing. When a popular program came on, everyone in the family gathered round the television, which was often in the *tokonoma*, the alcove that was traditionally reserved for displaying the family's most prized possessions. Lights were dimmed and voices were lowered, so as not to miss a gesture or a syllable. Television, be it the antics of the Crazy Cats on *Shabondama Holiday* (Soap Bubble Holiday) or the acting of Vic Morrow in *Combat*, mattered.

Not surprisingly, ratings reached heights that they have seldom approached since: 64 percent for the May 24, 1963 broadcast of a Rikidozan pro-wrestling bout, 53 percent for the November 29, 1964 broadcast of *Ako Ronin*, an NHK TAIGA DRAMA, and 50.5 percent for a January 11, 1963, episode of *Ben Casey.*

The next technological step was color, and this time Japan was an international leader, not a follower. Hitachi began the production of their first domestic color television in 1959, long before the local market was ready for them. At half a million yen for a twenty-one-inch model, early color sets were out of reach for most consumers. But the Olympics gave them a reason to dig deep into their savings for a color set and sales began to take off. By 1975, ninety percent of Japanese homes had made the switch to color and Japanese manufacturers were shipping 1.2 million sets abroad. Most went to the United States, where their high quality and low prices soon gave them an insurmountable lead over the U.S. competition. Japan had found not only an exciting new entertainment medium but a major new export industry.

The Three Sacred Treasures may have symbolized the rise of Japan's postwar consumer culture, but they were only a part of the flood of products that transformed the Japanese way of life in the space of a generation. The automobile was among the most important; it didn't number among the treasures because back in 1955 so few people

could even imagine owning one. Japan's auto companies were still turning out mostly trucks and taxis. The small number of private passenger cars were only for the rich and privileged.

In the 1950s the main forms of motorization for the masses were motor scooters, motorcycles, and mopeds, all of which were were relatively cheap and easy to ride. There was no legal need for a license or a helmet: just get on and go. The two most popular scooters were Fuji Heavy Industries' Rabbit and Mitsubishi's Silver Pigeon. Hardly macho names, but the target market included women, dating couples, and salarymen who didn't want to muss their suit as they putt-putted to work. Japanese motorbikes, including models by such famous names as Honda, Suzuki, and Yamaha, were already winning races abroad and the hearts of young men at home, while the moped was viewed as a high-class mode of transportation best suited to well-born young women on their way to their private tennis club.

By the end of the decade, however, not only car makers but the Japanese government wanted to see more passenger cars on the roads. Led by the Ministry of International Trade and Industry, the government was eager to stimulate the domestic economy—in 1960 Prime Minister Hayato Ikeda announced a policy of doubling the average worker's income by the end of the decade— and a key element in its GNP expansion scheme was motorization. Planners began drafting blueprints for the superhighways of the future and manufacturers started gearing up for mass production.

The potential market was huge. In 1959 total production of passenger cars amounted to only 87,992 units and only 1 Japanese in 131 owned a car, compared with 1 in 2.6 people in the United States and 1 in 30 worldwide.

To get more Japanese behind the wheel, MITI had proposed in 1955 the development of a small, lightweight car that would seat three or four passengers, have an engine displacement of between three hundred fifty and five hundred cubic centimeters, and cost no more than 250,000 yen. Makers who could meet these and other conditions would be eligible for financial support. That same year Fuji Heavy Industries announced a plan for an auto that would be only two-and-a-half times heavier than its popular Rabbit motor scooter and far cheaper than any passenger car on the road.

A supplier of aircraft to the Japanese military during the war, Fuji had the know-how needed for designing what was essentially a plane cockpit on wheels. In 1958, it launched the Subaru 360, a car that bore a striking resemblance to a ladybug and cost only 420,000 yen. Used to seeing large American cars lumbering about the streets, Japanese consumers were surprised by the Subaru's smallness and pleased by its price, so much so that Fuji was able to keep the 360 in production, essentially unchanged, until 1970. Altogether, Japanese consumers bought four hundred thousand 360s, making it most successful of the early minicars.

In 1960 Hiroshima Toyo Kogyo, a maker of three-wheeled trucks, introduced a four-passenger car called the Matsuda R360 Coupe that cost only 310,000 yen, or 20,000 yen more for an automatic transmission. This competitor to the Subaru 360 had a two-cylinder air-cooled engine and generated sixteen horsepower. It later metamorphosed across the Pacific as the Mazda.

About the same time Mitsubishi brought out its first passenger car, the Mitsubishi 500. Priced between the Subaru 360 and the Matsuda R360, the 500 offered a rear-mounted two-cylinder air-cooled engine that produced twenty-one horsepower. Its real selling point, however, was a four-wheel independent suspension system that made it ahead of its time.

The Subaru, Matsuda, and other so-called "K cars" (the "K" refers to *kei*, or "light") may have looked like motorized toys to owners of "real"—i.e., American—cars, but they were perfect for buzzing around Japan's narrow streets and, more importantly for government planners, made car ownership possible for the bike-peddling and scooter-riding masses.

Meanwhile, makers of standard-size passenger cars were also competing feverishly to bring out low-priced new models and ride the motorization wave. In August 1959 Nissan launched the Datsun 310, better known as the first of its hugely popular Bluebird series. The 310 had a thirty-four horsepower engine with a displacement of one thousand cubic centimeters and a top speed of one hundred five kilometers per hour. The low price, 680,000 yen, made it a big hit and orders flooded in. By 1961, only two years after its launch, Nissan had sold one hundred thousand—a huge number for the time.

In 1961 Toyota, which had previously concentrated on more expensive models, including its Bluebird rival, the Toyopet Corona, brought out the Publica for 380,000 yen. The first passenger car in its class to be priced under 400,000 yen, it soon became a bestseller.

The age of motorization for the masses had arrived, as the ownership of "my car" or *mai kaa*—a popular Japlish term for a personal passenger car—exploded. In 1960 total production of passenger cars amounted to 460,000 units. By 1965 this number had grown to 2,180,000 and by 1970 to 8,780,000.

The rise of Japan's mass consumer culture had a profound impact on the culture at large. Freed from household drudgery, which in early postwar Japan meant an endless round of chores from dawn to dusk, Mom was now free to cultivate her own interests or simply doze off in front of the tube (according to a cynical saying of the time the housewife's job description entitled her to *sanshoku hirune*— "three meals and a nap"). Though her liberation was far from complete and she could not easily take a full-time job, she had emerged from her traditional place in the kitchen into the larger world outside, with no intention whatsoever of looking back.

Meanwhile, the kids were abandoning traditional pastimes for the delights of TV cartoons and *manga*. The marbles, tops, and *menko* went into the closet, seldom to emerge. Also, the marriageable daughters of the family were giving up their traditional "housework apprenticeship"—a polite euphemism for waiting until the right man came along—to continue their education, take a job, or in some cases pursue a career.

Dad still went for his after-work drink with his office buddies—some things never change—but on Sundays and holidays he would often take the family out for a spin in his new Bluebird, thereby contributing to the growth of the leisure industry and the advent of the seventy-kilometer-long traffic jam.

The electrification and motorization of Japanese life, in short, had much the same effects as in the West, though over a much shorter period of time. In two decades, Japan went from a culture that, despite such Western innovations as radio and films, still maintained vital links to the cultural and literary traditions of the pre-modern world, to one that had largely severed those links and created new mass forms of entertainment and new ways of life in the waning years of the twentieth century.

DORAEMON

The Japanese, goes the cliché, are stolid, unimaginative types who, when younger, dream prosaic dreams of a high entrance-exam score and, when older, a low golf handicap. Not a few Japanese perpetuate the cliché, taking a rather perverse pride in being "worker bees" (*hataraki bachi*) who have no time for flights of fancy.

But many of those same bees spent their youths enthralled by a blue robot cat whose mission in life is to make even the wildest dreams come true. Named Doraemon, he made his debut in December 1969 in four educational magazines for kids published by Shogakukan Inc. In the decades since, Doraemon and his ten-year-old companion,

Nobita, have become a national institution—the Japanese equivalent of Snoopy and Charlie Brown. (And like the characters of Charles M. Schulz, they have also become an enormously profitable multimedia franchise.)

Most children first become acquainted with Doraemon through the half-hour TV show that Asahi National Broadcasting Company has aired since 1979. Kids also turn out in droves for the latest Doraemon movie, which is released each spring and inevitably ends up in the year's domestic box office top ten. Eventually, they start reading the Doraemon comic (*manga*) published monthly in *CoroCoro Comic* and buying the paperback collections, of which more than one hundred million have been sold.

Doraemon's creator was Hiroshi Fujimoto, a member of the most prolific and successful creative duo in *manga* history. Following their debut in 1952 with *Tenshi no Tama-chan* (Little Angel Tama). Fujimoto and collaborator Abiko Motoo created forty-nine *manga* series over the next three decades under the collective pen name Fujiko Fujio. Their most popular collaboration was *Obake no Q-Taro* (Q-Taro the Ghost), which became a pioneering TV cartoon program in the 1960s. But their true collaborations were few; they usually preferred to work independently. In 1988, Fujimoto and Abiko came to an amicable

Take-copters secured, Doraemon and Nobita fly off to a new adventure.

parting of the ways. In 1996, at the age of sixty-two, Fujimoto died of liver disease.

The *manga*'s central character is Nobi Nobita, a fourth-grade boy who lives in a Tokyo suburb with his office-worker father and housewife mother. Like his American counterpart, Charlie Brown, Nobita experiences life as a series of (often self-inflicted) calamities, both large and small. At school, he ranks at the bottom of his class and spends much of his day standing out in the hall. At home, he is forever being scolded by his mother for not doing his homework, cleaning his room, or getting up on time in the morning. His classmates tease him because he is poor not only at school work but everything boys consider important. He can't hit a baseball, build a plastic model, or even ride a bicycle.

Despite his troubles, Nobita is a happy-go-lucky kid who is always looking for the easy way out. He wants his parents and teachers to praise him, his friends to like and admire him, but he doesn't want to make an effort to change. And when change becomes necessary, he tries to make it as painless as possible by calling on Doraemon.

Doraemon is a time-traveling robot from the twenty-second century with a very specific mission to save Nobita from his future. Knowing that Nobita is doomed to end as a henpecked bankrupt whose debts will still be burdening his descendants a hundred years hence, Nobita's great-great-grandson, Sewashi, sent Doraemon to guide Nobita along the path to happiness and success in the *manga*'s first episode.

Though a robot, Doraemon is not Nobita's slave: He has a will and personality very much his own. Also, unlike Charlie Brown's Snoopy, he is not a mute (to humans) figure of whimsy, but something of a moralizing, indulgent maiden aunt who is forever urging Nobita to study hard, finish his homework on time, and be more self-reliant. But when the boy comes to him in tears asking for help out of his latest scrape, Doraemon always responds by reaching into a kangaroo-like pouch and pulling out a gadget from the twenty-second century.

The best known is the *take*-copter (bamboo-copter), a small, double-bladed propeller that can be attached to the body and, at the touch of a button, be used as a miniature helicopter. But the *take*-copter, like so many of the marvels in Doraemon's pouch, has its dangers. In the *manga*'s first story, Nobita discovers one when he attaches the *take*-copter to the seat of his short pants and takes off. Soon after, we see the pants flying alone, minus their owner. (The best place to attach the *take*-copter, Nobita soon learns, is the top of the head.)

Over the years, Doraemon has pulled more than a thousand gadgets out of his pouch. Some, like the *take*-copter, are familiar to nearly every Japanese, just as Snoopy's biplane is familiar to most Americans. Others appear once and are never seen again.

The best known after the *take*-copter is the *dokodemo* door (anywhere door), an ordinary-looking pink wooden door that opens to anywhere in the world at the user's command. Nobita, Doraemon, and their neighborhood gang often use it when setting off on a big adventure. In the book-length *Nobita no Daimakyo* (Nobita's Big Magic Kingdom), they pass through the *dokodemo* door into the African jungle—and back again to hide a test paper, set the videocassette recorder, and use the bathroom. Finally, a big, ham-fisted kid named Jaian says he will slug the next one who spoils the mood of their safari with a trip back to the real world. Soon after, however, Jaian (a nickname that is a Japanese transcription of "giant") goes through the door himself to explain his absence to his terror of a mother—and returns covered with bruises.

As these examples indicate, Doraemon's gizmos are less future technologies than magic lamps that fulfill every conceivable wish—and teach gently humorous but ultimately serious lessons about our technological and human limitations. Instead of H. G. Wells and George Orwell, with their grimly pessimistic future worlds, Fujimoto was closer in spirit to C. S. Lewis and Lewis Carroll, with their didactic fantasies of alternative realities.

He was also a prolific and imaginative inventor. The *dokodemo* door might be a near cousin to Lewis's wardrobe, but Fujimoto also improved on and went beyond his models. One example is the *time furoshiki* (time wrapping cloth), a Japanese wrapping cloth with a clock-face design. Covered by the red side of the cloth, an old object becomes new, an old person, young. But with the blue side down, the *furoshiki* has the opposite effect—a new car becomes an instant junker.

Though the gadgets may be pure fantasy, Doraemon and Nobita's Japan is firmly, comically down-to-earth. Together with his father and mother, Nobita lives in a house in suburban Tokyo. And though he is, untypically, an only child, he belongs to a close-knit neighborhood gang whose members are familiar schoolyard types. One is Jaian, the aforementioned bully, who may be quick of fist and loud of voice, but is also brave and good-hearted. Another is Suneo (whose name roughly translates as "Sneaky"), a scheming kid who is drawn to resemble a *kappa*, the trickster water-sprite of Japanese folklore. Suneo lives in a big house, has all the latest toys, and plays the role of Jaian's brainy sidekick (and frequent punching bag).

The three boys thus present a microcosm of Japan's class system, and illustrate the way those classes are perceived, with Suneo representing the arrogant, materialistic, self-centered upper-middle; Nobita the nice, ordinary but much-put-upon middle; and Jaian the impulsive, crude, but salt-of-the-earth lower-middle.

Finally, there is Shizuka, a typical *ojo-sama* (i.e., a well-educated, well-groomed, well-behaved young lady). Often presented as blandly nice, Shizuka can be surprisingly strong-willed and spunky. She serves as the manga's love interest.

Like *Peanuts,* the *Doraemon manga* offers an idealized vision of suburban childhood. Although Nobita's neighborhood and school may be the scenes of his numerous defeats and humiliations, they are basically child-friendly environments where the temptations and disruptions of modern life are largely kept at bay. Instead of a game center or convenience store, Nobita and his pals hang out at a vacant lot, where they sit or nap on an always present pile of sewer pipes (the construction workers would seem to be on a permanent lunch break). The lot is a refuge from adult expectations and pressures, a jumping-off point for adventure; the American equivalent might be Huck Finn's raft.

Though hardly Huck Finns, Nobita and his friends are more carefree than most Japanese children their age. Despite Nobita's homework, Shizuka's violin lessons, Suneo's cram school, and Jaian's chores at his parents' store, the children seem to have plenty of time to hang around the vacant lot, play sandlot baseball, and explore the wooded hill behind the school. Needless to say, these are not activities that most suburban Tokyo children can indulge in; the open spaces where children used to play have long since disappeared in the course of relentless development.

For all the stories' many variations, their basic pattern is set and simple. Doraemon is forever pulling new gadgets from his bottom-less pouch and Nobita, ignoring the cat's warnings and instructions, is forever misus-ing them. The result, inevitably, is a debacle. In *Time Furoshiki* (Time Wrapping Cloth), which appears in the second volume of the paperback series, Doraemon and Nobita are overjoyed when the family's ancient black-and-white TV finally goes on the blink; now his mother will be forced to buy a new color

Doraemon, as the banner proclaims, is still "Japan's number one" cartoon idol.

set. (The paperback was published in 1974, when most Japanese had already made the switch to color.) But when his mother temporarily fixes the TV with a karate chop ("The secret is to hit it here at a sixty-degree angle," she explains), Doraemon decides that rather than ruin his eyes watching wavy lines, he will repair the TV once and for all by covering it with a time *furoshiki*. After reviving the TV, mother's old washing machine, and father's old camera, Nobita has the brilliant idea of using the *furoshiki* to make money. Doraemon, less wise to Nobita's ways at this early stage of the series, readily agrees.

But after Suneo spies them turning a boxful of junk into brand-new, and presumably saleable, goods, he steals the *furoshiki* and sets into motion a comedy of errors. Jaian promptly snatches the *furoshiki* from Suneo and accidentally hatches eggs that he was delivering to a customer. In the course of the story, a tree becomes a sapling; a new car, a junker; and a bald head, one badly in need of a haircut—all because of the flying *furoshiki*. When Suneo finally recovers the *furoshiki*, his mother tells him to return it to its rightful owner. First, though, she tries it on her old crocodile-skin bag. The *manga* ends with her running for her life from a dazed-looking crocodile crawling out from underneath the cloth.

But no matter how many disasters he causes (if he hadn't carelessly left the *furo-* shiki hanging on a branch, Suneo wouldn't have taken it) and no matter how many times he vows to do better, Nobita remains Nobita. "When a *manga* hero become a success, the *manga* suddenly stops being interesting," said Fujimoto. "So the hero has to be like the stripes on a barber pole; he seems to keep moving upward, but actually he stays in the same place."

The Doraemon movies, nineteen of which had been released by spring 1997, also follow a pattern, but one far more grandiose than the *manga* or the TV show. With Doraemon at their side, the children travel to another time or world. Although their trip may begin as a vacation outing, they soon find themselves involved in a titanic struggle to thwart an evil power. With the aid of Doraemon's gadgets (and, often, the timely intervention of his sister from the twenty-second century) the children manage to triumph.

The 1993 Doraemon movie, *Doraemon Nobita to Buriki no Labyrinth* (Doraemon and Nobita and the Tin Labyrinth) is typical. Nobita discovers a magic door in a mysterious suitcase that leads to the Tin Hotel, where everything, including the hotel staff, is made of tin. The trees, grass, and even the snow in the nearby mountains are also artificial. Nobita is delighted; the whole place is a spoiled city boy's dream. The hotel is free, the service is excellent, and the snow isn't cold.

But—and here is the film's message—this technology-provided ease and comfort come at a price. When Nobita asks Doraemon for a pair of never-fall superskis, the cat replies crossly that a kid who wants everything done for him will never learn to do anything well. Nobita gets his skis, however, and as he buzzes down the slope to disaster, the story moves into high gear. An evil-genius robot named Napogisutora (a combination of Napoleon and Hitler?) and his robot cohorts have seized power from the good people of the planet Chamocha. Formerly mechanical servants, these robot despise their human masters as obsolete.

Doraemon, Nobita, and the rest of the gang are recruited to the human cause by Sapio, the son of the Tin Hotel's builder. The robots have imprisoned his father and the planet's other humans in a giant concentration camp. Sapio, who can only move about with the aid of a special capsule (the result of his society's overdependence on robots), needs the help of Doraemon and the four "Earth warriors" to save Chamocha from the robot dictatorship. After many perils, they succeed.

Like the other series entries, *Doraemon Nobita to Buriki no Labyrinth* was technically not much more than a big-screen version of the TV show; the backgrounds were simple, the colors primary, the animation limited. Also, the good-versus-evil storyline, with its boy's-adventure plot twists, was aimed squarely at a ten-and-under audience, with little to interest adult ticket buyers. Even so, the film was a hit, earning distributor Toho 1.65 billion yen (14.87 million dollars) and finishing in the annual domestic box-office top ten.

Despite the sameness of the *manga* and the movies, in *Doraemon* Japanese children can find characters at once individual and universal (in some sense, we are all Nobita) and a comic mind that understands and entertains them, without regard for adult expectations and standards. For kids whose lives are often so regulated, Doraemon represents a welcome breath of freedom and a glimpse of a funnier, friendlier world where all dreams, even foolish ones, can come true.

DOWNTOWN

Japanese television comedians usually work in pairs. Yes, the kimono-wearing monologist known as a *rakugoka* sits alone on his cushion, but he is usually not so much a comedian doing an original routine as a practitioner of a traditional performing art, telling stories whose punch lines are often over a hundred years old. And yes, comedy troupes like **THE DRIFTERS** still perform, but the basic unit of modern Japanese comedy is the two-man team of the dimwit, or *boke*, and the straight man, or *tsukkomi*.

This style of comedy called *manzai*—the wild and wacky dimwit stirring the straight man to irritation and anger—is hardly unique to Japan, but it is in Kansai, the area of western Japan centered on the three cities of Osaka, Kobe, and Kyoto, where it has put down its strongest roots. Kansai *manzai* duos have dominated the comedy scene in Japan for much of the television era, including the *manzai* boom of the early 1980s, which put dozens of Kansai comics, however briefly, in the national spotlight.

Various explanations have been offered for this phenomenon. Though the heart of the Kansai region and the nation's second-largest commercial center, Osaka is outside the government and business power loops, which are centered in Tokyo. Osakans have long resented their second-class status vis-à-vis Tokyo, but it has also given them a skeptical view of authority—a useful tool for a comedian.

Also, unlike the stolid, straitlaced samurai of Edo (the premodern name for Tokyo), who lived off their government stipends, distrusted novelty, and dreaded change, the merchants of Osaka had to hustle for their rice and were forever on the lookout for the next new thing. At the same time, they liked to live in style and have a good time, which often meant having a good laugh. Their modern descendants have carried on this tradition, including the traditional respect for people with a comic gift.

It shouldn't come as a surprise, then, that the most popular comic duo of the 1990s is from the Osaka area. But while emerging from the heart of the Osaka *manzai* culture, this duo has gone its own, sometimes defiant way in redefining the meaning of comedy—and cool—for their generation.

Called Downtown, the duo of Hitoshi Matsumoto and Masatoshi Hamada work a lot of gigs that may have little to do with real comedy, but are common status signifiers for

successful Japanese comics. Together they have hosted prime-time infotainment and variety shows and served as TV pitchmen for a convenience store chain. Separately, they have written best-selling collections of comic essays, with Hamada's 1995 *Yome!* (Read This!) selling eight hundred thousand copies and Matsumoto's 1994 *Isho* (Last Will and Testament) moving nearly four million. Hamada, the straight man of the duo, has starred in TV dramas and cut two records, "Wow War Tonight" and "Going Going Home," with the former selling 2.1 million and the latter 1.26 million copies in 1995.

These extracurricular activities have been handsomely rewarded. In 1996 Matsumoto had the dubious honor of paying more income taxes than any other entertainer in Japan: 263.4 million yen, while Hamada was number two on the list, at 236.4 million yen. Though Hamada feigned embarrassment to the press when their tax payments were made public, saying that he and Matsumoto were "two klutzes who couldn't find any loopholes," their rankings were widely recognized proof that Downtown were the kings of not only comedy but the Japanese entertainment world.

Hitoshi Matsumoto (left) and Masatoshi Hamada (right) looking bemused at a 1996 press conference to announce that they are the entertainment world's biggest taxpayers.

But while raking in more yen than most of their colleagues (Matsumoto admitted that some comics were more interested in padding their bank accounts than heading the tax office's list), Downtown was still doing the heavy lifting of the comedy profession: appearing together regularly on stage without props, partners, or gag writers to make audiences laugh.

That made them unusual indeed among Japan's comic elite. Most of the biggest comic duos of the past three decades, including Kiyoshi Nishikawa and Yasushi Yokoyama, Jiro Sakagami and Kin'ichi Hagimoto of Konto 55 Go, and Kiyoshi and **BEAT TAKESHI** of the Two Beats, stopped doing standup routines and eventually went their separate ways after reaching the top. Though Nishikawa, Hagimoto, and Takeshi—the more successful halves of these duos—certainly made audiences laugh as singles, usually as variety-show emcees, they had long since distanced themselves from their standup roots.

Downtown, on the other hand, carefully nurtures those roots and regards standup as its raison d'être. Instead of a funky underground club, however, their main venue for standup comedy is a weekly show called *Gaki no Tsukai ya Arahende!!* (This Is No Job for Kids!!). Debuting on a Kansai station in October 1989 and moving to the NTV net-

work in October 1991 as part of a late-night program called *Shogeki Den'eibako* (Laugh Attack Electrical Shadow Box), *Gaki no Tsukai* has long been the most unusual and, its many fanatically loyal viewers would claim, hippest comedy show on Japanese television.

Airing at 11:00 P.M. on Sunday, *Gaki no Tsukai* begins with a short comic sketch. In one, an off-camera Matsumoto solemnly discusses the dangers of parking without a concrete backstop, as Hamada slowly, inexorably backs a car through the walls of an apartment building set that has been constructed in a real parking lot. The panicked occupants, including a dentist and nurse fornicating in the dentist's chair, escape unharmed, but after Hamada parks his car and calmly exits, it seems to explode in a roar of flame. This, we see from Hamada's startled expression, wasn't in the script. Then Matsumoto strolls on camera with a canary-eating look on his face: the explosion—made by igniting a ring of powder around the parked vehicle—was a practical joke.

Though funny enough to anyone with a thirteen-year-old mind, these sketches are only a warm-up to the main event of the thirty-minute show. Appearing on stage before a live audience, Matsumoto and Hamada essentially wing it for the rest of the program, relying only on viewer postcards drawn at random from a box for inspiration.

This, as Matsumoto insists, may sound easier than dreaming up routines or rehearsing skits, but it isn't. "Young guys who want to be comics tell me they want to do improv like Downtown. I say 'go ahead and try it' but they can't do it: they're just two guys standing around talking."

This is certainly not the case with Matsumoto and Hamada. Friends since junior high school, partners since they entered the Yoshimoto Kogyo talent agency's Osaka training school together in 1982, they are completely in synch with each other's comic rhythms, creating a ceaseless flow of wisecracks, put-downs, and free-associating stories that may appear out of the ether, but are often hilarious in their spot-on timing and off-the-wall inventiveness.

The one doing most of the free-associating is Matsumoto. Taller and more ruggedly built than the average Japanese man, with the heavy eyebrows that are considered a symbol of macho good looks, Matsumoto may not have the physical tools of a typical *boke* clown (save for teeth that look as though they could use the attention of a good orthodontist), but he possesses a permanently unhinged mind.

Like Jonathan Winters, Robin Williams, and other masters of improvisation, Matsumoto can instantly create fully realized characters, from a fairylike creature called, for reasons known only to Matsu-

moto, Exciting, to a resolute turd who refuses to be flushed. Playing himself, he is possessed of an infinite variety of comic attitudes, from Jack-Benny-like foppishness to Eddie-Murphy-like aggressiveness, switching from one to another with an abruptness that itself is a source of laughs.

On one show, he was loudly disparaging Hamada's performance in a running race, which his partner had entered as a gag, when Hamada suddenly and seriously challenged him to a marathon. Instantly dropping his teasing banter, Matsumoto fixed Hamada with a coy, wondering stare and held it for what seemed an eternity, as Hamada mocked him for his wimpishness. Finally Matsumoto broke his silence. "I would rather . . . *help*," he said. "Pass out sponges, water bottles, stuff like that." The timing of "help" was Jack-Benny perfect and the audience roared.

Though ostensibly the straight man, Hamada is as much actor as reactor, constantly prodding his partner to new heights of outrageousness. With his boyishly round face, Hamada looks like a cute kid in a grown man's body, but there is nothing childish about his comic attack. Unlike *tsukkomi* who live up to their names (the term comes from the verb *tsukkomu*, which means to thrust or shove) by constantly—and predictably—hitting their partners upside their heads, Hamada's favored weapon is his tongue, which is as fast and sharp as any in Japanese show business. At the same time, he is a gifted physical comedian who can get laughs by frantically leaping gazellelike across the stage or by squatting, his back to the audience, in a heap of feigned embarrassment.

During their improv sessions on *Gaki no Tsukai*, Matsumoto and Hamada are not playing their assigned roles of dimwit and straight man so much as simply playing— with words, personas, reality itself. Talking about a man who had won a banana-eating contest on a recent TBS special, Matsumoto conjures up the image of a human banana whose sides squirt out when tromped on by a giant foot. Or he suddenly begins spinning the tale of an imaginary surfing expedition to New Zealand, during which he rescues a local boy with a high fever by riding him to the doctor's on his surfboard. While Matsumoto is flying ever higher with his fantasies, Hamada is trying to bring him back to earth with skeptical snorts, mocking questions, and remonstrating raps on the head. The laughs come not so much from Matsumoto's airy (and deliberately airheaded) free associating as from his winking obliviousness to Hamada's reactions— an obliviousness that sends his partners into new paroxyms of comic frustration and the audience into new fits of laughter.

This style of free-form humor, which respects no rational boundaries or social taboos, may have become Downtown's comic signature, but it was not always popular. When they started the show's ratings were abysmal. Even the studio audience was sitting on its hands. Used to the broad, obvious gags of so many Japanese TV comics, they didn't know what to make of these two speed-rapping madmen. But instead of changing their act, Matsumoto and Hamada persisted, and they succeeded in educating the audience to appreciate their brand of humor. Five years after its start, the show's ratings passed the twenty-percent mark and Matsumoto was being proclaimed as his generation's comic genius.

That genius was nurtured in Amagasaki, a suburb of Osaka, where Matsumoto and Hamada were born in 1963. Although the boys went to the same elementary school, they did not become friends until they entered the local junior high. Though Matsumoto was hardly a diligent student— he later reminisced that he spent more of his adolescence in coffee shops than classrooms—he was already a budding comic: Matsumoto's stagehand father often took the family to performances of *manzai, rakugo*, and comic stage plays with free tickets from his son's future employer, Yoshimoto Kogyo, and the young Matsumoto eagerly memorized the gags and routines.

In Hamada, a boy whose quick mouth and bad attitude matched his own, Matsumoto found a soul mate. Soon the two boys were trying out standup routines on their classmates and playing pranks on the neighbors, including a foreign woman who went to get her laundry from the washing machine in front of her apartment and found Hamada extracting a pair of her panties. (This story was to become one of Matsumoto's on-air favorites.)

In high school, the boys went their separate ways, with Hamada enduring three years of exile at a boarding school known for the strictness of its discipline and Matsumoto drifting through those same years at a commercial high school notorious for its anything-goes atmosphere (Matsumoto later reminisced that his classmates popped cans of beer during the lesson, while he lounged in the back of the room, chain-smoking cigarettes).

After graduation, Hamada toyed with the idea of becoming a motorboat racer, while Matsumoto was determined to become a comedian ("Comedy is what saved me," he later said. "Making people laugh was the reason for my existence. . . . [Without it] I'd probably be a middle-aged man selling superballs.") After failing the exam for the motorboat racing association's school, Hamada happened to run into his old friend, who persuaded him to apply for the

training school of Yoshimoto Kogyo, the biggest talent agency in the Kansai area. Hamada agreed: by going back to school he could goof off for another year before getting a real job. The boys were accepted and began their comic careers.

It wasn't obvious at first that those careers would be brilliant. After their first television appearance, host Yasushi Yokoyama—then one of the most popular comedians in the country—stormed over and told them they knew nothing about the art of *manzai* comedy. "You guys are just a couple of punks talking," he sneered. Matsumoto wanted to punch the bespectacled comic, but was later glad he restrained himself: Yokoyama had the power to break them and might well have used it.

Given this experience, it was not surprising that the boys never attached themselves as apprentices to a senior comedian, then a standard practice for budding *manzai* comics. Matsumoto picked the name Downtown out a magazine because it was given as the English translation of *shitamachi*, the premodern working-class heart of the city, where entertainment for the urban masses first flourished.

The heart of the Kansai area, where Yoshimoto Kogyo had three theaters, is where Downtown got their start, performing for bored housewives who often paid more attention to their box lunches than the chatter on stage. Eventually, however, Downtown developed a strong following among teenage girls who liked their looks (Matsumoto, in particular, has since developed a reputation as a womanizer), stylish casual fashions (no rumpled salaryman suits for these dudes!), and most of all, their brand of comedy, which may have been occasionally crude, but was always aggressively cool.

By 1987, they had their first regular show, an afternoon program on a local TV station that featured Downtown's stage act at a landmark Osaka theater. In 1988 they began appearing as regulars on their first Tokyo TV show, *Renren!! Tokimeki Club* (Passionately!! Heartthrob Club) and radio show, *Lotte Young Star Number 1*. In October 1989, they got their first network program, *Gaki no Tsukai*. Downtown had finally made it to the big time.

Another career milestone was reached when, after scoring high ratings on two special comedy shows called *Downtown no Gottsu Ee Kanji* (Downtown's Feelin' Good), they got a regular program of the same title on the Fuji TV network. Debuting in December 1991, it was their first in prime time.

Unlike *Gaki no Tsukai*, the new show was scripted from beginning to end, but because Matsumoto was Matsumoto, the sketches that finally appeared on the air almost never followed the original script. Another important departure from *Gaki no Tsukai* was that instead of carrying the burden of the show almost entirely alone, Matsumoto and Hamada worked with young comedians whom they knew from the Yoshimoto agency. Still another was that Matsumoto and Hamada were able to create continuing characters instead of dreaming them up on the spot. The result was a program that was more structured and domesticated than *Gaki* but still had an offbeat and even bizarre approach compared with other prime time comedy shows. Imagine *Saturday Night Live* with bathroom humor but no political jokes.

The show's sketches, which later became chart-topping bestsellers on video, ranged widely in quality. One of the best features Matsumoto and Hamada as two washed-up middle-aged comedians wearing Afro wigs and technicolor jackets straight from a seventies lounge act. When two young comics return to the dressing room from the stage, with applause still echoing in the hallway and confetti thrown by enthusiastic fans still clinging to their hair, the has-beens begin to criticize their trendy getup, right down to their sunglasses and headbands, and complain that newcomers no longer know how to treat their seniors with respect.

Affecting an air of weary dignity and irritated superiority (Hamada adds the perfect touch by dragging elaborately on his cigarette holder à la Noel Coward), the two has-beens accept the bows and apologies from the young comics and their manager and then, when they leave the room, pounce on the very stuff that they had found so offensive only moments before. When the young comics suddenly return to the dressing room to retrieve something they had forgotten, they find the has-beens wearing sunglasses, headbands—and stupid grins on their faces. It's hard to avoid the feeling that Matsumoto is finally getting his revenge on his early tormentor, Yokoyama.

Among the show's low points are a hysterical dance instructor, played by Matsumoto, who gets his kicks by knocking over his cowering female students like tenpins, and a dim anti-superhero named Aho Aho Man (Stupid Stupid Man), another Matsumoto creation, whose costume includes yellow-and-brown stained undershorts.

But despite these lapses (or given the tastes of a large segment of the Japanese viewing audience, because of them), *Downtown no Gottsu Ee Kanji* became a long-running hit and another of Downtown's signature shows.

Widely hailed as the funniest men in Japan and widely criticized for their bad effect on kids—the complaint that has followed popular Japanese comics since the dawn of television—Matsumoto and Hamada now face a problem that many of their colleagues would love to share: audiences, which were once Great Stone Faces, laugh at everything they say. "I get angry when they laugh at even our bad routines," Hamada told *Bart* magazine. "That is dangerous. It's like the *manzai* boom, which went way up, but soon came crashing down. There seems to be this feeling now that everyone can understand Matsumoto's humor. I want to tell them that they have no idea how funny Matsumoto really is."

THE DRIFTERS

The Japanese, many Japanese will tell you, have no sense of humor. A samurai, goes the saying, is allowed to crack a smile once every three years. The samurai's successor, the salaryman, is also expected to be a serious sort, who grins only when he surpasses his sales quota.

Television, however, tells another story. Japanese viewers, including salarymen, love shows that make them laugh. Even programs that don't fall into the comedy genre, including the omnipresent infotainment shows, frequently feature comedian hosts who go for the yocks. On most channels except sober-sided NHK, the sound of laughter in primetime—from the guests and studio audience, never from a laugh track—is as nearly constant as the surf at Kamakura.

The Drifters in a relaxed moment at the height of their TV popularity.

The show that probably made viewers laugh loudest and longest was *Hachiji Da Yo! Zen'in Shugo!* (It's Eight O'Clock! Get Together Everybody!), a comic variety hour that debuted on TBS in 1969 and ran until 1985. Averaging a 27 percent rating during its sixteen years on the air, *Zen'in Shugo* reached as high as 50.5 percent in April 1973 and, during its peak in the early 1970s, rarely fell below 40 percent.

Hosted by the Drifters, five comedians who had gotten their start in 1964 as a comedy band (they opened for the Beatles when they played the Budokan judo arena in 1966) the show was about as subtle as a Three Stooges' rubber hammer to the skull. *Zen'in Shugo* was built around skits, many of which got laughs from goofy slapstick gags or broad sexual innuendo. One Drifter, Cha Kato, was known for his male striptease number. Another, Ken Shimura, played a character called *hen na ojisan* (which roughly translates as "middle-aged pervert") who strapped a stuffed swan's neck to his crotch and bobbed the head at giggling female guests.

Other big laugh-getters were the show's sets, often enormous Rube Goldberg contraptions that seemed to have a life of their own. One favorite was a house that blew down in an on-stage typhoon and popped up again when the wind died down. Another was a full-size singing staircase.

A golden rule of the Drifters' comedy was bigger is better. Even props tended toward the gargantuan. In one routine the Drifters competed in a relay race, but every time a runner handed off the baton, it got bigger. Finally, the anchor, played by Kato, staggered across the finish line carrying a baton six meters long.

Some of the show's sight gags were not only grotesque but downright dangerous, including sending a real car crashing into the sets or covering the stage with real ice and having the show's expensive talent slip and slide on it.

Though *Zen'in Shugo* was the jewel of TBS's prime-time schedule, it deliberately courted controversy with its blatant disregard for what guardians of public morals regarded as good taste. A women's group protested the on-air food fights as "causing a problem for children's education." Outraged traditionalists even started a petition campaign to have the show canceled because they felt that Shimura's irreverent rewrite of a much-beloved sentimental children's song "distorted its spirit."

As might be expected, this utterly lowbrow show, which parents' groups routinely condemned as the worst on television, was a big hit with kids, who memorized the routines and made the catchphrases a part of schoolyard slang. *Zen'in Shugo* seemed destined to roll on forever.

Over the years, however, the show encountered its share of problems. In 1974, the oldest member of the Drifters, Chu Arai, announced he was leaving because he could no longer stand the physically strenuous pace. His replacement, Ken Shimura, was hardly an Olympic athlete, but had the advantage of youth—and a permanent leer. In 1976 Shimura and Drifters leader Koji Nakamoto were arrested for betting on the ponies with a bookie. Until their case was settled in court, the two comedians were barred from the show and nearly kicked off

it permanently by the image-conscious network. But the thought of continuing *Zen'in Shugo* without two of its funniest performers led TBS to reinstate them.

What finally killed the show was not enraged parents, zealous cops, or nervous network execs, but the competition. Although it beat off several challengers, including a 1980 show starring the then king of prime time comedy, Kin'ichi Hagimoto, it began to fade with the debut of the comedy show *Oretachi Hyokinzoku* (We Are Wild and Crazy Guys) on Fuji TV in 1981.

Starring some of the new standup comic duos that were then the rage of young audiences, *Hyokinzoku* did not try to beat *Zen'in Shugo* at its own game, but reinvented the rules. Although the show used *Zen'in Shugo*'s live-audience format, it rejected its rigid lowest-common-denominator formula. Instead, it was closer in spirit to an anything-goes late-night variety show for hip insomniacs. The show's core performers, including **BEAT TAKESHI**, Samma Akashiya, and Kuniko Yamada, were not hosts so much as resident crazies who seemed to drop in when the spirit moved them. Also, rather than rely on the usual numbskull humor to get laughs, *Hyokinzoku* developed a new style characterized by bizarre parodies of pop-culture icons and a ceaseless stream of ad-libs. The young audience liked *Hyokinzoku*'s brand of off-the-wall comedy and began turning off *Zen'in Shugo*. The Drifters reign as ratings kings had come to an end.

After *Zen'in Shugo*'s cancellation, TBS featured Shimura and Kato in a show of their own called *Kato-chan Ken-chan Gokigen Terebi* (Kato and Ken's Feeling Good TV). Though it never reached the ratings heights of *Zen'in Shugo*, the show proved popular. One regular segment on home videos contributed by viewers became a nationwide sensation and latter metamorphosed across the Pacific as *America's Funniest Home Videos*.

The Drifters have also kept plugging away, appearing several times yearly in comedy specials. But the old wildness is gone—and never a peep is heard from the PTA.

ELEVEN P.M.

Like *The Tonight Show* in the United States, *Eleven P.M.* owned late-night TV in Japan for decades. Launched in 1965, when miniskirts were first appearing on the streets of Tokyo, the show lasted until 1990 on NTV, when the sexual revolution had run its course and weekly magazines were printing scare stories about the spread of AIDS in Japan. In the beginning, there was nothing else on the air like it. By the time it ended, it had spawned several generations of imitations and spin-offs.

Conceived as the televised version of **HEIBON PUNCH**, a popular weekly magazine for men modeled on *Playboy*, *Eleven P.M.* debuted in a snazzy "nightclub" set and offered viewers everything from scantily clad girls and celebrity guests to hard news, in five minute segments.

Initially, network execs were skeptical that the show would fly; how many early rising salarymen would stay up to watch it? Even the NTV (then NET) workers union frowned: too many late-night hours. The show's producers compromised by having affiliate station Yomiuri TV in Osaka produce the Tuesday and Thursday night shows.

Unlike the *Tonight Show*, *Eleven P.M.* didn't center around a single personality, but the host who became most closely associated with the show was Kyosen Ohashi. Appearing on Friday nights for twenty years and on Monday nights for seventeen, the round-faced, jovially smiling Ohashi, with his trademark black-rimmed glasses, was a self-proclaimed "genius of play." The show needed this genius. When he took over Monday night, ratings were languishing; NET's hard-news slant was putting viewers to sleep.

Ohashi revamped the show with "gentleman's play-guide" segments, including guides to mah-jongg, horse racing, fishing,

Kyosen Ohashi in a familiar pose—in front of the microphones.

and driving. Although the segments contained plenty of how-to advice, they were mostly unscripted, relying on Ohashi's quips for their appeal. Viewers started tuning in and the ratings started perking up.

During the show's peak—from 1965 to 1975—Ohashi lived out the average salaryman's fantasies, jetting off to Europe and other points beyond Japan's shores to explore their pleasure spots, particularly ones where the sex industry flourished. At that time, foreign travel was out of reach for all but the well off and well connected. Also, many Japanese men regarded Western women as exotic, unobtainable creatures. Ohashi, however, treated these jaunts as a big lark and, far from being overawed by the fleshpots of the West, seemed to enjoy them hugely. Through Ohashi's eyes, the distant and forbidding suddenly seemed nearer, more familiar. Viewers wanted to go along for the ride.

Another host who had a major impact on the show was Giichi Fujimoto, an Osaka scriptwriter who appeared on Tuesday and Thursday nights for the show's entire twenty-five-year run and, off the set, won the prestigious Naoki Prize for literature. With a cocktail from the studio bar in front of him, Fujimoto would chat with the guests in slangy, macho-sounding Osaka dialect. The liquor and the use of nonstandard Japanese were both departures from the then straitlaced TV norm, but they endeared the white-maned Fujimoto to his salaryman viewers.

Even more endearing, however, were Fujimoto's erotic adventures, including segments on women sumo wrestlers and hot-springs geisha, who are better known in Japan for their performances in the futon than on the shamisen.

Although Fujimoto drew a contrast between Ohashi's "high-class" eroticism and his own earthier variety, both the Tokyo and Osaka shows relied heavily on sex for their appeal. The show's erotic displays were mild by latter standards—the strippers had to settle for seminudity—but they earned *Eleven P.M.* the enmity of women's groups and the punning nickname *Erobun P.M.*, a combination of *erosu* (eros) and *erebun* (the Japanese transcription of "eleven").

The show was more than the sum of its soft porn, however. In April 1968, when Lyndon Johnson called for a pause in the bombing of North Vietnam, the show pre-empted its regular programming to broadcast a special report, scooping the straight media. In 1972 *Eleven P.M.* even won a Galaxy Award—the Japanese Emmy—for its exploration of such topics as sex education and Japan-Korea relations—then both taboo on mainstream Japanese TV.

But as the show entered its second decade and Japan was swept up in the 1980s economic boom, viewers began to tire of the program's vicarious pleasures. Flush with cash in the palmy days of the bubble economy, less inhibited by traditional mores than their fathers and older brothers, younger salarymen began to take overseas trips and attend the live sex shows in Amsterdam themselves. Instead of seeming racily advanced and daringly underground, the show now was, if not passé, nothing special. And those searching for on-screen sexual kicks could find more thrilling ones in the neighborhood video rental racks than the show could ever hope to offer.

As the news race heated up among the commercial nets in the late 1980s (see **NEWS STATION**), NTV began pushing the show's time slot back to make room for its evening news program. In its last days, *Eleven P.M.* was going on the air at 11:45 P.M.—too late for all but the most dedicated fans or hard-core night owls. Finally, in 1990, the show was canceled.

Late-night TV lived on, but with a difference. By the mid-1990s, a popular figure on an *Eleven P.M.* successor was Ai Ijima, a red-headed former porno actress who spoke her mind about topical issues and dissed her male colleagues with raunchy talk. The days when the biggest thrill on TV was ogling miniskirted girls on the streets of the Ginza were like a dimly remembered dream.

GODZILLA

In the days before Hideo Nomo, a polling organization asked Americans to name as many famous Japanese as they could. The list was short, headed by Bruce Lee, Hirohito, and Godzilla. Unfortunately, two of the top three were not Japanese. The Emperor doubtless qualifies, though he does not carry a Japanese passport, vote in national elections, or possess that ultimate proof of Japanese citizenship, a family register. Kung Fu action star Bruce Lee was from Hong Kong. Finally, Godzilla may have often visited (and visited destruction on) Japan, but was born off the Bikini Atoll, in the wake of a U.S. hydrogen bomb test.

In the decades since his debut in the 1954 *Gojira* (Godzilla), the big guy has come to stand as a symbol of: (1) campy, cheesy monster movies, and (2) mindless destruction. Actually, the original film, which was directed by Inoshiro Honda, with special effects by Eiji Tsuburaya, was an A-list title for Toho, then as now one of Japan's largest film companies. In addition to spending sixty million yen—three times the studio norm—on state-of-the-art special effects, producers engaged an all-star cast headed by Takashi Shimura, who later become internationally known for playing a samurai leader in another Toho production of 1954, Akira Kurosawa's *The Seven Samurai.*

Godzilla, whose name is derived from the Japanese words for gorilla (*gorira*) and whale (*kujira*), and was inspired by an overweight press agent in Toho's publicity department, may have stomped Tokyo in his first movie, but his debut vehicle was intended as a sincere protest against nuclear destruction. Mess around with those hydrogen bombs long enough, the movie seems to say, and this is what can happen.

The producers even sabotaged the possibility of a sequel—the schlockmeister's Grail—by killing off Godzilla at the end of the movie. "Believe it or not," said Honda. "We had no plans for a sequel and naively hoped that the end of Godzilla was going to coincide with the end of nuclear testing."

Some hope. But the movie was a big hit, so much so that it attracted the attention of Columbia Pictures, which in 1956 released a version titled *Godzilla, King of the Monsters.* The Columbia film cut twenty minutes from the original and added new footage, directed by Terry Morse, of Raymond Burr as an American reporter in Tokyo. Backed by ads proclaiming that "Godzilla makes King Kong look like a midget!" the film became a hit with American audiences.

In 1955 Toho revived Godzilla for another movie, *Gojira no Gyakushu* (called *Gigantis—The Fire Monster* in a 1959 American version), which featured a titantic struggle between Godzilla and Angirasu, a stubby-legged monster modeled on the anklyosaurus. Kids in the audience, especially the pro-wrestling fans among them, loved it; it reminded not a few of the recent heavyweight bout between **RIKIDOZAN** and judo champ Masahiko Kimura.

Deciding that audiences wanted monsters, not a monster, again and again, the studio gave Godzilla a seven-year rest while entertaining moviegoers with a variety of creatures both odd and awesome, including Radon the pteranodon, Varan the lizard, and Mothra the moth. Finally, in 1962, at the prompting of American producer Joe Beck, it brought back Godzilla for a battle royal with King Kong in *King Kong tai Gojira* (King Kong vs. Godzilla).

Although Honda directed and Tsuburaya handled special effects, this Godzilla movie was not intended as a protest against anything. (Honda, however, suggested that Godzilla's fire-breathing defense of his adopted homeland against a foreign invader symbolized the wartime struggle between Japan and the United States.) In fact, the film was little more than a goofy entertainment aimed at kids, with a memorable scene of King Kong climbing Tokyo Tower and a climactic battle on Mount Fuji that was, like its 1955 predecessor, a pro-wrestling bout writ large. The Big G, of course, emerged the winner, with King Kong swimming back to his island home in the South Seas. This new formula was a huge success; *King Kong tai Gojira* was, with twelve million admissions, the biggest draw in the history of the series. In 1963 Universal released a revised version featuring a newscaster at the United Nations relaying a blow-by-blow account of the bout via satellite to a breathless world.

Thinking that it had developed an indefinitely replicable, predictably profitable product, Toho proceeded to stamp out Godzilla movies the way Volkswagen did Beetles: the same basic model year after year, with a few changes here and there to give buyers the illusion that they were getting something new.

Over the next thirteen years Toho matched Godzilla against a procession of monsters, but whether the opponent was a giant moth (Mothra again), a three-headed space dragon (King Ghidorah), or a mammoth mechanical reproduction of the big guy himself (MechaGodzilla), Godzilla triumphed, even though a few national landmarks disappeared in the process. (Eventually Japanese cities would vie for the honor of being Godzilla's new stomping ground.) Beginning with the 1964 *Sandai Kaiju Chikyu no Saidai Kessen (Ghidorah—The Three-Headed Monster)* he also morphed from a terrifying force of destruction into a savior of mankind (though Radon and Mothra, his comrades in the struggle against the film's bad guy, the flying space dragon Ghidorah, deserved some of the credit).

As the series continued, Toho added bizarre twists to hold audience attention—in one installment a baby Godzilla joined Big G in the battle against the baddies—but exhaustion finally set in. If the first Godzilla movie had aspired to profundity, the series entries of the 1960s and 1970s descended into campy mediocrity. In 1975, after disappointing returns from *Mekagojira no Gyakushu* (Revenge of MechaGodzilla, or as retitled for U.S. release, *Godzilla vs. the Cosmic Monster*), Toho retired its biggest star again. The monster who had once beaten America's best—if King Kong, after his sojourn in New York, can be considered an honorary American—was now being thrashed at the box office by glitzy Hollywood special-effects shows. Traditionalists may have thrilled at a man in a Godzilla suit tromping toy cities, but younger moviegoers were flocking to the scarier realism of *Jaws*. The year of Godzilla's final humiliation at the hands of Steven Spielberg was also the year that the Japanese movie industry's market share fell below fifty percent for the first time.

After the failure of *Mekagojira no Gyakushu,* Honda never directed again, though he did serve as technical advisor on five films of close friend Akira Kurosawa. He died in 1993, with his first film still his best remembered. Godzilla, however, lived on. Though new Godzilla movies were no longer being made, revivals drew big crowds and Godzilla character goods continued to sell.

Realizing that it had a national icon on its hands, Toho brought Godzilla out of retirement once more. The 1984 comeback recycled the title of the first movie, to make it clear that the big guy was getting back to basics. No more Mr. Nice Guy: this Godzilla was going to be scary!

Second, there would be special effects that Star Wars fans could respect. Producers, however, made a concession to tradition and budgetary realities: a man in a Godzilla suit would once again play the lead.

Kempachiro Satsuma, the man they chose, appeared in all the remaining installments of the series. A master of judo, karate, and horseback riding (not that he needed the last skill in his biggest role), Satsuma portrayed Godzilla so convincingly that in 1985 North Korea's Dear Leader Kim Jong II—a Godzilla buff with filmmaking ambitions—invited him to play the monster in a movie that Kim was planning to produce with South Korean director Shin Sang-ok. Satsuma accepted the offer and later wrote a tongue-in-cheek book about his experiences titled *North Korea as Godzilla Saw It.*

But though Satsuma may have seen the absurdity of Godzilla rampaging around the People's Republic (What could he tromp, one wonders, statues of the Great Leader?), he took his job seriously. Speaking to reporters on the set of *Gojira tai Supeesu Gojira* (Godzilla vs. Space Godzilla), a 1994 film made to celebrate the fortieth anniversary of the series, Satsuma said that his conception of the role involved more than simply acting out. "After a rampage, Godzilla always returns to the sea," he said. "I try to express with my back the silent message that Godzilla will always come back and fight as long as people keep making nuclear weapons."

Lured by a massive PR campaign, including a hotline for fans to phone in story ideas, and curiosity as to how Godzilla would look and act after a ten-year layoff, moviegoers flocked to *Gojira.* It became the second-highest-earning domestic film of the year, making 1.7 billion yen for distributor Toho. Retitled *Godzilla 1985,* with additional footage of Raymond Burr reprising his 1956 role as an inquiring American reporter, the film was also released by New World on 1,500 screens in the United States.

Instead of immediately capitalizing on its success, however, Toho spent three years in script development before starting production of the next installment. Released in 1989, *Gojira tai Biolante* (Godzilla vs. Biolante) was another box-office winner. Starting in 1991, Toho made a new Godzilla movie annually for the peak New Year's season. Produced for an average budget of 1 billion yen—big for a Japanese movie—these 1990s entries all become hits, with the 1992 *Gojira tai Mosura* (Godzillavs. Queen Mothra) reaching a series earnings peak: 2.22 billion yen on 4.2 million admissions.

Though Toho tried to give the big guy a nineties edge with snazzier special effects and a makeover that included a double row of teeth and more pumped-up look, the lameness of the story lines, with their mix of far-fetched international intrigue, belabored techno-jargon, and predictable finales made the series a critical disaster. Not campy enough to be a hoot, they were simply over-produced bores.

Abroad, the image of the series was largely derived from the "classic" period of the 1950s and 1960s. Even so, the central image—a man-created mutant lizard powerful enough to destroy the greatest works of modern civilization—held a universal fascination that survived the critical lambastings visited on later series entries.

Thus the inevitable Hollywood remake. In 1992 Tristar Pictures bought the international rights to the character from Toho with the idea of producing an American Godzilla movie. Originally budgeted at fifty million dollars, the project hit a production snag when director Jan De Bont quit after the studio refused his request for more spectacular effects. Finally, in May 1996 Tristar signed *Independence Day* director Roland Emmerich and co-scriptwriter Dean Devlin to make a Godzilla movie with a reported budget of one hundred million dollars—ten times that of Toho's latest entry.

Rather than compete with this high-powered Hollywood newcomer, Toho bowed out of the Godzilla business. In July 1995 Toho executive producer Shogo Toyama announced that the entry for that year's New Year's season—*Gojira tai Desutoroia* (Godzilla vs. Destroyer) would be the last. "Because the Godzilla movies are serialized, some constraints came to be imposed on the character of Godzilla and the background story," he explained. "That's why we decided to end the series."

Others within Toho, however, have suggested that, more than story problems, the company is concerned about cannibalizing box-office returns from the Tristar Godzilla series, which Toho will distribute in Japan. So Toho has sent its own Godzilla into retirement until its American cousin finishes its theatrical run. "We are going to develop a new Godzilla for the twenty-first century," said International Business Division deputy general manager Yoshihisa Nakagawa. "We are not going to abandon this character."

But will they keep the Godzilla suit?

GURUME

Food fetishism is hardly a new trend in Japan; Japanese with the means and inclination have long sought out gourmet delights, including some that Westerners might consider less than delightful (squid and octopus on the sushi menu are just the beginning, as anyone who has sampled raw horse meat, fried grasshoppers, and pit viper wine can testify). Japanese gourmets have also long appreciated not only the taste but look of food, a tendency exemplified most famously by the tea-ceremony cuisine called *kaiseki ryori*, whose bite-sized courses are as

exquisitely presented as they are delicately flavored. But gourmet dining was traditionally the passion of a privileged few, especially in the early years after the war, when average Japanese were more concerned with filling their stomachs than critiquing what went into them.

During the boom years of the 1980s, however, many Japanese found themselves, for the first time in their lives, with the income to pursue their passion for fine food, both at home and abroad. To satisfy this growing legion of gourmets, restaurants specializing in all the major world cuisines, and more than a few of the minor ones, began to spring up in Tokyo. French restaurants, which could once be counted on the fingers of one hand, suddenly seemed to be in every suburban neighborhood. At the peak of the gourmet boom, in the late 1980s, there were more than one thousand in Tokyo alone.

Television was quick to pick up on the trend. The pioneer was *Banzai! Oishimbo* (Hurray! Taste Quest), a two-and-a-half minute program that debuted on Fuji TV in 1975 and, more than two decades later, is still being aired four days a week from 9:54 P.M. As the title implies, the show features a robust-looking male celebrity (usually with an expanding waistline) who tours the countryside sampling—or scarfing—local specialties.

During the bubble years, this program, as well as the perennial afternoon cooking shows for housewives, were joined by a flood of new shows, several in primetime. By 1991, just as the bubble burst and the Japanese economy entered its long recession, the six Tokyo TV stations were broadcasting twenty-two cooking shows a week, for a total of more than seventy programs. Including "gourmet corners" on shows that otherwise had nothing to do with cooking, the total rose to nearly one hundred.

Following the pattern set by *Banzai! Oishimbo,* the new *gurume* (gourmet) shows were usually anything but stuffy. Instead of food critiques by picky connoisseurs, they often featured on-the-scene reports by bubbly young female talents who would gasp at outlandish ethnic concoctions, coo at kitschy pastries, and, putting fork to mouth, utter the standard one-word critique: *oishii* (delicious)!

The *manga* industry also did its part to boost the *gurume* boom. In 1983 *manga* artist Tetsu Kariya debuted *Oishimbo* (Taste Quest), a *manga* about the search of two young newspaper reporters for the Ultimate Menu to celebrate the paper's hundredth anniversary. Though the *manga* had its melodramatic elements, including a bitter rivalry between one of the reporters and his estranged gourmet father, Kariya included plenty of solidly researched information on food production and expert advice on food preparation. The *manga* became an enormous hit whose fifty-five paperback volumes have sold seventy million copies.

In 1996 Shochiku released a film based on the *manga* series, starring Rentaro Mikuni as the crusty old gourmet, Koichi Sato as his rebellious son, and Michiko Hada as the son's cub-reporter colleague. In the movie, the ultimate gourmet delight turns out to be special home-cooked beans from the heart of the heart of the country, far from corrupting Western influences. Needless to say, they never see the inside of a can.

The *gurume* boom spawned a variety of food fads, both banal and bizarre. One was for *ikizukuri,* or fish taken live from a tank, sliced and diced and placed, still wriggling, on a plate or in a soup bowl. Far from being a modern invention, *ikizukuri* had long had a place, albeit a minor one, in Japanese cuisine. Instead of waiting until they returned to shore, hungry fishermen would often pop some of their catch into their mouths.

The *gurume* boom brought *ikizukuri* into the mainstream. Restaurants specializing in live fish began to proliferate. At one, Chunagon in Tokyo's exclusive Ginza area, waiters brought the entrees, eyes moving and tail flapping, whole to the table, where they gutted and served them to the waiting gourmets. Smaller aquatic animals, including eel and firefly squid, were consumed in one piece—or gulp. Live, however, did not mean cheap; a full-course dinner at Chunagon could set a diner back one hundred twenty dollars.

Japanese cuisine was not the only inspiration for fads. In 1990, *Hanako,* a trendy city magazine for Tokyo women, surveyed the then-current craze for Italian food and decided that tiramisù—a sweet made of mascarpone cheese, chocolate, and espresso, with a dusting of cocoa powder on top—should replace cheesecake as the dessert of choice among young fashionables.

Where *Hanako* led, millions of young women followed. Tiramisù was soon the most-ordered dessert at Tokyo's rapidly growing number of Italian restaurants. Those that didn't have tiramisù soon put it on the menu.

Food and beverage makers quickly exploited the trend, launching tiramisù soft drinks and candy bars. Fast food chains were not far behind; in February 1991 Kentucky Fried Chicken added a frozen tiramisù dessert to the menu. Wendy's and two Japanese chains, Mos Burger and First Kitchen, came out with their own tiramisù concoctions soon after.

Needless to say, when tiramisù became as common as a Wendy's Frosty, young trendies realized that it wasn't trendy anymore and stopped ordering it. (It didn't help that the products masquerading as tiramisù would

make any self-respecting Italian dessert chef throw up his hands in horror.) Soon importers were wondering what to do with their hastily ordered shipments of mascarpone cheese, and convenience stores were selling their tiramisù candy bars at discount to untrendy school kids.

The early demise of tiramisù didn't spell the end of the *gurume* boom, however. Even when the bubble economy burst in 1991 and Tokyo's French restaurants started to look like sets for *Last Year at Marienbad,* young gourmets latched onto new fads better suited to recessionary times. One was *motsu nabe,* a stew made of animal entrails that older Japanese associated with wartime rationing and postwar poverty, but the younger generation revived as a reverse-chic *gurume* treat. Now that bonus payments were shrinking, companies were laying off workers, and jobs for new graduates were becoming harder to find, it also didn't hurt that *motsu nabe* was filling and cheap.

Despite the popularity of old-fashioned poverty-row cuisine, *gurume* shows on TV became, if anything, even more frantic in their search for the new and the trendy. The competition to stay ahead of the *gurume* curve forced producers not only to make their shows more sophisticated ("delicious!" was no longer an acceptable restaurant review) but create new formats for them.

One such show that attracted media attention and generated high ratings following its 1993 debut was *Iron Chef,* which might be described as Julia Child meets the World Cup meets the Metropolitan Opera.

Hosted by Takashi Kaga, who impersonated a rich European nobleman with a deep, booming voice, a theatrical manner, and a passion for good food, the show pitted one of the three master chefs of its Iron Chef Academy against a challenger.

Using a carefully selected seasonal ingredient, the master chef and challenger were required to prepare from three to five dishes in their specialty—Japanese, Chinese, or Western cuisine—in sixty minutes or less. During the frantic preparation period, the show's announcers commented on the action with breathless intensity, while cameras zoomed in for dramatic close-ups of slicing and stirring. Finally, three judges sampled the results and announced the winner, basing their decision as much on artistry and originality as taste.

Explaining the show's success, Fuji TV International Sales and Marketing Director Ansei Yokota noted that "Japanese are fanatics about food. It's often said that they make the best spaghetti outside of Italy, the best French cuisine outside of France. Another example is the movie *Tampopo,* which is about making the perfect bowl of ramen (Chinese noodles). As a general rule, no other Asians are as particular about what they eat as the Japanese." In short, unlike the bubble economy that spawned it, the *gurume* boom shows no signs of going bust.

HEIΒON PUNCH

In 1964 Japan was in the midst of the most rapid economic expansion in its history. Wages were rising and ownership of televisions, audio sets, cars, and other consumer goods was soaring (see **CONSUMER CULTURE**). As though to proclaim to the world that it had arrived, Japan was holding its first-ever Olympics in a Tokyo that seemed to be transforming itself daily.

No longer struggling to survive, young people were looking for new ways to have fun, including fun with the opposite sex. That year an editor at the Magazine House publishing company named Tatsuo Shimizu created a weekly magazine for young men with time on their hands, spare yen in their pockets, and young women on their minds. Called *Heibon Punch* (*heibon* means "ordinary"), it became Japan's version of *Playboy*—a seminal publication that brought sex out of the dirty bookstore and into the mainstream.

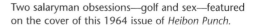

WEEKLY

平凡パンチ

6/17
130yen

Entertainment for men

性を媒介とした世直しの道

SEX探求
女は汗にまみれてベッドイン
伊東商高ゴルフ部の徹底した クラブ活動

Two salaryman obsessions—golf and sex—featured on the cover of this 1964 issue of *Heibon Punch.*

picked up *Punch* on the newsstand, the more immediate attraction was a sexy cover illustration by Susumu Ohashi—selected by Shimizu and his staff from among eighty candidates—and a center foldout titled simply "A Girl of Paris." The first issue sold 550,000 copies—then a huge number for a men's magazine, particularly one whose main selling point was a nude foreigner. The Japanese publishing industry had never seen anything like it.

But though *Heibon Punch* made an immediate hit, it was swimming against a current of official repression. Trying to clean up the country's image in preparation for the Olympics, authorities in Tokyo and across Japan were launching crackdowns against the sex industry. In January 1964 the Cabinet decided to amend to the morals law to abolish all-night coffee shops, seen as dens of vice, although their customers usually limited their wickedness to heavy petting. In May the Ministry of Health urged prefectural and local governments to forbid massueses at the notorious Turkish baths (which, as was often noted, were neither Turkish nor baths) from wearing then-standard bathing suits. Instead, said ministry bureaucrats, they should don white uniforms, though what effect this satorial change would have on the services the masseuses performed was not

At first, Magazine House's middle-aged editor-in-chief didn't think that such a magazine would fly. "If young guys have enough money to buy a magazine, they'll spend it on ramen or cigarettes instead," he said. But Shimizu, who later said that "it's dangerous if everyone agrees with your idea— that means it's not new," finally won the necessary editorial consensus and, in 1965, Magazine House launched *Heibon Punch.*

Showing that it understood the materalistic aspirations of its target readers, the premiere issue featured a quiz with a new car as first prize. But for many of the men who made clear. In July, in reaction to the fashion novelty of the moment, the topless swimsuit, Tokyo police gave notice that anyone caught wearing this shameless garment in public would be prosecuted.

Heibon Punch, however, escaped from the crackdowns unscathed. One reason was that its approach toward sex was cool rather than hot. Instead of the lurid personal confessions or heavy-breathing red-light reportage found in under-the-counter men's magazines, *Heibon Punch* ran stories of sex that former editor Akira Amakasa later described as being "like student essays" in their abstract intellectuality. But this softcore policy, together with plenty of inside info on cars, sports, and fashion, and an editorial style that addressed readers with older-brotherly informality and directness, proved to be a winner. One year after its launch *Heibon Punch's* circulation had nearly doubled, reaching one million.

As the magazine advanced into the sixties, it began to acquire a tougher, cheekier, more antiauthoritarian attitude. This attitude was exemplified by *Heibon Punch* photographer Osamu Nagahama, who once hired a model to pose in front of cops guarding a student demonstration and, at the appropriate moment, open her coat to reveal that she was wearing nothing underneath.

Although he received a visit the next day from members of the National Security Force—Japan's FBI—Nagahama refused to reform. In another flight of inspiration, he persuaded a drug-using delinquent to not only tell her story in the magazine but return home to her remote mountain village and, as an act of purification, pose nude in front of her ancestors' grave. Other *Heibon Punch* photographers followed Nagahama's adventurous and iconoclastic lead. One traveled to San Francisco to shoot the Hell's Angels in action, while another photographed a model urinating from the roof of a building. The magazine also covered countercultural phenomena in a more serious light, publishing an analysis of why a radical group's plan to occupy the prime minister's residence and seize the centers of power had failed to materialize.

But as the sixties gave way to the seventies, *Heibon Punch* began to mellow out—and sell out—interviewing the Bay City Rollers and running fawning photo spreads on popular idol singers that differed little from those in teenybopper fanzines, while letting the Punk Rock revolution pass it by. By now, having made nudity acceptable in mass-circulation weeklies and become thoroughly mainstream itself, the magazine was losing its raison d'être and, eventually, its readership.

In the early eighties Magazine House brought in one new editor after another to shake things up and stop the circulation slide, but *Heibon Punch* had become too set in its ways (or, as its critics said, too brain dead) to respond. One feature instructed readers on methods of guzzling beer, while another hymned the joys of anal intercourse. Mindless seasonal and topical motifs dominated the photo pages, with nude models gamely frolicking in the snow at ski resorts, and porno actresses donning bald wigs to mark the election of a shiny-domed prime minister. A kind of low was reached when, for a Year of the Monkey special issue, the magazine posed a baby monkey between the spread legs of a Shinjuku sex worker.

Even on its last legs, however, the magazine occasionally produced stories that recalled its chance-taking glory days, including a report by Shigeru Endo on the inner workings of an Osaka *yakuza* gang, in which he asked a gang boss how many men he had killed and whether he had taken out life insurance. By this time, however, it was too late to stanch the flow of red ink. Finally, in October 1988 the staff published the last issue, whose cover illustration showed a man in bed with the covers pulled over his head and a caption announcing that *Heibon Punch* was going into "hibernation." And there it remains today, living in fond memory for a generation as the first magazine to give them the promise of a heretofore unimagined personal freedom, in a garden of earthly delights.

INSTANT RAMEN

Instant ramen is to Japan what the hamburger is to America: a national junk food, symbol, and obsession. Japanese consumed about 5.02 billion instant ramen packs or cups in 1993, or 40.2 for every man, woman, and child in the country. These quick, easy meals—just add hot water, flavoring powder, wait one minute, and presto!—can be found not only in expected places such as supermarkets, convenience stores, and vending machines but also at ball parks (thermos-toting vendors hand you your cup of ramen piping hot), in earthquake preparedness kits (instant ramen is light, virtually indestructible, and lasts forever), and office desk drawers (instant ramen is a favorite hot snack of the nation's late-working salarymen).

Instant ramen is also a favorite of traveling Japanese who can't abide the local cuisine and want a taste of home. One of the common images of the Japanese abroad, found in such movies as the 1989 *Torajiro no Tabiji* (Torajiro's Journey), is of the culture-shocked traveler in a foreign hotel room

A meal in a minute for the masses—instant ramen.

sucking ramen noodles out of a styrofoam cup. **TORA-SAN**'s case of culture shock is more severe than most; he doesn't even know that he's in Vienna (why would take too long to explain). The task of ordering and paying for a meal is so far beyond him that he probably would have starved if it weren't for instant ramen, that most quintessentially Japanese of junk foods.

Like the hamburger, however, ramen is an import-gone-native. Its origins, like so much of Japanese food culture, lie in China. No one knows exactly when this noodle soup arrived in Japan, but according to Keiko Kosuge, a food expert who teaches at Sugino Women's College, feudal lord Tokugawa Mitsukuni was the first Japanese to taste ramen, in 1665.

The first ramen shop—at the least the first one that can be definitely dated—was the Rairai-ken, which opened in Tokyo in 1910. It did not start a ramen boom, however. It was not until after World War II and the introduction of American-style convenience foods that manufacturers began to see ramen as a product for the masses. In 1958, Nisshin launched Chicken Ramen—the first instant ramen in a pack. Total production that year was a mere thirteen million packs, but Japanese consumers were soon hooked and sales soared.

In 1971 Nisshin introduced another innovation: instant ramen in a cup. This meal-in-a-minute, which came with its own styrofoam container for heating and serving, was the first of its kind and offered even greater convenience. By 1989 ramen-in-a-cup was outselling ramen-in-a-pack and has lengthened its lead in the years since.

Instant ramen, as nearly everyone now knows, is no longer a Japanese-only treat. Japanese food companies began exporting it in 1960 and launched overseas production in 1970. They also started to expand their product lines: over the years instant ramen leader Nisshin has debuted Pork Chowder, Beef, Seafood, Vegetable, and, in 1982, a spicy Chili Tomato ramen that helped generate the fad for "ethnic" foods. Today instant ramen is sold in more than eighty countries and foreigners slurp down seventeen billion packages a year. Japanese instant-ramen makers have even taken their product back to ramen's birthplace: China. In 1994 demand in China was officially estimated to be two billion units a year, but some industry observers claimed that actual consumption was much higher—five to six billion units, rising to ten billion by 1995.

But though the Chinese may have taken instant ramen to their hearts, it is the Japanese who turned ramen making into an art, with professional ramen tasters employed by leading food companies traveling the country to define regional variations, famous chefs competing on national television to make the ultimate bowl of ramen, and gourmets patiently enduring long lines outside of tiny eight-seat shops that food critics have hailed as ramen meccas.

Instant ramen, of course, is far too humble a dish to aspire to snob appeal. Though some brands position themselves as ur-Japanese soul food, using images of old-fashioned ramen pushcarts (still to be found on busy urban streets, especially after dark, when ramen is supposed to be tastiest), others present themselves as a wild, zany, childishly sinful snack (an image not too far from the truth; a diet heavy on instant ramen, with its sky-high sodium count and low nutritional value, is a frequently cited cause of malnutrition, especially among young adults living alone). In 1989 Nisshin introduced a new wrinkle in ramen TV-commercial wackiness by hiring Arnold Schwarzenegger to pose heroically in a black T-shirt, swinging giant brass teakettles in each hand (though neither, thankfully, was filled with hot water). The aim was to emphasis the "power" in the product by associating it with Arnie's rippling muscles.

But whether pitched by an old-timey ramen vendor or the toothily grinning star of *Terminator 2*, instant ramen is here to stay as the real taste of today's Japan.

ISHIHARA, YUJIRO

He was the "Tough Guy," a symbol of Japanese macho for more than three decades. In his later years, with his puffy jowls, crinkly eyes, sagging paunch, and gravelly voice, he was a stolid figure who looked as though he had smoked too many Mild Sevens and drained too many glasses of Suntory Old. Still tough, but in a battle-weary, middle-aged, salaryman way.

The "Tough Guy" hadn't started out so tough, however. Back in 1956, when he appeared in his first film, *Taiyo no Kisetsu* (Season of the Sun), Yujiro Ishihara was a tall, gangly boy with a pretty, chubby face and a mischievous, sexy grin. The movie, which featured Yujiro in a bit role as the boxer friend of the hero, was a big hit. Though Yujiro was already projecting a rebellious image, filmgoers could see that he was really a likable kid with loads of star charisma. And the teenage girls in the audience couldn't take their eyes off his long, lanky legs—then an uncommon sight in Japan. A star was born.

Yujiro had lucked into the role through a family connection; his older brother, Shintaro Ishihara, had written the book on which the film was based. (Years later, as a Liberal Democratic Party politician, Shintaro wrote another book, *The Japan That Can Say No,* that caused an international uproar.) Still a student at Keio University, he was regarded as the representative of the book and film's "Sun Tribe," or *Taiyo-zoku* (see **ZOKU**), by adoring fans.

The Sun Tribe were kids who had grown up in postwar Japanese society, in all its chaos and freedom, and now rejected adult values. Instead of dying for the emperor or slaving for the company, they just wanted to hang out on the Ginza or Shonan Beach near Tokyo, listen to groovy sounds, and work on their attitudes. Their elders regarded them as spoiled and wild; they could not have cared less. They were, in fact, the Japanese counterparts of another Sun Tribe on the opposite side of the Pacific that was busy creating the culture of surfing, hot-rodding, and fun, fun, fun in the warm California sun.

Yujiro later claimed to be embarrassed by his media image as a Sun Tribe chieftain. In a 1958 book titled *Waga Seishun Monogatari* (The Story of My Youth) he wrote that "com-pared with older teenagers today I feel that I'm rather old-fashioned."

Old-fashioned or not, Yujiro was a gilded youth compared with most of his contemporaries. His father had been a shipbuilding company executive and, though he had died when Yujiro and his brother were still young, his sons had grown up relatively unaffected by the hardships of the early postwar years. Shintaro had attended elite Hitotsubashi University and Yujiro had been admitted to Keio University from its affiliated high school, without having to sweat through entrance exams.

A private university attended by the rich and privileged, Keio offered Yujiro a punched ticket to the good life. Instead of grinding away at the books, he spent his college days sailing his boat off the Zushi coast, playing sports, and drinking with his friends at university bars—a typical Keio student, in other words, but with uncommon good looks and a self-confidence that bordered on arrogance. And he could even sing.

The movie industry, however, wondered whether Yujiro was the real thing. When the Sun Tribe set, would his career fade? Yujiro himself talked of returning to his studies at Keio. But he was too much of a good thing: Japan's own Elvis Presley and James Dean rolled into one. Nikkatsu cast him as the romantic lead in film after Sun Tribe film. Soon, he was simply "Yu-chan" to millions.

Yujiro Ishihara drums up a storm in a poster for *Arashi o Yobu Otoko.*

These films were not all exploitation vehicles. The 1956 *Kurutta Kajitsu* (Crazed Fruit) by Ko Nakahira, which gave Yujiro his first starring role, sent François Truffaut, then an influential young film critic, into ecstacies over its raw depiction of amorality among Sun Tribe youth. Based on a novel by Shintaro, *Kurutta Kajitsu* was the first Japanese film selected for preservation, at Truffaut's strong recommendatation, by the Cinemathèque Française film archive.

Another well-remembered film from this period was the 1958 *Hi No Ataru Sakamichi* (The Sloping Road in the Sunlight) which was based on a novel that Shintaro had modeled on *East of Eden.* Working with veteran director Tomotaka Tasaka, Yujiro played the James Dean part of a love-starved boy in a wealthy family with an appealing vivacity that won him more critical plaudits and brought Nikkatsu yet another hit.

Though his Sun Tribe movies about disaffected youths did well, he soon found even greater success in another genre: hardboiled action films. In the 1957 *Arashi o Yobu Otoko* (The Man Who Started a Storm) he played a wild Ginza kid whose ambition is to become a jazz drummer but who has more of a talent for finding trouble than for stroking the skins. The movie was one of the year's five biggest boxoffice earners and pulled then-struggling Nikkatsu out of the red. Fans went crazy, clapping and yelling their approval, when he began singing about being "a drummer, a no-good drummer, when I get mad, I start a storm." Industry veterans, who had watched dozens of stars come and go, had never seen anything like it.

Yujiro's husky-voiced singing in *Arashi* and other films of the period, including the 1957 waterfront actioner *Washi to Taka* (The Eagle and the Hawk), launched him on a second, highly successful career as a crooner. His records, mostly of the genre of soulful Japanese ballads called *enka*, soared to the top of the charts (he cut a total of 218 albums and 235 singles in his career).

Yujiro was also a trendsetter in his adoption of things new and Western. In his films he played the trumpet and saxophone with a boyish insouciance and practiced ease. Off screen, he not only drove fancy foreign cars and wore expensive designer clothes—standard movie star stuff, even for 1950s Japan—but was an expert skier and yachtsman, accomplishments that made him an exotic rarity in a Japan still emerging from postwar poverty.

While Yujiro's Westernized looks and style were thrilling to his teenage female fans, his macho persona captivated the boys as well; they imitated his casual, over-the-forehead hair style, his blue-denim look, and even the hitch in his walk. More than a few followed him to the seaside or the slopes, hoping to taste the carefree, adventurous life that he seemed to embody.

Meanwhile, like Elvis in his post-Army film career, Yujiro became a one-man studio, grinding out formula flicks by the dozen, often opposite the hot young actresses of the day, Mie Kitahara and Yuriko Asaoka. And like Elvis, the refreshingly uninhibited rebel of Yujiro's early films quickly gave way to the conventional hero who upholds good and defeats evil. This character may have looked dangerous to the parents of nubile young women, but never really threatened conventional standards of morality. Though he may have set the old folks straight, as James Dean did in *Rebel Without a Cause,* he was polite and respectful, not wild and heartstricken like Jimmy. In the 1960 *Ajisai no Uta* (The Hydrangea Song) he even hoisted a fainting Mom up on his broad, manly back in an admirable performance of traditional filial duty, or *oyakoko.*

Yujiro's constant proximity to Mie Kitahara—he costarred with her in seven films in 1958 alone—soon led to an off-screen romance. In January 1960 Yujiro and Mie flew to Hawaii on what the press dubbed a "secret honeymoon." Their lack of a marriage certificate, however, caused a scandal. Finally, in December, they were wed at the Nikkatsu Hotel, which was owned, conveniently enough, by Yujiro's studio. One hundred guards patrolled the grounds during the four-hour ceremony to keep frenzied female fans from storming inside.

In the sixties, Yujiro's interests and ambitions widened beyond grinding out increasingly routine action films. In 1963, with brother Shintaro at the helm, Yujiro sailed in the Transpacific Yacht Race aboard the thirty-nine-foot sloop *Contessa III.* The only Japanese boat in the 2,225 mile annual race, the *Contessa III* survived thirty-knot winds to finish second in its class. Yujiro returned home a hero, this time for real.

In 1965 he appeared in a big-budget Twentieth Century Fox comedy, *Those Magnificent Men in Their Flying Machines.* Starring Sarah Miles, Terry Thomas, Robert Morley, and Gert Frobe, this movie about the early days of aviation today looks corny and coy, but Yujiro acquitted himself well, portraying an accident-prone Japanese air racer with an amused panache that contradicted then-prevalent Hollywood stereotypes of typical "Japanese" behavior, as exemplified by Mickey Rooney's frenetic performance as the Japanese photographer in *Breakfast at Tiffany's.*

In February of the same year, Yujiro's tough-guy image got an unwanted boost when cops raided his house looking for pistols. An acquaintance who described himself as Yujiro's bodyguard had been arrested for selling smuggled heaters to *yakuza* gangsters and the police suspected that Yujiro was also involved. The search, however, turned up nothing but a Japanese sword and the head of a lance—both lacking the necessary licenses. Yujiro vigorously denied any connection with either the bodyguard or the gun-smuggling ring. Finally, in September, after lengthy and highly embarrassing questioning, he was cleared of any wrongdoing.

Seeking to escape the studio grind and become his own boss, Yujiro founded his own production company in 1965 and began making films, with the money coming from corporate sponsors. Though *Kurobe no Taiyo* (The Tunnel to the Sun) and *Safari 500* may not have won critical plaudits, they earned big yen at the box office. Yujiro started to dream of making international movies with Hollywood stars. His wish list included such names as Richard Widmark, Charlton Heston, and Steve McQueen.

In the early sixties, however, Japanese moviegoers began abandoning the theaters in large numbers for the small screen. Although Yujiro remained immune longer than most to the precipitous slide in admissions, he began to lose his hit-making touch in the early 1970s, turning out ill-concieved "humanistic" pictures that pleased neither critics nor fans. Also, with his expanding middle and puffy face, Yujiro no longer looked the part of the young rebel hero.

After having vowed that he would never appear in a TV series because of the cheesy quality of Japanese TV production, in 1972 Yujiro succumbed and agreed to play the lead in *Taiyo ni Hoero* (Howl at the Sun), a police detective series. The show, with its weekly gun battles and high-speed car chases, may have stretched the limits of credibility (real Japanese cops avoid both like the plague), but *Taiyo ni Hoero* found favor with viewers, who reveled in the interplay between the fatherly section chief that Yujiro portrayed, who spoke little but knew all, and his devoted if occasionally brash subordinates, including the young **YUSAKU MATSUDA** as the long-haired, blue-denimed Detective Jiipan. The show stayed on the air for fourteen years.

As Yujiro advanced into middle age, his smoking, drinking, and partying to live up to his Tough Guy image began to take its toll. On April 25, 1981, he collapsed on the set during the filming of another TV cop show, *Seibu Keisatsu* (Seibu Police). After being rushed to Keio Hospital, he was diagnosed with a coronary aneurysm. So many well-wishers descended on the hospital—twelve thousand in all—that the hospital staff set up a tent outside to receive them. In addition to the usual flowers and folded-paper cranes—symbols of good fortune—fans sent two thousand stuffed dolls and cakes, including one in the shape of a yacht, and three thousand orders of sushi.

Yujiro recovered and returned to work,

A voyeur's dream: the platform fan-dancers at Juliana's.

but fell victim to liver cancer. After a six-year battle, he succumbed on July 17, 1987, at the age of fifty-two. He left 1.748 billion yen in assets, including a thirty-room house in Tokyo's exclusive Seijo neighborhood, a villa near Lake Yamanaka, and two homes in Hawaii.

Within days after his death record stores had sold out their stocks of his records, including the entire pressing of a new thirteen-album boxed set titled, simply, "The Big Man" (another of his nicknames), that contained 154 songs and cost a hefty twenty-five thousand yen. Like two of his American role models, Elvis and James Dean, Yujiro was an even bigger earner dead than he had been alive. Nearly a decade later, though no one sights him in supermarket parking lots, his legend is alive and well.

JULIANA'S

Juliana's was the disco to end all discos, at its height a nationally known symbol of late-bubble-era excess and decadence, a creator of fashions in music, fashion, and sexual display. Conservative guardians of morals and taste railed against it, while the trendy, the curious, and the just plain lecherous longed to walk through its fabled portals and gaze at its multifarious wonders.

Located in a former warehouse in Shibaura, a district of Tokyo better known for its drab office buildings than its night life, Juliana's was built as a high-class, high-tech monument to boogie. After being vetted by a tall, imposing foreign doorman for age, dress, and overall hipness, patrons walked through the large fractured-glass doors and past the official greeters—six Japanese women in glittering green minidresses, all bowing in unison—to a cavernous room that would have made a great setting for a high-life scene in a James Bond film.

Underneath a huge chandelier imported from California, splashed by multicolored beams of laser light, bodies seethed to the Eurobeat produced by the twenty-six-thousand-watt sound system. On stage, foreign professional dancers dressed in minimalist assemblages of leather and metal gyrated in fifteen-minute shifts, while a bank of forty-nine monitors behind them showed music videos. Rich, famous, and other elite patrons who wanted a respite from the high decibels and masses of tightly packed bodies—Juliana's could fit up to three thousand people into its one thousand two hundred square meters of space—could retreat to two luxuriously appointed VIP lounges overlooking the dance floor.

Juliana's was also a cut above the competition in its service. Its large staff of waiters, waitresses, and bartenders—numbering

nearly sixty altogether—were attentive, polite, and actually able to smile. Among Tokyo's trendy discos, where many of the hired help regarded surliness as a mark of sophistication, this made Juliana's unusual indeed. Not surprisingly, the media gave this 1.5 billion-yen dance emporium glowing reviews after its May 1991 opening.

A joint venture of Wembley PLC, the largest leisure management and services group in the U.K., and Nissho Iwai Corporation, one of Japan's Big Five trading companies, Juliana's was intended as the flagship of a disco network that would extend throughout Japan. It was designed, said Wembley Japan Executive Director Simon Rees, "to appeal to a somewhat older, higher spending clientele who may be fed up with the quality of other clubs. We want to prove to the market that it's still fun to go dancing, whatever your age."

What Juliana's clientele found the most fun, however, were the raised platforms, or *tachidai,* next to the dance floor, where the bolder of the patrons could show off their moves. Soon after the club opened, young female office workers and college girls could be seen swaying demurely on the platforms in "body-conscious" (*bodikon,* or tight-fitting) suits, their feet planted firmly on the floor and their eyes staring blankly into space. Contrasting this rather staid scene with the wilder clubs of the West, a foreign visitor couldn't help concluding that, for all their outward cool, the Japanese young were shy, unadventurous types.

But over the weeks and months, the platform performers began to shed their inhibitions—and their clothes. Instead of dress-for-success suits, they came to Juliana's in slinky miniskirts. Some brought feathered fans, less for cooling off than performing impromptu dances à la Sally Rand. The male patrons couldn't help noticing that Juliana's platforms offered the best show in the place, if not in town.

The escalation continued. The women started wearing G-strings under their microminis and bumping and grinding with abandon, while the floor in front of the platforms became packed with gaping, leering men. More and more of the onlookers were cameramen and reporters from weekly magazines and sports newspapers. Soon pictures and stories about the platform dancers were appearing in the national media. The Juliana's craze had begun.

While it lasted, the platform show at Juliana's was a voyeur's dream come true. It also represented a marketing bonanza. The club became a hot destination for tourists from all Japan and CDs of Juliana's disco mixes became big sellers. Imitators, some of which were little more than dance-on-the-bar strip joints, began to appear in towns and cities across the country. One enterprising manufacturer even brought out a Juliana's doll, complete with a *bodikon* dress and plastic fan.

Then came the inevitable complaints from Juliana's more conservative neighbors. The crowds were becoming too rowdy and the dancers too flagrant, changing from street clothes to their G-strings in alleyways and public lavatories. It didn't help that in June 1993 a local magazine ran photos, shot with management's cooperation, of nearly nude women on the platforms. In November 1993, the Tokyo Metropolitan Police told Juliana's management that the platforms "were not a preferable place for the customers to dance." The following month, Juliana's replaced the platforms with a "crystal stage" for professional dancers only and tightened up its dress code to keep the immodest off the premises.

The new policy pleased the cops, but emptied out the disco in no time flat. From a peak of five thousand a night, attendance fell to a disastrous two hundred fifty. Unable to cover its sky-high overhead—the joint venture partners were paying Juliana's Leisure Group 137 million yen a year to operate the club—Juliana's was forced to close in August 1994. It went out in style, with an eight-day celebration that brought back forty thousand of the faithful, including the women in the microminis. "It's so depressing," one of the platform dancers told the *Washington Post.* "This is the only place we could have fun. This was my place for making my stress melt away. Now where am I going to go?"

KADOKAWA, HARUKI

Shortly after 6 P.M. on August 29, 1993, Chiba Prefectural Police arrested Haruki Kadokawa, the president of Kadokawa Shoten Publishing Company, at his home in Ogikubo, a Tokyo suburb. The charge: Kadokawa, fifty-one, had instructed his close aide and photographer, Takeshi Ikeda, to smuggle cocaine from the United States into Japan.

On July 9 police had nabbed Ikeda at Narita airport, after finding him carrying eighty grams of coke with a Japanese street value of 5.6 million yen. According to the police investigation, Ikeda had received 1 million yen from Kadokawa and bought the coke from an L.A. dealer for 800,000 yen. Ikeda had made five other trips to L.A. between June 1992 and July 1993, all at company expense and all, the cops suspected, for the purpose of adding to Kadokawa's coke supply.

On August 11, the police also arrested Kyoko Sakamoto, a board member of an entertainment agency that was a Kadokawa Shoten affiliate, after finding 100 grams of marijuana in her Shibuya condo. Kadokawa had been living with Sakamoto and police suspected that he had also partaken of the weed.

Kadokawa's arrest was the Japanese show-business scandal of the century. Japan's most flamboyant and controversial producer, the last of the big risk takers and innovators in a business increasing dominated by salaryman bean counters, Kadokawa had made some of the highest grossers of the past two decades and had often been hailed as savior of a moribund industry. His disappearance from the scene—in Japan's drug-phobic society, his cocaine bust made him an instant industry pariah—was widely regarded as a body blow the movie business would not soon recover from.

At the same time, Kadokawa had been attacked by critics for churning out mediocre or downright awful movies—he had made a total of sixty films prior to his bust—and hawking them with slick, saturation ad campaigns to the unwitting public. Within the industry he had been notorious for spending huge amounts on promotion while forcing his backers and distributors to pick up the tab on unsold tickets and his company bookkeepers to hide the sea of red ink generated by his cinematic misadventures. (By the time of his arrest his film production company, Kadokawa Haruki Jimusho, was said be carrying losses of nearly twenty billion yen.)

Kadokawa was also accused of running his film and publishing empire as his personal fiefdom and treating his staff with all the consideration of disposable paper towels. In 1992, he forced his younger brother, Tsuguhiko, from a vice president's post, to make room for his son, the twenty-five-year-old Taro Kadokawa. When Tsuguhiko launched a new publishing startup, Media Works, Kadokawa employees resigned in large and damaging numbers to help him start five computer game magazines that were clones of five Kadokawa rivals, right down to the titles. It was as though the former employees, now free from their boss's arbitrary transfers and firings, were thumbing a collective nose.

Five months after Tsuguhiko's ouster and Taro's promotion, a male staffer filed suit against the new VP for sexual harassment. When the media began running lurid stories about the sex life of the man it now called "Homotaro"—a play on the name of a well-known fairy-tale character, Momotaro—Tsuguhiko could celebrate yet another victory in his war against his estranged brother.

After Kadokawa's bust, a company labor union leader told the press that employees were helpless to resist Kadokawa's "reign of terror" and added that "he got what he was asking for." A company vice president anonymously commented that Kadokawa made all the decisions and forced his board of directors to rubber-stamp them. "There was no discussion," he said. "Things were run by presidential orders." When Kadokawa submitted his resignation in September, it took the board all of five minutes to choose a replacement—and zero time to express "regrets" over Kadokawa's departure.

Kadokawa had taken over Kadokawa Shoten from father and company founder Gen'yoshi in 1975, when it was a modestly prosperous midsized publishing house with a solid, serious reputation for its literary and educational titles. "From now," he had reportedly told his board of directors, "I am the Godfather."

Kadokawa was determined to turn the company into an industry powerhouse by publishing blockbuster bestsellers. A key element in that strategy was films. By turning his literary properties into hit movies, Kadokawa believed he could create a synergy that would generate revenue throughout the media stream, including sound-track records and merchandise. He had this flash of insight, he later said, after seeing *The Graduate* in 1967 and hearing how the success of the movie had propelled the book onto the bestseller lists and the sound-track composers, Simon and Garfunkel, to worldwide stardom. His father, however, was a conservative highbrow, and Kadokawa knew that it was pointless to approach him with his moviemaking plans.

In 1976, soon after taking over, Kadokawa made his first film, a murder mystery titled *Inugamike no Ichizoku* (The Inugamis) and spent 300 million yen to publicize it (the ad campaign's catchphrase was simple but to the point: "Should you see the movie before or after reading the book?").

Written and directed by Kon Ichikawa, the movie earned 1.92 billion yen in distribution revenues and finished at number two in the year's domestic box office top ten.

Kadokawa followed this success in 1977 with *Ningen no Shomei* (Proof of the Man), a cross-cultural mystery that featured U.S. locations and U.S. actors, including George Kennedy, the reigning king of disaster movies. Aided by a massive TV ad campaign—a first for a Japanese film—and publicity from a nationwide contest to find the scriptwriter, the movie raked in 2.26 billion yen for distributor Toei.

For his 1978 *Yasei no Shomei* (Proof of the Wild), about an amnesiac girl who is the sole survivor of a massacre in a remote Tohoku village, Kadokawa cast Hiroko Yakushimaru, a thirteen-year-old schoolgirl with big eyes, a Kewpie-doll face, and an appealing childlike directness. Asked to imitate the robotic gyrations of the **PINK LADY** pop duo at her audition, Yakushimaru said flatly, "I can't do that." Her refusal—the only one among 1,234 hopefuls—impressed producers and earned her the lead role. Yakushimaru became an immediate sensation and *Yasei no Shomei* became another Kadokawa superhit, earning distribution revenues of 2.19 billion yen.

Kadokawa's big film for 1979 was *Sengoku Jieitai* (Time Slip), an unintentionally wacky sci-fi fantasy about twenty-one Self-Defense Force soldiers who find themselves, together with their tanks, helicopters, and guns, in the middle of a medieval war, pitted against an army of twenty thousand samurai. Unlike most films of the time, which were made, distributed, and promoted by the same studio, *Sengoku Jieitai* was distributed by Toho and publicized by Toei, while several different record companies released soundtrack songs. The movie became a smash and Kadokawa was hailed as a marketing genius for his ground-breaking multicompany, multimedia strategy.

In 1980, Kadokawa made *Fukkatsu no Hi* (Virus), a disaster film about the survivors of a plague and nuclear war who flee to the Antarctic. Filmed with a budget of 2 billion yen—a record for a Japanese film—*Fukkatsu no Hi* featured an international cast that included Glenn Ford, Chuck Connors, Sonny Chiba, Olivia Hussey, and the ever-reliable George Kennedy. But though it earned 2.39 billion yen—more than any Kadokawa movie to date, this plodding, weakly plotted movie hit the U.S. market after the cycle of disaster movies had run its course and its U.S. box-office take did not live up to Kadokawa's expectations.

In 1982 Kadokawa made his directorial debut with *Yogoreta Eiyu* (The Last Hero), an action film about a motorbike racer. During filming Kadokawa reportedly carried a knife with him as a reminder to fulfill his public

Hiroko Yakushimaru blows away the baddies in a still from *Sailor Fuku to Kikanju*.

school girl who becomes the boss of a *yakuza* gang. In the film's memorable climax, Yakushimaru charges into the rival gangsters' headquarters wearing—what else?—a sailor suit and blows them away with—what else?—a machine gun in orgasmic slow motion while mouthing the word *kaikan*: ecstasy. Fans were so ecstatic about Yakushimaru herself that when she made a stage appearance at an Osaka theater on the day of the film's release, more than 3,500 who had arrived after 7:00 A.M.—too late to buy a ticket—blocked the streets outside until city officials called out riot police to disperse them.

In 1983 Tomoyo Harada drew the crowds to Nobuhiko Obayashi's *Toki o Kakeru Shojo* (The Girl Who Ran Through Time). Starring Harada as a high school girl who travels through time with the aid of a mysterious lavender-smelling liquid, *Toki* earned Obayashi critical accolades for its imaginative and skillful blending of fantasy and romance, while producer Kadokawa once again scored a box-office coup. Playing together with a Yakushimaru and **YUSAKU MATSUDA** vehicle, *Tantei Monogatari* (Detective Story), the film earned 2.81 billion yen—a Kadokawa record—while the theme song, written by New Music Queen Yumi Matsutoya (see **YUMING AND THE BIRTH OF NEW MUSIC**) and sung by Harada, sold six hundred thousand copies.

promise to slit his stomach if the film did not earn more than 1 billion yen. It passed that mark easily, despite complaints from the critics that Kadokawa had turned the offbeat novel on which the movie was based into simplistic hash.

Kadokawa's best-remembered movies from the 1980s, however, featured Hiroko Yakushimaru and another teenage idol star, Tomoyo Harada. In 1981 Yakushimaru sent her already tremendous popularity soaring to new heights with her performance in *Sailor Fuku to Kikanju* (Sailor Suit and Machine Gun), a gimmicky film about a high-

Kadokawa had other hits with Yakushi-maru, including the 1983 *Satomi Hakken Den*, a period drama with sci-fi fantasy touches reminiscent of Star Wars. But in 1984 key production staff, fed up with Kadokawa's dictatorial and penny-pinching ways, began to desert the producer, and his star at the box office started to fade. After flopping with *W no Higeki* (The Tragedy of W), a backstage drama starring Yakushi-maru as an ambitious young actress, Kadokawa did not produce another movie for the remainder of the decade.

He was hardly idle, however. In addition to running his publishing empire, he pursued a wide range of interests. A poet since childhood, Kadokawa composed haiku and *tanka,* the latter an ancient thirty-one-syllable form that had long been a favorite of the Japanese imperial court. He published in poetry magazines (not ones owned by his company) and his efforts won him praise from Japan's poetry establishment.

Kadokawa was also fascinated by Japanese traditions and myths, as embodied by the Shinto religion. He founded a shrine, Asukonomiya, in Tsumagoi, Gumma Prefecture, that received official recognition as a religious organization in 1974. Kadokawa and his common-law wife, Kyoko, served as priest and shrine maiden and officiated at monthly Shinto rituals, which were attended by friends and associates from the literary and cinema worlds. After Kadokawa's arrest, rumors flew that the post-ritual entertainment at the shrine included dope smoking and coke hoovering by Kadokawa and his inner circle. Also, in September 1993 police investigators learned that three of the four buildings on the nine-thousand-square-meter shrine site had not been properly registered with the authorities.

Kadokawa had other interests that were less traditional. He was a big fan of *Mein Kampf* and even included a paean to Hitler's autobiography in one of his *tanka,* describing it as a "magic book." Also, in a 1988 interview, he proclaimed himself a believer in UFOs and casually claimed to have spotted one the day before. When Kadokawa turned to staff members for confirmation of this sighting, they nodded their agreement. The boss may have been spacey, but he was still the company Führer.

In 1990 Kadokawa returned to directing in grand style with *Ten to Chi to* (Heaven and Earth), an epic period drama with a budget of five billion yen—the highest ever for a Japanese movie. To film his story about rival warlords in turbulent sixteenth-century Japan, Kadokawa journeyed to the Canadian Rockies (the actual historical settings had been rendered unfilmable by the trappings of twentieth-century civilization) where he used three thousand extras—mainly local college students—and one thousand horses to shoot a climatic battle that occupied more than thirty minutes of screen time.

To cover the enormous cost of this epic—the Japanese film industry's *Waterworld*—Kadokawa printed nearly five million advance tickets, of which his thirty-eight corporate backers took three million, distributor Toei one million, and Kadokawa's own company the remainder. He calculated that to break even the film needed to attract at least ten million moviegoers, or nearly one-tenth of Japan's entire population.

Ten to Chi to didn't draw nearly that many, but despite its glacial pace and tangled storyline the film earned five billion yen in distributor revenues—the third-highest total ever for a Japanese film. Kadokawa needed foreign earnings to clear a profit, but the film's take in the United States, where audiences were unfamiliar with the film's crowd of samurai heroes (even domestic audiences needed subtitles to keep them straight) and unimpressed by the marching-band precision of the big climatic battle scene, amounted to only two hundred thousand dollars.

Undeterred by his film's lack of international success. Kadokawa renewed his assault on the U.S. market. In 1991 he backed an eight-million-dollar musical version of the James Clavell novel *Shogun* that closed after only two months on Broadway. He also spent twenty-five million dollars making *Ruby Cairo,* a continent-spanning suspense film starring Andie MacDowell that failed to find to a U.S. distributor.

In 1991 he made another kind of grab at international recognition when he completed a three-year project to build a 3.14 million-dollar replica of Christopher Columbus's flagship, the *Santa Maria*. After blessing the ship in a Shinto ritual, Kadokawa piloted it from Barcelona harbor on the start of a 27,200 kilometer trip around the world. "If I am to have a place in the future, it may be as a man of achievement," he told reporters. "If we complete this voyage, and the twenty-first century is peaceful, I will be very pleased."

Following the successful completion of his oceanic adventure, Kadokawa finally refocused on the home market with *Rex*, a sci-fi fantasy about a girl and her pet dinosaur. The girl was played by preteen heartthrob Yumi Adachi, while her cute little T. Rex was designed by Carlo Rambaldi of *E.T.* fame. Riding on the dinosaur boom generated by *Jurassic Park,* Rex drew large crowds following its July 1994 release and was on its way to becoming the biggest hit of the summer.

But in September, following Kadokawa's bust, distributor Shochiku withdrew the picture, afraid that an association with an indicted cokehead might tarnish its corporate image. Not long after, the distributor of

Kadokawa's last prebust film, an animated feature titled *Coo* about yet another cute dinosaur, blanked out the producer's name from the movie's posters and fliers. The man who had made seven of the twenty top-earning Japanese movies of all time had become a nonperson in the industry he was credited with saving.

In December 1995, after one year and three months of detention, Kadokawa was released from Chiba Prison on one hundred million yen bail. While in the slammer, Kadokawa had continued to write haiku, including a poem in which he compared his own predicament to Icarus's fatal flight into the sun, and another in which he complained of prison conditions:

wrists tied up like a dog,
warm autumn day.

After his release, Kadokawa continued to protest his innocence of all charges. Prosecutors, however, claimed that he had instructed Ikeda to buy cocaine on at least thirty-six separate occasions and had embezzled thirty million yen in company funds to pay for it.

In March 1996 Kadokawa announced plans to produce a remake of his 1983 hit, *Toki o Kakeru Shojo* (The Girl Who Ran Through Time). He had reportedly asked the original film's director, Nobuhiko Obayashi, to helm the film and approached his old stars, Tomoyo Harada and Hiroko Yakushimaru, about appearing in supporting roles.

In June, however, the Chiba District Court sentenced Kadokawa to four years in prison for cocaine smuggling and embezzlement. In handing down the sentence, the judge noted that Kadokawa had never expressed remorse for his crimes and had instead tried to blame everything on his subordinate, Ikeda. Kadokawa claimed throughout the trial that, as a dedicated Shintoist, he could have never done anything as rotten as smuggle coke. "When I was arrested, I thought the gods were testing me with such a big challenge," Kadokawa said in court. "I decided to maintain my innocence throughout the trial as a means of spiritual training."

But though he may continue that training in prison, Kadokawa will find it difficult to make his film, unless he can somehow smuggle in the heroine's time-traveling liquid—and send himself back to 1983.

KARAOKE

Where can't you karaoke in Japan? What was once an after-hours pastime for sodden salarymen has now become a generation-spanning leisure-time favorite, right up there with playing home computer games and watching movies on the VCR. In short, karaoke has moved out of the nightlife ghetto of sleazy bars and clubs into the mainstream of Japanese life. Grade schoolers pick up the mike at McDonald's while their teenage brothers and sisters sing with their friends at the karaoke clubs found in nearly every urban neighborhood. Later in the evening, while Dad is crooning with office colleagues at a bar (made much classier by its laser-disc karaoke system and Las-Vegas-in-miniature stage), Mom and Grandma sing along with their favorite song show on the TV, as they read lyrics that appear on the bottom of the screen.

To those who know the country only from movie and media images of stoic samurai and nerdy salarymen, it may seem strange that the Japanese would have not only invented karaoke but embraced it with such a passion. Isn't Japan supposed to be a shame culture, where standing out is considered a sin? What could be more embarrassing than to make an idiot of yourself in front of a roomful of strangers? And yet many Japanese not only volunteer but vie for the mike, even if they know that their vocal chords are instruments of pain. Isn't there a contradiction somewhere?

But consider *Twenty-four Eyes (Nijushi no Hitomi)*, a 1954 Keisuke Kinoshita megahit about a teacher and pupils on a small Inland Sea island that is one long tear-jerking song fest. Or the enduring popularity of **NODO JIMAN** (Proud of My Voice), a four-decade-old NHK amateur hour that gives folks from Hokkaido to Kyushu a chance to display their singing talents with a live band before a big hometown crowd. Or pre-karaoke banquets that inevitably featured inebriated revelers wailing their favorite oldies at the top of their not-always melodic voices.

As these examples indicate, Japanese loved to sing long before karaoke and had fewer inhibitions about strutting their stuff in public than most Westerners. Instead of the Western tendency to critically compare an amateur's mangling of "My Way" with the Frank Sinatra original, the Japanese put a greater stress on the attempt. They were willing to forgive even the tone deaf their acts of butchery, as long they "gave it a good try" (*issho-kemmei ni yatta*). The seed, in short, fell on fertile soil.

Karaoke's invention remains a matter of dispute, though all claimants are from the Kansai (Osaka-Kobe-Kyoto) area. The basic idea was simple: a machine for playing the song tapes that professionals use to hone their acts, with an orchestral backing but no melody line (*kara* means "empty" and *oke*, "orchestra"). Handed a mike, bar patrons could make like **HIBARI MISORA** or **YUJIRO ISHIHARA**—a heady feeling.

One claimant to the title of karaoke's inventor is Kisaburo Takashiro, who was managing a record store in Osaka in the early seventies when he discovered that local snack bars were hiring organists to accompany crooning patrons at five hundred to one thousand yen a pop. Feeling that he could do the job better and cheaper, he built a machine containing the tapes of four hundred songs, installed it in a snack bar, and charged one hundred yen a tune. The machine was popular with patrons and in three months Takashiro earned his money back. The first karaoke boom was under way.

Early karaoke, however, left much to be desired. Besides being clunky, with bulky eight-track tapes and mikes heavy enough to stun hecklers with one blow, the first karaoke machines had all the subtlety of a high-school P.A. system. The vocally challenged sounded truly awful, making a visit to a karaoke bar a test of endurance until you got your own turn at the mike (and a chance to take revenge on your tormentors).

In addition, many of the early bars were poorly sound-proofed. As the evening wore on and inebriated Saburo Kitajima and Frank Sinatra wannabes began bellowing ever more loudly, noise complaints from the neighbors flooded into the local police.

Finally, the selection of tunes often ranged from World War II military songs to slightly mildewed *enka* ballads: a hopelessly unhip lineup to younger Japanese and foreigners with a taste for contemporary rock and pop. For years, karaoke was viewed as the afterhours recreation of middle-aged men with retro tastes and auditory nerves as sensitive as rhinoceros hide.

The second karaoke boom came in 1983 with the introduction of compact and laser discs. The new discs provided not only audio but visual accompaniment that helped singers get into the mood. Also, the subtitles on the screen allowed them to belt away without referring to bulky lyrics books.

But what transformed karaoke into a truly national obsession was the invention of a Nagoya entrepreneur that debuted in 1986: the karaoke "box." Originally abandoned railway cars partitioned into booths and outfitted with karaoke gear, the karaoke box had the advantage of privacy and cheapness. Instead of peeling off ten thousand yen notes to buy a bottle of Johnny Walker, the company of a barely bilingual Thai hostess, and a chance to fight for a mike with a roomful other salarymen, patrons could sing to their heart's content for a low hourly charge and bring their own cans of Asahi Dry beer.

Soon karaoke boxes (also called cabins and clubs) were proliferating like the proverbial bamboo sprouts after a rainstorm. At first educators and parents voiced concern that these tiny rooms containing little more than a table, sofas, and a giant karaoke machine might become dens of iniquity, where teenagers unable to afford the price of a love hotel would unbridle their passions and imbibe illegal substances. Their concerns proved to be largely unwarranted, however. "We've found that once young people get caught up in singing they don't have time for anything else," said Yuji Yamamoto, general manager of the Presidential Affairs Office of Daiichi Kosho, which operates hundreds of Big Echo karaoke clubs throughout Japan. "Teenagers, especially, will try to see how many songs they can sing in thirty minutes or one hour. They don't want to waste a second." To thwart the few who do have libidinous intentions, owners installed corridor windows and instructed their staff to check in periodically. As a result, an afternoon in a karaoke box is usually like a day at Disneyland: good, clean fun.

In its new incarnation, karaoke proved attractive to women, who had shied away from the smoky karaoke bars filled with drunken, leering, middle-aged men. Discovering that karaoke boxes were a convenient, hassle-free way to party, more schoolgirls, office workers, and housewives began to frequent them with their friends and soon became karaoke fanatics. Today nearly sixty percent of the patrons of the nation's twelve thousand karaoke clubs are female.

Boosted by this third boom, the karaoke industry now boasts an annual take of nearly one trillion yen (more than eleven billion dollars). Its products are enjoyed by sixty million people—about half the population—on more than six hundred thousand commercial karaoke systems nationwide.

The initial lure of easy profits, however, has long since given way to the realities of fierce competition. To thrive, clubs today have to set themselves apart from the pack.

For many that difference is special discounts and low prices to keep their rooms filled during the daylight hours and lure in teenagers and others with tight budgets but a strong desire to sing. In Tokyo's Kabukicho entertainment district, where the struggle for survival is the among the toughest, karaoke fans can enjoy a ninety-minute session for a little as five hundred yen—dirt-cheap in an area where the standard cover charge for a karaoke-equipped hostess club is ten thousand yen.

Other clubs located in the suburbs lure housewives and their children with special lunch sets and daytime rates. Some even stock cassette tapes or laser discs of children's songs so that kids won't become bored out of their minds while their moms eat their pilaf and pore over their song books.

Japan's king of fast food, McDonald's, has filled the lost-cost karaoke-for-kids niche by installing in many of its party rooms in Japan karaoke equipment called, appropriately enough, MacSong. Groups with children pay only five hundred yen an hour, compared to one thousand yen for adults, and kids can choose from hundreds of children's songs on the playlist. "It hasn't made a radical difference in our bottom line, but it's a popular service that has turned a lot of kids into McDonald's fans—and that's our aim," says McDonald's spokesman Kenji Kamiya.

Clubs in the Ginza and other high-rent nightlife districts are setting themselves apart from the crowd by packaging karaoke as upscale entertainment for the expense-account elite. A former Ginza hostess club, the Namiki, charges ten thousand yen an hour for a group of five or less to use any of its eight luxuriously appointed rooms. One, with a small Japanese-style garden, is presumably reserved for aficionados of *enka* and other impeccably traditional musical genres.

Other entrepreneurs are blazing new trails for karaoke in unlikely places, including public transportation. Yukio Iwai, a taxi driver in Sakai City, near Osaka, offers a free karaoke service to his passengers. His onboard system includes four video monitors, a laser-disc player, and a video library with four thousand selections. The total cost:

ten million yen. Iwai told the weekly magazine *Shukan Yomiuri* that nearly seventy percent of his passengers take advantage of the free service. "Some have even requested that I keep circling the Hanshin Expressway until they finish singing," he said.

Karaoke can also be found on the train. The Hankai Tramway Company operates a karaoke car between Osaka's Naniwa Ward and Sakai City that features a playlist of more than one thousand selections and rents for forty-eight thousand yen for two hours. Some of the singers getting off at Sakai Station no doubt luck out and catch a ride home in Iwai's cab.

Karaoke has even penetrated that most un-show-business-like bastion of traditional culture: the Japanese public school system. Nearly one thousand elementary schools across the country now have karaoke equipment in their music rooms. Instead of listening to a teacher bang away on a battered upright and warble folk songs in an uncertain alto, kids can sing along to professionally produced videos on fifty-inch screens.

As karaoke widens its reach, karaoke software and hardware makers keep fine-tuning the technology. Sony Music Entertainment has introduced a software package that features vocals arranged for easy harmonizing. Fans of pop megastars Chage & Aska can take Chage's part and feel that they are really a member of the group.

Daiichi Kosho, the Tokyo-based company that has been in the karaoke business since 1973, has gone Sony one better with a software package called Hamorun that allows singers to harmonize with their own voices, in five parts no less. Another Daiichi Kosho package called Daburin gives singers who have trouble hitting the high notes digital assistance.

But the technological innovation that has really revolutionized karaoke in the nineties is the on-line services that digitally pipe thousands of songs over telephone wires to clubs, where they are stored on computer hard disks and CD-ROMs for easy replay. When karaoke-on-demand was first introduced in 1992 by arcade-game maker Taito Corporation, the sound quality was not nearly as good as the laser discs that were then the industry standard. Also, the on-line systems could not send background voices or video images because conventional copper wires did not have the capacity to handle the necessary data. Clubs had to supply videos from their own libraries to accompany the music.

Even so, the huge selection of songs available—more than ten thousand on the most popular systems, including many current hits—made karaoke-on-demand popular with customers, especially younger ones who were tired of the oldies-but-goodies selections at most clubs. By March 1996, twenty-five percent of the nation's half million karaoke systems were on-line.

Some of them are offering more than just music. Sega Enterprise's Prologue 21 on-line system, which debuted in December 1994, can be combined with Sega's SegaSaturn, a 32-bit video-game machine with multimedia features. While their friends are agonizing over their next song selection, patrons can play video games or even catch up on the latest sports and weather news.

In the summer of 1996, music system designer Timeware introduced yet another karaoke advance: a virtual karaoke system that allows singers to select not only a tune but a virtual concert hall in which to perform it. Using a special mixer, data processing sound board, and power amps, the system can reproduce the acoustic characteristics of famous concert halls or, if so inclined, the singer can design a hall that best suits the sound of his or her voice. Electronic instruments and videos can also be used with the system to make the experience even more like the real thing. All that's lacking is the applause.

Still other companies are busy commercializing the next generation of karaoke technology: home karaoke-on-demand transmitted via cable TV lines or over the Internet. Together with IBM Japan, Daiichi

Kosho has been testing a karaoke-on-demand service in Kyoto. Part of a large-scale multimedia project being carried out by a private enterprise umbrella organization called the Broadband ISDN Business Chance Culture Creation (BBCC), the test has been a smashing success, says Daiichi Kosho's Yuji Yamamoto. "People have been saying that karaoke is the business best suited to multimedia and we're proving them right. The service is very popular with consumers."

So popular in fact that, after Taito launched the first home karaoke-on-demand service, X-55, in October 1995, the company predicted that in its first eighteen months the service would attract one million subscribers. Several other companies are planning to join Taito on-line, including Xing, Pioneer, Sega Enterprises, and Victor Company of Japan. Even foreign companies are trying to grab a share of the burgeoning Japanese home karaoke market. In January 1996, Microsoft tied up with Nikkodo, a major karaoke equipment and software company, to launch a home karaoke service in Japan over the Microsoft Network. In the spring of 1996 the service began beaming ten thousand Nikkodo-supplied tunes to users' homes.

One of the partners' aims is to tap the still largely undeveloped international market via the Internet. Though thousands of singers in Beijing bars and London pubs have discovered the pleasure of karaoke, the overseas karaoke boom has yet to reach Japan-size proportions. But in developing their international businesses, warns Yamamoto, karaoke suppliers have to take cultural differences into account. "Pioneer tried to introduce the karaoke box concept to the United States, but it didn't work," he explains. "Unlike Japan, where houses are small and people enjoy socializing in clubs with company and school friends more than at home with family members, Americans like to have home parties. That's the market we have to serve if we want to expand our business in the United States."

In Japan, meanwhile, karaoke has become far more than a fad; two decades after its introduction it has become as integral a part of the culture as sakè and cherry blossoms. (These days cherry blossom viewing parties are often karaoke parties.) One indication of karaoke's impact is the decline of another Japanese institution: the drunken salaryman. According to a 1994 study by Tokyo police researchers, the number of drunks taken into protective custody has declined to one-third of the mid-1970s peak of 35,000. The reason, says researchers, is karaoke. In 1976, the year karaoke first became popular, the number of drunks escorted to the slammer fell by 4,000. The start of the second karaoke boom, in 1982, witnessed another sharp drop. Following the introduction of karaoke boxes later in the decade the number plunged again. "Our findings may appear odd," a police official told *The Japan Times,* "but there is no doubt that karaoke, as a means to vent frustration, is helping to reduce the number of people who get drunk and lose control of themselves."

Those who do lose control and find themselves behind bars can sing the blues about their bad luck. But drunk tanks are still one of the few places in Japan where an amateur Johnny Cash can't find a mike.

KIMI NO NA WA

In April 1952, when memories of the chaos and poverty of the early postwar period were still fresh but Japan was finally moving away from the shadow of the Occupation—the signing of the San Francisco Peace Treaty in 1951 had returned Japan to the ranks of sovereign nations for the first time since 1945—a new weekly thirty-minute radio drama debuted on NHK. Titled *Kimi no Na wa* (What Is Your Name?), it told the story of Mariko Ujiie and Haruki Atomiya, who meet

on Ginza's Sukiyabashi Bridge during the Great Tokyo Air Raid in March 1945. Mariko and Haruki fall in love, pledge to reunite at the bridge in six months, and part without asking each other's names.

But, as in *An Affair to Remember,* which the radio drama preceded by five years, the protagonists find it hard to make their date. Encountering various obstacles to reuniting with her ideal, Mariko finally marries another man. Of course, she is soon miserable and longing for Haruki, and Haruki never stops longing for her. But unlike Cary Grant and Deborah Kerr, the two lovers never make it to the happy ending.

Written by Kazuo Kikuta, with music by Yuji Kozeki (who played the theme song on the Hammond organ at the beginning of each episode) *Kimi no Na wa* belonged to the "ships in the night" (*sure chigai*) genre of dramas about lovers who are destined never to unite. Before the war the most popular representative of the genre had been the 1938 *Aizen Katsura* (The Compassionate Buddha) about a doctor (Ken Uehara) and nurse (Kinuyo Tanaka) who fall in love but are kept apart by the doctor's parents. *Aizen Katsura* had shattered box-office records and spawned two sequels.

But in writing *Kimi no Na wa,* Kikuta had more in mind than wringing audience tears. In the December 1952 issue of *Hoso Bunka*

(Broadcast Culture) magazine, he said that he wanted to describe "the people who have lived in this country for the past seven years, from the end of the war to the present, much as they really are." In other words, he wanted to make not melodrama but social drama with a semidocumentary flavor. In the course of the show's long run, various postwar types appeared: war widows, war orphans, discharged soldiers, prostitutes, and mixed-blood children. The show also dealt with social issues, including the eternal Japanese war between wife and live-in mother-in-law.

Even so, for *Kimi no Na wa's* millions of female listeners, the core of the show remained the star-crossed romance between Haruki and Mariko. Broadcast live on a nationwide network, with Michiko Asato as Michiko, the show soon won a devoted following who breathlessly listened for every new development in the two lovers' tangled lives.

Seven months after the show began, a novelization of the radio drama was published and became an immediate bestseller. Shochiku bought the movie rights and made a film starring Keiko Kishi and Keiji Sada in the leads. Released in three parts, the first in September 1953, the second in December 1953, and the third in April 1954, *Kimi no Na wa* become a runaway hit, with

parts two and three topping the box office for their respective years, and part one finishing at number two. The copy for the ad campaign was "the women's side of the public bath becomes empty," a reference to the often-repeated observation that, when the radio show began broadcasting at 8:30 P.M., public baths across the country reported a dramatic drop in the number of female customers.

The movie even inspired a national fashion craze, with women everywhere buying the "Mariko" shawl that Keiko Kishi had worn for her famous scene at Sukiyabashi Bridge. Also, a bridge on Sado Island, a rock near the Kyushu town of Obamacho, and Lake Kussharo near Bihorocho, Hokkaido, where the two lovers had briefly reunited became popular tourist attractions.

The *Kimi no Na wa* boom finally faded, but for audiences of the early 1950s, the radio show and film seemed to capture the mood of the early postwar period, when life was uncertain, happiness fleeting, and the country was filled with lost souls looking for values that seemed to have fled with defeat. Beginning in 1962 on Fuji TV, four TV remakes of the story were broadcast, but none achieved anywhere near the success of the originals. Raised in more properous, stable, and Westernized times, younger viewers seemed to prefer their on-screen lovers to finish in a happy Hollywood embrace, not with a sad, final, ships-passing-in-the-night farewell.

KOHAKU UTA GASSEN

The most popular show ever on Japanese TV celebrates Japan's biggest holiday: the New Year (not Christmas, which is mainly an excuse for unscrupulous confectioners to sell cardboard-like cakes to the undiscerning and for young men to lure young women into expensive hotel rooms). The *Kohaku Uta Gassen* (Red-and-White Song Contest) is, appropriately, gaudily overproduced and earnestly trendy in its details, while being rigidly traditional in its essentials. It is, in fact, less a show-biz extravaganza than an annual national rite that, for the Japanese entertainment world, is the equivalent of the Academy Awards or the Queen's Honors List.

The basic format is simple: two teams, a Red Team for the women and a White Team for the men, take part in a singing contest, with male and female singers appearing in turn before a live audience. The audience and a panel of judges—celebrities who may or may not have any professional connection with music—then select the winning team. Trophies are presented, everyone joins in a rousing chorus of "Auld Lang Syne" (which is sung with Japanese lyrics and is assumed by many to be a traditional Japanese song), and at fifteen minutes to midnight the show ends. The New Year is then ushered in, not with pop singers making lame wisecracks and belting their latest hits (or, in the case of veterans, their golden oldies), but scenes of quiet snow-covered rural temples and the sounds of worshipers ringing the temple bell to cleanse away sins of the past year. The atmosphere is closer to the chanting of midnight mass at Saint Paul's than the lowering of the ball in Times Square.

Kohaku Uta Gassen was the brainchild of NHK producer Tsumoru Kindo, who initially conceived of the show in 1945 as spiritual R&R for a defeated and poverty-stricken nation. Worried about the revival of militarism, Occupation authorities forbade the use of *gassen* (which also means "battle") in the title. The first show, rechristened the *Kohaku Uta Shiai* (Red-and-White Song Competition), was broadcast over NHK radio with a total of ten singers, five for each team. A former government agency reborn after the war as a public broadcaster, NHK still had a monopoly on the nation's airwaves.

The show's real beginning, however, is considered to be January 3, 1951, when NHK revived it after a five-year hiatus. Once again, the program was on NHK radio, but this time *gassen* was in the title and there was a live audience in the studio. Starring fourteen popular singers, the hour-long program was an immediate hit. The following year it was expanded to an hour and a half and six singers were added to each side.

What really solidified the show's status as a yearly ritual was its move, in its fourth edition, to New Year's Eve. It was the first big special program to appear on that day and the first *Kohaku Uta Gassen* to be broadcast on TV. At a time when the price of a television was beyond the reach of most, it stood out like a big, glowing beacon. As the television viewing audience grew in the late 1950s and early 1960s, so did *Kohaku*, becoming bigger and splashier every year. The program itself tried to offer a little something for everyone, including jazz, chanson, and even rock, to go along with more traditional fare like Japanese folk songs and *enka* ballads. Later viewers of the show, who know it only as a showcase of Japanese popular music (with token appearances by foreign talent), may be surprised to learn that in the show's early days *Kohaku* performers were warbling such traditional Japanese numbers as "High Society," "Que Sera Sera," and "Be Bop A Lula."

By 1965, with the introduction of color TV, stars were competing fiercely to be on the show and the decisions of NHK's selection committee were breathlessly reported in the media. The singers chosen to appear in the final slot on each team were considered to have reached show business heaven. On the other hand, to be dropped from the program, especially after appearing on it for years, was regarded as a major, even career-wrecking, embarrassment. (Some singers, however, made headlines for returning to the show after years of languishing in the outer darkness.)

Kohaku reached its peak of popularity in the 1960s and 1970s, when ratings regularly passed the 70 percent mark, soaring as high as 81.4 percent in 1963. By the mid-1960s, 90 percent of all households had TVs, but VCRs and TV computer games had not yet distracted viewers from the tube and New Year vacations to ski slopes and island resorts were still options only for the affluent few.

During this period, the show largely reflected what a majority of the show's viewers, young and old alike, were actually listening to. Although many of the show's stars had launched their careers in the pre-TV era and sang *enka* ballads, with their often lugubrious laments about separation and loneliness, a growing number were so-called "idol" singers who sang light, bouncy, Western-influenced pop tunes with lyrics that were often a surrealistic mishmash of Japanese and English. Both *enka* and Japanese pop were mainstays on the music programs that occupied choice prime-time slots and drew high ratings. It was during this period that *Kohaku* established a pattern it still follows today: Japanese pop music for the young in the first half of the show and *enka* for the old folks in the second half.

NHK has long prided itself on choosing its *Kohaku* lineup according to average viewers' tastes. Actually, the network's own input into the selection process is not a small one. NHK picks performers based on the results of three surveys. The first is a nationwide poll that asks respondents to name their favorite male and female singers. The second poses the same question to contestants on the NHK **NODO JIMAN** (Proud of My Voice) amateur singing program. The third, however, is an in-house survey of NHK employees. Critics have charged that this selection process, which effectively gives NHK brass a veto over selections, makes it easier for NHK to pressure top-line talent into appearing on *Nodo Jiman* and other NHK programs for a fraction of the fees they would command from commercial networks.

NHK has also tried hard—and some would say, acted unfairly—to maintain the show's sanitized image, dropping *enka* queen **HIBARI MISORA** in 1973 because of her younger brother's *yakuza* connections and refusing to invite Misato Watanabe in 1986 because she had sung at a *yakuza* gang's New Year party, even though she had the year's biggest hit record, "My Revolution."

The public broadcaster has also been accused of favoring certain singers, especially those who make the above-mentioned "contributions" to NHK by appearing on its programs, and discriminating against others who don't. In 1978 **PINK LADY**, a popular song-and-dance duo, fell into the latter category when they performed on the New Year's charity program of a rival commercial network instead of *Kohaku*. The following year, they were not invited to appear on *Kohaku* even though they had several best-selling records on the charts.

But as the 1970s gave way to the 1980s, *Kohaku's* ratings began to slip, finally falling into the fifties. NHK hadn't changed its selection system, but the viewing audience had changed its way of spending New Year's Eve. Instead of sitting around the television with the whole family, young adults were often polishing their parallel turns on the slopes or soaking up rays in Guam.

Also, musical tastes had diversified. Instead of *enka* and Japanese pop performed by idol singers, more people were listening to rock, reggae, rap, and New Music (see **YUMING AND THE BIRTH OF NEW MUSIC**), a genre that had grown out of the Japanese contemporary folk music scene. Many of the big stars in these genres had little interest in appearing on the TV music shows that were mainly showcases for talent-agency-packaged idol singers, and NHK had little interest in having many of

them on *Kohaku*. As a result, fans of these genres turned elsewhere for New Year's entertainment—and ratings dropped.

Enka fans remained loyal to their favorites, but *Kohaku*'s long parade of *enka* stars reminded young viewers, especially, that the show had become stuck in a time warp. Kimonoed veterans who had not had a top-ten hit in years kept racking up *Kohaku* appearances, while rock groups and singers that sold out stadiums were excluded.

Beginning in 1987, NHK decided to overhaul the show. While usually reserving a place of prominence at the end for *enka*— considered the most "Japanese" form of pop music—the producers invited a wider spec-trum of artists, including foreigners (Cho Yong Pil in 1987, Cyndi Lauper and Paul Simon in 1990, Andy Williams and the Ventures in 1991), and offered a broader range of genres, including traditional Japanese folk songs, chanson, and even opera arias.

Despite talk of canceling *Kohaku* after its fortieth edition, NHK pressed on with its reform effort. In 1990, the show was broadcast in two parts of two hours each, the first devoted mainly to youth-oriented pop music, the second to standards for the older folks. Though the rating for the second half, 47 percent, was the lowest in the show's history, the first half managed a better-than-expected

38.5 percent. The following year, to NHK's relief, ratings climbed above the 50-percent mark. *Kohaku* seemed more likely to survive.

One thing about *Kohaku* had not changed, however: NHK's allergy to anything smelling of scandal. In 1989 pop singer Akina Nakamori was dropped from the invitee list following a suicide attempt. In 1991 model-actress-singer **RIE MIYAZAWA** got the ax for appearing in a nude photo book.

NHK has kept fiddling with the *Kohaku* formula throughout the decade, dropping foreign artists in 1992 after ratings revealed that viewers were tuning most of them out. Though traditionalists welcomed the change, ratings remained low compared to the show's peak. Given that the days when everyone from eight to eighty was watching the same music show on the same television are gone for good, they will probably never reach that peak again.

But on New Year's Eve of 1995, *Kohaku* clobbered the competition with a 44.9 percent rating for its first section, which featured a bigger-than-ever lineup of hot pop singers and groups, and a 50.4 percent rating for its second, which offered the usual *enka* stalwarts. Meanwhile, *The Beatles Anthology* on TV Asahi could manage only a measly 3.3. Half a century after its start as a one-shot radio program, *Kohaku* shows no sign of singing "Auld Lang Syne" for the last time.

KOMURO, TETSUYA

In the early 1990s the Japanese pop music scene resembled that of the West in its fragmentation and cross-fertilization. Want rap in the Osaka dialect? Folk rock with an Okinawan accent? Spacey ambient grooves in no known human language? We got it. Former pop music categories, consequently, became largely meaningless or changed their meaning altogether. To make things simple for record buyers, stores began classifying all contemporary Japanese pop music as "J Pop" while applying the *kayokyoku* label, which literally means "Japanese popular music" and was formerly reserved primarily for the pop products of "idol" singers and groups, to collections of *enka* ballads.

But while thousands of groups were catering to tiny cliques of fans in clubs and concert halls, a few artists were racking up incredible sales numbers in the mainstream pop marketplace. The number one single of the 1980s, "Dancing All Night" by Monta & Brothers, sold 1.6 million copies. In the first four and one-half years of the 1990s, eighteen singles on the *Oricon* chart—Japan's equivalent to the *Billboard* chart—surpassed that figure, with six going over the two million mark. Album sales also went stratospheric: a trio called Dreams Come True moved 3.2 million copies of their *The*

Swinging Star album in 1992 and all of the top twenty albums released from December 1989 to May 1994 surpassed sales of 1.6 million.

One reason for the bigger numbers was the CD revolution, which made pop music more easily accessible and affordable to the nation's teenagers. Another was the **KARAOKE** boom, which gave pop music another, highly effective venue for sales and promotion. Songs that were karaoke-user-friendly often became chartbusters. Still another was the increasingly common practice of using contemporary Japanese pop music as theme songs for TV ad campaigns and TV programs, principally the dramas and cartoon shows most popular with young viewers. A snippet of a song on a shampoo commercial, played hundreds of times a week on national TV, could boost sales of the CD single into the millions.

Although these trends were obvious to anyone in the music business at the beginning of the decade, one man had the marketing savvy and musical talent to incorporate all of them into an explosively profitable pop formula. His name was Tetsuya Komuro and, by the mid-nineties, he was the most successful record producer in Japanese pop music history. In 1995—his breakout year—Komuro's CDs earned a total of 26.8 billion yen, nearly 282 million dollars at then-current exchange rates, and the appearance of his name in his trademark lower-case Roman letters (which he also tended to use for many group names and song titles) on a record was enough make it a hit. In April 1996 five of the top ten best-selling singles were Komuro productions—a feat that underscored his domination of the world's second-largest music market.

A slight, delicately handsome man with lank, auburn-dyed hair, who bore a passing resemblance to the young Andy Warhol, Komuro was far more than a mere record producer; he served as composer, lyricist, arranger, synthesizer programmer, promoter, and all-round Svengali to the artists under his charge. In short, he did almost everything but sing and dance for them.

Although nearly all of the members of what he called the "Komuro Family" were hit makers—how, with Komuro behind them, could they miss?—the biggest until recently was the group trf, consisting of one female vocalist, one DJ, and three dancers who performed to Komuro's pre-recorded sounds. In 1995 trf sold 3.78 million singles and 5.23 million albums. Sales of their fifth and biggest album, *dance to positive*, totaled 3 million copies.

As implied by their name, which stood for "Tetsuya Komuro rave factory," trf's specialty was Eurobeat rave music that, with its busy-but-insistent rhythms and simple-but-catchy hooks was easy to sing, easy to dance to, and, once heard, nearly impossible to dislodge from the brain.

Another Komuro Family megastar was Namie Amuro, a diminutive Okinawan-born singer who caught Komuro's eye in January 1995 for her work on "Try Me Watashi o Shinjite" (Try Me Believe Me), a hit single that featured the same kind of Eurobeat sound Komuro had marketed so successfully through trf. Komuro negotiated Amuro's transfer from Toshiba EMI to Avex Trax, the label that had released all of trf's hits, and produced a single, "Body Feels Exit," that sold 800,000 copies—a promising start. Amuro's second Komuro-produced single, "Chase the Chance," broke the million sales barrier with 1.3 million copies. In her first year with Avex Trax, sales of her CDs amounted to eight billion yen, or nearly eighty million dollars.

In 1996, Amuro's career continued to soar. Her first album, *Dance Tracks Vol. 1,* sold two million copies and in August she held a concert at Chiba Marine Stadium—the first-ever stadium show for a Japanese teenage female singer. Her second album, *Sweet 19 Blues,* sold an astounding 3.7 million copies in the first two months following its July 22 release.

Meanwhile, schoolgirls all over Japan were imitating the Amuro look: short pants, miniskirts, high boots, and shoulder-length hair dyed a coppery shade that complimented Amuro's dusky beach-girl complexion. But though nearly the same tender age as her legions of fans, the nineteen-year-old Amuro belted out her hits with an unsmiling intensity that was meant to be erotic and represented a dramatic departure from the sweet-but-sexy image preferred by the previous decade's idol singers.

Amuro's own charisma contributed to her enormous popularity, which has surpassed even trf's, but it was Komuro's distinctive sound that transformed her from a newcomer with one medium-sized hit into the hottest female singer of her generation.

Komuro began the search for that sound early. Born in 1958 in Tokyo's Setagaya Ward, near the youth mecca of Shibuya, Komuro studied violin from the age of three. In 1970 at the Osaka Expo, he saw and promptly fell in love with his first synthesizer. While still a junior high school student, he secretly pawned his guitar, violin, and electronic keyboard to buy one of his own—the Roland SH1000—for 160,000 yen. He was on his way.

After entering Waseda University, a prestigious private university located in Tokyo, Komuro joined a band called Speed Way. In 1983, he and two Speed Way members, Naoto Kine and Takashi Utsunomiya, formed a technopop group called TM

Network and, in 1984, released their first album, *Rainbow Rainbow.*

While recording and performing with TM Network, Komuro began to produce records for other artists. In 1986, a song he wrote and produced for Misato Watanabe, "My Revolution," sold seven hundred thousand copies—Komuro's first major hit. He also worked with such big-name talents as Miho Nakayama, SEIKO MATSUDA, Kyoko Koizumi, Yoko Oginome, RIE MIYAZAWA, and Akina Nakamori.

TM Network had its share of hits, including "Get Wild" and "Self Control," but in 1988 Komuro decided he wanted to further his pop-music education by going to the source: London. During his year abroad, Komuro learned about not only the Western way of producing music but the British way of having fun at wild all-night dance parties called raves.

After returning to Japan, Komuro knew that he would rather produce than perform. But rather than work with established talent he wanted to develop his own stars, his own style. His first discovery was the lead singer of trf, Yuki, whom he found at an amateur disco dance contest in 1992. The crowd booed her when they learned she was a pro who had danced with a group called Zoo, but Komuro thought she had the right moves and look for what he was soon calling the "trf project." Best of all, as he heard at a later audition, she had the right pop singing voice: high, bright, and strong enough to carry Komuro's musical message over the background pound, straight to the audience subconscious.

His idea for the new group was dazzlingly simple: kids liked to sing at karaoke clubs and dance at discos. Why not combine these two forms of popular mass entertainment into one sound? Avex Trax, a young label that specialized in dance music, liked Komuro's idea, signed his group, and released their first album, *EZ Do Dance.* It became a hit and by mid-1996, twenty-one million albums and singles later, trf had made Avex Trax a powerhouse in the Japanese pop music business.

Although Komuro's original idea for trf may have been simple, his execution was anything but. An obsessive worker, he supervised every detail of his project, from the composition of the music to the type font on the album jacket. Also, once the trf project had fulfilled his goals, including the goal of making Komuro the most successful and powerful record producer in the business, he did not slack off but remained constantly on the prowl for new talent, sounds, and trends.

He haunted Roppongi clubs to see what young women—his target audience—considered cool in fashion, hairstyles, makeup, and music; scoured data from karaoke on-line services to find out what tunes they liked to sing; and scanned the media to spot new movements on the younger generation's trendscape. Quietly and deliberately, he turned himself into a one-man market-research company.

Then, huddled in his Tokyo Bay studio with his state-of-the-art electronic music gear, Komuro would begin to put together his next hit, using the thousands of rhythms and melodies from every known pop genre that he had input into his Synclavia synthesizer. Critics charged that Komuro was simply recycling Western pop for Japanese tastes, that he was less an original composer than a master at the craft of pastiche. But no matter what sources he used—the latest Eurobeat sound or a half-forgotten 1970s pop tune—he made music that was distinctly Komuro, with hooks short enough to catch the ear in a fifteen-second TV commercial but carefully constructed to stand up to repeated listenings.

Critics also scored his lyrics for being childishly artless. But though sentiments like "singing every night, I can enjoy being alive" ("Overnight Sensation") and "I won't cry, I just want to keep looking at you" ("Koishisa to Setsunasa to Kokorozuyosa to," or "Sweetness, Sorrow, and Strength") were never going to make anyone forget Lennon and McCartney, they had the desired impact on his fans, many of whom, after all, were young kids whose own use of the Japanese language was anything but sophisticated.

Like the editors of **SHONEN JUMP**, Japan's most popular *manga* magazine, Komuro was fond of what he called "keywords," i.e., words that expressed the dreams and aspirations of his target audience. To find them, he often called women to his table at the VIP room in the Velfarre—a Roppongi disco that he made his after-dark headquarters—and asked them to write, on a coaster or napkin, their favorite words and phrases. Komuro would then take these verbal scraps back to his studio and plug them into his lyrics.

After writing and recording the song came the business of selling it and, in this area of the music business as well, Komuro demonstated his mastery. A key element in his marketing strategy was network television. Japan lagged far behind the United States in the licensing of radio stations and the building of cable and satellite networks. In the middle of the decade radio stations played relatively little contemporary Japanese pop music and no cable music channel had a mass youth audience equivalent to MTV's. Knowing that one of the few places kids could hear new sounds was network TV, Komuro placed nearly all of his early hits as TV commercial songs or drama series themes. Soon sponsors were lining up to use his material, even though they complained that viewers often paid more attention to Komuro's song than the ad.

While churning out hit after hit, Komuro continued to recruit new members for his family, including a second-rank idol singer named Arisa Tomine whom Komuro not only raised from late-night-show-sex-kitten obscurity but gave a new name—Tomomi Kahala—that happened to have the same initials as his own. In 1995 he launched Kahala as the first artist on his new label, Orumok—Komuro spelled backwards. Released in September 1995, Kahala's debut single, "keep yourself alive," reached number eight on the *Orikon* chart and sold four hundred thousand copies. Her second single, "I Believe," climbed to number seven and became a million seller. "Her voice stimulates the tear ducts," said Komuro, in explaining why he had decided to produce her. Another reason for his interest in the twenty-one-year-old singer's career: she soon became his live-in lover.

Yet another demonstration of Komuro's hit-making power was his response when Masatoshi Hamada of the comedy duo **DOWNTOWN** jokingly asked him to write a song for him on the October 22, 1995 broadcast of the TV show *Hey! Hey! Hey! Music Champ*. Answering in the affirmative, Komuro quickly composed two tunes for Hamada—"Wow War Tonight" and "Going Home"—that became million sellers. "I had never heard Hamada sing, but his voice when he was shouting during a comedy routine was exactly right for the musical genre called Jungle," explained Komuro. "So that's the kind of music I had him record."

In 1996 Komuro also launched "dos project," a group whose name means "dance of sound." Although Komuro conceived dos as a showcase for the talents of his latest find, a second-tier idol singer called Taeko Nishino, he recruited, rehearsed, and even named the group on a segment of *Asayan*, a weekly music show broadcast on the TV Tokyo network. Called "Komuro Garcon"—a play on the well-known Japanese designer label Comme des Garcons—the segment offered viewers a glimpse into the inner workings of the Komuro hit machine. Naturally, there was also a commercial tie-up, with a TV ad campaign for a Shiseido brand shampoo. Released in March 1996, dos's first single, "Baby baby baby" debuted at number six on the *Oricon* chart and sold eighty thousand copies its first week. Komuro had yet another hit on his hands.

Having conquered Japan, Komuro is moving into international markets. In December 1996 he closed a deal with Rupert Murdoch's News Corporation to establish a joint venture called tk news for scouting, developing and promoting new Asian artists. Launched in

February 1997, the new Hong-Kong-based company will not only nurture the trfs and Namie Amuros of Taiwan, Hong Kong, China, and other Asian countries, but broadcast their music via the tk news satellite channel throughout Japan and the region. Eventually, the partners plan to beam Komuro's artists across the United States on the new A Sky A satellite TV platform.

Not all is rosy in Komuro's world, however. In June 1996 a biography, *Komuro Tetsuya, Eiko to Satetsu* (Tetsuya Komuro, the Glory and the Failure), appeared that portrayed the producer as an insatiable womanizer, habitual drug user, and ruthless exploiter of talent who casts aside his completed "projects" and is only interested in advancing the career of Tetsuya Komuro. But despite the book, that career will continue to flourish as long as "with t. komuro" on the back of a CD means the coolest groove in Japanese dance music.

KUROYANAGI, TETSUKO & "TOTTO-CHAN"

In Japan, as elsewhere, a celebrity autobiography is usually the ghosted story of the author's fabulous career, with occasional stops along the way for self-glorification and self-justification. Unlike in the West, lurid personal revelations are relatively rare, since confessions of one's addictions and affairs are more likely to damage one's image than stir sympathy or elicit approval.

There are, however, exceptions to the rule, sometimes large ones indeed. In 1981 *Madogiwa no Totto-chan* (Totto-chan: The Little Girl at the Window) by TV personality Tetsuko Kuroyanagi not only resembled no other Japanese celebrity autobio ever written but also became the biggest bestseller in the postwar history of Japanese publishing. In its first year of publication, the book sold 4.55 million copies—breaking the record of 3.5 million sales set by *Nichibei Kaiwa Techo* (U.S.–Japan Conversation Notebook), an Occupation-era English conversation text. In its first two years, sales reached 5.5 million copies—a figure never since equaled.

Totto-chan's publisher, Kodansha, had no idea that the book would become Japan's publishing sensation of the decade, if not the century. It was assigned to an editor, Keiko Iwamoto, who hadn't had a bestseller in years and considered herself a corporate dropout in danger of losing her job. The first printing was twenty thousand copies—not a large number considering that Kuroyanagi had been appearing regularly on Japanese television almost since its inception and was currently hosting a popular afternoon talk show, *Tetsuko no Heya* (Tetsuko's Room).

The first few weeks after its publication in March 1978, *Totto-chan* sold briskly, but not extraordinarily well. Then came the explosion: orders for the book started flooding in from all over the country. When Iwamoto submitted a request for a new printing of eighty thousand copies, one of the company directors asked her if she had lost her mind. "What are you doing, printing so many?" he asked. But instead of sitting in the warehouse, as the director had feared, the copies sold so quickly the bookstores couldn't keep them in stock. To satisfy the demand, the book's printer, Kyodo Insatsu, installed special high-speed rotary presses and ran off copies as though they were newspaper extras.

As *Totto-chan* graduated from bestseller to social phenomenon, NHK made it an item on its evening news broadcast, and Iwamoto, a corporate dropout no longer, was flooded with interview requests from more than one hundred media organizations. Even after the boom died down, *Totto-chan* continued to sell steadily, and not only in Japan. Translations were published in more than twenty foreign countries and, as of March 1996, sales of the book totaled 7.7 million copies.

What made *Totto-chan* different from the dozens of other celeb autobios published before and since? For one thing, Kuroyanagi wrote it herself, with no prompting from a publisher and no help from a friendly ghost. After meeting Iwamoto several times socially, Kuroyanagi told her that she had woken up one night and "started writing some sentences." Those "sentences" became *Totto-chan.*

For another thing, Kuroyanagi the celebrity never makes an appearance in the main text of the book (though she does, briefly, in the afterword). Instead, writing in the third person, she tells the story of a little girl nicknamed Totto-chan (Kuroyanagi's childish pronunciation of "Tetsuko") who lives in Tokyo and is expelled from school in the first grade for misbehavior. One time, she went to the window and shouted to a passing street musician, who came over and gave Totto-chan and her classmates an impromptu concert. Another time she nearly drove her teacher mad by opening and closing her desk top hundreds of times because she liked the movement and sound.

Realizing that Totto-chan is not going to adapt to a normal school environment, her violinist father and housewife mother enroll her in Tomoe Gakuen, a small private elementary school founded by Sosaku Kobayashi, a pioneering progressive educator. Totto-chan loves the place from the moment she sees it. Instead of the usual imposing concrete pillars, the entrance is framed by two small trees. And instead of the usual barracks-like school building, there are old electric train cars, converted into classrooms.

Imagine going to school in a train! It is six-year-old Totto-chan's idea of paradise.

The book is series of vignettes from Totto-chan's years at Tomoe, illustrated with pastel drawings by Chihiro Iwasaki. Kuro-yanagi writes not as an adult looking back but with the eyes of the child she once was—simply, directly, unpretentiously. Not surprisingly, many of the book's early readers were young women, who could more easily accept the book's offer of a passport back to girlhood.

Kuroyanagi makes that girlhood seem wonderful, especially to millions of Japanese who spent their own school days in rule-obsessed, overcrowded classrooms, stuffing their heads with facts to pass tests and stifling their individuality to avoid the wrath of their teachers and the ridicule of their peers. While "conform or perish" is the unspoken motto of much modern Japanese schooling, the key word of Kobayashi's educational philosophy is "freedom." At Tomoe, Totto-chan and her classmates are free to sit where they want, and to study what they want when they want. In the afternoon their teacher often takes them on a walk to a nearby temple, giving impromptu nature talks on the way. A lot more fun—and instructive!—than grinding away at a textbook.

Kobayashi's "freedom" does not mean anarchy, however. Though he firmly believes in the individual worth of his charges and rarely scolds them ("You are really a good child," he is forever telling Totto-chan), he does make rules, which are often childlike in their simplicity. (One that particularly captivates Totto-chan is the rule that every child's lunchbox contain "something from the mountains and something from the sea.") And he often works, godlike, behind the scenes to boost his students' self-esteem. For the shortest boy in Totto-chan's class he designs field-day races that turn his disability into an advantage, yet without causing resentment by advertising the principal's altruistic intentions.

For the talkative, hyperactive Totto-chan, Kobayashi sets aside the better part of an afternoon to hear everything the girl has to say about her pet dog, her family, and her life. No other adult had ever listened to her so long and intently before.

Though few of Kuroyanagi's readers ever encountered a paragon quite like Kobayashi, her affectionate account of her teacher and his school falls squarely into the Confucian tradition of respecting one's teacher and valuing one's education, a tradition with which all Japanese, even the dropouts, are familiar. Kuroyanagi noted in the afterword that she and her former Tomoe classmates still get together once a year to reminisce about old times and renew friendships. Although these reunions testify to the lasting impact of their Tomoe experience on their lives, they are hardly unusual

The Japanese and English editions of Japan's biggest bestseller ever.

in Japan, where even nursery-school classmates keep in touch over the years.

Many Japanese also retain fond memories of their favorite teacher and many books, films, and TV programs are panegyrics to teachers: Yoji Yamada's 1993 *Gakko* (School) is a winningly folksy example of the genre, Akira Kurosawa's 1993 *Madadayo* (Not Yet), a sentimentally overbearing one. Though Kuroyanagi's approach may be unconventional, her anecdotes of Kobayashi and his methods are of a type familiar to her Japanese readers.

But for all its nostalgic, sentimental, and traditional appeal, *Totto-chan* was also intended as a counter to trends in Japanese education that Kuroyanagi found distressing, including school violence—an issue much in the news when the book appeared. This, *Totto-chan* says on nearly every page, is the way we can, and indeed should, educate young children. Shocked by media stories of kids trashing schools and beating teachers, a lot of readers were eager to listen.

After Kuroyanagi struck such a resounding chord, other celebrities from sports and show business tried their hand at autobiographies and many of these books joined *Totto-chan* on the bestseller list (it should be mentioned that singer **MOMOE YAMAGUCHI** was

also a generator of this boom, with her best-selling 1980 autobio *Aoi Toki*, or "Green Time"). Kuroyanagi followed up her success with *Totto Chaneru* (Totto Channel), an account of her early days as a radio and TV actress and personality, and other books with "Totto" in the title.

In addition to writing Japan's best-selling-ever book, Kuroyanagi holds what must be a record for TV appearances in a career that began four decades ago, almost simultaneously with the birth of Japanese broadcasting. Among her long list of credits of is *The Best Ten,* a pop-music program she hosted together with Hiroshi Kume (see **NEWS STATION**) on TBS from 1978 to 1989. During its eleven-year run, *The Best Ten* launched the careers of several Japanese pop superstars, including **MOMOE YAMAGUCHI,** Junko Sakurada, Masako Mori, and **YUMING**. But the longest-lived of Kuroyanagi's shows is the aforementioned *Tetsuko no Heya*, which celebrated its twentieth anniversary on the air in February 1996. Broadcast Monday through Friday at 1:15 P.M. on TV Asahi, this forty-minute program is usually a one-on-one interview by Kuroyanagi of a celebrity guest. For those used to the quips of Jay Leno or the confessions of Oprah Winfrey, the show may seem rather tame: two adults having a real, extended conversation in what looks to be a real living room. But Kuroyanagi, who is still the same motor mouth she was as a six-year-old chewing off Kobayashi's ear, keeps things moving at a smart pace.

Not always though; once, when she asked Ken Takakura why he was still acting after having made his name and his fortune in the movies, the strong-but-silent star mulled for one agonizingly long minute before answering "I guess because I want to pursue happiness." Kuroyanagi not only waited patiently until Takakura had spoken his piece, but kept the dead-air time in the program. "If we had edited out the silence, it wouldn't have been Takakura any more," she told an interviewer. Her teacher Kobayashi, who was all for free expression, or even free inexpressiveness, would have no doubt approved.

Editing as little as possible is also the rule for other guests, to make the show as live as possible. Kuroyanagi made two other "iron rules" when she started the program twenty years ago: (1) don't change the staff and, (2) don't ask guests embarrassing questions about their latest scandal. The object was to encourage staff loyalty and make guests—a total of 3,173 by the twentieth anniversary—feel at ease.

Kuroyanagi also set some informal rules for herself. Although she always wears the same trademark hairstyle—an onion dome with helmetlike bangs that come down to her eyebrows—she changes her outfit for every show, having gone through more than five thousand in the first twenty years. Kuroyanagi, however, is not a show-business Imelda. Every year for the past twenty years she has donated the greater part of her wardrobe to a charity bazaar for needy children. She also donates herself. Since 1984 she has served as a goodwill ambassador for UNICEF, traveling all over the world to publicize the plight of children in underdeveloped countries.

Another rule is that the show must go on. Kuroyanagi never missed a single one of the 5,082 broadcasts during the program's first two decades, even skipping her father's funeral to make a taping session. She has proclaimed that she wants to "keep talking [on the program] until I'm one hundred." If anyone can do it, it's Kuroyanagi, aka Totto-chan, the irrepressible iron lady of Japanese television.

KUWATA, KEISUKE & SOUTHERN ALL STARS

Can rock translate into Japanese? In the early 1970s this question divided Japan's rock community into two opposing camps: the purists, who believed that only English-language rock was real rock, and the realists, who knew that without Japanese lyrics rock was forever doomed to the pop-music fringe. Commercially and artistically, the question was soon settled, with realists winning a decisive victory.

But though Japanese-language rock had its share of successes in the first half of the decade, including the Sadistic Mika Band and the wildly popular greaser-rock group Carol, mainstream pop music was still dominated by idol singers and groups whose songs may have contained a smattering of English words but whose sound was bright, bubbly, and smilingly insubstantial.

Then in 1978 a group called Southern All Stars released "Katte ni Sinbad" (Sinbad In Your Own Way) whose title spoofed two recent pop hits—**PINK LADY**'s "Nagisa no Sinbad" (Sinbad on the Beach) and Kenji Sawada's "Katte ni Shiyagare" (Do What You Want). Like so many Japanese pop hits, the lyrics were a mixture of Japanese and English, but the song itself was like nothing else in the top ten. The group's lead vocalist, Keisuke Kuwata, sang the Japanese words as though they were English, with a feeling that came directly from American soul music. At the same time Kuwata wasn't trying to self-importantly pass himself off as a Japanese Ray Charles. A natural entertainer with a rapid-fire stage patter and a talent for clowning, he gave the song's Latin rhythms an infectious energy and comic lift that made it an immediate hit. Also, the lyrics, with their references to romantic good times at Shonan Beach—a swimming and surfing beach southwest of Tokyo—had a summery Beach-Boys-like appeal.

Born in 1956 in Chigasaki, Kanagawa Prefecture, near Shonan Beach, Kuwata formed Southern All Stars with five members of a music club at Aoyama Gakuin University. In 1977 the group entered a Yamaha-sponsored amateur-band contest and performed a song titled "Onna Yonde Boogie" (Get the Girl Boogie), whose frankly lubricous lyrics and raucous sound blew the crowd away.

Unlike many New-Music artists (see **YUMING AND THE BIRTH OF THE NEW MUSIC**), Kuwata did not disdain that prime venue of mainstream pop: television. But though Kuwata and the Southern All Stars had no qualms about performing on *The Best Ten* and other pop music shows, they took a different approach to the business of being pop idols. For his debut on *The Best Ten*, Kuwata appeared live from a funky Tokyo club, wearing nothing but short pants and a tank top and rocking until the sweat poured down. At a time when the typical TV pop idol was expensively costumed and coifed to present a glamorous show-biz image, the rawness of Kuwata's act hit the airwaves with an explosive force.

The song that solidified Kuwata's pop stardom was the 1979 "Itoshii no Ellie" (Ellie, My Love). A soulful ballad, it was used as the theme song for *Fuzoroi no Ringotachi* (Odd Apples) a hit TV drama that depicted the lives and loves of six young people from college days to adulthood. Selling 710,000 copies, "Itoshii no Ellie" later became a karaoke standard and, in 1989, was recorded in English by Ray Charles—further proof to Kuwata's millions of fans that his music was indeed the real thing.

In the 1980s Southern All Stars became Japan's top rock band, releasing a string of ten straight number-one albums, including *Tiny Bubbles* (1980), *Stereo Taiyo-zoku* (Stereo Sun Tribe, 1981), *Nude Man* (1982), *Kirei* (Pretty, 1983) and *Kamakura* (1985), while trading heavily on their Shonan Beach goodtime image. Not surprisingly, the beach itself, which had been known primarily as the setting for Yuzo Kayama's 1960s **WAKA DAISHO** (Young Captain) movies and as a hangout for motorcycle gangs (see **ZOKU**), became all the rage among young people who wanted to live the lyrics of Southern All Stars' songs.

In 1985 the band members embarked on solo careers. Working with an ensemble called The Kuwata Band, Kuwata scored two number-one singles and recorded two albums, including *Nippon no Rock Band* (Japan's Rock Band), an all-English album that won the Japanese music industry's 1986 Album of the Year award. In 1987 Kuwata also acquired international cachet by recording with Darryl Hall and John Oates on a track titled "She's a Big Teaser."

The Kuwata Band broke up in February 1987. In 1989 Kuwata reunited with Southern All-Stars to record the band's twenty-sixth single and their first ever number-one hit, "Sayonara Baby" (Good-bye Baby). In the 1990s, the band continued to top the singles chart with such tunes as the 1991 "Neo Bravo," which was used as the ending theme of a late-night news program, the 1992 "Namida no Kiss" (Tearful Kiss), the theme song of the TBS drama *Zutto Anata ga Suki Datta* (I've Liked You For a Long Time), and the 1993 "Erotica Seven," the theme song of the Fuji TV drama *Akuma no Kiss*

(Kiss of the Devil). With 1,727,000 copies sold, "Erotica Seven" became the group's biggest hit ever.

In 1990 Kuwata directed his first film, *Inamura Jane,* a nostalgic look at the Shonan Beach scene of the 1970s. Filled with hit tunes of the period from both sides of the Pacific, including the songs of the Southern All-Stars, *Inamura Jane* earned 1.83 billion yen for distributor Toho and became the fourth-biggest domestic grosser of the year.

In the nineties, however, Kuwata began to tire of his image as Japan's minstrel of summertime fun. In 1993 he took part in a concert to raise money for AIDS research and in 1994 released a solo album, *Kodoku no Taiyo* (Lonely Sun) that contained tunes about Japan's money politics, prostitution, and AIDS—and not a single song about love at the beach. "I'm more complex [than my public image], not that happy-go-lucky," he told an interviewer. "I think it's time Japanese musicians thought about social issues."

MARIO

Do Nintendo video games really count as a Japanese pop-culture phenomenon? After all, the name of the most famous Nintendo character comes not from Japanese history or legend but the landlord of the company's first U.S. headquarters, a chap called Mario. In the United States, Mario has not only sold millions of game cartridges but starred in a television series and, in 1993, a big budget, effects-laden movie (that was also, with 20.9 million dollar U.S. gross, a disappointment at the box office). To a lot of his young U.S. fans who wouldn't know Tokyo from Timbuktu, he is no doubt as American as Mickey Mouse, Donald Duck, and, now, the POWER RANGERS.

Even so, Nintendo is a Japanese company, which started by selling playing cards in 1889, and Mario did spring from a Japanese mind, that of Nintendo game designer Shigeru Miyamoto. The year was 1981 and Miyamoto was designing an arcade game called Donkey Kong, whose main character was a gorilla. As one of the supporting players, Miyamoto came up with a tiny mustachioed figure called Jumpman. But when Nintendo exported the game to the United States, the local staff decided that Jumpman bore a striking resemblance to their landlord. Thus the name change, which Miyamoto quickly agreed to. The early Mario, however, was a crude creation. Given the technological limitations of the time, Miyamoto could use only three colors, which made it hard to draw the hair, eyes, and mouth of the tiny figure without lines of black running together. To solve the problem, Miyamoto gave his little man a floppy

Mario: saving the princess and conquering the world computer game market.

cap. Also, to make it easier to see his arms move against the background of his body, Miyamoto dressed him in a pair of blue overalls. The result of these shifts and compromises was Mario, whose profession became plumbing, though he fixed as many leaky pipes as Elmer Fudd shot rabbits.

For some time after his debut, Mario and other Nintendo characters were known mainly to teenagers with a few spare quarters and time to kill in an arcade. That changed with the introduction of the eight-bit Famicom home video-game system in Japan in July 1983 (which was called the Nintendo Entertainment System ® when it went on sale in the United States in 1985). At the time of the system's launch, Nintendo was a relatively small player in the video-game business. Six months later, sales had skyrocketed and Nintendo owned a fifty-per-cent market share. Famicom had beaten the competition in both technology and price—and it had Mario on its side.

In 1985, Mario, together with brother Luigi, graduated to star status with the debut of the home version of the Super Mario Bros. arcade game. Players guided Mario across a surrealistic landscape that included underground passageways and ocean bottoms, while clearing obstacles and defeating enemies, including man-eating flowers. Having survived these challenges, Mario came at last to a giant turtle called Kuppa (Koopa in the American game). If he could beat this formidable foe, he could rescue the Piichi Hime (Daisy in the American version) and win the game. The same year, the Nintendo Entertainment System, with Mario as part of the lineup, crossed the Pacific and enjoyed the same explosive success in the United States as it had in Japan.

Nintendo didn't stop with Mario, however. Not long after the Super Mario Bros. game debuted, the company brought forth Dragon Quest, a pioneering role-playing game that became a smash hit in Japan, with lines of customers snaking around game stores the day it went on sale. Boosted by sales of these two games and the introduction of new hardware like the hand-held Game Boy, Nintendo achieved near total dominance in the Japanese market by the end of the decade.

Despite a spirited challenge by Sega and its Sonic the Hedgehog, Nintendo maintained that dominance into the 1990s. In August 1995 Nintendo released its first new Mario game in four years: Super Mario World 2: Yoshi's Island. Once again, the theme was dramatic rescue, this time of Baby Mario from the evil clutches of the Evil Magi-koopa, Kamek. Players had to carry Baby Mario back to his parents in the Mushroom Kingdom while dodging traps and dispatching Kamek's henchmen, including winged koopa troopers, through the six worlds of Yoshi's Island. In the first month after its Japanese release the game sold more than 1 million copies, well on its way to equaling or even exceeding the 3.4 million unit sales of its predecessor, Super Mario World.

Also, despite the introduction of rival thirty-two-bit games, Nintendo's sixteen-bit Super Famicom continued to be a hot seller in Japan, moving a total of 15 million units by September 1995, compared with 19 million in the much larger American market (where it is known as the Super Nintendo Entertainment System ®). In October 1995, Nintendo announced the sale of its one billionth video game—or one for every teenager in the world. Of those one billion cartridges, forty-four percent sold in Japan and forty-two percent in North America. Worldwide, designers had created nearly one thousand games for Nintendo machines.

And the original Super Mario Bros. cartridge? In the twelve years since its release it has sold forty million units. Not bad for a pair of pint-sized plumbers.

Nintendo still has big plans for its biggest star. Together with Silicon Graphics of California, It has developed the Super Mario ® 64 game for its Nintendo ® 64 game system, the first in the industry to offer sixty-four-bit action. Using a "3-D stick," players can step inside a three-hundred-sixty-degree lifelike virtual environment. Now that Mario is three-dimensional and mobile in all directions, he would seemingly have no new technical worlds to conquer, except for leaping out of the screen to repair that nagging leak in the faucet.

MATSUDA, SEIKO

To the Japanese entertainment world, the media must often seem a giant, ravening pack, ceaselessly searching for fresh meat and sniffing potential victims for signs of weakness. The media maw is a huge one, including sports newspapers, weekly magazines, TV "wide shows" (daytime magazine shows that cover everything of interest to the viewing housewife, including celebrity scandal), and other media outlets with an interest in entertainment news. When hard news is lacking, the maw is happy to fasten on rumor or sheer speculation. And when the maw happens upon a particularly juicy morsel, it feeds on it voraciously, relentlessly, regardless of the damage to reputations or careers. Photo magazines like *Focus* and *Friday* stake out a celebrity twenty-four hours a day, hoping to snap a photo of a late-night tryst in a restaurant or an early-morning exit from a lover's apartment. Other weekly magazines run features with titles like "The Celebrity I Hate the Most" or "Japan's Fifty Most Scandalous Women" that are little more than forums for celebrity score settlers or media character assassins.

And where one mag goes, dozens, if not hundreds, must follow. U.S. reporters watching the Japanese media pack dog Hideo Nomo's every step during his first season in the Major Leagues became fascinated by its size, intensity, and tenacity. Wasn't there any letup? They began to wonder. Wouldn't they ever give the poor guy a break? The answer, as any celebrity who has been in the maw's grip could tell them, is "not this side of the grave."

Not a few celebrities have retired (**MOMOE YAMAGUCHI**), retreated into silence (**SAYURI YOSHINAGA**), or torched their own careers (**RIE MIYAZAWA**), partly or largely because of pack maulings. The worst-mauled celebrity of all is pop singer Seiko Matsuda. As of August 1995, some 3,313 mostly negative stories had appeared about her in Japanese magazines, the highest total for any postwar public figure. Even so, Seiko-chan, as her fans once universally called her, has not only survived but thrived. In the process she has become a role model for thirtysomething women and changed the relationship between the Japanese media and the entertainment world. The pack's bark, she has proven, can be worse than its bite.

One reason for Seiko's survival is sheer star power. During the peak of her popularity as an idol singer in the 1980s she spun out twenty-four straight number-one singles—a record that no other Japanese pop star or group could match. Like the Western pop star with whom she is most often compared, Madonna, Seiko accomplished this feat less through beauty or talent than canny manipulation of her own image, always staying one step ahead of the media and fans.

Another is changing morals and mores. During the late 1980s and early 1990s, when Seiko was being regularly bashed in the male-dominated media for putting her high-powered career and freewheeling sex life ahead of hearth and home, young Japanese women were rebelling against traditional role models and seeking out new life paths and pleasures. While the media was excoriating Seiko for leaving her husband and infant daughter behind in Tokyo to live in New York and try to break into the

U.S. music market, her fans were thrilled by her determination and boldness. And while the press was painting a big red "A" on her forehead for her dalliance with an unemployed actor named Jeff Nichols, her fans were reveling in the romanticism and daring of it all.

Even when this "Queen of Scandal" was running through men the way other women ran through panty hose—local magazines have romantically linked her with more than thirty, not including her husband—she still sold out concert after concert. Though Seiko's adulterous liaisons may have seemed tame indeed compared with Madonna's experiments with bondage, lesbianism, and other nonstandard forms of sexual expression, they struck many young Japanese women as liberating. One didn't have to abandon one's dreams and desires just because of marriage, particularly a marriage that had become strictly pro forma, as Seiko's so obviously was (and as so many marriages in Japan's divorce-adverse society were and still are).

Yet another reason for Seiko's show business longevity, perhaps the most important one, is character. A notorious public figure in a society known for pounding down the proverbial nail that sticks up, she seems to thrive on the media abuse. The harder she is hit, the stronger she bounces back, more like a round, weighted *daruma* doll than a nail.

Even her detractors have come to privately admire her toughness while remaining publicly flabbergasted by her lack of shame.

Seiko was hardly an obvious candidate for superstardom. Unlike so many Japanese show business legends, including Momoe Yamaguchi and **HIBARI MISORA**, she didn't have to battle against poverty or overcome a dysfunctional family background. Born Noriko Kamachi in Kurume, Fukuoka Prefecture in March 1962, she was the daughter of a city government employee and a full-time housewife, who occasionally supplemented the family income by working at the city race track or sewing buttons on clothes at home. Her parents had one other child, a boy eight years older than Noriko. Theirs was an average middle-class family, living a quiet life in a small provincial town.

After she entered junior high school, her fascination with show business grew. Every day after class she would get together with two friends and sing and dance along to the records of her favorite group, **PINK LADY**. She also worked hard at charming those around her, particularly the boys and teachers. But the girls, who saw her as an artful schemer and showoff, voted against her in the eighth-grade school-council election and caused her defeat. She wept hot tears in the teacher's room, but quickly recovered her poise—a pattern often repeated in later life.

After enrolling in a high school in Fukuoka—the largest city on the island of Kyushu—she started taking singing lessons at a local pop-music academy. In 1978, she entered the "Miss Seventeen Love Idol Attack Contest" sponsored by CBS-Sony and the Shueisha publishing company and finished first out of 4,500 contestants.

She hid the first-place medal from her straitlaced father, who strongly disapproved of her singing ambitions, but later screwed up the courage to approach him about taking part in the national contest, held in Tokyo. He flatly refused his permission. Rather than give up, she kept taking singing lessons, with the encouragement of CBS-Sony music director Muneo Wakamatsu. Finally, in 1979 she journeyed alone from Kyushu to Tokyo to audition for the Sun Music talent agency. Impressed more by her determination than her talent, Sun president Hideyoshi Aizawa decided to sign her.

In April 1980, Noriko—now performing under her new stage name of Seiko Matsuda—made her recording debut with "Hadashi no Kisetsu" (Barefoot Season). The seventy million yen promotional budget for her single, thirty million yen of which came from Sun and the remainder from CBS-Sony, was extraordinarily large for an unknown singer, but Aizawa said he needed it to make his new star stand out from the six hundred other newcomers making their recording debuts that year. With a boost from a Shiseido TV ad campaign for a new face cream that featured a snippet of the song, and aired it two thousand times the first week, sales of "Hadashi no Kisetsu" soared to 288,000 copies.

Seiko's next two singles also benefited from TV commercial tie-ins: "Aoi Sangosho" (Blue Coral Reef) reached number two on the singles chart, with 602,000 copies sold, and "Kaze wa Shushoku" (The Wind Is the Color of Fall), hit number one, with 796,000 copies sold. In Seiko's first year as a professional singer, total sales from her records amounted to eight billion yen. The seventy million yen Sun had invested in her first promo budget had been repaid more than one hundred fold.

This was the age of the made-for-TV idol, whose music, choreography, look, and even press-interview answers were the products of record-company and talent-agency handlers. Right from the beginning, however, Seiko resisted manipulation, insisting on her own clothes and hair style. Her handlers had wanted to make her look older than her eighteen years. Instead, with her miniskirts, frilly blouses, and soft bangs, Seiko came across as a coy child in a woman's body. This woman-child swept the newcomer's awards in 1980 and sobbed with gratitude for the cameras when she received them, but cynical reporters on the scene could detect nary

Seiko in an early 1980s incarnation: a *burikko* for the ages.

a drop of moisture in her eyes. They also noted, unkindly, that her legs were bowed, her proportions were less than generous, and her accent was that of a Kyushu country bumpkin. None of that mattered; Seiko charmed TV audiences much as she had charmed her male classmates and teachers in Kurume. Yes, she may have been faking it, but she faked it so sincerely that it was hard not to admire her sheer brass.

The uncharmed called her a *burikko,* a woman who acts childish and cute—eighteen going on twelve—often to win male approval. But rather than grow up, Seiko wore this label proudly—and soon millions of young women across the country were following her lead. Watching these *burikko* legions cavorting and giggling girlishly on the tube, in the classroom, and on the street, feminists, particularly foreigners, could feel their blood boiling. To them, Seiko represented all that was wrong about Japanese pop culture, which infantilized and trivialized women in the most blatant ways imaginable. How could she let herself be exploited and degraded this way, they asked? What her feminist detractors didn't know, however, was that, against initial opposition, Seiko was simply underscoring what she felt to be her strong points, particularly her faux naive charm. Like Madonna, she knew that the first law of show business was to make an impression. Political correctness could wait.

Seiko was also quite capable of speaking her mind and she was soon telling the world that, more than anyone else, she wanted to meet Hiromi Go, a baby-faced idol singer Seiko had admired since she was a schoolgirl. Now a star herself, Seiko easily found an opportunity for an introduction, on the set of an NHK pop music program called *Let's Go Young.* Smitten, she courted her ideal the same way she had pursued her career ambitions: directly, persistently, effectively.

By November 1982, Seiko was confessing

Here comes the bride: Seiko's marriage to actor Masaki Kanda was the biggest show-business event of 1985. Twelve years later, they called it quits.

on late-night radio that "if there's one man I like, it's Hiromi." Hiromi made it clear he felt the same way about her.

This time, Seiko was not faking it; she and Hiromi really intended to marry. There was one barrier standing in the way, however. Hiromi, a typically conservative Kyushu male, wanted Seiko to give up her career and become a full-time housewife. By now, however, Seiko was the top female pop star in Japan, with a lengthening string of hits. Unlike Momoe Yamaguchi, the pop queen of the 1970s who retired in 1980 after marrying Tomokazu Miura, Seiko wasn't sure she wanted to give it all up for her man.

Fate offered an answer to her dilemma. In November 1984, while on location in Mexico making a movie called *Caribu: Ai no Symphony* (Carib: Symphony of Love), Seiko fell ill with food poisoning. Costar Masaki Kanda, the only one on the all-Japanese set able to speak English, arranged for medical assistance and stayed up all night nursing her. Seiko fell in love again, this time with a man more willing to sacrifice himself for her needs, including her need for a career.

In January 1985, after returning from a trip to Hawaii, Seiko told a packed press conference that she had decided not to marry Hiromi. "He compromised and told me that he didn't mind if I wanted to continue working, but I don't think that [marrying me] would be good for him. . . . If I were reborn

again, I would definitely want to be with him." Seiko ended her emotionally wrenching, and oddly contradictory, statement in a flood of tears, but a week later she was admitting to the press that she and Masateru were an item. Five months later, in June 1985, Seiko and Masaki were married in a church ceremony and feted at a reception at the Hotel New Otani that cost a total of two hundred million yen—extravagant even by Japanese entertainment-world standards. In October 1986, Seiko gave birth to a daughter, Sayaka.

This, according to then-prevalent social conventions, should have been the end of the story. Seiko was expected to settle down to married life and motherhood, while putting her career on hold. She intended nothing of the kind; by March 1987 she was performing again. "I like being Noriko Kanda," she often told intimates, "but I also like being Seiko Kanda."

As the weekly magazines were soon reporting, she also liked being with other men. Within a year after returning to work, she was romantically linked no less than three: director Yoshitaro Negishi and actors Hiroyuki Sanada and Eiji Okada.

By 1988, women's weekly magazines were embroiled in a raging debate over whether Seiko and Masaki would get a divorce, with the "divorce" faction in the majority. The aim of this brawl was to build

circulation, but the constant stream of stories about their imminent breakup put undeniable pressures on the couple's marriage. To celebrate their third anniversary and scotch rumors that they were splitsville, Seiko and Masaki sang a love duet on a program called *Music Station*. But this lovey-dovey pair didn't tell their public that they were in fact separated; Seiko was living with Sayaka at her parents' house, while Masaki remained alone in their apartment in the exclusive Seijo section of Tokyo.

Seiko also made headlines that year for her decision to conquer the U.S. market. Though Masaki gave Seiko his blessings, he refused to accompany her or let her take Sayaka. Seiko got on the plane to New York alone.

Her record company, CBS-Sony, backed her in this attempt, but company execs told her flatly that she would have to change her style. The *burikko* affectations that had charmed so many fans in Japan would strike Americans as simply childish. She would have to begin from the beginning, with singing, dancing, and English lessons. Seiko threw herself into her task with her usual dedication (while taking time out for a date in New York with pop singer Masahiko "Matchi" Kondo that photo mag *Friday* captured for readers back home).

Her American sojourn worked a dramatic change in Seiko. The sweetly accommodating *burikko* quickly transformed herself into a straight-talking woman who opened a press conference for a "midterm progress report" on her U.S. recording session with a blunt question: "You're really here to ask about my divorce, aren't you?" The media didn't get their long-awaited divorce story, but they did get a new take on Seiko, one that they weren't sure they liked. Sun Music also discovered the new, independent Seiko; in July 1989 she announced that, after ten years with the agency, she was striking out on her own.

Less than a month later, Seiko found her name in the headlines again when Akina Nakamori, a pop singer whose popularity rivaled Seiko's own, slashed her wrists in the Roppongi apartment of her lover, Masahiko Kondo. Matchi's New York tryst with Seiko had evidently prompted her suicide attempt.

The resulting scandal was enormous— almost trashing Akina's career and knocking yet another gaping hole in Seiko's sexy-but-innocent *burikko* image. Although her new single, "Precious Heart," hit the top of the charts in its first week on release, it soon dis-

appeared from sight, while membership in her fan club plummeted from a prescandal peak of eighty thousand to eight thousand. Then came the crowning blow: she was dropped from the lineup of NHK's KOHAKU UTA GASSEN (Red-and-White Song Contest), the year-end song fest that was the biggest event on the Japanese show-business calendar. All was not lost however; tickets to her December concert in the Budokan—the country's second-largest indoor arena after the Tokyo Dome—sold out in a few hours.

In February 1990 Seiko met a young waiter and actor named Jeff Nichols at a Second Avenue eatery called Mulholland Drive, the beginning of her most serious affair and the one that was to have the biggest impact on her career. In June, she released her first U.S. album, *Seiko,* and single, "The Right Connection," the latter a duet sung with New Kids on the Block vocalist Donnie Wahlburg. But despite a massive push from CBS-Sony, neither record made much more than a blip on the charts, and the Japanese music industry wrote off Seiko's American adventure as yet another failure by a local artist to woo U.S. record buyers.

Then in October 1990 photo mag *Focus* ran a story, complete with damning photographic evidence, of Seiko and Jeff together on a hot date in Japan. Following up on its scoop, *Focus* had reporters sneak into the room next to Jeff's at the Akasaka Prince

Hotel. The magazine's writer described "voices that seemed to echo with the love of a man and woman." Even more shocking to these hardened entertainment-beat reporters was the daytime visit that Jeff and Seiko paid on Seiko's mother and Sayaka. As this foursome left a French restaurant, reporters heard the four-year-old Sayaka calling Jeff "Daddy." How much more brazen, they wondered, could this woman get?

Plenty, as it turned out. In March 1991 Seiko began an affair with a dancer on her concert tour, Alan Reed. In May, she flew Jeff in from New York to Osaka, where she was giving a concert, and introduced the two men: the lover on the way out, and the lover on the way in. But even after reportedly setting Alan up in a 120,000-yen-a-month apartment and paying him a fat monthly retainer, Seiko couldn't quite forget Jeff. In October 1992 *Josei Jishin* magazine ran a pic of them kissing in a New York hotel.

Alan, however, was also along on this trip—and Jeff soon realized that he was no longer part of Seiko's plans. Rather than gracefully bow out, in March 1994 he published a tell-all book, *Shinjitsu no Ai* (True Love). Even more ironically, just before the book's publication date, Seiko and Masaki appeared in a commercial for fried noodles that hymned their happy domestic life.

After the book hit the shelves, Masaki called a press conference to assure the world

that "Noriko Kanda is my wife and will always be my wife." This touching testament of loyalty, juxtaposed with Jeff's base disloyalty, turned the tide. Fans began to see Seiko as a victim, and Jeff and the media pack as victimizers. A growing number even viewed her as a New Age heroine, living her own life in defiance of old-fashioned morality. Buoyed by this surge of popularity after such a long season of bashing, Seiko broke off with Alan and signed a contract to appear in a cosmetics ad campaign. The campaign's catchphrase was *nudishu senden* ("nudish declaration"), a Japlish phrase implying that the product "stripped" the skin to its original freshness. To bring this message across more effectively, Seiko had herself photographed stripped to the waist, embracing a Caucasian male model. The ad aired in July 1994 and, in a revised version that featured a passionate kissing scene, again in August. The campaign created a nationwide sensation and started a rumor that Seiko's involvement with the model was more than professional. The rumor happened to be right; the model was Alan, who had been restored to favor.

The most telling sign of Seiko's comeback, however, was NHK's invitation to appear on the 1994 *Kohaku Uta Gassen*—her first in six years. Also, her nationwide concert and dinner-show tour that year was a complete sellout. The formerly reviled Seiko could do no wrong. Even the publication of two more books by Jeff, the second of which contained stories of wild nights of drugs and sex in New York, documented with passionate faxes and scandalous photos, did little to dent her new popularity. When Jeff's books failed to sell, his Japanese agency canceled his contract and he returned to the States.

This triumph did not mean that Seiko was ready to settle down. In July 1995 *Focus* snapped her on a late-night date in Roppongi with an African-American video director. And beginning in the fall of 1994 rumors flew that she was about to appear in a nude photo book, with her fee a stunning 150 million yen (nothing has yet come of this project, however).

Her star again on the ascendant, Seiko began to make new career moves. In July 1995 she ended her long relationship with CBS-Sony and signed to record for Mercury Music Entertainment, a Polygram label. Her contract, however, was with Polygram International, whose artists included such superstars as Bon Jovi and U2. In October 1995 Seiko returned to the States to make yet another assault on the U.S. record charts, with her first Mercury release scheduled for May.

The initial signs were good. In February Seiko made the cover of *Billboard* magazine, the first Japanese recording artist ever to be so honored. A&M Records, her sales compa-ny in the States, took out a full-page ad in *Billboard* to coincide with the release of her first single, "Let's Talk About It," on May 14. Soon after, nearly 1,800 radio stations across the country gave Seiko's new single airplay. How could it miss?

It not only missed, it didn't even make the charts. Her English-language album, *Was It the Future* also went nowhere. Meanwhile, her new Japanese-language single, "Anata ni Aitakute Missing You" (I Want to See You—Missing You) hit the top spot on the *Oricon* chart on its first week of release, becoming her first number-one single in eight years. It went on to sell more than one million copies, the first of Seiko's records to reach that magic number. Her Japanese-language album, *Vanity Fair,* which was released in May, also became a hit.

Despite these and other hometown triumphs, including a sellout national tour in the summer of 1996, Seiko's most recent failure to crack the U.S. market represented a major setback (She did score a minor victory, however: in September the video for "Let's Talk About It" hit the top of the CVC national club video chart). But, says Seiko publicist Shin Miyoshi, though beaten, she remains unbowed. "When she made her first attempt eight years ago, she was riding an escalator, with other people in control," explained Miyoshi. "This time she's doing it on her own and she's determined to carry on. She sees [the release of the single] as an initial step to her eventual success. . . . She is very aware that, because of her age, it won't be easy, but her motto is 'never give up.'"

On January 10, 1997, however, she finally gave up on her marriage with Masaki. On that day the couple issued a joint statement to the press in which they said "we both found it troublesome to combine family and work" and that "by separating we hope to start anew."

The media pack, quite naturally, had a field day trying to find out the real reasons for the split. With no recent infidelities to blame, they came up with the fundamental incompatibility as the culprit: Masaki wanted Seiko to spend more time in Japan, playing her role as housewife and mother. Seiko, meanwhile, was eager to resume her assault on the American music market, with or without her husband and daughter.

None of this should have been news to anyone, but the press played up the divorce as the show-business story of the newly born year. It made sports paper headlines and dominated the morning "wide show" chat sessions.

Only two days after making her announcement, Seiko boarded a flight to Los Angeles to make a new record and start a new life in a beachfront condo in Santa Monica. As she walked to her plane, wearing a black down jacket and sunglasses, photographers scrambled for a shot and reporters shouted questions. Seiko, however, only smiled, shook hands with fans, and continued on her way, without a comment for or a backward glance at the media horde. Free at last to live her American dream.

MATSUDA, YUSAKU

Though Japan has relatively few show-business Dead Legends of its own, it has imported them enthusiastically from the West. James Dean, Marilyn Monroe, Elvis Presley, and John Lennon all enjoy the same iconographic status in Japan that they do in the United States, appearing in advertisements (James Dean has been a silent-but-effective pitchman for Levis jeans), on memorabilia (Marilyn in the gold lamé of her Screen Goddess period was long a favorite of sidewalk poster peddlers), and in the persons of numerous impersonators (one Japanese Elvis won a major Elvis look-alike contest in the U.S., even though his physical resemblance to the King was less than perfect).

Although his face may not appear on T-shirts or coffee mugs, Yusaku Matsuda has come closer than most deceased Japanese stars to Dead Legend status. He was extraordinarily talented, attracted an intense, loyal following, and died in his prime, just as he was on the brink of international stardom. More important to his fans, he created a new definition of cool for his time, a definition that, decades later, still retains its appeal.

Matsuda is perhaps best known in the West for playing the take-charge tutor in *Kazoku Geemu* (The Family Game), Yoshimitsu Morita's 1983 black comedy about family life in modern Japan, and the take-no-prisoners gangster in *Black Rain*, Ridley Scott's 1989 hyper-charged cop action film, whose image of Osaka as a dark, smoky human anthill was a borderline racist fantasy extrapolated from *Blade Runner*.

In both films Matsuda portrayed extreme characters with precision, authority, and a sense of humor that dryly illuminated rather than smugly self-congratulated. Though an actor who strove for economy of means, Matsuda was also capable of the sudden, bold gesture that might amuse (i.e., his use of a pro-wrestling hold on his recalcitrant student in *Kazoku Geemu*) or chill (i.e., his use of a plastic bag on Michael Douglas in *Black Rain*), but was always characteristic and original.

Matsuda appeared in a total of twenty-five movies, ranging from such mass-audience fare as **HARUKI KADOKAWA**'s 1977 mystery-thriller *Ningen no Shomei* (Proof of the Man) to such critically acclaimed films as Yoshimitsu Morita's 1985 *Sore Kara* (And Then), an overly long but sensitively told

drama based on a novel by Natsume Soseki that depicted the love of a self-proclaimed idler, played by Matsuda, for the wife of a socially conforming school friend.

But though Matsuda's screen career was certainly successful—by the time of his last film, *Black Rain*, he was widely considered the leading actor of his generation—it also coincided with the steady decline of the Japanese film industry following the emergence of television in the early 1960s. So it shouldn't be a surprise that some of his most fondly remembered characters appeared on the tube.

Born in Shimonoseki on the southwestern tip of the main island of Honshu in September 1949, Matsuda was raised in a brothel where, as he later recalled, the nights were marked by wild drunkenness, jealous stabbings, and suicide attempts. "The scars [that remained from my early life] later became my treasures," he told an interviewer for the Japanese edition of *Playboy*. "There was a time in my life that, while selling those scars one by one, I was trying, in a half-assed way, to make myself look mysterious and invent my own legend."

It was during these early hard times that, in the company of his older brother, he became a regular at the local movie theater and a big fan of Nikkatsu action films starring **YUJIRO ISHIHARA**, Jo Shishido, and Akira Kobayashi. "The movie world totally captivated me," he later said.

When he was a sophomore in high school, Matsuda went to San Francisco to live with his mother's older sister and, in 1968, entered the prelaw course of a local college. But Matsuda's English was next-to-nonexistent and he spent more of his time working at part-time jobs than hitting the books. After a year, he gave up his law career and flew back to Japan, but instead of returning to Shimonoseki went to Tokyo, where he graduated from high school and entered Kanto Gakuin University.

After seeing a production by the off-off Broadway theater troupe La Mama, Matsuda decided to change course again and become an actor. Dropping out of college, he worked backstage for the Rokugatsu Gekijo theater troupe, studied acting, and wrote film synopses.

While a student at the training school of the Bungakuza theater troupe, which has given many well-known Japanese stage and screen actors their start, he was scouted by a producer for a role in *Taiyo ni Hoero* (Howl at the Sun), a police detective series that was one of the most popular shows on television.

Beginning in July 1973 Matsuda played Detective Jiipan, a newcomer to the detective squad whose long, permed hair and all-denim outfit marked him as a hippie—and an affront to the sensibilities of his conservative colleagues. The nickname they gave him, Jiipan or "Jean Pants," was not intended as a compliment. But the women working at the station house adored his long-legged good looks and dug his hang-loose, peace-loving attitude (he never carried a gun, preferring to subdue baddies with karate). Meanwhile his all-wise boss, played by a pudgy-faced **YUJIRO ISHIHARA,** liked his sincerity, persistence, and fearlessness, even if he did not always approve of his unorthodox methods.

Though the gimmick of a hippie cop may seem quaint now, in 1973 it struck viewers as exotically new. In no time at all, Detective Jiipan became a schoolyard hero and Matsuda a hot actor for his ability to project toughness, sexiness, and cool-dude indifference to the jibes of the uptight squares around him. As for the last quality, it was not faked; Matsuda disliked what he perceived as the grind-it-out hack ethic of the *Taiyo ni Hoero* cast and staff and they responded in kind. Soon he was having run-ins with everyone from the assistant directors to the producers and, despite his popularity, Detective Jiipan was written out of the show.

By now, however, Matsuda was considered a rising young action star and, starting with a role as *yakuza* punk in the 1974 *Abayo Dachiko* (So Long Dachiko), launched a busy and successful film career. But he also made tabloid headlines for playing the tough guy off-camera, slugging a magazine reporter in

甦れ！

探偵物語

松田優作にもう一度会いたい

日本テレビ

The enduring popularity of *Tantei Monogatari* prompted the publication of a 1994 book about the series that quickly went through several printings.

March 1975 and a prep-school student in July of the same year. Ironically, the following year he portrayed a teacher who tames high school gangbangers in *Boryoku Kyoshitsu* (Violent Classroom).

In 1978 Matsuda starred in Toru Murakawa's *Mottomo Kiken na Yugi* (The Most Dangerous Game), the film version of his *Daitokai* (Big City) TV series about a long-haired, shades-wearing hitman-for-hire. Although intended as a low-budget B programmer, this film and the two series entries that followed were hits for the Toei studio and further solidified Matsuda's reputation as a tough-guy action hero who could crack wise, make love, and waste the bad guys with a panache more reminiscent of Hollywood than Shimonoseki.

The series attracted the attention of super-producer Haruki Kadokawa, who had cast Matsuda as the returned-from-America detective hero in his 1977 hit *Ningen no Shomei* (Proof of the Man), but now saw him in a different, darker light—in short, perfect for the lead role in his next big film, *Yomigaeru Kinro* (The Return of the Golden Wolf). Matsuda portrayed an ordinary salaryman who, at night, transformed into a hard-bodied high-stakes con artist. The movie earned one billion yen—the mark of a domestic blockbuster.

By now, however, Matsuda was tiring of his image as Japan's premier purveyor of hardboiled urban action. He knew that the studios and TV networks would be quite happy to let him play the same roles forever, or at least until audiences tired of him. He also had ideas that he wanted to try, other sides of his personality that he wanted to express. Fortunately, by this time he had the clout to make his dreams a reality.

His vehicle was *Tantei Monogatari* (The Private Detective Story), a new series that debuted on the NTV network in Septermber 1979. Matsuda played Shunsaku Kudo, a P.I. who had spent five years learning his trade in San Francisco and now occupied a tiny, rundown office in Tokyo that doubled as his living quarters. During his sojourn in the States, Kudo had acquired not only an all-American knack for streetfighting and contempt for authority, but outlandishly foreign habits and tastes. He always wore a black fedora with a white band, solid-color ties (usually loosened) with colored dress shirts, and, when the occasion demanded it, round-framed shades. He smoked Marlboro cigarettes, which he lit with the lighter flame on high, drank blend coffee with a drop of sherry, and slept in pink pajamas, wearing an eyeshade. His favored form of transportation was a white Vespa P150X scooter, which stood out amidst the Hondas, Suzukis, and Yamahas of Tokyo traffic like Sophia Loren at a Shinto wedding.

Kudo, in short, was an outrageous dandy

who would rather make love than war, but he was also a pro who could sniff out a rotten alibi, talk his way out of an unpleasant situation, and keep his soul clean in a dirty world. His smart mouth, bad attitude, and habit of skirting the law were forever getting him into trouble with the local cops, especially the short-tempered Detective Matsumoto (Michihiro Yamanishi) and his foppish, cynical, casually corrupt boss, Chief Detective Hattori (Mikio Narita).

Other characters included a woman lawyer (Mitsuko Baisho), who may have been a knockout but proved braver in the clutch than Kudo, and an American fashion model (Nancy Cheney) who lived in Kudo's building and helped out at his office, lending an international air to his one-man operation.

The show's episodes contained plenty of action, often of the frantic slapstick sort (in the first episode Kudo and a furiously protesting Japanese nun were chased hither and yon by the *yazuka*), but the stress was definitely on Kudo's ad libs and antics.

Tantei Monogatari had a laid-back, wryly humorous, anything-can-happen quality like nothing else on Japanese television. At the same time, Matsuda was a perfectionist on the set, constantly adding new lines to the script and inventing new pieces of business. But though he could be demanding, he showed few signs of his legendary tem-

per. Reminiscing about the show years later, former cast and crew members noted instead his energy, enthusiasm, and ability to create an atmosphere of one big family that, despite the inevitable clash of egos, was usually happy. "We all felt like we were making something together," said guest star Yutaka Nakajima. "A lot of actors only really care about their own parts, but Yusaku tried hard to get everyone to make the show a good one."

Viewers thought he had succeeded; *Tantei Monogatari* earned high ratings in its first weeks on the air. The show also brought Matsuda an unexpected bonus: he met his future wife, the then seventeen-year-old Miyuki Kumatani, while making the first episode.

Despite the show's success, he had no intention of tying himself permanently to the tube. Most TV series then on the air, including *Taiyo ni Hoero,* had several main cast members to carry the load, but *Tantei Monogatari* was essentially a one-man show. "Physically and mentally it was quite wearing," said NTV producer Tsuyoshi Yamaguchi. "He only wanted to do the show for one year."

After making twenty-seven *Tantei Monogatari* episodes, the last of which aired in April 1980, Matsuda returned to his film career. In 1980 he appeared in Toru Murakawa's *Yaju Shisubeshi* (The Beast Must Die), a remake of a 1959 Eizo Sugawa action film starring Tatsuya Nakadai. In portraying a former Vietnam War photographer who turns to crime, Matsuda lost ten kilograms and had four back teeth pulled to give his loner character the right gaunt, wasted look. He even thought seriously about having his legs surgically shortened by five centimeters. Clearly, Matsuda took his acting with the self-sacrificing seriousness of a Robert De-Niro. He might still play a tough-guy hero, but his would be a different tough-guy hero who would further open the way to other, non-tough-guy roles.

The following year, Matsuda finally found one such role. In Seijun Suzuki's *Kageroza* (Heat Shimmer Theater), he portrayed a Shimpa playwright who is led into a destructive world of illusion by his love for a mysterious woman. The film marked a clear break with Matsuda's cinematic past: he was now ready to move on to *Kazoku Geemu*, *Sore Kara*, and the other films that would establish him as a major dramatic actor with an international following before his death of cancer at the age of forty.

Tantei Monogatari may have represented little more than a interlude in Matsuda's career—film writer Takeshi Yamaguchi devoted less than a page to it in his Matsuda biography—but over the years it has acquired a cult following. In 1994 NTV brought out a book about the series,

Yomigaere! Tantei Monogatari (Come Back! Detective Story) that contained photos and synopses of all the episodes, together with comments from surviving cast and staff. The book quickly went through several printings.

Also, Toei Video released the entire series and, noted company spokeswoman Naoko Watanabe, it remains the most popular of the actor's work on video. "Boxed sets of his films appeared on the third and seventh anniversaries of his death and sold quite well," Watanabe said. "His real fans probably like the *Yugi* (Game) series the best, but *Tantei Monogatari* is what most people remember him for. After all, it was on television."

MISORA, HIBARI

When singer Hibari Misora died in 1989, at the age of fifty-two, the Japanese media marked the passing of not only an entertainer but a postwar symbol. Despite a career spanning four decades, during which she made 1,700 records and 150 movies, Hibari was indelibly identified with the early postwar period, when people were trying to scratch out a living in the rubble and find hope in a society whose values had been blasted into oblivion together with its cities.

Songs such as "Kanashiki Takebue" (Sad Whistle), "Tokyo Kid," and "Ringo Oiwake" (Apple Blossom Song) evoked the struggle and pain of those years for Japanese of a certain age. Younger music fans, who had no memory of anything but prosperity, found her dark image a drag, her kimono-clad stage presence and "Queen of Enka" repertoire hopelessly old-fashioned. Many of the forty-two thousand mourners who attended her funeral at Aoyama Funeral Pavilion in Tokyo or the thirty thousand who paid their respects at seven special centers around the country were matrons in their fifties, fans who had grown up and suffered with her.

But Hibari had something more than a merely nostalgic appeal. Her steely will, strong family loyalty, deep loneliness, streak of self-destructiveness, and talent for expressing these qualities nakedly and unforgettably in song made her the quintessential Japanese pop singer.

Born the daughter of a Yokohama fishmonger in 1937, Hibari (her birth name was Kazue Kato) was a prodigy who was said to have memorized ninety-two of the one hundred poems in the traditional *hyakunin-isshu* card game by the age of three. When she appeared in an NHK amateur singing contest at the age of nine and performed "Kanashiki Takebue," the applause from the audience was thunderous, but the judges didn't ring the gong to announce a winner;

they were shocked by this kid singing an adult song in an adult voice and what one judge later described as "the sensuality of a thirty-year-old woman." Children were supposed to sing like children, not miniature grownups. They had never seen anything like her. The critics in the mass media were quick to label her a fake adult and a sideshow freak who, as one put it, "represents the sick tastes of a defeated people."

Despite the knocks from NHK and the media (Hibari was to bear grudges against both for the rest of her life), she persevered and in July 1949 released her first record, a snappy jazz tune titled "Kappa Boogie-woogie." "Even as a child, at the age of ten, I thought that I would kill myself if I couldn't become a singer," she later wrote.

That same year Hibari's second single, "Kanashiki Takebue," rocketed up the charts, selling four hundred thousand copies. Ignoring the critics, the record-buying public was fascinated by this pint-sized phenomenon with the unusual voice and the oversized talent. The 1950 "Tokyo Kid," with the lyrics "I have dreams in my right pocket, chewing gum in my left pocket," symbolized the poverty and hopes of the early postwar years for a lot of listeners, who made it a number-one single.

In 1952 "Ringo Oiwake" (Apple Blossom Song) evoked a nostalgia for the countryside at a time when country folk were streaming

The various faces of Hibari Misora: from child star to *enka* queen.

into the cities in large numbers looking for a better life. Written as the opening song for a Radio Tokyo (later TBS) drama called *Ringoen no Shojo* (Girl of the Apple Orchard), it sold seven hundred thousand copies, making it the biggest hit since the end of the war. Ironically, it was released as the B-side of the "Ringoen no Shojo" theme song. The composer, Masao Komeyama, had knocked it off quickly and didn't think much of it, but Hibari, feeling that the instrumental interlude was too long, added a lyric about "watching the white cotton clouds float lightly, lightly from the summit of Mount Iwaki" that made the song a chart buster.

In the 1950s Hibari also launched a thriving movie career, starring in films as part of a trio called Sannin Musume (The Three Girls, not to be confused with an early sixties trio of the same name). Harmless fluff that were little more than showcases for the singing talents of the three stars, the Sannin Musume movies were wildly popular, especially among teenage girls. Izumi Yukimura played a with-it rock'n'roller who sprinkled her conversation with English words. Chiemi Eri was a good-natured, tomboyish country girl who sang Japanized versions of American pop tunes. Hibari was the old-fashioned Japanese girl, who betrayed no hint of foreign influence in speech or song and stood foursquare for traditional values.

Her fans loved her for it, much as Elvis fans of the same generation loved the King for being a patriotic American, God-fearing Christian, and good to his mother. In a 1957 poll by *Heibon* (Average), a teen fanzine, forty-five percent of the respondents mentioned Hibari as their "most respected person" because, as one said, "although she's young and makes a lot of money, she takes care of her parents."

Hibari certainly did make a lot of money; in 1957 she was the country's best-paid entertainer, with an income of 30,180,000 yen, a staggering sum for a twenty-year-old pop star. In January of that year, she also encountered an occupational hazard of the rich, famous, and charismatic: an obsessed nineteen-year-old fan splashed hydrochloric acid on her face while Hibari was waiting to go on stage at the Kokusai Theater in Asakusa. After her arrest, the girl said she had done it because, though she loved Hibari's singing, she wanted to make her "an ugly, boring girl like me." Hibari recovered, but actor Shinichi Nishimura, who was standing next to her when the acid flew, was blinded. "I realized to the core of my being what popularity, of which I had been so enamored as a teenager, really was," she wrote in the *Tokyo Times*.

Off stage Hibari wasn't always the proper Japanese girl of her image. After her comeback, in July 1957, she told columnist Al Ricketts that she would rather sing in English than Japanese and expressed a liking for the music of Julie London and Nat King Cole. Her dream, she said, was to have an American screenwriter write a real Hollywood-style musical for her. "I know it isn't possible," she said, "But I'd like to read one, just to see what it's like."

But for all her dreams of Hollywood glory, Hibari was loyal to her family in the best Confucian tradition, to the detriment of her career. Her fiercely protective mother alienated scores of journalists and industry figures over the years with her sharp tongue and combative ways. Hibari, however, refused to go anywhere without her, even taking her on overseas trips.

Also, though her ne'er-do-well younger brother, Tetsuya Kato, was constantly getting into scrapes with the law, Hibari supported his singing ambitions by featuring him in her stage show. In February 1973, after reports of Tetsuya's links to a criminal gang surfaced in the media, public halls and cultural centers around the country began to cancel her show or demand Tetsuya's removal from it. At first Hibari denied the reports, but soon caved in and dropped her brother from the bill. None too soon, as it turned out: in March Tetsuya was arrested for mah-jongg gambling and, in September, for illegal possession of firearms.

Then came the biggest blow of all, when in December public broadcaster NHK omitted Hibari from the lineup of **KOHAKU UTA GASSEN** (Red-and-White Song Contest), the New Year's Eve song show that is the highlight of the Japanese show-business calendar. Hibari had been a fixture on the program for seventeen straight years; NHK's rejection was a public slap in the face. Although NHK said that Hibari's family troubles had nothing to do with the decision, everyone knew that if it weren't for Hibari's gangster brother the public broadcaster would have invited her to appear. Hibari never forgave NHK; until her death she refused to appear on any NHK programs, including *Kohaku Uta Gassen.*

Though NHK may have spurned her, Hibari was still a popular performer on the commercial networks, specializing in the sad, soulful, Japanese ballads called *enka.* Several, such as "Kanashii Sake" (Sad Sakè) and "Kawa Nagare no Yo ni" (Flowing Like a River) became megahits and karaoke standards. Beginning in 1964, she also became a frequent attraction at Shinjuku's Koma Theatre, performing in a stage show that combined lavishly staged musical numbers with snatches of samurai drama. By the time she finished her last show, in 1986, she had appeared on stage 1,815 times before 4.4 million people. She made

such a large contribution to the theater's coffers that the management named a new annex the Apple Theater in honor of her biggest hit.

The *enka* genre that Hibari did so much to popularize had its origins in the 1880s, when members of the popular rights movement or *jiyu minken undo,* who were agitating against Japan's authoritarian government, began to compose songs to promote their cause among the common people. Among the earliest was "Oppekepe-bushi" a martial-sounding tune written by Otojiro Kawajiri. In the 1890s, with the promulgation of the Meiji Constitution, the founding of the national parliament, and Japan's victory in the Russo-Japanese War, the popular rights movement died and its songs fell from favor.

That didn't mean the end of *enka,* however. In the early years of the new century a singer named Azembo Soeda popularized a new style of *enka* with lyrics that commented satirically on recent trends and historical events. During the Taisho Period (1912–26), *enka* singers, or *enkashi,* began to widen their repertoire with romantic songs about loneliness and loss—themes that were to become genre staples over the coming decades.

Many *enka* singers at this time made their living as wandering minstrels, going from bar to bar, often accompanying themselves with a guitar or accordion. With the coming of the phonograph and radio, they could bring their songs to a wider public and, in the 1930s, *enka* tunes became nationwide hits.

Originally based on Japanese folk songs, *enka* used a minor scale called *yonanuki*—so called because it did not use two degrees in the Western scale—together with a kind of vibrato called *yuri* and a style of high-pitched vocal production called *jigoe.* Though often called "Japanese blues," *enka* was technically in a category of its own.

Enka also set itself apart from Western pop music by its frequent gender crossing, with male singers crooning plaintively in the persona of a lovelorn woman and female singers, including Hibari, dressing in samurai drag to perform macho ballads.

In her personal life, unfortunately, Hibari enjoyed less success than she did as an *enka* queen. In 1962 she married Nikkatsu tough-guy star Akira Kobayashi in the hope of living a normal life out of the media glare. Two years later, the couple divorced, with Kobayashi claiming that Hibari lacked "humility" and "a sincere attitude toward life." She never remarried. A bigger trauma, however, was the death in 1981 of her mother, who had been Hibari's constant companion since childhood. She never recovered from the loss.

Health problems also plagued her in her later years. In April 1987 she entered a hos-pital in Fukuoka to receive treatment for a deteriorated hip joint. Although the media reported that that she might never walk normally again, in April 1988 she gave a gutsy comeback performance at the Tokyo Dome, singing forty songs and bringing the crowd to its feet.

Her triumph was to be short lived, however; decades of heavy drinking had weakened her liver. In March 1989 she was hospitalized at Tokyo's Juntendo University Hospital for chronic hepatitis and bone nephrosis. Early in the morning of June 24, she died of pneumonia.

Hibari, who once said that "a star never attains true happiness," was unlucky even in death. Because she had left a pile of debts and neglected to find tax shelters for her earnings, her 2.1-billion-yen fortune shrank to 400 million yen after the creditors and tax-men got through with it. The son of the now deceased Tetsuya, whom she had legally adopted, inherited the entire amount. Japan's favorite child singer had no children of her own.

By the time of her death, however, *enka* was a pop music institution, with millions of fans. Top *enka* singers such as Shin'ichi Mori, Hiroshi Itsuki, Saburo Kitajima, Harumi Miyako, and Sayuri Ishikawa appeared on TV music programs so often that Japanese pop music for adults seemed to be *enka* and little else. That impression was strengthened by the repertoire of middle-aged karaoke singers, which rarely strayed from *enka* standards, and the year-end *Kohaku Uta Gassen* show, which always climaxed with a procession of *enka* stars. Oddly, this popularity was not reflected in record sales—after the rise of Western-style Japanese pop in the 1960s, *enka's* share of the music market slipped, until by the mid-1990s it accounted for only three percent of the total—but the genre was so pervasive on the tube that it didn't really seem to matter (except, of course, to the performers and their record companies).

In the early 1990s, however, *enka* faced hard times. The disappearance of TV music shows left singers with fewer venues and the rise of the karaoke "boxes" or clubs, with their crowds of young J Pop fans, pushed *enka* from its position atop karaoke play lists. Also, the genre's biggest stars were advancing into middle age and beyond.

But *enka* has proven surprisingly hardy. New young stars, such as Kaori Kasai and Ayako Fuji, have brought needed fresh blood. Also, *enka* superstar Harumi Miyako, who retired in 1984 saying that she wanted to be an "ordinary middle-aged woman," staged a triumphant comeback in the 1990s, adding a World Music flavor to her sell-out stage shows. If anyone needed any proof that *enka* was still a vital genre, the second section of the 1995 *Kohaku Uta Gassen* show, which was dominated, as usual, by *enka* singers—walloped the competition with a 50.4 rating.

If Hibari had been around to witness this resurgence, she probably would not have offered her congratulations to NHK, but she would no doubt have been happy to find *enka* still thriving and her own music—all four decades of it—still very much alive in the heart of her fellow Japanese. The once and future queen of *enka* still reigns.

MITO KOMON

Period dramas, or *jidai geki*, are to Japan what the Western is to the United States: repositories of national myths and cultural values. But just as Westerns have changed with the times, so have *jidai geki*. The genre parody of Kaizo Hayashi's *Zipang*, with its campy hero and dazzling MTV-inspired imagery, is a far cry indeed from the dead-serious posturing of the classic samurai movie or even the amusing antiheroics of Toshiro Mifune in Akira Kurosawa's *Yojimbo*.

The Japanese, however, have felt less need than Americans to keep reinterpreting and updating their national myth. The values and attitudes of the samurai on primetime TV are still closer to those of 1797 than 1997.

Thus the seeming changlessness of the period-drama shows. The samurai you saw

on the tube ten or even twenty years ago will probably be much like the one you see tonight. This is not to say that all such shows are the same; some, like NHK's **TAIGA DRAMA**, attempt a semblance of historical accuracy. But others tell simplistic tales of good versus evil that are about as faithful to history as Kevin Costner's made-in-America Robin Hood in *Robin Hood: Prince of Thieves*.

Perhaps the most simplistic and certainly the most enduringly popular of the period-drama shows was *Mito Komon*. Broadcast every Monday night on the TBS network for twenty-eight years, beginning in August 1969, the series described the adventures of feudal lord and high shogunate official Mito Komon, a minor historical figure whose life

has, like Robin Hood's, become obscured by legend. Posing as a retired merchant, Mito traveled about the countryside with his loyal retainers, upholding justice and righting wrongs. Portrayed as a stubborn codger with a snowy white goatee and a heart of gold, Mito kept his real identity hidden until, at the crucial moment, retainer Kaku typically flashed his lord's official seal at the villains and roared "Silence! Silence! Can't you see this crest!" At which point the rowdy, threatening bad guys fell silent in terrified awe and abased themselves before the representative of shogunal power.

Not all of the episodes followed this pattern, however. The show's creator, TBS producer Minoru Itsumi, counted thirteen basic

Retainer Kaku flashes his lord's official seal as justice triumphs yet again in *Mito Komon.*

plots, including Mito's struggle to thwart an evil bailiff (shades of the Sheriff of Nottingham?) and expose a Mito Komon imposter. The show's writers added variations to maintain the illusion of newness, but Hikaru Nishimura, the second of the three actors to impersonate Mito, once admitted to an interviewer that his years of work on the show "made me realize the difficulty and importance of not becoming bored with playing the same role again and again."

Even so, Nishimura stuck it out for ten years, until 1993, more than enough time to make dozens of fictional grand tours of Japan. The most indefatigable traveler, however, was the first Mito, Eijiro Higashino, who played the role for thirteen years, until 1982. By these standards the last Mito, Asao Sano, barely got his walking legs. In the show's first quarter century, Mito and his hardy band traveled an estimated fifty thousand kilometers by land and twenty thousand more by sea—nearly three times around the globe.

As these numbers indicate, the show was not only a fairy tale for grown-ups but a travelogue that offered glimpses of famous sights, bits of local lore, and tastes of regional delicacies. The actors, however, rarely ventured far from Kyoto, where Toei, the show's production company, has a studio. Over the years, the producers became adept at making a local hot springs pass for the wilds of Hokkaido or a local nature trail look like the famed Tokaido road that wound from Edo (premodern Tokyo) to Kyoto.

In the show's early days, its ratings soared into the forties, and even toward the end of its long run they were among the highest for the period-drama genre. Most viewers were on the far side of fifty and as loyal as Mito's trusty retainers, Kaku and Suke. "I want to keep [the show] going as long as possible," Itsumi told an interviewer. "The sight I saw once at a nursing home, all the old folks gathering around the TV when the program started, still brings tears to my eyes."

In December 1996, however, TBS decided to cancel *Mito Komon* and another period drama that aired after it on Monday night. In the fall, the network said, it would premiere a "new style of period drama" in the same time slot. One reason for the cancellation was that, though *Mito*'s ratings may have been high, its demographics were wrong; the young viewers that advertisers wanted to attract didn't tune in. Another reason was Itsumi's death in late 1995. Without the man who was its creative heart, the show had begun to falter.

Mito Komon almost didn't get made in the first place. When Itsumi suggested it to his bosses at TBS, they reminded him that the network had just broadcast an installment from the Mito Komon film series, starring Ryunosuke Tsukigata. Also, an NHK Taiga

Drama set in the same era had just flopped. No one wanted period drama any more, they said. Matsushita Electric liked Itsumi's idea, however, and its advertising agency, Dentsu, commissioned an independent production company to make the show. TBS agreed to air it and Mito began his long journey into TV history. In September 1997, with the show's eight-hundredth episode, that journey came to an end.

MIYAZAKI, HAYAO

Disney animation has long been an object of veneration among Japanese animators. OSAMU TEZUKA, who was revered as the "god of *manga*," watched Bambi eighty times, until he had memorized every frame, and dreamed of equaling or surpassing Disney realism in his own animation. It was not to be; Japanese TV networks simply didn't have the money and Tezuka had to use limited animation in creating Japan's first TV cartoon series, *Tetsuwan Atomu* (Astro Boy), which debuted in 1963.

But the Japanese animator who finally beat Disney at the local box office, Hayao Miyazaki, never really cared that much for even the classic Disney films. He thought them too simple, too superficial. Realistic movement, yes. Realistic human emotions,

no. The film that made Miyazaki want to become an animator, as a teenage boy in 1958, was *Hakuja Den* (The White Snake), a tragic love story based on an ancient Chinese legend that was the first animated feature by Toei Doga, a studio founded in 1956 to challenge Disney's supremacy in the Japanese market.

This is not to say that Miyazaki is an *anime* nationalist, disdainful of foreign influences. Some of his most popular films are visual and thematic grab bags, with bits and pieces gathered from the the far corners of the globe. The setting of one, the 1989 *Majo no Takkyubin* (Kiki's Delivery Service), is a seacoast town that mixes Italian and Scandinavian port architecture with a dash of San Francisco street cars, while the story of another, *Tenku no Shiro Lapüta* (Lapüta: Castle in the Sky) was inspired by *Gulliver's Travels*.

Miyazaki melds these bits and pieces into films that closely reflect his tastes, interests, and concerns, while appealing to everyone from kids to adults and winning high critical marks both at home and abroad for their originality and excellence. In an industry where mass-audience animated movies are usually little more than feature-length versions of popular TV cartoons and are aimed squarely at an under-twelve audience, Miyazaki and long-time collaborator Isao Takahata stand out as serious *anime* auteurs

The 1989 *Majo no Takkyubin* (Kiki's Delivery Service) featured an incandescent flying sequence directed by Hayao Mizaki himself.

whose Studio Ghibli happens to make hit movies with almost metronomic regularity. Worldwide, Disney may have a far larger audience, but when Miyazaki's *Mimi o Sumaseba* (Whisper of the Heart) became the highest-earning domestic film of 1995, with distributor revenues of 18.5 billion yen, it marked the fifth time in a row Studio Ghibli had gone head-to-head with a Disney film—this time *Pocahantas*—and out-performed it at the box office.

Born in Tokyo in 1941, Miyazaki was the second of four brothers. His father was the director of an aircraft parts company that made rudders for the Zero fighter plane, while his mother spent much of Miyazaki's youth in a sickbed, battling spinal tuberculosis. An intelligent woman and voracious reader, she often expressed her disdain of the intellectuals who had rapidly changed from rabid nationalists to fervent democrats after Japan's defeat in the war. Miyazaki later said that he inherited his questioning and skeptical cast of mind from her.

At Gakushuin University, an elite private college with close ties to Japan's imperial family, Miyazaki majored in political science and economics and was strongly influenced by Marxist thought (given the political climate of the time, and the fact that he was the guilt-ridden son of a wealthy bourgeois, Miyazaki's transformation into a student radical was all but inevitable). At the same time, he was a member of a children's literature study circle, where he nursed his ambition to become an animator.

After graduating in 1963, Miyazaki joined Toei Animation, then as today the largest animation studio in Asia, where he worked as an in-betweener—the lowest rung on the animation ladder—for 19,500 yen a month. This was an unusual choice of occupation for a Gakushuin graduate, but Miyazaki was a diligent and talented animator who soon attracted the attention of his seniors. One was Isao Takahata, who first supervised Miyazaki as a director on the 1964 TV series *Okami Shonen Ken* (Ken the Wild Boy). Miyazaki and Takahata also worked together as activists in the company union.

In 1965 Miyazaki joined the production team that director Takahata and animation director Yasuo Otsuka were assembling to produce a full-length animated feature, *Taiyo no Oji Horus no Daiboken* (The Little Norse Prince Valiant). Anxious to make a film able to compete with the TV animation that was killing off the feature *anime* market, Takahata and Otsuka opened their storyboarding meetings to all members of their team, regardless of rank or experience. Miyazaki jumped at the chance. Bombarding his superiors with ideas, he played a key role in developing the film's style and storyline.

While the rest of the *anime* industry was sacrificing quality to cut costs and recycling tried-and-true fairy-tale and comic-book formulas, Takahata, Otsuka, and Miyazaki decided to head in the opposite direction and make their film as different from the TV *anime* product as possible. Instead of relying on childish gags, slam-bang action, and simplistic plots, they set out to prove that animation could depict real feelings and tell a complex, layered story as well as a live-action movie.

This film about villagers banding together to protect their homes and families against an evil witch won critical and popular acclaim when it finally appeared in the summer of 1968, three years after the start of production. A reviewer for the monthly magazine *Taiyo* wrote that after seeing both *The Jungle Book* and *Taiyo no Oji Horus no Daiboken,* he realized that "in one corner of the world, there now exists a commercial animation that has surpassed Disney and started to make rapid advances."

With this success behind him, Miyazaki left Toei in 1971 and joined Takahata at a new animation production company, A-Pro. Together they made *Panda Kopanda* (Panda, Panda Cub), a 1972 feature that may have exploited the panda boom of the early 1970s, but realistically portrayed the inner world of its young heroine. In 1973 Miyazaki and Takahata left A-Pro to join Zuiyo Pictures, where they made *Alps no Shojo Heidi* (Heidi), the first Japanese TV *anime* series based on sketches and information gathered by animators at a foreign location, in this case Switzerland. It stood out among the frenetic TV *anime* of the time for its calm, unhurried, intimately detailed portrayal of life in a nineteenth-century Alpine village and became a fondly remembered hit.

But though his more high-minded projects may have enhanced his industry prestige, Miyazaki was also responsible for *Lupin III: Cagliostro no Shiro* (The Castle of Cagliostro), a 1979 feature about a dashing, debonair, but wacky French thief that was about as socially redeeming as a James Bond movie (in a 1994 interview with *Yom* magazine Miyazaki expressed a desire to make a film "that is frowned on by the PTA").

The film that propelled Miyazaki to the forefront of the Japanese film industry and first brought him international attention was the 1984 *Kaze no Tani no Nausicaä* (Nausicaä of the Valley of the Wind), an epic eco-fable about a young girl's struggle to survive in a poisoned world inhabited by warring tribes and giant mutant insects. Takahata served as producer, while Miyazaki scripted and directed the film and drew the *manga* on which it was based. Begun in 1981, the *manga* finally ran to fifty-nine episodes and did not conclude until 1984. Miyazaki departed from the film's storyline to explore the relationship of God and man, the eternal battle between good and evil, and the nature of life itself.

In Nausicaä, for the first time, Miyazaki created a deeply imagined, highly complex world that went far beyond the bounds of here-and-now realism while remaining firmly grounded in present-day concerns, the foremost of which was ecological disaster caused by commercial greed. *Nausicaä* won a slew of awards and accolades, including the Grand Prize at the Second Japanese Anime Festival and a commendation from the World Wildlife Fund. It was screened at sci-fi film festivals in Paris and Zagreb, where it won first prize, and was voted the best Japanese movie of the year by the readers of *Kinema Jumpo,* Japan's oldest film magazine. But most heartening to distributor Toei was the 740 million yen the film earned in distribution revenues, a figure that proved sci-fi anime could appeal to more than a cult audience.

For foreign fans the Nausicaä *manga* and *anime* revealed thrilling new possibilities in formats previously derided as eye candy for kids. Though Miyazaki's basic themes may have been familiar, he developed them with a strikingly original visual vocabulary and a brilliantly fertile imagination. *Superman* had never been like this. Together with **KATSUHIRO OTOMO**'s *Akira*, another intricately imaged post-apocalyptic fable, *Nausicaä* was instrumental in launching the worldwide *manga* and *anime* boom.

Miyazaki's theatrical follow-up to *Nausicaä* was *Tenku no Shiro Lapüta*, mentioned above, a fantastic adventure tale about the search for the lost flying island of Lapüta. As in *Nausicaä*, a spunky princess was the heroine and the story contained a respect-nature-or-die subtext, but the action element was more central, the plotting less labyrinthine.

Lapüta, however, was something of a disappointment at the box office, earning only

Totoro and a friend waiting for the Cat Bus in *Tonari no Totoro* (My Neighbor Totoro).

summer, the time, an indefinite nostalgic past that feels like a Japanese version of the Ozzie and Harriet 1950s. Dad is an infinitely patient and understanding, if slightly woolly-headed anthropology professor, who has come to this country retreat to write a book, while saintly Mom lies several kilometers away in a hospital sickbed (echoes of Miyazaki's own youth here), recovering from an undefined illness.

Although not quite the box-office success of *Nausicaä*, *Totoro* also acquired the status of an instant classic. If anything, it has become even more popular over the years in Japan, with adults and children alike. According to a recent NHK poll that asked respondents to rate their all-time favorite films, *Totoro* came in second among domestic movies, after Akira Kurosawa's *Shichinin no Samurai* (The Seven Samurai).

In 1993 *Totoro* was released in several U.S. cities, where the critical reaction was mixed; some reviewers praised the beauty of the animation and the gentle humanism of the story, while others scored it for being rambling and slow (Roger Ebert gave it a thumbs up, Gene Siskel, a thumbs down).

Beginning with the 1989 *Majo no Takkyubin* (Kiki's Delivery Service) the productions of Studio Ghibli, the studio Miyazaki and Takahata had launched to produce *Laputa*, morphed into megahits.

580 million yen. In the 1988 *Tonari no Totoro* (My Neighbor Totoro), which he wrote and directed, Miyazaki took a different tack, spinning a leisurely paced, loosely plotted fantasy about the encounter of two young sisters with magical forest spirits.

Two of the most memorable are an enormous owlish/catish creature called Totoro, and the Cat Bus, a twelve-legged, bus-sized cat that comes complete with doors, windows, furry seats, and headlight eyes. The setting is a paradisical countryside in mid-

The story of young witch Kiki who is sent by her mother—a witch married to a mortal man—on a year long quest, the film has a typical coming-of-age movie arc, but the flying scenes, in particular, are stunningly realized (Miyazaki is an aviation buff) and the port city that Kiki decides to call home is a charmingly eccentric blend of styles and periods. The streets are filled with 1930s automobiles, while the houses boast microwave ovens.

Kiki makes friends with a good-natured baker's wife, a big-sisterly teenage artist, and a pesky thirteen-year-old boy; she lands a job as a broom-riding delivery girl, and temporarily loses her powers, but as in *Totoro*, the twists and turns of the plot are less important than the small, magical moments that reveal character or simply delight with their beauty and humor. More mass-audience friendly than *Nausicaä,* more visually dynamic than *Totoro, Majo* became the biggest domestic box office hit of 1989, with distribution revenues of 2.17 billion yen.

Ghibli's follow-up film, the 1991 *Omoide Poroporo* (Only Yesterday), was executive produced by Miyazaki but written and scripted by Takahata. Since Miyazaki's success with *Nausicaä,* Takahata had retreated into the background of the partnership. This was partly a matter of temperament: Miyazaki was talkative, opinionated,

quotable—in short, the ideal media celebrity. A tireless worker and natural leader, pouring forth an endless stream of ideas, he seemed born to run an animation studio. Takahata, on the other hand, was a quiet, studious type who could spend years working on a pet project, but was also quite capable of speaking his own mind and getting his own artistic way. (In the program notes to *Omoide,* Miyazaki compares his long-time colleague, affectionately, to a sloth with a sharp claws that can wound, while calling himself a beaver.)

Although the two men had over the years developed what might be called a Ghibli house style, Takahata's Ghibli films were, with their greater emphasis on realism of character and story, their stronger tug on the heartstrings, distinctly different from Miyazaki's. His 1988 *Hotaru no Haka* (Grave of the Fireflies), a story of children adrift in wartime Japan, which played on the same bill as *Tonari no Totoro,* wrenched tears from nearly everyone who saw it.

Like *Majo, Omoide* is about a voyage of self-discovery. This time, however, the voyager is a twenty-seven-year-old Tokyo office worker named Taeko who visits her married sister in the countryside and, on the way, travels mentally back to her tenth year. Why, she wonders, is the little girl of 1966 so important to the woman of 1982? Like the girl about to become a woman, Taeko is on the cusp of change. Tired of her humdrum existence and her single state, she longs for something new. Then, at her sister's home, she finds that something in the person of a chipperly earnest young farmer.

This abrupt transition from sensitively developed inner dialogue to conventional love story may have weakened the film, but the lushly detailed scenes of country life, drawn to the last verdant branch, bud, and leaf, helped make *Omoide* yet another Ghibli hit.

The studio's biggest box-office success was yet to come, however, in the 1992 *Kurenai no Buta* (Porco Rosso). Scripted and directed by Miyazaki, this tale of a loner pilot-turned-pig who battles air pirates over the Adriatic Sea in the days after World War I had all the Miyazaki trademarks—breathtaking flying sequences, a feisty young heroine (who works as an aircraft designer), and a gloriously realized fantasy world. The story, in which the pig pilot duels a pirate leader, while carrying a torch for a sultry chanteuse, is sub-Hemingway silly, but the animation is among Miyazaki's exuberant and lovely best. Recording 2.71 million yen in distributor revenues, Kurenai became Japan's biggest animation box-office hit and the top-grossing film of 1993, beating out *Hook, Basic Instinct,* and *Beauty and the Beast.*

Interestingly, Kurenai was originally planned as a humble animated short for the inflight entertainment program of Japan Airlines, but the project gradually grew, until Miyazaki decided to make it as a feature film.

In 1994, Takahata returned with *Heisei Tanuki Gassen Pompoko* (Pom Poko), an eco-fable about a clan of *tanuki* (Japanese badger-dogs) who battle developers to save their idyllic homes in Tama Hills, just outside of Tokyo. These overfed cousins to the raccoon are known in traditional stories and legends for changing their form to baffle pursuers and trick intruders. Takahata's *tanuki* transform into everything from iron pots to Tokyo salarymen, while calling on a wild and wonderful assortment of storybook monsters and goblins in their struggle against human invaders. But though there is more morphing than in ten **POWER RANGERS** episodes put together, Takahata keeps the film firmly grounded in the real world—and real-world environmental issues.

Pom Poko not only trounced *The Lion King* handily at the box office (the local press called their summer season face-off "the battle of the *tanuki* and the lions"), but all the domestic competition as well. The film also garnered several awards, including Best Animation Prize at the 1994 Mainichi Film Concours and a Special Award at the 1995 Japan Academy Awards.

Tanuki band together to save their Tama Hills home in Isao Takahata's *Pom Poko.*

In 1995 Studio Ghibli's summer entry was *Mimi o Sumaseba* (Whisper of the Heart), a simple love story about a fourteen-year-old girl who wants to write and a fourteen-year-old boy who wants to make violins in Cremona, Italy. Though first-timer Yoshinobu Kondo directed, producer and scriptwriter Miyazaki gave Mimi his characteristic touches, including an incandescently gorgeous dream flying sequence that Miyazaki directed himself. The film topped the Japanese box office with earnings of 18.5 billion yen—by now a routine accomplishment for a Ghibli product.

But while besting Disney at the Japan box office, Studio Ghilbli is by no means a Disney-sized giant. Although its studio, located in a quiet Western Tokyo suburb, is spacious and modern by the rabbit-hutch standards of the Japanese animation industry, it employs a staff of only one hundred, fifty of whom are animators. Also, Studio Ghibli uses nothing like the advanced computer graphics of Disney; its animation is still very much hand crafted.

Far from being offended by their Japanese rival's acts of commercial lèse-majesté, the ever-pragmatic folks at Disney studios decided that, if they could not beat Miyazaki, they might as well join him. In July 1996, Disney's distribution arm Buena Vista linked with Tokuma Shoten Publishing—Studio

Ghibli's sales company—to distribute nine Studio Ghibli titles worldwide, including Miyazaki's next film, *Mononokehime* (The Princess Mononoke), which is scheduled for release in Japan in July 1997.

Although this deal does not mean that Miyazaki will soon find his name on the marquees of U.S. mall multiplexes—the films are mostly bound for the video shelves—it does offer further proof that his brand of animation is no longer only a local taste or cult phenomenon, that its magic can appeal to moviegoers everywhere.

Despite being Japan's most successful commercial filmmaker for the past decade,

Miyazaki is still very much the iconoclast, the idealist, the social critic. "Japanese today have nothing to rely on in their minds," he told an interviewer for *Pacific Friend* magazine. "They have alienated themselves from their own natural and spiritual environment.

"In my movies for children I want to express, before anything else, the idea that the world is a profound, multifarious, and beautiful place. I want to tell them that they are fortunate to have been born into this world."

Takahata claims that he doesn't "feel a sense of rivalry" with Miyazaki, while admitting that he would "never be able to equal him" if he tried. "He has a wonderful sense of fantasy, while I'm more interested in creating a feeling of reality in my films," he explains. "To use an expression from *sumo,* I want to fight my bouts in a different *dohyo* (sumo ring). In that way, I think we can better enrich Japanese animation and please Japanese audiences."

But whatever their differences of theme and approach, says Takahata, he and Miyazaki share one thing in common. "Whether the story leans towards fantasy, as his tend to, or realism, as mine tend to, we want the audience to feel that what they're seeing on the screen really could have happened. We want to make animation that the audience can believe in."

MIYAZAWA, RIE

Every year the Japanese entertainment industry produces dozens of new female "talents" (*tarento*) whose only discernible talent is an ability to project certain qualities thought desirable or fashionable at the moment (girl-next-door cheerfulness, disco-diva sluttishness). Most are little more than decorative presences on TV shows or commercials, and are as interchangeable as the *ikebana* arrangement on the host's desk. Others eke out evanescent careers as singers (who can't carry a tune or write their own songs) or actresses (whose effusions would never pass muster at a high-school drama-club audition).

Some, however, manage to become pop goddesses, representatives of the current zeitgeist, or notorious for challenging *tarento* convention. One such, in the early 1990s, was Rie Miyazawa. Observing her skillful manipulation of the media, some compared her to Madonna. Others, reacting to her frothy-but-sexy persona on screen and her self-destructive behavior off it, drew parallels with Marilyn Monroe and, more recently, Karen Carpenter.

Born in 1973 of a union between a Dutch father and Japanese mother, Rie made her TV debut as an eleven-year-old pitch girl for Kit Kat candy bars. She was one of the first *bishojo,* or pretty young girls who appeared on TV commercials, posters, and telephone cards and quickly displaced girl-next-door types in the affections of the public.

It could be argued that the *bishojo* boom was simply another example of Japan importing a Western product—in this case, Brooke Shields—and reshaping it in its own image. But the *bishojo* was also an innovation of sorts. Instead of a bubbly, air-headed Miss Average—the then-standard public persona for young female talent—the *bishojo* often presented herself as a cut above the common herd not only in looks but in upbringing: her public image was that of a well-dressed, well-mannered, well-educated young lady. The *bishojo* was a fitting symbol for a Japan that, in the 1980s, was eager to assert not only its economic superiority but its cultural superiority as well.

But though the *bishojo* boom soon faded, Miyazawa's career continued to thrive. In addition to her lucrative work as a "campaign girl"—the smiling face of an ad campaign—she appeared on teen-targeted variety shows, TV dramas, and even wangled a starring role in a 1989 comedy called *Bokura no Nanokakan Senso* (Our Seven-Day War), about a group of teenagers who declare war against the adult world. Also, by posing in only a loincloth for a hugely popular calendar, she left her *bishojo* image behind for good.

The main force behind Rie's drive for suc-cess was her mother. A former dancer who had divorced her Dutch husband before Rie was born, Mitsuko Miyazawa had raised her daughter alone and was totally dedicated to advancing her career. The talent agency she started in 1990 had only one client—Rie—and mother and daughter were inseparable.

By the fall of 1991, Rie was representing Japan Telecom Company, Limited, and seven other corporate clients for annual contract fees that ranged from fifty to sixty million yen each. According to an August 1991 survey published by Nikkei Entertainment magazine, she ranked twentieth in name recognition among all TV commercial *tarento*. Her popularity was especially high among high school and college boys.

Two months later, her name recognition soared from 72.5 percent (according to the Nikkei survey), to nearly 100 percent, literally overnight. The trigger for this amazing jump was a full-page nude ad of Rie for a photo book titled *Santa Fe* that appeared in the morning editions of two national newspapers. The ad, which appeared on pages normally devoted to international news, caused a nationwide uproar.

While TV commentators solemnly speculated about the impact the ad would have on newspaper advertising policies (would we suddenly be seeing unclad cuties cavorting daily on the pages of the *Asahi Shimbun*?) and Rie's career (nude photo books were usu-

Rie, the naked teenage goddess, in a shot from *Santa Fe*.

ally the resort of the unknown and desperate not, like Rie, the famous and upwardly mobile), orders for the book flooded into the offices of the publisher, *Asahi Shuppansha*. Within three months after publication, 1.5 million copies of *Santa Fe* had been shipped and the book had become the publishing phenomenon of the year, if not the decade. It seemed to many, especially in the foreign press, that this eighteen year-old commercial "campaign girl" and actress had the Material Girl's magic media touch.

After *Santa Fe* transformed Rie from just another pretty face peddling telephone cards into a figure of nationwide notoriety, some criticized her mother for forcing her daughter to strip for photographer Kishin Shinoyama's camera. Mitsuko, however, insisted that the decision to pose for the book had been Rie's own. In any event, the main object of the book project—to send Rie's name recognition soaring, had been achieved.

Rie then proceeded to nearly end her career when in October 1992 she accepted the phoned-in marriage proposal of twenty-year-old sumo superstar Takahanada (see **THE SUMO DYNASTY OF THE HANADA's**). After meeting in December 1989 at a joint interview arranged by a sports newspaper, Rie and Takahanada had hit it off, even though their "dates" were largely limited to interviews and other public appearances. Hailed as the celebrity couple of the (Japanese) century—comparisons were made with Marilyn Monroe and Joe DiMaggio—Rie and Takahanada were scheduled to tie the knot at the Hotel Otani on May 28, 1993, with baseball home-run king Sadaharu Oh serving as go-between. The media feeding frenzy soon reached a peak, with NHK reportedly offering one billion yen for the TV rights to the wedding reception.

Then, on January 27, 1993, Takahanada held a press conference to call off the engagement and apologize for his "irresponsibility." At her own press conference Rie said that they had grown apart during Takahanada's long absences from Tokyo; he had, she said, never called her once since leaving on tour in December. But the press speculated that the real reason for the breakup was unreconcilable differences between the future in-laws, with Takahanada's stablemaster father and former-model mother insisting that Rie follow sumo tradition and give everything up for her man, and Mitsuko demanding that Rie's talent—and the years she had spend nurturing it—not go to waste.

Is there talent? Although Rie has appeared in such dreck as *Erochikku na Kankei* (Erotic Relations), a 1992 Koji Wakamatsu detective thriller that seemed to have been made by dirty old men for dirty old men, she acquitted herself well in Hiroshi Teshigahara's *Gohime* (The Princess Go), a 1992 period drama in which she portrayed three decades in the life of a sixteenth-century princess. Though not convincing as a forty-year-old, Rie showed real fire as a teenager who runs away with the stud-muffin family gardener. In Kon Ichikawa's *Shiju Shichinin no Shikaku* (Forty-seven Ronin), a period drama based on the famous story of the forty-seven samurai who revenge their master's death, she displayed a bubbly charm as she romanced the sixty-three year-old Ken Takakura in slightly off-key Kyoto dialect. (Can a comparison be made with MM in *How to Marry a Millionaire*? Why not?)

After breaking up with her sumo hunk, however, Rie seemed to be spiraling, MM-like, out of control. In September 1994, while in Kyoto to promote *Shiju Shichinin* at the Kyoto International Film festival, she was found unconscious in her room after cutting her wrist with a broken water glass. Rie claimed that the cut, which required a week to heal, was an accident. But the tabloid press, noting a noisy spat with her mother after Rie's return from a drinking session with people from the *Shiju Shichinin* production company and her subsequent tearful flight to a nearby hotel, reported it as a botched suicide attempt.

The new year did not bring an end to Rie's troubles. In February 1995 she suddenly exited from a starring role in *Kura*, a big-budget period melodrama about a blind women who inherits a sakè brewery in prewar Niigata Prefecture. In October, photos taken of her gaunt form at a charity golf tournament renewed speculation that she was suffering from anorexia. Then, on November 29, she quit the cast of the musical *Koyote,* just a week before it was scheduled to open, and, on December 8, flew to Los Angeles with her mother. Though Rie cited artistic differences with the show's staff, the weekly magazines—noting her skeletal frame—said that real reason for her departure was the fragile state of her health; she was flying to L.A., they claimed, to receive treatment for her anorexia from a noted specialist.

She returned, but at the end of January *Shukan Hoseki* published what it claimed was "a complete record of Rie Miyazawa's 350-day struggle with illness." Seeking to avoid the resulting media uproar, Rie secretly flew off to L.A. again for what the press speculated might be a protracted stay in the United States.

As it turned out, the press was right; Rie went into near seclusion in Los Angeles, while receiving treatment for anorexia and recuperating from the media bashing she had received in Japan. Finally, she agreed to an interview with novelist Shizuka Ijunin that appeared in two parts in the April 22 and May 13, 1996 issues of *Bart* magazine.

Rie revealed little concrete about her life in America but, from the evidence of the photos that accompanied the interview and her own testimony, she seemed to be gaining weight and confidence.

In May, she went to France to report on the Cannes Film Festival for a Japanese network. Though still looking fragile and wan, she managed to project some of her old charm. Although the show ran in a late-night time slot, it indicated that Rie was starting on the comeback trail.

Then in August she went to Australia for the filming of a Fuji TV drama series called *Hanayome Kaizoebito* (The Bridesmaid). In October she completed her comeback with a lead role in a new TBS drama, *Kyosokyoku* (Concerto). Playing opposite SMAP heartthrob Takuya Kimura, she still looked angular, but gave an effervescent performance that helped propel the show to a 28.2 percent rating for its debut episode—the highest of any drama that week. After her long, hard slide from the heights, *Kyosokyoku's* success was sweet music indeed.

Rie may well make media comparisons to Madonna and Marilyn irrelevant as she shapes her own, unmistakably individual star image—much as her earliest foreign role model, Brooke Shields, has done. But whatever the outcome, triumphant or tragic or somewhere in between, Japan will long remember her in the incarnation that launched her to national notoriety: the naked teenage goddess standing demurely by the scalloped double doors of an old Spanish house in Santa Fe.

MUSEKININ OTOKO

Westerners tend to think of the Japanese "salaryman" as a species of worker bee, devoting his entire life, unquestionally, to the cause of a bigger market share and a higher GNP. But while such self-sacrificing workaholics exist, this stereotype is outdated. Like his counterparts throughout the industrialized world, today's salaryman is worrying more about downsizing and restructuring, and believing less in the company as a surrogate father that will always do right by its loyal sons.

Back in the boom days of the 1960s, though, the stereotype was still alive and well. Labor was scarce, business was good, and companies worked their staff to the bone. In compensation, they gave them a promise of lifetime employment, ever bigger bonuses, and a lengthening list of perks. Many salarymen lived for and even at their companies, slaving away nights and weekends, taking only token vacations. The thought of changing jobs to get better pay and conditions was considered almost sacrilegious and, in any case, suicidal. Who would hire a traitor to the sacred corporate cause? Thus the image of salaryman as worker bee was born.

But as the corporate warriors—another popular image—marched off to battle in the early 1960s, a movie series that comically challenged the official salaryman ethos did terrific business among the very salarymen it was lampooning. The first entry, released in 1962, was titled *Nippon Musekinin Jidai* (Japan's Irresponsible Age) and starred comic Hitoshi Ueki, a member of The Crazy Cats, a popular comic jazz band. It told the story of Hitoshi Taira (a name that loosely translates as "Joe Average"), a scapegrace salaryman who schemes his way to the top while indulging himself to the hilt and doing nary a lick of real work. It was *How to Succeed in Business Without Really Trying*, Japanese-style.

After worming his way into a job with a liquor company by telling the president about plans for an impending takeover bid that he'd overheard at a bar, Hitoshi shows up for work late every day and, when he is scolded by the boss, blithely urges him to lighten up. But when his offbeat attempts to prevent the takeover fail, he is fired. Unperturbed by this change in his fortunes,

Hitoshi Ueki mugging as a Crazy Cat (top row, left), and charming the ladies in *Nippon Musekinin Jidai.*

he cheerily bids his former associates farewell and sails out into the streets.

Soon after, he approaches the new president of the company, who mounted the successful takeover, and coolly tells him that it's pay-back time. The president hires him and, by assiduous brown-nosing, Hitoshi rises to the post of PR manager. But when he is discovered buying a car for a geisha with company money, he gets the boot yet again.

The ever-resilient Hitoshi soon talks his way into a job at a client company and, following the death of its president, deftly steps into his shoes. Then, at the wedding of the liquor-company president's son, he has his final triumph. Striding into the reception as an invited guest—his company is, after all, a valued customer—Hitoshi proudly announ-

ces his own engagement to the pretty secretary of the liquor-company president. The moral: scum rises to the top.

Filled with wacky comic songs and dances, loaded with punchy one-liners, *Nippon Musekinin Jidai* became the second-biggest box office hit of the year, after Akira Kurosawa's *Tsubaki Sanjuro,* and generated three sequels, none of which equaled the success of the original.

The ground work for the series had been well-laid. Ueki's theme song, "Sudara Fushi" (Hang Loose Melody), which was featured prominently in the movie, had sold more than six hundred thousand copies following its August 1961 release. The dance that accompanied the song, which featured goofy arm swings, was soon being imitated in schoolyards across the country, much to the alarm of the PTA, and the lyrics "I know it, but I just can't help it" (*Wakatcha iru kedo yamerarenai*) became a national catch-phrase.

Ueki and The Crazy Cats appeared on a hit TV program on NTV called *Shabondama Holiday* (Soap Bubble Holiday) that, since its start in June 1961, had firmly fixed Ueki's "irresponsible" persona in the public mind. He also appeared in two films in 1962 as his wild-and-crazy character: *Sudara Fushi: Wakatcha Iru Kedo Yamerarenai* (Hang Loose Melody: I Know It, But I Just Can't Help It) and *Sarariman Donto Fushi: Kiraku na Kagyo to Kitamonda* (Salaryman Ding Dong Melody: It's Easy Work If You Can Get It). By the time *Nippon Musekinin Jidai* came out, in July 1962, audiences were ready to see Ueki as Hitoshi Taira. In fact, it was impossible to imagine anyone else taking the part.

Hitoshi Taira, of course, was a fantasy figure, but the movie's scriptwriter, Yasuo Tanami, claimed that, in creating him, he was offering a message of hope to his audience. "Instead of complaining about having no money or freedom, change your way of thinking," he said. "Then, you can be free, even though you are an ordinary salaryman." Unfortunately, if any real-life salaryman adopted Hitoshi's way of thinking, he would soon find himself looking for another job.

Be that as it may, in the uptight world of 1960s corporate Japan, Hitoshi represented a welcome breath of fresh, anarchic air. Even worker bees, it seemed, could dream of making easy honey.

Off-screen, Hitoshi Ueki was nothing like his Hitoshi Taira character. The son of a social-activist Buddhist priest, Ueki was a serious type who didn't drink or gamble and often said that his best stress reliever was coming home to his family. In the hard-drinking, fast-living Japanese entertainment world, this straight-arrow attitude made him a standout.

Equipped with a melodious, classically trained voice, Ueki started his musical career strumming a guitar and singing sentimental ballads in Tokyo clubs. But he did not find success until he unleashed his funny streak in the form of "Sudara Fushi"—and shocked the fans and friends who had only known him in his soulful crooner incarnation.

In 1990, at the height of Japan's bubble economy, Ueki made a comeback with a new version of "Sudara Fushi." In the wake of the song's success, theaters began screening revivals of the *Musekinin* series and drawing packed houses of fans, most of whom were born after the series had ended in 1964. Ueki even got his own late-night talk show, on which he reminisced about his days of glory with The Crazy Cats and played the part of show-biz elder statesman. Now in his sixties, he looked, with his thinning gray hair and dignified manner, more like a real company president, less like the wacky clown of yore. The irresponsible man had finally come of age.

NAGASHIMA, SHIGEO

He was, quite simply, the most popular player ever on the most popular team ever in Japan's most enduringly popular sport: baseball. Sadaharu Oh, his long-time teammate on the Yomiuri Giants, may have hit more home runs—and broken Hank Aaron's home-run record in the bargain—but Shigeo Nagashima won the hearts of the fans. To them he is, and probably always will be, "Mr. Giants," "Mr. Baseball," or just plain "Mister."

It's not that Nagashima lacked the stats. He ended his seventeen-year career in 1974 with a lifetime batting average of .305, 2,471 hits, 1,522 RBIs and 444 home runs. He was batting champion six times, setting a league record; home-run champ twice; and RBI leader five times. Playing third base, he was a fielding marvel, winning the Diamond Glove Award in 1972 and 1973, the first two times it was given. He was voted the Central League's Most Valuable Player five times and named to the All-Star team a record sixteen times.

Nagashima had more than numbers going for him, however; he had a charismatic presence and showman's instincts. A schoolboy star at Rikkyo University, he signed with the Giants in 1957 for eighteen million yen—a rookie record. The experts doubted he was ready for the bigs and in his pro debut, batting against the league's best pitcher, Shoichi Kaneda of the Swallows, he fanned four straight times. But Nagashima soon adapted to the pro game and by the end of season led the league in home runs and RBIs. He played with a speed, intensity, and flair that made him a standout in the often gray world of Japanese baseball. The golden boy was the real thing. To the surprise of no one, he was named Rookie of the Year.

Off the field, his open manner and sunny personality won him fans everywhere, even among confirmed Giants haters. Though in many ways a role model—manly but modest, a fierce competitor but a team player who never made demands—Nagashima was also notorious for his absent-mindedness. Once, he wore a teammate's uniform onto the field. Another time he hit a home run, but forgot to touch base and was called out. Still another time, he was running from first to third on a hit and run play when the outfielder caught the batter's fly ball.

Instead of rounding second to tag up, he made a beeline for first base—only to see the umpire's raised thumb. Unbelievably, he made the same blooper again in another game and the fans never let him forget it.

The fog didn't clear when he left the diamond. Once he stayed behind in the locker room after all his teammates had left, searching desperately for his car keys. He had forgotten that he had come to the stadium that day by chauffeured limousine. Another time while out driving he saw a detour sign— but kept heading straight toward the surprised road crew. Luckily, he stopped the car before they became road kill.

Instead of damaging his image, these gaffes only made Nagashima more lovable to his fans. Here was a superstar who was human, all too human.

He also pleased them by playing the showboat on the field. When he struck out, he hit his bat on the plate to show his frustration. When he swung and missed, his helmet often went flying. Fans thought he was making a superhuman effort to send the ball into orbit. Instead, he wore a helmet one size too big to give the crowd a thrill.

Batting fourth in the lineup, right after Oh (sportswriters referred to these two as simply "ON," in roman letters) Nagashima powered the Giants to nine straight pennants and Japan Series titles from 1965 to 1973, a string that has never been equaled. This was also the period of Japan's postwar economic miracle, when the GNP was growing by double digits every year. For many Japanese, the triumphs of the Giants seemed to symbolize the country's rise to wealth and prominence.

Even those who resisted this connection— Giants hating was as popular a sport in Japan as Yankee hating used to be in the United States—could hardly miss the headlines trumpeting Nagashima's latest sayonara (last-inning, game-winning) home run in the *Yomiuri Shimbun,* the flagship newspaper of the media group that owned the Giants, or the Giants games on the Nippon Television Network, another Yomiuri Group company.

When they retreated to the neighborhood bookstore, Giants haters were confronted with books and *manga* glorifying the Giants, including the enduringly popular comic series, *Kyojin no Hoshi* (Star of the Giants), about a boy who undergoes incredible hardships to play for his favorite team. There was no escape: the Giants, as personified by the on-field exploits of Nagashima, had become a national institution.

When Emperor Hirohito attended his first baseball game, at Korakuen Stadium on June 25, 1959, it was, appropriately, to watch the Giants. Even more fittingly, the hero of the game was Nagashima, who powered a sayonara home run to beat the archrival Hanshin Tigers. The Emperor, after seeing the clutch hit of a lifetime by the best all-round player in Japanese baseball, never attended another game. But with that one stroke, Nagashima created a sports legend.

Nagashima went on to many other triumphs and solidified his reputation as the game's best money player, while leading the Giants to nine straight Japan Series championships, a streak that the Japanese sports papers referred to ever after as simply "V-9"—no need to explain what "V" or "9" meant.

Finally, even Mr. Giants reached his limit and announced that the 1974 season would be his last. Though the season was not the triumphal procession his fans might have hoped for—Nagashima ended it with a .240 average and the Giants finished second in the pennant race, after the Chunichi Dragons—in his final game he smacked four hits, including one last dinger, in powering his team to a double-header sweep against the Dragons. During his postgame retirement ceremony the fans gave him a standing ovation. Few cared that the Dragons, having already clinched the pennant, were resting their best players for the Japan Series.

Though Nagashima's active career was over, the Giants couldn't bear to part with him. The following season he took over as team manager, with high hopes that, after the previous season's lapse, the Giants would return to the path of glory. Instead, they plunged into the cellar. Although Nagashima later recovered from this humiliation by winning two pennants, his Giants were never able to defeat the former doormat Pacific League in the Japan Series. Finally, in 1980, after three disappointing seasons, Nagashima resigned as manager.

Though Nagashima went on to a successful career as sports commentator, baseball ambassador, and commercial pitchman (he plugged a line of suits called "Mister Sanyo" after his "Mister" nickname), a cloud hung over his head. By not winning a Japan Series victory, he had failed the Giants, baseball, and the nation. But when the Taiyo Whales offered him a managing job in 1983 and a sports paper reported, erroneously, that Nagashima had accepted, fans were upset; they couldn't imagine him as anything but a Giant. They needn't have worried; Nagashima turned down the offer. One sports commentator suggested that Nagashima didn't want to make life harder for former teammate Oh, who was then managing the Giants and under heavy pressure to win the Japan Series to mark the team's fiftieth anniversary.

In 1992, when most fans had given up hope of ever seeing Nagashima in a Giants uniform again, he signed a five-year contract to manage his former team. "I know that Giants fans won't wait long for a pennant," he told reporters.

Though the 1993 season was a disappointment—the Giants finished third and Nagashima was criticized for putting his weak-hitting son, Kazushige, into the line-up—in the first half of the 1994 season the Giants built a big lead over their Central League opponents, blew it in August, then came back to win a dramatic three-way battle for the pennant in the final game. Fans who had been drifting away from baseball to pro soccer, Formula One racing, and sumo started watching Giants games on NTV again and packing the Tokyo Dome, the Giant's home stadium. Thanks to Nagashima and his team, baseball was Japan's number-one sport once more.

Although the Giants had the slugging power of sophomore sensation Hideo Matsui and veteran Hiromitsu Ochiai, as well as the strongest pitching staff in the league, Nagashima got credit for providing canny-but-inspiring leadership. Mellowed since his first stint as Giants manager, when he would often bawl out players and even smack them around, Nagashima kept a cool head as his team's lead melted away in the midsummer, while juggling the lineup to rest his aging veterans and pump life into his team's fading offense. Then, in a nail-biting seven-game series with the Seibu Lions, the team came though again—and Mr. Giants had his first Japan Series title as a manager.

The Golden Boy was shining again.

NARUHODO THE WORLD

Early Japanese TV quiz shows were essentially copies of U.S. originals: From 1955 to 1967 *I've Got a Secret* and *What's My Line?* found new life in Japan as NHK's *Watashi no Himitsu* (My Secret), on which four celebrity panelists tried to guess the secret or the secret identity of the mystery guests. As Japanese TV matured, producers began to try out their own ideas. One was punishing the losers. Contestants on TV Asahi's *Quiz Time Show* were jacked high up in the air and, when they gave an incorrect answer, sent whirling down to earth with gut-wrenching speed. Another was to adapt the show to local tastes. Horse racing is wildly popular in Japan, so the producers of TBS's *Quiz Derby* turned the celebrity contestants into jockeys and the quiz into a race for the finish line. But the most innovative show of the 1980s not only Japanized the quiz-show format (so much so that the network could never manage to sell it in the United States and Europe, even after years of trying to reshape it for Western audiences) but created a new genre

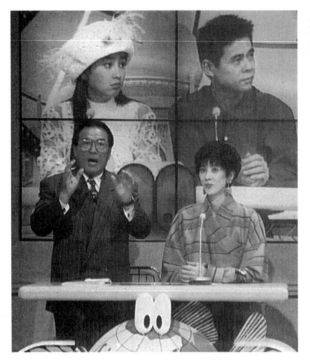

Naruhodo the World emcee Kin'ya Aikawa explains a fine point as co-host Eriko Kusada (foreground) and guests Rie Miyazawa and Shigesato Itoi listen.

that was to have an enormous impact on Japanese TV.

The show was *Naruhodo the World* (*naruhodo* means "I understand" or "I see"), which debuted on Fuji TV in October 1981. Unlike the other quiz shows of the day, *Naruhodo* was not studio bound. Instead of an emcee reading questions, the show presented video clips of foreigners (and in one segment, Japanese) doing and using strange, exotic, and, to most viewers, completely inexplicable things.

Working in pairs, the celebrity panelists had to guess what in the world the people in the clips were up to, with the husky-voiced host, Kin'ya Aikawa, moving briskly from one pair to the next, feeding them rapid-fire hints and slamming his hand down on their

table to indicate that their time for guessing was up. The atmosphere was that of a raucous game of charades, with the emphasis more on having a rollicking good time, while learning a few offbeat facts, than picking winners and losers. In fact, the pair with the most right answers didn't always end the show as a winner; the final round gave the lowest-ranking pair a shot to reach the top with one right answer or lucky stab in the dark.

Also, instead of the approach of NHK travelogue presenters, with their serious, responsible air and cultured, measured tones, the reporters for the show's video clips came across as unabashedly wide-eyed and breathlessly hyper about the wonders they were presenting.

The most hyper of all was Yumi Masuda, who worked on the show for its first six years and defined its much-copied style. Rejecting the cutesy-cute persona that was then standard for female talents, Masuda was a rough-and-ready type who often looked as though she had spent a few days hiking through the bush. She was, however, a peerless scatterbrained comedian who deftly caricatured the stereotypical Japanese abroad—she sometimes appeared in tour-guide garb, clutching a little flag—while exhibiting a boundless enthusiasm for her job.

She needed it. During her grueling stint on the show, Masuda traveled to more than ninety countries, many in the more remote regions of the Third World. Frequently, she was shown sprinting to her latest discovery, with the cameraman and soundman struggling to keep up. This anything-can-happen, you-are-there style gave her segments a bubbly excitement and visceral rush completely absent from the travelogue shows then on the air.

Naruhodo's co-host, the tall and talkative Eriko Kusuda, also represented a departure from the norm for women emcees on shows of this type, who were expected to play a passive, supporting role, opening their mouths only to lead into a commercial or express agreement with their male partner's pearls of wisdom. Kusuda, however, projected a frank, forthright, endearingly flaky persona—she was known for her outlandish costumes—that blithely violated rules of acceptable female TV talent behavior.

The show broke the new ground in other ways, including its hour-length (half an hour was then considered the maximum for quiz programs), its 9:00 P.M. time slot (most quiz shows aired early in the evening), and its high production costs (at least three times those of comparable shows). It represented, in fact, a sizable gamble for the Fuji TV network.

The gamble, however, paid off handsomely. Beginning in November 1983, the show passed the thirty-percent rating mark for eighteen straight weeks, reaching a height of 36.4 percent in December—numbers that obliterated the competition and inspired other nets to churn out an endless stream of imitators, including shows that focused on foreign foods, prices, and jobs. Some of these knockoffs, including *Sekai Marugoto How Much* (How Much in the World Is It?) and *Quiz Sekai wa Show-by Shoobai!!* (The World Is a Show, The World Is a Trade Quiz!!), became long-running hits and made *Naruhodo's* infotainment format a prime-time staple.

Though *Naruhodo* struck a chord with Japanese viewers, it rubbed not a few resident foreigners the wrong way. The usual criticism was that the show presented non-Japanese as so many sideshow freaks and their customs as bizarre departures from the Japanese norm. But though the show was undoubtedly pushy, intrusive, and obsessed with the weirder aspects of the more than one hundred twenty countries it visited, most of the laughs came from the clowning of the reporters and often lame-brained answers of the panelists.

Also, though *Naruhodo* was intended as pure entertainment, during its fifteen years on the air, it made even the most parochial and xenophobic viewers aware that the world outside Japan not only existed but was excellent fun to explore. And by satirizing the behavior of Japanese abroad, including the mad rushing about of the typical group tour, the program may even have persuaded a few viewers to strike out on their own and actually learn about the cultures of the places they were visiting, though most did not imitate the redoubtable Masuda in sampling snakes, scorpions, and other local delicacies.

The show may have succeeded too well. When it started, in 1981, four million Japanese traveled abroad, with most flying to "safe" destinations like Hawaii and the U.S. West Coast, where homesick tourists could always find signs in Japanese or a comforting bowl of ramen. By the mid-1990s, however, the number of overseas travelers had risen to more than ten million and more were venturing to places previously considered off the beaten path. Instead of snapshots of Waikiki Beach, travelers were returning with videos shot on Himalayan treks or in the villages of Thai hill tribes. *Naruhodo's* cultural surprises were no longer as surprising and its ratings began to drop. Finally, in March 1996, Fuji TV decided to cancel the show.

Given *Naruhodo's* popularity, longevity, and cross-cultural theme, one might expect that the show would have found a second life abroad. But despite years of trying, Fuji TV has only been able to sell the format to South Korea and Thailand. The West, says Fuji TV senior director of business development Ansei Yokota, has been a hard market to crack. "In Japan, no one cares who wins; they just want to see how the contestants respond," explains Yokota. "In the West, however, interest is much more focused on winners and losers."

Whereas the Japanese program used only four or five video clips in a hour, filling in the rest of time with repartee between the hosts and panelists, U.S. producers insisted that a local version would need many more—too many to turn a profit. "They finally decided that it wouldn't be worth it," said Yokota, with a sigh. *Naruhodo.*

NEWS STATION

News shows on Japanese television used to be good, gray, and deadly, deadly dull. The typical newscaster on the nation's leading news network, NHK, was a middle-aged man wearing a dark business suit and a somber expression, reading a story about the latest trade imbroglio or Ministry of Finance White Paper off the teleprompter in clearly enunciated syllables. His language was excruciatingly polite, his tone emotionally neutral, his stance rigidly objective. When the story called for analysis, he would question an expert, be it an NHK staff commentator or university professor, as though he were leading a postgraduate seminar. As

Redefining TV news for the 1990s: *News Station's* Etsuko Komiya and Hiroshi Kume.

the jargon flew and the charts detailing import sales and interest-rate trends filled the screen, it was hard to fault the professionalism and dedication of the news staff—and to keep one's eyelids propped open.

The commercial networks tried to interject more life into their newscasts—unlike public broadcaster NHK, they had to worry about ratings—but their basic format was the same: talking heads, boring graphics, dense language, minimal entertainment value. That, the news professionals would argue, is the way things ought to be; the news was serious business, not a show.

Then, in October 1985, a new type of news show debuted on the TV Asahi network. Called *News Station,* it started at 10:00 P.M., a time slot usually reserved for adult-oriented entertainment shows, and ran for ninety minutes, far longer than rival evening newscasts on the other commercial nets and NHK. But the biggest difference, it soon became apparent, was the show's anchor, Hiroshi Kume.

A former comedian whose previous job had been hosting the highly rated infotainment show *TV Scramble*, Kume had no TV news or journalistic experience. Instead, he had a telegenic presence, a quick tongue, an irreverent sense of humor, a lively curiosity, and a stubbornly independent mind. He also had no intention of following TV newsroom convention. Good-bye teleprompter, good-

bye dark suit (Kume's impeccably tailored clothes were chosen by his fashion-coordinator wife), good-bye bland scripts and, most important of all, good-bye objectivity.

In addition to reading the news, Kume would add his own explanations and comments. Some of his interjections were little more than quips designed to liven up the proceedings, but others were bluntly critical or straightforwardly emotional.

His object, he said, was to make the news understandable to even junior high school students. But the show's low ratings in its first weeks seemed to indicate that not many viewers of any age were paying attention. Then came the *Challenger* space shuttle disaster and the revolution in the Philippines that overthrew the Marcos regime. Viewers tuned into *News Station* to follow these major stories and liked what they saw. Ratings rose to twenty percent and even as high as thirty percent. By the end of its first year, *News Station* was a solid hit—and had other networks running scared.

Kume was not the whole show, of course. He shared his news reading duties with co-anchor Etsuko Komiya, while commentator Ikki Kobayashi supplied background and analysis. They were supported by the TV Asahi news department, which claimed to be the best among the commercial nets. Even before Kume's arrival, TV Asahi had billed itself as "the news network."

But it was Kume whom his journalistic critics attacked, blasting his lack of credentials and his unorthodox approach to the news. Kume shrugged off his bad reviews. "I don't consider myself a newscaster—I am merely the emcee of the show," Kume told an interviewer. "Given that it's a television show, it has to be entertaining."

Kume tried to make the show entertaining not only by editorializing but by interviewing his guests, many of whom were powerful politicians, as though they were real people and not a separate, exalted species. On one early show, he started an interview with former Foreign Minister Shintaro Abe—a Liberal Democratic Party boss with ambitions to become prime minister—by bluntly asking why he had accepted the invitation to appear. "You turned us down so many times before," Kume blandly commented. A flustered Abe, not used to this kind of cheek from the reporters who followed his every move, fumbled for an answer. Later, though, when Abe made a

mild joke about Japanese politics, Kume laughed uproariously, a reaction that put his guest in a relaxed, expansive mood. The interview was a success.

Kume's other on-air antics, however, were not designed to ingratiate him with the ruling LDP, or the business community that supported the party. When Kume heaped scorn on the LDP for betraying its 1986 election promise not to impose a general consumption tax, the Toyota Motor Corporation withdrew its sponsorship from the show. Unrepentant, Kume claimed that he had never directly spoken against the consumption tax itself, only the LDP's devious ways. The show producers backed their star; plenty of other sponsors were eager to fill the gap.

But as the show's popularity grew and Kume became more confident (some would say "entrenched") in the anchor's chair, his role began to change from sprightly gadfly to crusader with an agenda. In 1992, when seventy-eight-year-old LDP kingmaker Shin Kanemaru received a slap-on-the-wrist fine of 1,700 dollars for taking 4 million dollars in illegal campaign contributions, Kume reported the news, then looked straight into the camera and asked viewers "Do you think that's right?"

Most, as it turned out, did not. Over the following weeks, as Kume reported almost nightly on the aftermath of the Kanemaru scandal, including provincial assembly resolutions condemning the lawmaker and an opinion poll in his home district indicating that nearly eighty percent of his constituents wanted him to resign, more and more Japanese began to express their outrage in demonstrations, petitions, and letter-writing campaigns. Finally in October 1992, Kanemaru left the Diet in disgrace—with many attributing his downfall to Kume.

Not surprisingly, Kume's success spawned imitators. Though attempts to go head-to-head with *News Station* failed—TBS pulled a short-lived 10:00 P.M. news show called *Prime Time* in 1990—other network anchors began to lighten up and say what they felt about the news. Even stodgy NHK, after being thrashed repeatedly in the ratings by *News Station,* began allowing its news readers to make the occasional mild comment.

In recent years, as the pressures and responsibilities of the job have taken their toll, Kume has changed his own style. Once a free-spirited sort on the air, who vowed to shave his head if his beloved Hiroshima Carp lost the 1989 Central League pennant to the Yomiuri Giants—and carried through when the Giants won—Kume has become more sober-sided and evenhanded. He still has a long way to go, though, before he becomes NHK material.

As *News Station* approached its tenth anniversary, Kume began to publicly complain that he was becoming an "imitation journalist" and say that every show had to come to an end. He also started to freelance occasionally, appearing as a guest on a radio show in February 1995 for his old employer, TBS (Kume had started out in the business as a radio announcer) and in March as a host for a TBS TV show called *Kan Kan Pittashi '95* (Burning Right '95).

Not surprisingly, this outside activity fueled speculation that Kume was about to leave *News Station.* Kume, however insisted that he wanted to stay around for at least the Atlanta Olympics in 1996 and the reversion of Hong Kong in 1997. "Television is not interesting unless appealing people appear," he told a press conference in March. "Recently, I've really been wondering whether I still fit into that category. I've been appearing on other programs to refresh myself."

Anxious to fill the gap should Kume change his mind and depart, TV Asahi recruited new talent for the show in 1995, including former NHK announcer Maoko Kotani and, in a public audition that drew 1,630 applicants, former NTT International Department assistant general manager Satoru Nagami.

But no one is likely to duplicate Kume's feat of changing the course of Japanese TV journalism. For a while, at least, he made it fun to watch the news.

NODO JIMAN

Japanese pop singers and groups can be accused of many things, from blandness to plain bad singing (though the latter is less of a problem in these days of electronic vocal enhancement), but the ones signed to major labels and talent agencies are rarely guilty of amateurish spontaneity. The fresh-faced teenager who trills so innocently on the tube has often been packaged to project a certain image, with little left to chance, from the lyrics of her songs to her dance steps and hand gestures.

Though millions are obviously enthralled by these slick entertainers, Japanese TV's longest-lived musical show is also its corniest and most unsophisticated. On the air since 1946, in the radio days of broadcasting, *NHK Nodo Jiman* (which literally translates as "NHK Proud of My Voice," though its official English title is "Amateur Singers On the Air") is a traveling amateur hour. Every Sunday the show appears from a different area of Japan and features local singers who compete to be that week's champion.

Selected from a preliminary audition that often attracts hundreds of wannabes, the twenty-two contestants range widely in age, talent, and musical styles, though perform-ers of rap, heavy metal, and other outre Western genres never make the cut. On the air, they perform one number each with a live band. If a panel of judges passes them with three gongs, they become finalists eligi-ble for the championship. One gong, how-ever, and they are out, even if they are only three bars into their number. The judges tend to be strict, giving their three gongs only to a lucky few.

The one-gonged contestants nearly always accept their humiliation with no whines, complaints, or scenes. An embar-rassed grin, a slight bow, and the loser trots off the stage. Sometimes the kindhearted emcee even interviews a loser, especially if he or she happens to be a wrinkled pen-sioner. And at the end, everyone, winners and losers alike, returns to the stage for the awarding of the week's championship and another moment in the spotlight.

The **KARAOKE** boom has made it possible for crooners in the hinterlands to polish their favorites to perfection (or as close to it as their talents will take them) and, as a result, the show is somewhat easier to listen to than in the off-key old days, but *Nodo Jiman* is still for real amateurs; truck drivers, salarymen, housewives, school girls, and others whose only connection with show biz is the neigh-borhood karaoke club. Newcomers with seri-ous professional aspirations usually make their TV debuts elsewhere.

Until 1970, NHK sponsored a national contest in which *Nodo Jiman* champions vied for the title of the best amateur singer in

Japan. Using the contest as a springboard, several contestants went on to successful professional careers. But when the show's ratings started to fall in the late 1960s, the producers decided that the audience preferred to watch average folks sing for their family, neighbors, and a shot at fifteen minutes of fame (though the champions barely got enough air-time to accept their trophy and smile at the camera). NHK ended the contest and widened its scouting net to include a broader cross-section of the population, even if they didn't have voices like Saburo Kitajima or Hiroshi Mifune—popular professional singers who were *Nodo Jiman* contestants. Ratings recovered and the show went on to celebrate its fortieth anniversary

on TV in 1993—the same year that Japanese TV broadcasting marked the start of its fifth decade.

A Sunday afternoon institution as long as most of its viewers can remember, *Nodo Jiman* offers a glimpse of a down-home Japan far removed from economic-super-power stereotypes. The mood is closer to that of a rural banquet (*enkai*) than a professional music show. While the crowd claps and cheers them on, contestants belt out their numbers with energy, spirit, and a surprising lack of self-consciousness. Even if they blow a few notes no one (except the judges) seems to mind. The emcee always makes a few complimentary remarks on the local sights and delicacies and, when talking with the contestants, tries hard to draw them out, while taking care never to put them down. Tatsuo Kaneko, who served as emcee for nearly eighteen years until 1987, once called himself the show's "twenty-sixth contestant" (at the time there were twenty-five contestants instead of the current twenty-two) to underline his empathy with the show's amateur vocalists, who had to sing their hearts out while dreading the sound of the fatal gong.

The contestants run the generational gamut. On a given week one might see a kid with long, red-dyed hair shyly confessing that he is on the show to impress a girl, or a middle-aged salarymen on assignment in the hinterlands sending his greetings to the wife and kids back in Tokyo. And every show seems to feature at least one *min'yo* (folk song) by an elderly singer who inevitably gets a big round of applause, even though her voice has seen better days.

These are the folks who never get their pictures taken at trade-talk photo ops, but represent the Japanese heartland. For the millions living in the big cities, a generation or less away from their rural roots, the show is a window into an unpretentious, gently human world that they seldom see in the frantic, impersonal crush of the metropolis, but still lives in their memory—and on the stage of *Nodo Jiman*.

ONYANKO CLUB

Foreigners seeing Japanese TV for the first time often comment on its air of amateurishness: the comedians who crack up in the middle of their own jokes, the young female singers who lack any discernible talent, and the real amateurs who are constantly turning up as quiz-show contestants, singers, mimics, and interviewees.

The main reason for this amateurism is bottom-line business. Large segments of the Japanese audience actually like seeing amateurs—or pros acting amateurishly—on the tube. Japanese society, as we are too often reminded, doesn't care for nails that stick up. The ultimate expression of this truism is television, where even the talented seem to spend much of their time proving that they are really Mr. or Ms. Average, even if it means deliberately fluffing lines or otherwise playing the fool.

After decades of show-biz folks trying to make TV as nonthreatening as possible by dumbing down their acts, the audience, the younger segment of it in particular, has finally gotten the message. Though supposedly living in a shame culture, in which expressions of embarrassment are considered signs of good breeding, a surprising number of ordinary Japanese keep their cool

in front of a television camera, acting as though they were appearing in a home video for family and friends (which, in a sense, they are).

The apotheosis of on-air amateurism was a mid-1980s show called *Yuyake Nyan Nyan,* which literally translates as "Meow, Meow at Dusk." Starting at 5:00 P.M., when its target teenage audience had just returned from school but hadn't started cracking the books, the show featured a group of twenty-four high school girls known as the "Onyanko Club," or "Kitty Cat Club."

The girls sang, danced, chatted with the emcee and otherwise did normal TV variety-show things. But what impressed viewers—and made the show a hit—was the girls' averageness. Instead of show-biz prodigies who had been taking dance lessons since they could walk and acting lessons since they could talk, the Onyanko Club members were ordinary teenage girls living ordinary teenage lives. All were amateurs who had been selected for the show in auditions.

On the show, they seemed to be utterly themselves, making no pretense of trying to "perform." They chitchatted about the usual high-school girl stuff, using high-school girl slang. When they took midterm tests, they had to miss the show—and the other club members expressed sympathy with their plight. The viewers at home, who were often taking those same tests, could identify. The show's ratings soared. "[This] sense of fraternity and amateurism is the main cause of their popularity," show producer Yasushi Akimoto told the *Asahi Shimbun*. "Ordinary girls happen to be discovered and become idols. That's the era the Onyanko Club has created."

The show also created a bonanza. Beginning with their debut single in July 1985, the Onyanko Club had one smash after another, each selling from three hundred thousand to five hundred thousand copies in a industry that then considered sales of fifty thousand copies a hit. The girls, of course, didn't write the songs themselves and few could sing them particularly well. It didn't matter. In their untalented everydayness, they appealed to kids who were intimidated by slick, sophisticated pop singers and groups. The girls in the audience could imagine becoming their friends or even appearing on the show themselves—new girls were always needed to replace the ones who graduated from high school and returned to blissful anonymity. The boys could fantasize about dating their favorite. And both sexes could get closer to their idols by buying their (admittedly mediocre) records.

The popularity of Onyanko Club and its imitators was short lived. Perhaps the sight of average girls behaving in an average way became, well, nothing extraordinary. Japanese viewers may like the amateurish, but they like the new even better.

OSHIN VERSUS IE NAKI KO

Japanese, more than most people, love a good cry, and TV soaps, called "home dramas" *(hoomu dorama)* have long loved to give it to them. It's no surprise that the most popular home drama of all, with a 62.9% peak rating, also wrung the most tears. Called *Oshin,* it appeared on public broadcaster NHK from April 1983 to March 1984 and spawned an *Oshin* boom. Politicians, including Ronald Reagan, mentioned it in their speeches, editorial writers analyzed it in their columns, and nearly ninety-eight percent of Japanese viewers tuned into at least one of the show's three hundred episodes. NHK later sold *Oshin* to broadcasters in more than forty countries, mostly in Asia and the Middle East, where it was often cited as a shining moral example for citizens of developing nations. (In Iran four TV executives were jailed for broadcasting a phone-in program in which a woman caller claimed that the show's heroine was a better role model for Iranian women than the daughter of the Prophet Mohammed.)

Based on three hundred letters solicited by a magazine about women's lives in pre-economic-miracle Japan, the show told the story of a girl named Oshin who suffered incredible hardships in the early years of the century but overcame every obstacle to become, in middle age, the owner of a super-market chain. Although three actresses—Ayako Kobayashi, Yuko Tanaka, and Nobuko Otowa—played the character in her life journey from age seven to eighty-three, it was cute newcomer Kobayashi who scored the biggest ratings. When her character, clutching a *kokeshi* doll, sailed away on a raft in the middle of a snowstorm to a new life as a maid for a timber merchant, her heart-rending cry of *"Okaasan!"* ("Mother!") had viewers shedding hot tears.

Though the destitution of Oshin's family in the northern Japan countryside drove her grandmother to commit suicide and her mother to attempt an abortion by wading in an icy river, even worse was in store for the poor girl in the months and years that followed. After escaping from domestic servitude—her pay at the merchant's was one bag of rice a year—she briefly found happiness at a rice shop in Sakata. But when a mean housemaid falsely accused her of thievery, Oshin found herself out in the streets again. An army deserter saved her from hunger, but was later arrested and shot. And so it went.

For many middle-aged and older women, the series' most poignant episodes depicted Oshin's marriage to the spineless third son of a rich landowner in Saga, a prefecture on the island of Kyushu. Left yenless when their small shop in Tokyo was destroyed in the Great Kanto Earthquake of 1923, Oshin and her husband returned to his home in Saga and the cold disdain of his mother, who disapproved of their marriage. Five months pregnant, Oshin was forced to slave in the fields from dawn to dusk, while the mother's own pregnant daughter lived the life of Riley, snacking on delicacies and doing no housework.

The mother-in-law explained this discrimination to her husband by saying that, though they were responsible for helping their daughter give birth to a healthy child, "Oshin is the wife of our third son and means nothing to us. She should contribute to her board and, if she can't do so, she should be divorced."

This attitude reflected the realties of the prewar Japanese *ie* or family system, in which mothers-in-law frequently tyrannized their daughters-in-law, but this character's outrageous behavior, which finally resulted in Oshin's miscarriage, prompted hundreds of Sagaites to protest to NHK that she was damaging the image of Saga women. Oshin scriptwriter Sugako Hashida and producer Yukiko Okamoto, both independent sorts

Toughing it out in pre-economic-miracle Japan: Ayako Kobayashi as Oshin.

big in the grocery business. Looking back over her long life at the age of eighty-three, she said, "Somewhere along the way, I feel that I've lost something."

What, a Western viewer might well ask, had she lost? During the national debate that swirled around the show, Japanese, especially ones raised before the war, answered that Oshin and many others of her generation missed the moral clarity that the old social system, for all its faults, offered. Younger Japanese, the old folks lamented, had been corrupted by the postwar reforms imposed on Japan by the Americans and no longer shared the values that had enabled the Oshins of this country to struggle against adversity and transform Japan into an economic superpower. Instead of being unselfish, uncomplaining, and hard-working, they thought only of making money and enjoying themselves.

Those same young folks countered that older Oshin fans, who had a sneaking longing for the days of prewar poverty, were all wet. "Many Japanese revel in that kind of thing, believing hardships are good for the spirit," a twenty-year-old flight attendant told *The Guardian*. "There's something sick about that way of thinking."

Sick or not, Oshin fans made their heroine a national byword. Takanosato, a sumo wrestler who had battled diabetes to reach the sport's highest rank, was labeled the

who had battled their way to the top in a mostly male business, stoutly defended the truth of their characterization. Several elderly *Saga* women came to their defense, saying that they had been subjected to similar treatment themselves and that they probably would have treated their own daughters-in-law the same way if the postwar Constitution hadn't dismantled the old family system.

Oshin finally escaped this hell, but another child died in World War II and, shortly after Japan's defeat, her husband committed suicide to atone for making profits as a military supplier while sending young men off to die in the war. Oshin, however, survived—her name contained a character for the word *shimbo* or perseverance—and finally made it

"Oshin grand champion." Political king-maker Kakuei Tanaka, who had been convicted of accepting bribes from Lockheed Corporation while prime minister, referred to himself as a "male Oshin," even though his hardships were self-imposed.

Does the Oshin ethic still live? Although weepy melodramas about long-suffering heroines still have their fans, audience tastes seem to have changed since the show set ratings records. More than than half a century after the end of World War II, it's becoming harder to find Japanese who are still nostalgic for Oshin's brand of strength through pain.

One indication of this change was the popularity of *Ie Naki Ko* (Homeless Child), a prime-time soap that scored a peak 37.2 percent rating—the fifth highest ever for a drama—on the NTV network in 1994. As the title suggests, the show was about an orphan girl named Suzu who struggles to survive in an unfriendly world. Disdaining the passive endurance of Oshin, Suzu is a gutsy little scrapper who is not above stealing money from her classmates to pay for her mother's heart operation or scheming to send an abusive stepfather to jail. The show's most memorable line, shouted with great conviction by Suzu in TV ad after ad, was "If you love me, give me money!"

The show made the saucer-eyed twelve-year-old who played Suzu, Yumi Adachi, a megastar. Next came a hit movie and a second season for the show—a rarity on Japanese TV, where even popular drama series usually disappear after a twelve-week run. But a comeback for Oshin, who never took a dishonest yen from anyone, is nowhere in sight.

OTOMO, KATSUHIRO

Manga and *anime* are no longer only-in-Japan phenomena. As a glance at Web sites on the Internet or the Japanimation sections of U.S. video shops clearly show, a growing number of overseas fans have become seriously (and at times strangely) devoted to these uniquely Japanese forms of comic art that many foreigners in Japan (not to mention adult Japanese) once routinely dismissed as grotesque, offensive, and obviously inferior to their American models.

One *manga* artist mainly responsible for this explosion of interest abroad, Katsuhiro Otomo, has also been hugely successful in Japan but still remains out of the Japanese pop cultural mainstream, more appreciated by a coterie (admittedly, a large coterie) of fans than by the mass audience. In 1995 HAYAO MIYAZAKI's romantic fantasy, *Mimi o Sumaseba* (Whisper of the Heart), earned 18.5 million dollars in distribution revenues,

Feral kids on electric bikes roam the streets of Neo-Tokyo in *Akira*.

compared with 1.5 million dollars for Otomo's three-part SF omnibus, *Memories*.

One reason is that while Miyazaki tries to entertain the way Disney does, by pushing mass-audience buttons with feel-good stories that everyone can understand (though Miyazaki's are more culture-specific), Otomo believes in faithfully realizing his own at times bizarre visions, even if it means exploding the boundaries of his art and blowing the minds of his audience. If **OSAMU TEZUKA** was the god of *manga*, who wanted to dominate the industry he had done so much to build, Katsuhiro Otomo is the *otaku* (see **ZOKU**), an *anime* and *manga* nerd who would rather rule in his own private worlds.

Born in 1954 in Miyagi Prefecture in the north of Japan, Otomo had what might be described as a typical *otaku* childhood. As a boy, he devoured *manga* and tried to copy his favorites, including the works of Osamu Tezuka and Shotaro Ishinomori. In high school he joined the art club and spent most of his time either drawing *manga* or watching movies, riding the train three hours to the nearest theaters in the city of Sendai. Among his favorites were American films such as *Bonnie and Clyde* and *Easy Rider,* **YAKUZA MOVIES** and Nikkatsu's soft porno (*roman poruno*) films.

Otomo thought of applying to art school, but hated the idea of sitting for entrance examinations. Instead, he decided to become a *manga* artist and went to Tokyo after graduation to seek his fortune, together with other young hopefuls from all over the country, for whom the capital was a *manga* mecca.

In 1973 Otomo made his *manga* debut in a supplement of the weekly magazine *Action* with "Jusei" (Gunshot), a story based on Prosper Mérimée's "Mateo Falcone." After drawing *manga* adaptations of works by Poe, Twain, and other writers, Otomo published his first original work in *Action,* "Hashi to Soshite" (The Bridge and Then) in 1974.

From 1974 to 1978 Otomo continued to draw *manga* for *Action* that violated the form's narrative conventions with their nearly plotless, character-driven stories and exhibited an artistic style that was complex but uncluttered, hyper-realistic but not boringly literal, with clean, fluid lines and dynamic compositions. Among these stories was "Around About Midnight," about an all-night game of mah-jongg played by four college students, and "Nothing Will Be as It Was," about a loner who murders a friend and cannibalizes his corpse. In 1979 Otomo drew "Fireball," a sci-fi story inspired by a Deep Purple song in which a super-psychic battles a mega-computer, for a special issue of *Action,* and published *Short Peace,* his first paperback collection of *manga* stories. Both created a sensation among *manga* fans and made Otomo a cult hero. "Fireball," in par-

ticular, marked a new direction in Otomo's work, toward more action-driven stories set in meticulously imagined future worlds. Other early book collections included *Highway Star* (1979), *Good Weather* (1981), *Hansel and Gretel* (1981), and *Boogie Woogie Waltz* (1982).

In 1980, Otomo began the serialization of *Domu: A Child's Dreams,* yet another seminal work. Inspired by a newspaper account of a spate of suicides at Takashimadaira Danchi, a large public-housing project in suburban Tokyo, *Domu* pitted a senile old man with dark paranormal powers, who caused people to leap from rooftops to their death, against a little girl with an equally formidable arsenal of psychic weapons. After run-

ning intermittently for two years, *Domu* appeared in paperback in 1983 and became a publishing sensation, selling half a million copies and winning Otomo the 1983 Science Fiction Grand Prix, the first time this prestigious award had ever been given to a *manga* artist.

In 1982, when he was reaching the peak of his popularity in Japan, Otomo began *Akira,* the *manga* that was to make him famous worldwide. Serialized in *Young Magazine, Akira* told the story of teenagers in the year 2019 who roam a Neo-Tokyo that has been rebuilt from ashes after a failed secret-weapons experiment in 1988. Scientists had tried to unlock the power of the human mind but instead unleashed a horribly destructive force that leveled Tokyo. The subjects of their experiments had been children whose psychic energies, the scientists had learned too late, were far more powerful than they had expected. The result of this miscalculation was World War III, which had been triggered by the Tokyo blast.

Now, three decades later, the government of Neo-Tokyo, under the control of an American-trained military dictator called The Colonel, has revived the secret project. The city has become a high-tech jungle of slums and super-high-rises, patrolled by feral kids on powerful electric bikes and infiltrated by resistance fighters bent on toppling the government.

One night, while speeding through the ruins of the old city, a gang of bikers encounters what looks to be a prematurely aged child wandering in the middle of an abandoned expressway. He is an escaped subject of the original experiments, who is called, simply, No. 26. One of the bikers, Tetsuo, is badly injured trying to avoid him and is quickly spirited away by the security forces. Meanwhile, the boy mysteriously vanishes. Tetsuo survives, however, and with the aid of psychic powers he acquires after taking a capsule in the government's mind-research lab, returns to join the struggle against the Colonel and his cohorts— and prevent a second apocalypse. The trigger for this catastrophe is a boy sleeping a dreamless sleep in the lab. His name: Akira.

Akira the *manga*, which Otomo later said had been partly inspired by *Star Wars*, ran more than two thousand pages and appeared for nearly a decade in *Young Magazine*. During that time it became a cult phenomenon in Japan and, in translation, worldwide. Since the publication of the first installment of the "Akira" saga by Marvel in the United States, thirty-eight paperback volumes have appeared in English, selling a total of two million copies. Akira has also been published in South Korea, Taiwan, Indonesia, France, Spain, Italy, Germany, Sweden, and Brazil, with worldwide sales, excluding Japan, totaling seven million copies. No other Japanese *manga* even approaches Akira's international success, though many have exceeded it in the domestic market.

While drawing hit *manga*, Otomo was also pursuing his other central passion: films. In 1982 he took a six-month break from the *manga* grind to make *Jiyu o Warera ni* (Give Me a Gun/Give Me Freedom), a 16-mm film about a group of adolescent gun enthusiasts riven by internal dissension, who finally take to the hills to settle their differences in a firefight to the finish.

Otomo also handled the character designs for the animated feature *Gemma no Taisen* (Harmageddon), created the opening titles for the NHK program *You*, and made

TV commercials for Suntory and Canon. In 1987 Otomo supervised the continuity of the opening and closing scenes of the animated feature *Robot Carnival* and directed the segment *Koji Chushi Meirei* (Order to Stop Construction) for the animation omnibus *Meikyu Monogatari* (Labyrinth Stories or, alternatively, Manie, Manie).

These relatively minor jobs did little to prepare moviegoers for the impact Otomo's animated feature version of *Akira,* which debuted in Japan in 1988 and became a mega-hit for the science-fiction anime genre, earning eight hundred million yen for distributor Toho.

The story, which basically followed the *manga,* was busy to the point of incoherence, but the film remained a dazzling exercise in future-world imagineering that equaled *Blade Runner* in its boldness of vision, artistic unity, and attention to detail. *Akira's* background artists drew every window in Neo-Tokyo's thousand-story buildings, using hundreds of nearly invisible lines. Animators designed gizmos and machinery right down to their inner workings even though they appeared for mere moments of screen time. They also drew light and shadow to reflect movement, place, and the time of day, with painstaking accuracy. Putting these various elements on the screen required extensive use of advanced animation technology, including computer motion control and optical effects, and superhuman labors from the *Akira* staff, who may have been experienced animators but had never done anything as technically complex or creatively ambitious.

The audacity of *Akira's* hyper-realistic images and the power of its hyper-violent action made mainstream American animated features, with their cutesy realism and child's storybook plots, look timid and bland. *Akira* not only gave U.S. animation fans a new on-screen world but a new way of thinking about the art of animated film. *101 Dalmatians* just didn't cut it anymore. Since its release, the video version of *Akira* has sold seventy thousand copies in the United States and one hundred thousand in Europe, compared with fifty thousand sold to date in Japan.

Following the international triumph of *Akira,* Otomo made, in 1991, *World Apartment Horror,* a low-budget film set in a run-down Tokyo rooming house inhabited entirely by foreign tenants—and one new gangster manager who wants to kick them out so a crooked real estate developer can tear the place down. But when the manager starts playing nasty tricks on the tenants, they respond in kind, with aid from supernatural forces.

Intended as an exploration of the relationship between the Asians flooding into Japan at the time and the Japanese around them, *World Apartment Horror* was an odd, if occasionally funny and absorbing, mixture of low comedy, serious social drama, and unbridled fantasy. Despite the Otomo name, it did indifferent business in its few art-theatre engagements.

After writing the script and providing the mechanicals for the 1991 video *anime Roojin Z*, Otomo turned to his next major animation project, the three-part omnibus *Memories*. Released in Japan in December 1995, *Memories* presented stories of outer space in the distant future, Japan in the present, and an Orwellian fantasy land where time has come to a stop. The animation was predictably stunning; Otomo had lost none of his talent for bringing his fantastic dreamscapes to highly realized life. Also, the advances in animation technology over the past several years had enabled him to expand his imaginative reach. Otomo, however, used his formidable technique to not just overawe, but to intelligently entertain. In the first two segments, especially, the approach was reminiscent of *The Twilight Zone* at its mind-bending best.

The last segment, "Cannon Fodder," was the strangest and most unsettling. The setting was a vaguely European city whose sole occupation seemed to be shelling distant targets with hundreds of cannons. The story was of a man who served on the crew of a monster cannon called Number 17 and his son, who dreamt of growing up to be the cannon's firer—the most prestigious job of all. The mood resembled that of *1984*: endless war, universal obsession with an unnamed, unseen enemy, and a wan-looking populace systematically programmed to perform a single task. The city of cannons, however, was less a possible future than a metaphor for the banal horrors of modern war. The mindless power of the cannons was finally as empty as the men who minded them.

Memories, which broke decisively with the dark utopianism of *Akira,* did not do nearly as well at the Japanese box office. It did offer new evidence that the ever-restless Otomo was not content to stick to a formula, however successful. He was still out ahead of his fans and his rivals, creating a personal artistic language that sounded very much like the future of animation.

OYAJI GYARU

Westerners have long stereotyped Japanese women as sweet, gentle, innocent, refined (the kimono! the tea ceremony!), and thoroughly squelched by their male-dominated society. Although the older image of the submissive, flowerlike geisha pouring sakè for her samurai master may have given way to the more up-to-date image of the submissive, flower-like OL ("office lady" or female clerical worker) pouring tea for her male boss, not much has changed, really, since the days of Cio-cio-san and Lieutenant Pinkerton.

Like all stereotypes, this one contains a grain of truth; compared with the West, Japanese society still defines its sex roles rigidly and practices discrimination openly. Women aspiring to job equality with men have long faced, not a glass but an iron ceiling to the upper reaches of the nation's business, political, and professional power structures.

Though the postwar female OL was offered opportunities that the prewar geisha could have never imagined, she could rarely expect to be more than a glorified assistant to a male superior, no matter how long or well she worked. Also, many companies expected (or forced) her to quit after marriage or the birth of her first child. And she had to hustle to find Mr. Right. If an OL was still single after the age twenty-five, her male colleagues would often call her a "Christmas cake" because they assumed that, like a holiday cake left unsold on December 25, no one would want her. In short, the OL was considered a "flower of the workplace": a pretty, pleasant, decorative object, whose brief career was largely irrelevant to the real business of running the company.

But in 1989, when the Japanese economy was booming and it looked as though the good times would roll forever, a young cartoonist named Yutsuko Chusonji announced to the world that the old image of the OL was outdated. Far from being fragile flowers or stale Christmas cakes, the OLs in Chusonji's "Sweet Spot," a *manga* that ran weekly in a magazine for young businessmen called *Spa!*, were formidable types who played golf, bet the ponies, swilled whiskey, sang at karaoke bars, and otherwise behaved like middle-aged businessmen on a spree.

Though Chusonji dubbed her creations *oyaji gyaru* (*oyaji* being an informal term for "middle-aged man" and *gyaru*, Japlish for "girl" or "girls"), they were not long-in-the-tooth toughies, but young, long-legged beauties whose dressed in sexy "body conscious" (*bodicon,* or body-hugging) clothes and wore their hair in the fashionable "one-length" (*wanren,* or straight and long) style. They also had loads of disposable income because they lived at home, spent hardly anything on the so-called necessities (Dad was still picking up the tab for boring things like food and shelter), and saved little for a rainy day (Mr. Right was supposed see to that).

It also helped that, in those wild, wonderful bubble years of the late eighties and early nineties, nearly any OL who could warm a seat could also could count on receiving a fat bonus check twice a year. It was the summertime of the Japanese economy and the living was easy.

Far from regarding their menial, dead-end clerical jobs as an insult to their intelligence and a violation of their right to self-realization, Chusonji's *oyaji gyaru* looked at their harried male colleagues slaving away on the fast track and thanked their lucky stars that they were OLs: inferior, interchangeable, but free. Blessed with looks, youth, leisure, and fat bank accounts, the *oyaji gyaru* were on top of the world. No longer bound by the traditional rules defining the proper behavior for unmarried women (good-bye kimono, good-bye tea ceremony), tired of the usual OL off-duty pursuits (shopping in Harajuku, discoing in Roppongi), the *oyaji gyaru* indulged their curiosity in all directions, including activities formerly considered exclusively male.

They took up golf because it looked like fun, not because they had a fierce desire to breach a bastion of male privilege. They did, however, enjoy tweaking the collective noses of the middle-aged male establishment.

Interestingly, Chusonji thought that not all *oyaji* were grumpy chauvinist troglodytes. "I think older men feel good about *oyaji gyaru* and welcome them as mates or comrades," she told an interviewer. "But young men are bewildered by *oyaji gyaru* because they can no longer trick them according to their 'date manuals.' "

In addition to hanging out with *oyaji,* these free-and-easy OLs spent their holidays skiing in Switzerland or shopping on Rodeo Drive—not activities that the average workaholic *oyaji* could take time out for or even afford. In short, they did it all and had it all. "Just as the fall of the Berlin Wall ended the Cold War, barriers to women's leisure pursuits fell in Japan, allowing young women to enjoy golf, horse racing, and other amusements once reserved for men," Chusonji later reminisced. "The message of the *manga* was that young women were discarding what was once considered 'womanly' and moving onto another level, by imitating men. They were creating a new borderless world."

Though the *oyaji gyaru* were based on Chusonji's own research (a daughter of a construction-company executive, she had never worked as an OL herself), she admitted that they were hardly typical. "An *oyaji gyaru* represented the evolution of the OL," she said. "There were still quite a few OLs who couldn't overcome the barriers. . . . My strip was about an OL's dreams."

But enough OLs wanted to live the *oyaji gyaru* life—and enough readers wanted to follow their adventures in *Spa!*—that Chusonji's *manga* became a national rage in the bubble years. "Men turn to ['Sweet Spot'] to find out what women are thinking," said *Spa!* editor Naoki Watanabe. "Our women readers—nearly all of them OLs—universally love [it]."

The *oyaji gyaru* had their detractors, who criticized them for leading shallow, boorish, materialistic lives, while sneering at their bosses, living off the fat of the corporate land, and refusing to pull their share of the work load.

But love her or loathe her, the *oyaji gyaru* is now as extinct as the flapper. With the bursting of the bubble economy, bonuses began to shrink and jobs to disappear. Instead of assuming that designer clothes and trips to Sweden were their birthrights, young female college graduates—formerly prime OL fodder—faced the cold, hard reality that, in a tough economic climate, office flowers were the first to be round-filed. Many of the women of the class in 1997 may not find jobs at all—unless, of course, they don't mind being caddies.

PACHINKO

There they sit, in row after row, as bells clang, lights flash, martial music blares, and clouds of cigarette smoke drift up toward the ceiling: salarymen, students, housewives, and punch-permed characters who look as though they have just stepped out of a police lineup. They are watching little steel balls rattle and clatter past gleaming pins arranged in patterns on a gaudily colored upright board protected by a pane of glass. Occasionally the balls drop into holes on the board, causing plastic flowers to open and catch the balls cascading in an arc, like steel fireworks. Most of the balls, however, roll through a large hole at the bottom and pass into oblivion. Meanwhile, the players sit in front of the game, their right hands grasping a knob that sends the balls shooting skyward, their faces masks as hard to read as a meditating monk's. Are they deeply absorbed, mildly thrilled, or bored out of their skulls?

They are, of course, playing *pachinko*, the pinball-like game that has become Japan's biggest leisure industry, with revenues in 1994 of 30.5 trillion yen (305 billion dollars) or one-quarter of all earnings in the service sector. By comparison, the Japanese broadcasting industry earned 2.19 trillion yen (21.9 billion dollars) the same year—less than one-tenth of *pachinko*'s take. And because *pachinko* parlor owners are notorious for under-reporting their income—they regularly end up on the top-ten list of tax evaders—*pachinko*'s real total was no doubt higher.

But you don't need statistics to grasp *pachinko*'s pervasive influence on the culture. In every corner of Japan, including rural hamlets an hour's drive from the nearest movie theatre, you are sure to find a *pachinko* parlor, lighting up the night sky with a neon display worthy of the Las Vegas Strip. Altogether there are eighteen thousand parlors (the Japanese prefer to call them "halls" or *hooru*) catering to fifity million *pachinko* fans. That compares with eighteen hundred cinema screens for the entire country.

What is the reason for *pachinko*'s appeal? You need look no farther than the blue plastic buckets full of steel balls piled at a few lucky players' feet. The balls can be exchanged for prizes—lighter flints being among the more common. Other prizes include perfume, pendants, bracelets, pipes, pearls, golf balls, coffee beans, thermometers, and, in the Kansai region, for some reason, paperweights. But the real payoff is usually outside, around the corner, at a hole-in-the-wall through which *pachinko* players push their flints and receive cold, hard cash from an anonymous hand.

Yes, *pachinko* is Japan's very own slot machine, and the parlors Japan's very own casinos, in a country where real casino gambling is prohibited (though playing the lottery and betting at the horse, bicycle, motorbike, and boating races are all okay). Thus the rigmarole with the lighter flints, which hardly anyone in this land of one-hundred-yen disposable lighters uses anyway. Everyone, including the cop at the local police

box, knows what's going on and no one does anything to stop it. The idea of the police cracking down, save for the occasional bust of a parlor owner who is ripping off customers by remote controlling his computerized machines, is patently absurd. When 30.5 trillion yen talks, even the usually stiff-necked Japanese authorities walk.

Pachinko has even shown its clout in Japan's foreign relations, albeit inadvertently. Many of the parlors are owned by second- or third-generation Korean residents who are loyal to the Pyongyang regime. In the early 1990s, when North Korea was trying to build its own nuclear arsenal, it was seriously suggested that by cutting off remittances by these Koreans to their homeland Japan and its allies might deliver a crippling blow to North Korea's foreign reserves and bring its communist leaders to the bargaining table. The *pachinko* card, however, was not played—and the remittances continue to flow.

Pachinko did not always play this weighty a role in the affairs of nations. It began in the United States in the 1920s as a children's toy called the Corinthian game. A primitive form of pinball, the Corinthian game was an elevated board shaped like an inverted U and punched with holes for scoring. Players fired little balls through a slot at the right side of the game board and tried, by varying the arc and velocity of their shots, to slide them past barriers of protective nails into the holes. The round patterns of the nails were said to resemble the round Corinthian columns of ancient Greek temples—thus the name.

The first Corinthian game appeared in Japan in 1924 where Corinthian was immediately shortened to Corinth and transcribed into Japanese as *korinto*. The *korinto geemu* ("Corinth game") quickly became popular among candy-store owners as a come-on for kids. But adults liked to play too, and the crowding inside the tiny stores soon became a problem. The solution, an anonymous innovator discovered in 1926, was to turn the *korinto geemu* machines upright.

The new game, called *gachanko,* was also a hit, but it wasn't until after World War II that, rechristened as *pachinko,* it truly came into its own. During those dark days of hard work and hunger, when amusement was scarce, *pachinko* became popular as a cheap way to kill time while earning a little spare cash.

But though *pachinko* parlors quickly spread throughout the land, they acquired a murky reputation as resorts of despised minorities (including the aforementioned ethnic Koreans), gangsters, and other fringe types. The gangs, with their strong roots in Japan's gambling subculture, naturally gravitated toward *pachinko,* managing the parlors or the hole-in-wall "gift-exchange centers" (*keihin kokanjo*) where *pachinko* patrons traded their prizes for cash.

Among their patrons were the professional players, or *pachipuro,* who made a living, sometimes quite a good one, from the machines. There were also the con artists, or *gotoshi,* who made another kind of living by surreptitiously fixing the machines, using a magnet to guide the balls toward the holes or inserting a piano wire or plastic strip behind the window to open the the tulip-shaped plastic "flowers" or "tulips" (*chuurippu*) that allowed players to snag more balls.

But in the late 1970s, as the Japanese GNP continued its upward climb and new forms of indoor recreation appeared, including Space Invaders, Pac Man, and other high-tech arcade games, it seemed that *pachinko* might be left behind in the cultural backwash, a relic of the hardscrabble post-war days.

Instead of being left behind, however, *pachinko* flourished and, in the 1990s, positively boomed. In the five years from 1989 to 1994 parlor revenues nearly doubled. One reason was that, as thrilling as Space Invaders, Super Mario, and their many successors may have been to teenagers with time to kill and a few yen in their jeans, they didn't pay off in anything more than points. No fun there for *pachinko's* addicted gamblers.

Also, *pachinko* itself began to change with the debut of new games and machines, such as *pachisuro,* a hybrid game that combined the revolving drum of the slot *(suro)* machine and the flying balls of *pachinko,* and digitalized machines called *dijipachi renchan* that gave winners the chance to hit the jackpot several times in quick succession. Debuting in the late 1980s, these new machines jacked up the odds—players at cold machines could easily send fifty or sixty thousand yen flying down the holes—but offered winners bigger payoffs.

Authorities, however, frowned on *dijipachi renchan,* which they felt "stimulated the spirit of gambling," and in March 1993 effectively prohibited their sale. The nation's *pachinko* machine makers responded to this threat to their livelihoods by developing CR (Card Reader) machines, which players operated with prepaid cards. First appearing in August 1992, CR machines were digitalized like the *dijipachi renchan* but did not give the same super-payoffs—a turnoff for many *pachinko* addicts.

The CR machines offered advantages for owners, however. Instead of relying on the services of a "nail artist," or *kugishi*—a highly skilled professional who adjusted the machines' pins to pay more or less, depending on the parlor's balance sheet—the owners could set the CR machines' payoff at three different levels, each with clearly defined odds, making the calculation of potential profits and losses easier. The machines still had pins, of course, but adjusting them became a simpler chore, requiring tweaks to only the most crucial ones. The *kugishi* soon found work harder to come by.

The CR machines also pleased the authorities. Because they recorded payoffs in their internal memories, the taxmen could check the machines' computer read-out against the parlor's tax statement and crack down on cheaters. Also, the cops could more easily tell if owners had rigged the machines to rip off customers. (Not a common offense, really; owners who skim more than the usual thirteen or fourteen percent soon find themselves with an empty parlor.) By 1996 the police had persuaded seventy percent of Japan's parlor owners to introduce CR machines.

The new CR machines, which required less skill to read and operate, initially leveled the *pachinko* playing field. But con artists were soon figuring out ways to beat them, including the manufacture of forged prepaid cards. For fiscal 1995, the suppliers of prepaid cards reported the loss of a staggering sixty-three billion yen caused by the fake cards. *Pachinko* parlors, which had been reimbursed by the card companies for the used cards—forged or not—were not affected by the scam.

After taking financial hits large enough to wreck the entire prepaid card system, card suppliers introduced card inspection machines (though sophisticated cheaters could still beat them) and temporarily invalidated prepaid cards of the two largest denominations, the most frequent targets of the forgers. Also, the police moved against the Asian gangsters who were supposedly the main card forgers. In February 1996, Tokyo police arrested members of a Chinese card-forging ring and confiscated 15,500 fake cards.

Parlor owners were not happy with this crackdown, however: in May a parlor owners association sent a letter to the two largest card suppliers, complaining about the cost of maintaining the CR machines and lamenting the loss of the five-thousand- and ten-thousand-yen cards. The card suppliers indignantly countered that more than a few parlor owners were cooperating with the forgers. Some owners were reportedly even opening up their parlors after hours to let favored customers play with fake cards.

In November 1996 representatives of two leading card makers visited the Japan Federation of Pachinko Business Industry Association of Tokyo, an organization of 18,000 parlor operators, to propose abolishing the 10,000 yen card altogether and delaying the reissue of the 5,000 yen card. Fearing a loss of business if high rollers could no longer buy the high denomination cards,

the Federation countered that stopping forgers and cheaters should come first. Talks between the two sides ended inconclusively.

While this dispute raged on, other less controversial technological developments were sweeping the *pachinko* world. In 1991, Nagoya-based Daikoku Denki introduced the Data Robo, an in-house *pachinko* data system that told players which machines had recently hit the jackpot and how much they had paid. Many owners, who had considered such information top secret, regarded this as a radical idea. The players, however, loved Data Robo and soon super parlors were installing it as a draw. Even the pros admitted that Data Robo made it easier to calculate the payoff odds on a given machine, though it didn't always pick a winner. (Given the owners' ability to fiddle with the settings, a machine that had drawn blanks 1,999 times straight would not necessarily pay off on game 2000.)

Today Data Robo offers more than odds; it can tell your fortune by studying your biorhythm, give you info about neighborhood restaurants and night spots, tell you the local train schedule, issues tickets for free parking and umbrella rental, and even post messages (but not, presumably, to the wife who is waiting at home).

In December 1995, to meet the needs of on-the-go types, Daikoku launched Pokerobo, a PDA (personal digital assistant) that

Bells clang, lights flash, and balls spin in pachinko, Japan's own home-grown gambling obsession.

gives players the latest *pachinko* machine updates wherever they might be, as well as serving as a phone book, calculator, and world clock. By the end of February 1997 Daikoku had sold more than 200,000 to parlors, who use them as exchange gifts.

Daikoku Denki has also gone on-line. In October 1994 it started sending odds info over a PC-VAN network to the P Arc Konoguchi parlor, and by February 1997 had expanded this network to five parlors, with more on the way. The company has also developed Pachinko Now, a broadcasting service that transmits *pachinko* info directly to players' homes via cable TV and satellite, allowing them pick their machine in the comfort of their own living rooms. In February 1996 Kasugai Cable, an Aichi Prefecture cable operator, became the first to offer Pachinko Now programs to its subscribers.

Yet another recent Daikoku innovation is Robo Card, the *pachinko* version of a smart card. Robo Card holders can record their winnings on the card and keep it when they leave the parlor, to play another day. One advantage for owners is that card holders keep coming back to try for bigger scores. Another is that, instead of cashing in their winnings, holders usually ask for prizes, which tend to be more stylish and expensive than lighter flints, helping parlors clean up their gambling-den image.

Robo Card holders can also use the card at forty thousand C-System outlets nationwide to purchase discount goods and services, including movie, plane, and train tickets. They can even have gourmet food delivered to their homes, send flowers, and obtain information about new and used cars.

In addition to offering more perks and services, many of which have nothing to do with *pachinko*, owners are trying to attract new players by building *pachinko* palaces that are the industry's answer to Circus Circus and Caesar's Palace. One, I-BIC Nagaoka in Nagaoka, Niigata Prefec-ture, which opened in March 1996, is a sprawling *pachinko* complex whose attractions include restaurants, a CD store, and a convenience store. Patrons can use their *pachinko* cards to pay for anything in the clean, well-lighted place. Another, Aizen Raga Ikebukuro, which debuted in the Ikebukuro sub-center of Tokyo in December 1995, offers eight floors of *pachinko* action, each with a different theme. There are a total of 584 *pachinko* machines, including all the popular new models.

As *pachinko*'s social position improves and its popularity spreads beyond middle-aged salarymen and other uncool types, more companies are viewing it as a promising growth business. Among them are arcade-game manufacturers, who see a log-

ical fit between their products and the new digitalized *pachinko* machines, both of which use colorful liquid-crystal displays. In 1991, Konami began to manufacture liquid-crystal displays for *pachinko* machines and, in 1994, opened its first parlor, Deruka Deruyo (The name roughly translates as "Will It Pay? It'll Pay"). Since then, Konami has begun making liquid-crystal displays with its own character logos and opened another parlor in Tokyo, while proclaiming that *pachinko*, game centers, and game software would become the three pillars of its business.

Another corporate powerhouse seeking its own *pachinko* synergy is the Daiei supermarket group, which began managing parlors through a group company called Pandora in 1994 and had opened thirteen by February 1997. "We are already operating hotels and an amusement park, Yokohama Dreamland. *Pachinko* makes a good fit with our other leisure businesses," said Daiei Public Relations manager Katsunori Tanaka. "We are trying to make our parlors places where anyone, including women, can feel safe to enter."

As might be expected, most of these parlors are located in shopping malls near a Daiei store. One of the newest, the Pandora Shin Kobe, which opened near Shin Kobe Station in October 1995, has installed special "couples seats" for dating couples and chilled lockers for patrons' groceries. The parlor operates a members' card club that sends members information about new machines and updates on all machines, including recent big jackpots. Also, the card used to record winnings is the OMC Card, the Daiei Group card. If the law prohibiting the exchange of *pachinko* balls outside the parlor for money and prizes is changed, it will someday be possible to use *pachinko* winnings on the OMC Card to pay for Daiei groceries, although some patrons may end up sending their grocery money down the *pachinko* hole.

These and other innovations aimed at making *pachinko* a socially acceptable leisure activity for both sexes and all ages (not quite all; the legal age for playing *pachinko* is eighteen) may draw more fresh-faced beginners, increase the take of parlor owners, and please the authorities, but they don't really explain *pachinko*'s strong hold on its Japanese fans—a hold so strong that in 1996 several female players made headlines for neglecting their children, including letting them suffocate in locked cars, while they satisfied their *pachinko* addiction.

PINK LADY

In Japan the 1970s was the golden age of the packaged pop star, who rose to fame virtually overnight on the popular prime-time TV music shows and became, for a brief season, as much a fixture on the tube as chocolate bar and INSTANT RAMEN commercials. In fact, for the talent agencies and record companies that packaged these stars, including their songs, clothes, stage choreography, and personal lives, a contract to appear in TV and print ads as the "face" of a certain product was a vital part of the money-spinning machine.

Rather than losing status by plugging a brand of potato chips or curry rice, the pop stars gained precious name recognition that translated into bigger record and concert-ticket sales. It was products selling products selling products. Of course, this particular wheel didn't turn forever; TV viewers tired of the pitchmen (or women) almost as quickly as they tired of the saturation ads, but by that time the packagers had already made their pile and were already grooming other young talents for instant stardom.

The stars who exemplified this process the most spectacularly were a singing and dancing duo called Pink Lady who skyrocketed to fame in 1976, reeled off nine straight number-one singles, and at the end of the decade plummeted to oblivion with the finality of an empty soda can disappearing into a compacter, drained to the lees by the media and public.

Hailing from Shizuoka Prefecture, Japan's nearest cultural equivalent to Kansas, Mitsuyo Nemoto and Keiko Masuda were a schoolgirl folk duo when they passed the audition for *Star Tanjo!* (Birth of a Star!), an amateur talent show that groomed a few lucky contestants for TV stardom (see **YAMAGUCHI, MOMOE**). When they made their first appearance on the show in February 1976, the girls wore bib overalls and had all the polished sophistication of Dorothy in her first encounter with the Great Oz. But they also had a fresh-faced energy and charm that persuaded the show's judges to pass them and show's producers to invite them back.

Six months later, when they appeared on TV to promote their debut single, "Peppa Keibu" (Pepper Police Inspector) they were utterly transformed. Gone forever were the overalls, replaced by slinky, spangly minidressses. Gone too were the plaintive chords of their girlish folk tunes, replaced by infectious disco rhythms and goofy-but-catchy lyrics that, once heard, were impossible to dislodge from the brain.

But what most astonished about the reborn Pink Lady was their dancing; an odd combination of youthful vitality, sexy moves, and robotic precision, as though they were cloned cyborgs who'd learned how to boogie. As repeated viewings on TV made clear, they'd been programmed to dance exactly the same way every time, as though executing a disco version of karate *kata*.

To the Japanese TV audience, used to seeing female pop singers make archly stylized hand gestures to accompany their bubble-gum melodies, the hard bootie-shaking of Pink Lady hit like a visual bombshell. At the same time, the strenuous athleticism of their dancing and the utter lack of suggestiveness in their songs seemed to reassure adults that, though they could disco like Americans, Mii and Kei, as they were soon universally known, were really good, clean, hard-working Japanese girls, who were about as threatening to the morals of youth as *Bon* festival folk dancers.

Kids loved them too; unlike the endless procession of look-alike, move-alike pop singers who came and passed like a blur on their TV screens, Mii and Kei were instantly recognizable, comfortingly predictable, and excitingly unreal, like living action dolls. Children's books appeared with step-by-step instructions on how to imitate the choreography of the latest Pink Lady song. Soon, even preschoolers were trying out the moves in front of the TV.

"Peppa Keibu" climbed to number four on the charts and sold 605,000 copies. In December 1976 they released their second single, "SOS." It became their first number-

Like cloned cyborgs who'd learned how to boogie: Pink Lady at their mid-1970s peak.

one record, selling 655,000 copies. The Pink Lady boom was launched.

Their moment at the top was brief, from the summer of 1976 to the end of 1978. But while it lasted, Mii and Kei owned the TV airwaves as no other performers had in the medium's history. They not only appeared on every pop music and variety show to plug their latest hits, bringing with them an instant two- or three-point gain in the ratings, but contracted as commercial pitchwomen for eleven companies, a total seldom equaled or surpassed.

When an educational magazine for kids hired them as "image talents" (*imeeji tarento,* or cover girls), it immediately surged to a sales lead of one hundred thousand copies over its rivals. An ice cream brand that had their picture on its package recorded a fourfold gain in sales. When a shampoo maker used them in its ads, suddenly kids all across the country were demanding to have their hair washed with the Pink Lady brand.

As hit followed hit and the duo's popularity reached its peak in 1978, the industry paid its respects with awards, including the Japan Song Prize for "Southpaw" (whose choreography included pitching motions) and the Japan Record Prize for "UFO" (a great favorite with the grade-school crowd).

In addition to receiving these accolades, Mii and Kei were busy expanding their professional range. In April they played their first U.S. gig, at the Tropicana Hotel in Las Vegas (Mii sang Nillson's "Without You," Kei, The Animals' "House of the Rising Sun"). In December they released their first movie, *Pink Lady Katsudo Daishashin* (The Big Picture of the Pink Lady on the Go) and had their first U.S. recording session for their first English-language single, "Love Countdown."

Toward the end of their miracle year, Mii and Kei were riding so high that they decided to turn down an invitation to appear on NHK's **KOHAKU UTA GASSEN** (Red-and-White Song Contest) in favor of a competing charity show on NTV called *Pink Lady Ase to*

Namida no Omisoka 150 Pun!! (Pink Lady's 150 Minutes of Sweat and Tears on New Year's Eve!!).

This, in Japanese show-business terms, was the equivalent of passing on the Grammy awards show to perform on a cable TV telethon in the same time slot. The mighty Pink Lady took a thrashing in the ratings—scoring only 8.2 percent compared with *Kohaku's* 72.2 percent. Also, when the duo's managers told the media that they were inviting students from a school for the blind to the taping session, school officials publicly complained that they hadn't been consulted about the announcement. It looked as though the Pink Lady were using blind kids to hype their TV show—and their squeaky clean image received its first serious blemish.

As it turned out, this New Year's fiasco signaled the beginning of the end. The Pink Lady's first release of 1979, "Jipangu," reached only number four on the charts, ending their streak of number-one hits. Their next record, "Pink Typhoon," was covered by The Village People, but ran out of gas at number six and sold a disappointing 290,000 copies. Though their single for July, "Nami Nori Pirates" (Surf Riding Pirates) used members of the Beach Boys as a back-up group, it stalled at number four.

Ironically, as their fortunes declined in Japan, Mii and Kei started to find more opportunities abroad. In the summer of 1979, they starred on a summer replacement show for the NBC network, whose ratings sailed as high as 32 percent. In July they had their first worldwide release, "A Kiss In the Dark," which reached number 37 on the Billboard chart (The B side was a remake of the Left Bank's "Let's Walk Away Renee"). Unfortunately, the show was gone by the fall and Pink Lady never released another record in the U.S.

After failing to find success in the U.S. market, Mii and Kei struggled on for another year in Japan, but by the end, they couldn't give their records away. In March 1981 they had their last hurrah—a concert at Korakuen Stadium—and disbanded. But for Hisashi Aku, who wrote their lyrics, Shun'ichi Tokura, who composed their songs, Hajime Doi, who choreographed their dance numbers, Hisahiko Iida, who produced their records for Victor, and T&S, the talent agency that managed their careers, the decline and fall of Pink Lady was only a temporary setback. These folks were among the best in the business and had other big-name clients dependent on their services, other young talents to turn into stars. They had little time to waste on regrets for has beens. As lyricist Aku reportedly told the president of T&S, "[Pink Lady] should have disbanded a year sooner."

Mii and Kei no doubt agreed. After it was all over Kei told an interviewer that, from the beginning, "I was very aware that we were a product." Mii simply said, "After we announced we were splitting up I felt tremendously relieved."

In 1982 Mii shed her Pink Lady image for good when she made a shocking comeback as the star of *Call Girl,* a movie about a woman who sells herself to save her former lover from a gang of Middle East terrorists. (She used the professional name MIE, written in Roman capital letters, as though to remind fans of her brief moment of international success.) Kei, who had planned to quit show business entirely, made occasional TV appearances. In 1988, they reunited for an appearance on *Kohaku Uta Gassen*—the show that had given Pink Lady its first serious setback and, the following year, had not invited them to appear, despite their still impressive string of hits. If Mii and Kei still had any hard feelings about these decade-old wounds they did not show them. It had all been so very long ago.

In the mid-nineties, Pink Lady became a hot nostalgia item; prices of Pink Lady posters, fanzines, and other memorabilia went through the roof and sales of the group's albums began to perk up. Seeing another boom to exploit, the T&S agency launched a Pink Lady copy group, called Pink Lady X (for Generation X?), in September 1996. Idol groups, like soda cans, may be discarded, but they can also be recycled.

POWER RANGERS

It's hardly news that the Mighty Morphin' Power Rangers show is not the all-American product it appears to be, that its action sequences were made in Japan. (Not that the majority of its audience cares). What may be news, however (good or bad depending on which side of the generation gap you sit), is that the show is just the tip of the software iceberg.

The original producer, Toei, has been turning out similar shows for more than two decades in Japan, since the debut of *Go Ranger* (Five Rangers) on TV Asahi in 1975. The formula—a band of masked, color-coded superheros battle various space monsters and, in the finale, climb into a giant robot and vaporize a giant robot opponent—has been set in concrete since the beginning. Despite the sameness and the silliness, Toei has managed to make what it calls its "five-hero" shows an inescapable part of growing up for Japanese boys (as well as for a few girls) and their parents.

For a five-year-old boy, a department-store expedition during the New Year's holiday (when kids get envelopes of New Year's money from parents and relatives) is not complete unless it ends with a few spinoffs from the latest show, from simple plastic replicas of the heroes to elaborate transformer toys that only an aeronautical engi-

neer—or a savvy kid—could master at first try.

Also, the entire cast of heroes and monsters changes every year with the arrival of a new TV season. By the time the next New Year holiday rolls around, the old show is dim in its audience's memory and the old spinoffs must be replaced by new ones that, to the adult eye at least, look nearly the same, the only differences being the shape of the heroes' helmets and the cut of their costumes. But these differences are vital to the five-year-old eye, so out comes the adult wallet and away fly a few more ten-thousand-yen notes.

Understandably, Toei was eager to export this money-spinning machine abroad and had great success with it, first in Southeast Asia, then in Europe and Latin America. In

the mid-1980s the "five-hero" shows were so popular in Brazil that stations were broadcasting three or four a day, until the inevitable audience burnout occurred.

Toei thought that kids in North America might respond with equal enthusiasm, but it found U.S. buyers a tough sell. The Big Three networks, in particular, had no interest in the shows, which they regarded as too bizarre and violent for American tastes. In 1988 Toei sold one series, *Metaldar,* to TV producer and distributor Saban Entertainment, but it never caught on. The outlook for cracking the world's most lucrative TV market was grim.

Then Saban bought another series, called *Kyoryu Sentai Ju Ranger* (Dinosaur Attack Force Beast Rangers) in Japan and *Galaxy Rangers* overseas, changed the title to *Mighty Morphin' Power Rangers,* and reshot the non-action scenes with American actors. Also, though the original show, which was broadcast in Japan in 1992, featured only one female Ranger, Saban added another and, to further ensure the show's political correctness, made one of them white and one Asian-American, while hiring one white, one African-American, and one Hispanic actor to play the three male roles.

To avoid offending parental sensibilities, Saban changed the realistic whams and bams of fist hitting flesh in the original sound track to metallic crashes that it hoped would not sound as violent. Thus prepared, Saban sold the show to the Fox Children's Network, which began broadcasting it in September 1993 on one hundred eighty stations. The show soon became a runaway hit and by the Christmas shopping season parents across the country were scouring stores for Power Rangers toys.

Japanese toymaker Bandai, which had been making toys for the "five-hero" shows since the beginning, watched the sales of its U.S. subsidiary soar to 39.6 billion yen in 1994, a jump of ten times compared with the previous year. "The key was Fox's decision to broadcast the program," said Bandai senior managing director Katsushi Murakami. "If they hadn't picked it up, the toys would never have become a hit. Also, the show filled a gap; there were no live-action shows for kids on American television. Finally, it was lucky in its timing; its dinosaur-based character designs fit right in with the dinosaur boom that had been launched by *Jurassic Park*."

But Murakami, who orchestrated the company's U.S. character-merchandising effort, admits that Bandai's decades of making and selling character goods in Japan also had something to do with the eye-popping sales figures. "We had enough confidence in our products to bring them to the American market unchanged," he said. "We knew that they would appeal to kids in America just as they had to kids in Japan—and we were right."

The Power Rangers craze couldn't continue at the same fever pitch forever, of course. In the summer of 1995, Twentieth Century Fox's forty-million-dollar *Mighty Morphin' Power Rangers* movie struggled to cover its production cost at the box office. Also, at Christmas kids did not put Power Rangers toys quite so high on their lists and sales sagged. But in 1996 the show, now in its third season, was still number one in its time slot and Saban was preparing its fourth Power Rangers series.

Toei and Saban were also finding new markets for their creation outside the United States: kids all over Southeast Asia were tuning in the show, as well as many in South America, Europe, and Africa. Toei even reimported the Power Rangers show to Japan and

TV Asahi began broadcasting it in September 1995, but the early time slot—6:00 A.M. on Saturday—held ratings down.

In partnership with Toei, Saban has produced two other superhero series for the U.S. market: *VR Troopers,* which it launched in syndication in the fall of 1994, and *Masked Rider,* which it debuted on the Fox Network in the fall of 1995. Like the Power Rangers, both used footage and storylines from the original Japanese programs and both became hits with young viewers. "No one makes these shows better than we do," says Toei sales manager Yukio Homma. "Others have tried, but it takes a certain know-how to do them right. After more than two decades, we have that know-how."

RIKIDOZAN

Television got off to a late start in Japan. The first commercial broadcasts, by the Nippon Television Network, did not begin until 1953, when all America was already going gaga over *I Love Lucy.* Also, the first fourteen-inch sets cost 140,000 yen at a time when the average monthly salary of a first-year civil servant with a high-school diploma was just 5,400 yen.

To stir up interest in the new media, manufacturers put TVs on stands in public places. Crowds, mainly male, gathered by the hundreds and thousands to watch *sumo* bouts and boxing matches. But the figure on those flickering black-and-white screens that attracted the biggest crowds and drew the biggest cheers was a beefy, bare-chested man in black leotards and high lace-up shoes. His name was Rikidozan and he was Japan's first TV star.

A former *sumo* wrestler who had quit the sport in 1950 after a falling out with his stablemaster—he cut off his own *sumo* topknot with a kitchen knife in a fit of anger—Rikidozan had turned pro wrestler in 1951 at the request of Tokyo's Torii Oasis Shrine Club. The Shriners were sponsoring a pro-wrestling benefit to raise money for disabled children and needed local heroes to step into the ring against American wrestlers led by former world champion Bobby Bruns. Though he had only a week's training in the sport, Riki acquitted himself well and found a new profession. He went twice to the United States, once for training under Bruns and once for a series of matches with American opponents. When Riki returned to Japan, he had slimmed from his *sumo* weight of 265 pounds to 250 pounds of solid brawn and could drop kick with the best of them.

As Japan's first American-style pro wrestler, Riki could find few homegrown victims to practice his new techniques on. So he did the logical thing: fight foreigners, or *gaijin.*

When the viewers of those open-air TVs saw Riki laying into a big, hairy *gaijin* with his trademark karate chop and toppling him like a rotten tree, they went wild. Japan had been beaten by the Americans in the war, ruled by the Americans during the Occupation, and outstripped by the Americans in so many ways, material, technological, and cultural. While Japanese were leading pinched existences in bombed-out cities and working day and night to fill their stomachs in the early postwar years, Americans were driving fancy cars, living in big houses, and pouring whiskey from cut-glass decanters (at least, that's how it looked in the movies).

But now this big, strong Japanese guy was putting it to the *gaijin,* with style! With every karate chop, Riki struck a blow for Japanese national pride. He became every boy's hero and almost single-handedly made pro wrestling a major spectator sport in Japan.

In 1955, at the then-enormous cost of seventy-five million yen, Riki built a five-story wrestling center in downtown Tokyo, complete with a gym, a dormitory, and a movie theater where wrestlers could polish their techniques by watching films of their bouts. Here Riki trained the next generation of grapplers and prepared himself for bouts against Asian champion King Kong—a man-mountain with a Wolfman Jack goatee—and Mexican champion Jesus Ortega.

But he attracted the biggest crowds and the most media attention—mainstream Japanese newspapers covered pro wrestling just as they would baseball or *sumo*—for his stompings of real (i.e., Caucasian) *gaijin,* including former heavyweight champ Primo Carnera, Pacific Coast pro-wrestling champ Tom Rice, and world champ Lou Thesz. (Following Riki's September 1958 victory over Thesz in Los Angeles, American wire services informed their Japanese newspaper colleagues that Thesz was only a self-proclaimed "champion," but Riki stoutly maintained that he was the real thing.)

Riki's most fondly remembered triumphs were those over Mike and Ben Sharpe, NWA tag-team champions. The brothers came to Japan in February 1954 for the first international wrestling match on Japanese soil. Riki and former judoist Masahiko Kimura's tussle with the Sharps, from which they emerged victorious, was broadcast live and attracted huge crowds at open-air TV sets.

In 1958 Riki, together with partner Kokichi Endo, faced the Sharps again during their six-week tour of Japan. Known for their nastiness in the ring, these two bad-guy brothers fell victim time and time again to Riki's mighty body slams and merciless karate chops. The culmination came on

Japan's first television star, Rikidozan wowed fans in the 1950s with his trademark karate chop.

May 4, 1958, when in front of twelve thousand screaming fans in Osaka, he pinned Ben with a toe hold to win the World Tag Team Championship. After scaling this height, what other worlds could he conquer?

Riki, though, was not quite the All-Japanese Boy that his fans loved and admired. He had been born Kim Shin-Nak in a village near the port of Wonsan, in what is now North Korea. Though Riki claimed that his birthdate was November 14, 1924, there is now considerable evidence, experts say, that he was actually born earlier, in 1921 or 1923. Korea was then under Japanese rule and, as Japanese subjects, Koreans were required to take Japanese names. Kim's was Mitsuhiro Kanamura.

Scouted by a former military police officer at an amateur *sumo* tournament, the teenage Kanamura came to Tokyo and entered Nishonoseki Stable. His stablemaster gave him his ring name, Rikidozan (Strength-Way-Mountain), which he kept throughout his career. Mercilessly teased by his Japanese stablemates because of his poor Japanese, Riki worked hard to master the language and was soon speaking it fluently enough to pass as a native. He tried to pass as a native for the rest of his life.

Not everyone was fooled, however. When Riki's former tag-team partner, Masahiko Kimura, challenged Riki at an All-Japan

Championship Bout in December 1954, it was rumored that one of his aims was to make the pro-wrestling champ of Japan a real Japanese. To that end, he and his handlers tried to persuade Riki to accept a tie, but Riki refused. When this attempted fix was exposed, Kimura claimed that there had been "a prior agreement" between the two sides. The bout itself was hard fought, with Kimura delivering kicks to the groin and trying other dirty tricks (at least according to Riki's supporters), but Riki emerged triumphant—and the secret of his origin remained a secret.

Many fans, however, knew that Riki liked to brawl outside the ring almost as much as he did inside it. A heavy drinker and habitual pub crawler, he frequently found his name in the papers for roughing up civilians, including a bar girl, a taxi driver, a building contractor, and several carpenters he had caught goofing off at the construction site of the Riki Turkish Bath Center, yet another of his businesses. But no matter how many eyes he blackened and jaws he dislocated, Riki never served time; he was too popular and powerful to be put away in the slammer.

Better hidden than his scrapes with the law, though, were his close ties with gangsters and his heavy debts, most of which he had accumulated in real-estate deals and construction projects. In addition to his Turkish bath, he built a sprawling apartment complex called the Riki Apartments, a glitzy nightclub in Akasaka called the Riki, and, in 1961, the Riki Sports Palace. A nine-story domed sports arena in Shibuya that covered 6,600 square meters and cost 400 million yen, the Palace was Riki's ultimate monument to himself.

It was Riki's hot temper that finally killed him. On the night of December 8, 1963 at the Latin Quarter Night Club, he got into an argument with a twenty-five-year-old gangster named Katsushi Murata. Later claiming Riki had insulted him, Murata drew a knife and drove it into Riki's stomach. Staggering up to the stage and grabbing a mike, Riki told the startled crowd that he'd been stabbed and asked them to go home.

Taken to nearby Sanno Hospital, he was treated and kept for observation. Though he seemed to be recovering well from the wound, a few days later he suddenly developed peritonitis. The doctors operated again, but Riki went into shock and died on December 15. According to a recent biography, Riki's death was caused by malpractice; after his second operation the doctor in charge prescribed several times the normal dose of painkillers, reasoning that Riki was far bigger and tougher than the average Japanese man. Riki then went into a coma and died not from peritonitis but the drug overdose.

Only a few days before the stabbing, Riki had successfully defended his Pro Wrestling World Championship for the nineteenth straight time in a title bout with yet another big American lug, The Destroyer. Like James Cagney in *White Heat,* Riki went out on top of the world.

ROCKABILLY, GROUP SOUNDS & THE BIRTH OF JAPANESE ROCK

Japanese have long been importing American pop-culture phenomena and making them their own, but few crossed the Pacific quicker than rock'n'roll. Soon after Elvis Presley started to shake, rattle, and roll America, a few enterprising Japanese youths playing in then-popular country-and-western bands switched their allegiance to a music they called *rokabiri* (rockabilly) and started practicing their hip swivels. Soon rockabilly clubs, such as Tennessee in the Ginza, were drawing big crowds eager to catch these Japanese cowboys singing "Louisiana Mama" and "Blue Suede Shoes."

What gave this genre its first big boost toward nationwide recognition, however, was the first Western Carnival, a week-long festival of country-and-western and rockabilly music held from February 8, 1958, at Tokyo's Nichigeki Theatre. The three biggest rockabilly stars—Masaaki Hirao, Keijiro Yamashita, and Mickey Curtis—appeared and drove the crowd, especially the girls, wild. Fans screamed, danced, and rushed the stage. Some of the bolder ones tossed streamers, confetti, and panties at the twisting, shouting, perspiring performers.

A total of forty-five thousand fans showed up for this first-ever rock festival in Japan—a house record. Few of them knew that the rockabilly artists were only covering songs by Elvis, Carl Perkins, Gene Vincent, and other American stars. They thought they were getting the real thing. (They did get a taste of the real thing when Paul Anka showed up at the third Western Carnival, in September, to sing his new hit "Diana," which is still a fixture in *karaoke*-club songbooks.)

Japanese rockabilly didn't remain purely imitative for long. For one thing, the singers needed new material to pad their still skimpy rock repertoire. Masaaki Hirao, who had been the lead singer for a country-and-western band called All Stars Wagon, arranged Japanese folk songs and even children's songs to a rock beat. Then in 1958 he released "Hoshi wa Nandemo Shiteiru" (The Stars Know All)—the first made-in-Japan rock song. It became a big hit, paving the way for other recordings by rockabilly stars. But rather than let them play the kind of music that made them famous, record companies made rockabilly artists record material that sounded suspiciously like Japanese pop music, with its sweet melodies and smilingly inoffensive lyrics, or, in some cases, even *enka,* emotion-drenched ballads about loss and loneliness that the Japanese themselves often describe as "Japanese country and western."

But despite their hassles with the music-industry Establishment, rockabilly artists became fashion leaders, especially among the urban young. Soon members of the "Rockabilly Tribe," or *rokabiri-zoku,* were cruising the Ginza in leather jackets and wide "mambo" pants, their hair sculpted in the waterfall "regent" style. These early greasers were joined by Japan's first motorcycle gangs—the so-called "Thunder Tribe," or *kaminari-zoku.* Rock'n'roll culture seemed here to stay.

But though these pioneers set styles that would influence teenage rebels through the decades, rockabilly proved to be a fleeting fad. For one thing, the older generation, concerned about its deleterious effect on youth, hated it. After the wild scenes at the early Western Carnival concerts were reported widely in the media, TV networks banned rockabilly acts from the air for two years and local authorities refused to give them permits to stage their shows.

For another, in America the raucousness of early rock was giving way to the softer, more melodic sounds of pop balladeers like Paul Anka, Neil Sedaka, and Connie Francis, sounds that local kids, who had been raised on *enka* and Japanese pop, not R&B, found more familiar and their parents found more acceptable.

In 1959 Fuji TV launched *The Hit Parade*—a music request show that was the first to offer a venue for Japanized versions of Western pop songs. Rockabilly star Mickey Curtis, sporting a neatly trimmed regent hairdo and wearing a suit, appeared on the show as a host. With the surge of television-set sales in the late 1950s, artists like The Peanuts—identical twin sisters who were chipmunk-cute, had a pleasing stage presence, and could even sing—became national stars for their interpretations of Western pop hits. The other commercial nets and NHK launched their own music shows, with names like *Spark Show, Hoi Hoi Music School,* and *Yume de Aimasho* (Let's Meet in Our Dreams), and by the early 1960s living rooms across the country were echoing with the strains of "Vacation," "Hey Paula," and "I Wanna Be Bobby's Girl," all sung by local performers in Japanese. Latin rhythms and European pop music also provided ample fodder for the Western music-show mill.

But while Japanese singers were cheerfully recycling the U.S. top forty on TV, local songwriters were using the new Western musical influences to create Japanese pop music. Among the biggest and certainly the best remembered of the early 1960s made-in-Japan pop hits was "Ue o Muite Aruko" (I'll Walk With My Head Up) by **KYU SAKAMOTO**, a former lead vocalist with the rockabilly group Paradise King. Released in 1961, this catchy song about smiling through your tears hit the top of the Japanese pop charts and, in 1963, shot to number one in the United States as "Sukiyaki."

But pop stars had to have wholesome good looks and charm as well as singing talent to thrive in a TV-driven musical marketplace, and big talent agencies like Watanabe Production were soon scouting and grooming young singers who fit the bill. Among the most popular were a trio of teenage girls—Mie Nakao, Yukari Ito, and Mari Sono—under contract to Watanabe. Following their appearance in the hit 1963 teen movie *Hai, Hai Sannin Musume* (Yes, Yes, The Three Girls), the agency billed them as—what else?—the Sannin Musume.

Together with such male stars as Hisahiko Iida, a sweet-voiced crooner who sang cover versions of Del Shannon and Gene Pitney hits, and Takashi Fujiki, a broodingly handsome singer whose nickname was "The Twist Man," they established a pattern for the hundreds of "idol singers" (*idoru kashu*) that the talent agencies would manufacture in the years to come. Though their music may have been heavily influenced by American sounds, the TV idol singers and their handlers passed it through a Japanese filter, straining out nearly all of the American-style rock rebelliousness. In tapes of TV performances by these early rock-pop stars, it's easy to hear echoes of the American models but almost impossible to spot an Elvis-like sneer. Instead, everyone looks bright, chipper, and eager to please, even when wailing "Hound Dog."

But just when Japanese pop seemed doomed to total cooption by the talent agencies, record companies, and TV networks, a music explosion occurred that changed the local scene forever. In February 1964, when the Beatles paid their first visit to the United States, they released their first single in Japan: "I Wanna Hold Your Hand," or as it was titled in Japanese, "Dakishimetai" (I Want to Hold You). Like the rest of the world, Japanese kids became Beatlemaniacs.

In March a copy band appeared called the Tokyo Beatles. The two lead vocalists couldn't play instruments, so the new foursome hired a drummer and guitarist to provide backup. In April, soon after the band played their first gig, they released a cover single featuring "I Wanna Hold Your Hand"

and "Please Please Me." Although the group was successful at generating publicity, their boomlet quickly ended when record buyers had a chance to listen to their ragged Japanese-language cover and compare it to the real thing. The Tokyo Beatles, it turned out, had more hair than musicianship. But though the Tokyo Beatles failed to wow local fans, other Beatles copy bands soon emerged, including the Three Funkies, Cool Cats, and Crazy Beatles.

These groups, not to mention the Beatles themselves, made guitar bands the hot thing. Until then, vocalists and choral groups had dominated the pop scene, but now pop stars had to play the electric guitar (*ereki gitaa*) as well as sing if they really wanted to be hip.

Beatles tunes were not the only foreign sounds to make a big impression and ignite the boom in what the Japanese called *ereki* music, however. In June 1964 a former rockabilly group named Takeshi Terauchi and the Blue Jeans released "Korezo Surfing" (This Is Surfing), Japan's first surf-music album, featuring instrumentals by the group's three guitarists and one organist, none of whom had even been near a surf board. In May 1964 Koichi Fuji released a cover single of the Astronaut's instrumental hit "Movin'" that featured Fuji's own scat lyrics.

But what really set off the electric tsuna-mi was the January 1965 Japan tour of The Ventures and The Astronauts. The Ventures had first come to Japan in May 1962, but had attracted little attention in the local media. Several local bands had tried to imitate their instrumental sounds, however. One was the aforementioned Takeshi Terauchi and the Blue Jeans. Another was Yuzo Kayama and the Launchers (see **WAKA DAISHO**). Started as a pick-up band by movie idol Kayama and several of his actor friends, the group began playing Ventures covers in 1962 and performed in Kayama's *Waka Daisho* series movies.

When the Ventures returned in 1965, however, they were no longer a favorite only among the rock cognoscenti but had become a nationwide sensation. Playing fourteen dates in five cities, the Ventures and another instrumental rock group, the Astronauts, attracted turn-away crowds wherever they went. Soon, not only professional musicians but amateur bands all across the country were buying electric guitars and practicing the chords to "Walk Don't Run" and "Pipeline." Domestic guitar makers couldn't keep up with the demand. To fill it, harmonica maker Tombo and electric-appliance maker Victor (better known abroad as JVC) started to produce electric guitars, as did companies with no connection to either music or electricity, including a maker of wooden clogs. In 1965 guitar production surged to 760,000 units, a number never since equaled.

In June Fuji TV debuted *Kachinuki Ereki Gassen* (Electric Elimination Battle), a battle-of-the-bands show that brought electric rock sounds into every home and gave a few lucky bands a shot at stardom. Inspired by the success of *Kachinuki Ereki Gassen*, music shows proliferated. Then in July The Ventures returned to Japan for a two-month, fifty-eight-date tour that drew 170,000 fans and had the whole country rocking.

The *ereki* boom didn't please everyone. As had rockabilly, the music upset conservative guardians of public morals, who cared for neither the sounds nor the reaction they produced in young fans. The Board of Education of Ashikaga, Tochigi Prefecture, banned the playing of the electric guitar in public, and police in Shizuoka Prefecture cracked down on electric-band dance parties, citing the Act to Control Businesses Which May Affect Public Morals. But though police chiefs, mayors, and other Establishment types vowed to drive the electric guitar from the land, the boom was too big to stop.

Unlike the rockabilly boom, which was largely confined to major urban areas, produced only a handful of stars, and generated little original music, the *ereki* boom was a grassroots phenomenon that made rock a permanent part of the local musical landscape. Although many of the hundreds of rock bands were amateur groups with no aspirations beyond playing at the school festival, dozens of others had serious professional ambitions; they toured, appeared on TV, and cut records.

Among the pioneers was the Spiders, a former rockabilly band that, in May 1965, released a single, "Furi Furi" (Shake, Shake), that was the first Japanese interpretation of the then-popular Liverpool Sound. Then in March 1966 the Blue Comets came out with "Aoi Hitomi" (Blue Eyes), a seminal record that had English lyrics but expressed a distinctly Japanese musical sensibility. In July the group's Japanese version of the same song sold half a million copies.

The impact of these two records on the local scene was huge; suddenly covers were no longer cool, instrumentals were passé. Both the Spiders and the Blue Comets went on to record other hits and lead local rock bands into what came to be known as the Group Sounds era.

Another important progenitor of a made-in-Japan electric sound was Yuzo Kayama. His *Waka Daisho* series entry for 1965, *Ereki no Waka Daisho* (Young Captain of the Electric Guitar) was essentially a movie musical whose signature number, a Kayama ballad titled "Kimi to Itsumademo" (Always Together with You), sold three million copies. The movie itself became the biggest box-office success of the series' seventeen entries

Tigers' lead singer Kenji Sawada (front) later metamorphosed into 1970s glam-rock star Julie.

and Kayama became the biggest single star of the *ereki* boom (though as his strings-backed singing on "Kimi to Itsumademo" indicated, he was really more of a pop crooner than a rocker). In 1966 he released *Exciting Sounds of Yuzo Kayama and the Launchers*—the group's first album. All songs were originals, some with English lyrics. It became an influential hit.

Group Sounds—or GS as it was soon abbreviated in Japanese—represented a break with not only the bland, derivative, TV pop scene but then-standard music-industry practice. Before the advent of the Group Sounds bands, songwriters who wanted to make records had to sign exclusive contracts with record companies and become, in essence, paid employees. The set up was like that of a hierarchical *sumo* stable: music directors trained songwriters who in turn built singers' careers with their hits. But the composer of "Aoi Hitomi," Jun Hashimoto, was a freelancer, and when his record become a hit for Columbia Records, with English lyrics no less, the doors began to open to other noncontract talent and the old closed system began to break down.

The year 1967 saw a horde of GS bands rushing to make their recording debuts. Among the nearly thirty new groups with first records that year were the Outcasts, Tigers, Golden Caps, Carnabies, Jaguars, Beavers, Tempters, Dynamites, and Mops.

Most adopted the longhaired Mod look of mid-1960s Britpop: heavy gold chains, long velvet jackets, frilly shirt fronts, and knee-high lace-up boots. To the white-shirted, blue-suited brigades who were then creating Japan's economic miracle, these fops with guitars looked merely outré. Unlike in the West, the male peacockery of the young barely touched the adult mainstream in Japan.

Among the 1967 crop of GS bands, the two most popular were the Tigers and the Tempters. Both had started as high-school bands in the post-rockabilly era and soared to national prominence through frequent TV appearances. Also, both were fronted by charismatic singers who later went on to long and successful careers: Kenji Sawada of the Tigers and Ken'ichi Hagiwara of the Tempters. In the 1970s Sawada morphed into a rouged and mascara'ed glam-rock star, taking the stage name Julie, while Hagiwara later became a popular light comic actor, appearing in TV dramas and films.

Backed by the powerful Watanabe Production talent agency, the Tigers produced records whose combination of romantic ballads and hard rockers soon had the press calling them Japan's Beatles. The music, together with Sawada's cute looks and the band's hip Mod fashions, won them a huge schoolgirl following. They were the first GS band to play as a single at the Budokan,

then the biggest indoor arena in Japan, and the first to hold a stadium concert.

The Tempters, who had a darker, edgier sound that appealed more to the rock cognoscenti, were dubbed Japan's Rolling Stones. They were the first Japanese group to record in Memphis, then regarded as the mecca of real rock.

But though the Tigers may have had a bigger local following than the Beatles and the Rolling Stones combined, there was one crucial difference between them and their British models: they didn't write their own songs. That chore was handled by Jun Hashimoto ("Aoi Hitomi") and Koichi Sugiyama, who also wrote for many other GS bands. Thus the scorn for the GS boom expressed by later generations of Japanese rock purists, who regard the Tigers and many other GS bands as simply manufactured and manipulated pop products—more like the Monkees than the Beatles and the Stones.

But as innocuous as the GS boom may seem in retrospect—the most popular GS songs were insipid love ballads crooned by foppish young men on TV, not anthems to revolution hymned by drug-addled anarchists—reports of injuries at a November 1967 Tigers concert, as well as news stories of kids running away from home and counterfeiting concert tickets to be near their favorite bands, upset the authorities, who began the by-now-standard crackdowns.

In 1968, at the peak of the GS boom, junior high schools and high schools across the country started suspending and expelling kids caught at GS group concerts. Some even posted teachers at concert hall entrances to nab offenders and printed the names of forbidden groups, including the most "dangerous" of all—the Tigers—in kids' school handbooks. City and prefectural governments did their bit for law and order by refusing to allow GS bands to hold concerts in their facilities. Public broadcaster NHK stopped inviting long haired GS groups to appear on its programs, while giving its seal of approval to short-haired bands like the Blue Comets and the Wild Ones.

Though official intolerance may have shortened the GS boom, what finally killed it was music industry greed. Rather than nurture the few bands with real talent, record companies began to mass produce GS albums and launch dozens of new bands in the hope of scoring with another Tigers or Tempters. By the time the boom passed its peak, in late 1968, nearly one hundred GS bands had released records, far too many for the local market to absorb. Also, the quality of the music itself declined as more groups tried to appeal to the Tigers' thirteen-year-old schoolgirl market with frilly pop fantasies. Sated by the glut of largely mediocre music, fans began to turn away. GS concerts no longer sold out and GS albums were consigned to cutout bins. Finally, in 1971, with the disbanding of the biggest GS bands—the Tigers, the Spiders, Ox, and the Wild Ones—the GS era drew to a close.

Rock, however, didn't disappear from Japan. Many GS musicians resurfaced with new groups and a new sound that derived more from Cream and Led Zeppelin than Gerry and the Pacemakers. But though some of the old faces were still around, in the late 1960s and early 1970s the hipper of the Japanese rock groups firmly rejected the crass commercialism of the Group Sounds era in favor of pure rock sounds. But real ass-kicking rock music appealed to only a small number of music fans, and rock became an underground genre.

In September 1969, in what amounted to a declaration of independence from the iron triumvirate of big record companies, talent agencies, and TV networks, several of the so-called New Rock (*nyuu rokku*) groups held an open-air concert in Tokyo's Hibiya Park, charging ten yen for admission. Though no one made any money, fans packed the park to see groups like Power House and Flowers. Hibiya Park became a mecca for the New Rock scene.

New Rock groups started much the way electric rock bands had nearly a decade earlier, by imitating their foreign idols—there were a lot of long-haired guitarists playing Eric Clapton solos note for note—but as the scene matured in the early 1970s, more groups began to write their own songs, with English being the language of preference. New Rockers felt, first of all, that English was the real language of rock; the music somehow didn't sound right in Japanese. Second, they associated Japanese lyrics and a rock beat with the discredited Group Sounds sellouts. Finally, the more ambitious groups wanted to take their acts on the international road, and they knew that the only way to do it was to sing in English.

Not everyone, however, followed the rock-is-English line. In 1970 a group called Happy End released *Yudemen* (*Boiled Noodles*), a debut album whose lyrics, by leader Takashi Matsumoto, convinced a lot of skeptics that a Japanese group singing in Japanese could really rock, with words that felt and sounded as though they belonged to the music. Other groups, including Hachimitsu Pai (Honey Pie) and Zuno Keisatsu (Brain Police), also began writing and recording in Japanese. More than a decade and a half after its rockabilly beginnings, Japanese rock had finally found its own voice. No longer a teenybopper fad, it had emerged as an authentic creative force in Japanese popular music.

THE ROSE OF VERSAILLES

Comics for girls, *shojo manga*, were long second-class citizens in the *manga* world. Most of the big-name *manga* artists of the 1950s and 1960s were men who targeted their work at a primarily male audience. Though the "god of *manga*," Osamu Tezuka, created a popular early girls' comic, *Ribbon no Kishi* (Princess Knight), the typical *shojo manga*, whose heroine was forever fluttering her huge, glittering eyes and whose story was full of perfervid romance, did not inspire a great deal of admiration in the *manga* community.

Then, in May 1972, a *manga* by a twenty-four-year-old woman, Riyoko Ikeda, debuted in *Margaret* magazine and, by becoming a big, influential success, brought *shojo manga* a new commercial and critical respect. Titled *The Rose of Versailles* (*Berusaiyu no Bara*), it told the story of French nobility in the days leading up to the Revolution. Its main characters were the French queen, Marie Antoinette; her dashing Swedish lover, Hans Axel Fersen; and the commander of the palace guards at Versailles, Oscar Francois de Jarjeyes. Oscar happened to be a woman whose father, a French general determined to have a son, had raised as a man. Oscar was loved from afar by Andre, a darkly handsome stablehand at her family estate.

Ikeda had gotten her start drawing *manga* paperbacks for the lending trade (i.e. *manga* published exclusively for the lending libraries of bookstores) but she was still an unknown when she approached *Margaret* with *The Rose of Versailles*. She found the editors a tough sell: too many historical romances had flopped, they said. Confident in the appeal of her material, she persisted, and was proven right when the *manga* become an immediate hit.

But Ikeda, who had placed the tragedy of Marie Antoinette at the center of her story, was surprised herself when *Margaret's* schoolgirl readers made Oscar their overwhelming favorite. An Oscar fan club was launched and thousands of Oscar fan letters poured into the offices of *Margaret* publisher Shueisha.

Perhaps she shouldn't have been so surprised. This, after all, was the early 1970s, the era of student unrest, Women's Liberation, and androgynous pop stars, from Mick Jagger in the West to Kenji "Julie" Sawada in Japan. The idea of a female hero who wore tight trousers over her long slender legs, looked like an idealized Peter Frampton, and led the storming of the Bastille, musket in hand and blonde curls flying, struck a contemporary note.

Even the culturally conservative could relate to Oscar: she was the latest in a long

Marie Antoinette (left) and Oscar (right) from *The Rose of Versailles.*

line of androgynous Japanese folk heroes, from Yoshitsune, a semilegendary fugitive general of the twelfth century who is portrayed on the Kabuki stage as a pale, delicate youth, to the players of men's roles, or *otokoyaku,* of the **TAKARAZUKA** all-women theater troupe.

The story contained the usual elements of historical fiction bestsellerdom—romance in high places, life-and-death drama, attractive heroes and heroines in gorgeous period costumes. But it also offered the then exotic spice of illicit love, between Count Fersen and Marie Antoinette. Although this love story firmly stressed lofty sentiment sincerely expressed, not crude lust explicitly portrayed, it was still pretty daring stuff for a girls' comic.

Instead of recoiling in alarm, however, *Margaret's* readers reveled in the romanticism of it all. One reason, ventured Hosei University professor Osamu Nakano, who wrote of a study of *shojo manga,* was that the characters were Westerners and thus fantasy figures. "This [lack of reality] made it easier for them to accept this depiction of [adult] love," he said.

When Oscar was shot by a Bastille defender and died, beautifully and bravely, in the arms of Andre, the *manga's* readers went into a collective state of shock. One girl wrote *Margaret* that she had been so upset she had stayed home from school for five days. At one girl's high school, an entire class burst into uncontrollable tears at the thought of Oscar's passing, until the teacher had to cancel the lesson for the day.

But though it may have disrupted some classes, *The Rose of Versailles* began appearing in others; the *manga's* liberal use of carefully researched historical facts inspired teachers to select it as a supplementary text and schools to purchase it for their libraries—a Japanese educational first. Also, the popularity of the *manga* generated an upsurge in the numbers of students in

French language and literature classes and tourists bound for France, with Versailles as the first stop on their itinerary.

In 1973, after eighty-two installments, *The Rose of Versailles* finally ended. Shueisha collected the *manga* into ten volumes that sold a total of twelve million copies—a *shojo manga* record. That, of course, wasn't the end: The character of Oscar, the nature of the story, and the huge success of the series made *Versailles* a natural for Takarazuka.

Certain conservative member's of the troupe's male management did not like the idea, however. The love story of Count Fersen and Marie Antoinette did not fit the pristine Takarazuka image. Also, Takarazuka had never done a play based on a *manga*. But the thought of expanding the theater troupe's audience base with a sure-fire hit persuaded the holdouts to change their minds.

When the cast of *The Rose of Versailles* was announced from the stage of the Tokyo Takarazuka Theater in April 1974, the applause was so deafening that Yuri Haruna, who had been cast to play Oscar, got goosebumps of excitement. At the same time, she later reminisced, "I felt my heart pound with fright."

She had good reason to be scared; fans had sky-high expectations for the Takarazuka's musical production of *Versailles*. One fan who did not approve of Haruna as Oscar sent her a razor in the mail, presumably for slashing her wrists. Fortunately, the show turned out to be a smash hit after its debut in August 1974. On opening night excited fans invaded Haruna's dressing room—strictly against Takarazuka rules—and in their rush to get her autograph tore her costume and smeared it with marks from their felt pens.

The *Versailles* fever soon spread nationwide. To satisfy the demand for the most popular show in its sixty-year history, Takarazuka sent all four of its troupes—Moon, Flower, Snow, and Star—to present *Beru-Bara,* as it came to be called, throughout the country. By the end of the musical's first run in 1980, Takarazuka had performed it 707 times before 1,595,000 fans.

In 1989 Takarazuka mounted another production of *Beru-Bara* and, in 1991, premiered *The Oscar Version*—a reworking of the musical that threw a stronger spotlight on the character of Oscar, played by Maya Suzukaze. These latter-day *Beru-Bara* were presented a total of five hundred times to 1,403,000 people. Altogether 2,998,000 fans have seen the various versions of the musical over the years.

In 1978, *Beru-Bara* returned home, as it were, when French director Jaques Demy filmed *Lady Oscar,* a French-Japanese co-production based on the *manga,* on location at

Versailles, with dialogue in English and a score by Michel Legrand. *Beru-Bara* was also turned into a forty-episode animation series for Japanese TV. The series has since been shown in France, Italy, Germany, and Singapore under the title *Lady Oscar*.

Meanwhile, Ikeda moved on to other projects, including a three-thousand-page saga about the Russian Revolution titled *Orpheus's Window (Orufesu no Mado)*. In April 1995, complaining that she was exhausted after "standing on the front lines of *shojo manga* for more that twenty years," Ikeda retired from *manga* drawing and entered the Tokyo College of Music to study voice and fulfill her girlhood dream of becoming an opera prima donna. Safe to say, though, that her stage debut will not be in yet another version of *Beru-Bara:* Takarazuka has salted away its most valuable property until the twenty-first century.

ROYAL WEDDINGS

Before World War II, Japan's royal family would hardly have been the subject of a book on popular culture. The only permitted public images were iconic—the emperor in full-dress uniform, mounted on his white horse—and the only permitted public attitudes were reverence and awe. Subjects were expected to greet their imperial rulers with bowed heads, lowered eyes, and dead silence.

After the war, all that changed. No longer divine, Hirohito toured the country to support his subjects' recovery efforts and demonstrate his own transformation into a constitutional monarch. He walked instead of riding a white horse and wore a suit and tie instead of a uniform. He looked very human indeed, which was both exciting and confusing for his subjects. How do you greet a god who has come to earth?

But though this campaign helped re-establish the popularity and legitimacy of the monarchy, in reality the Chrysanthemum Curtain—the veil behind which the imperial family lived, removed from the scrutiny of the public—remained tightly shut, with the drawstrings firmly in the hands of the Imperial Household Agency, the bureaucracy in charge of royal affairs.

For reporters, working the imperial family beat was like viewing a Noh play, in which the performances were dictated by ancient tradition and the performers wore impenetrable masks. The media could make only the blandest of comments about the play and players; no scathing critiques, no nasty backstage gossip. The idea of a tabloid press vacuuming up bits of royal dirt for mass consumption was inconceivable (one

Fifteen million viewers—the largest audience in Japanese TV's six-year history—tuned into the live broadcast of Crown Prince Akihito and Princess Michiko's wedding procession on April 10, 1959.

reason was the very real threat of retribution from Japan's emperor-worshiping rightists).

Then, in November 1958 the Chrysanthemum Curtain suddenly dropped with the announcement that Crown Prince Akihito—Hirohito's eldest son—had become engaged to Michiko Shoda, the daughter of a prominent businessman. Breaking with an imperial tradition stretching back to the legendary emperors of pre-modern Japan, Akihito had chosen a commoner for his bride.

The press immediately heralded this match as a symbol of Japan's new democratic ethos and a sign that the imperial family was becoming closer to the people. For many of their readers, it was a once-in-a-lifetime fairytale romance. Michiko immediately became everywoman's stand-in Cinderella.

Of course, Michiko, or "Michi" as the press was soon calling her, after her schoolgirl nickname, was hardly a typical young Japanese woman. Her father was president of the Nisshin Flour Milling Company and a powerful member of Japan's business elite. She had attended University of the Sacred Heart, an exclusive private women's college, where she had served as student body president and graduated with honors. Fluent in English and French, an accomplished pianist and a student of the tea ceremony and flower arranging, Michiko was universally proclaimed a paragon.

It was not her way with a tea ladle that the media was soon raving about, however, but her form with a tennis racket. The summer before, Michiko had met the crown prince on a tennis court in Karuizawa, a posh summer resort, where she had beaten him in a mixed doubles match, 7-5, 6-3. Her partner, a twelve-year-old tennis whiz named Bobby Doyle, hadn't realized that he was supposed to throw the game to the future emperor. Akihito hadn't minded his humiliation by a girl and a kid, however. He had been looking more at Michiko than the ball—and liking what he saw. After the game he snapped Michiko's picture as a keepsake. "It was a long game, wasn't it?" he asked. Thus the beginning of the romance that had the entire country talking.

By Western standards it was an odd courtship. Akihito met Michiko only at tennis clubs and only in the presence of others. Often they didn't play on the same court or exchange more than casual greetings. But while being discreet in public, the prince was burning up the wires between the palace and Michiko's house, keeping her on the phone for an hour at a time.

The prince was intent, but Michiko was hesitant. She knew that marrying a future emperor meant saying good-bye to privacy and control over her own life. Meanwhile, the Imperial Household Agency was conducting a thorough background check—

and finding nothing that would prevent her from becoming the prince's consort. In August 1958, with the pressure intensifying from all sides, Michiko accepted an invitation to attend an international college alumnae meeting in Brussels. That fall, while she was out of the country, her family rejected several offers of marriage from imperial messengers. Finally, she sent a letter to the prince himself declining the honor. Akihito wasn't easily discouraged, however; he pressed his suit by phone and, after three weeks of constant long-distance wooing, Michiko gave in.

On November 29, after the betrothal announcement, Michiko and her parents visited Akihito at the imperial palace and the couple found themselves alone for the first time—for thirty minutes. Soon after, as an engagement present, the phone company installed a private line from the palace to Michiko's house so that the lovers could always be in touch.

The wedding, held on April 10, 1959, was the Japanese TV's industry's first televised spectacular. The ceremony itself was held in strict privacy, in accordance with imperial custom, with two press-pool cameras allowed only a brief glimpse of the imperial couple within the palace walls (the crews manning the cameras were required to don formal morning wear).

The procession afterward, however, was televised live from beginning to end by NHK and two commercial networks, KRT (today's TBS) and NTV. The other two nets, NET (today's TV Asahi) and Fuji TV, had just started broadcasting and were not yet up to covering such a major event. Instead, they had to rely on feeds, NET from KRT and Fuji TV from NTV.

Before the ceremony, while the networks were competing fiercely for good camera positions along the nine-kilometer parade route from the imperial palace in the center of Tokyo to the prince's temporary residence (the best ones gave a clear view of Princess Michiko's face), the public was frantically buying black-and-white TVs to watch the big event (see **CONSUMER CULTURE**). In the week before the wedding, the number of sets in Japanese households passed the two million mark, double the number of the year before. On April 10, an audience of fifteen million tuned in, by far the largest in the six-year history of Japanese television.

The procession itself, with the prince and his radiant new bride riding in a carriage drawn by six horses on a lovely spring day, transfixed viewers across the archipelago. A nation of TV addicts was born.

Thirty-four years later, when the next crown prince, Naruhito, was searching for a bride, the situation was somewhat different. In a break with centuries-old palace tradition, Akihito and Michiko had raised their three children themselves instead of entrust-ing them to guardians, and had served admirably as royal emissaries, greeters, and all-round constitutional symbols, with nary a whiff of scandal.

Meanwhile, the weekly magazines— Japan's tabloid press—had become bolder in their reporting on the imperial family. In their speculations about consort candidates for Naruhito, they named names and gave readers the inside scoop on the Imperial Household Agency's bride hunt. One thing hadn't changed, however; the prince was having a tough time finding a princess. The reason was the same as in Akihiko's time; the Chrysanthemum Curtain remained a formidable barrier, especially for young women raised in the freedom of postwar Japan.

But the thirty-three-year-old prince was, if anything, even more persistent than his father; he pursued his ideal for nearly seven years, in the face of repeated rebuffs. Her name was Masako Owada, and she was the eldest daughter of an elite diplomat, a graduate of Harvard and Oxford, and one of the handful of applicants to pass the rigorous Ministry of Foreign Affairs employment examination. Fluent in English and four other languages, Masako was serving on the North American desk—the most prestigious in the ministry—when Naruhito began his romantic full-court press.

On meeting Masako at a reception in 1986, Naruhito had been immediately smitten. Masako, however, did not reciprocate his interest; she wanted a career, not a life circumscribed by the palace moat. Even so, while she was off studying at Oxford, the Imperial Household Agency ran the same background check on her as they had on Princess Michiko. The criteria were stringent: the royal handlers would settle for nothing less than a well-bred, well-educated virgin from an upper-crust family who was younger and shorter than the prince. Attractiveness and athletic ability were also pluses.

Masako did not pass in the height department; she was slightly taller than the prince. Also, one of her favorite athletic activities was not the upper-class sport of tennis but the classless game of softball. More seriously, she had a grandfather who been president of Chisso Corporation, a chemical company that had pumped toxic mercury into Minamata Bay in Kyushu in the 1950s and afflicted thousands of local residents with a lingering nerve illness called Minamata Disease. Her grandfather's tenure as president, however, had begun in 1964, after the dumping had stopped. With dozens of other bridal candidates either falling short or fleeing into marriage to avoid the royal clutches and media scrutiny, the handlers finally decided that Masako would have to do.

After the press ferreted out the list of candidates, she also become a media target, with paparazzi and reporters camping in front of her family's doorstep and following her around at Oxford. Princess Michiko, needless to say, had never suffered such indignities. The media feeding frenzy made Masako even more resolved to pursue her foreign service career and avoid an imperial marriage.

Naruhito, though, was determined to have her. To aid him in his pursuit, the Imperial Household Agency asked the media to impose a news blackout on the bridal hunt. Reluctantly, the dozens of the TV stations, magazines, and newspapers with reporters on the trail complied, but kept digging for information. When the blackout finally ended, they were prepared with in-depth stories on the bride-to-be.

In August 1992, four years since their last meeting, Naruhito finally wangled a date with Masako. They had tea together at a secret rendezvous, the home of a retired Foreign Ministry superior of Masako's father. In October, at a second meeting at the imperial duck hunting grounds, Naruhito popped the question, but Masako could not decide. Then, taking a hint from his father, Naruhito launched a telephone campaign at beginning of November, calling Masako nightly for three weeks straight. Finally, on December 12, after a three-hour heart-to-heart, Masako agreed to become the next empress.

The press ban was not supposed to end until February 1993 but in January the

Washington Post decided to disregard it and print a story on the couple's engagement. The day after, the local news pages and air waves were flooded with reports on Masako, many of which had obviously been prepared weeks, if not months, beforehand.

There was, predictably, a Masako boom, just as there had been a Michiko boom three decades earlier. Female office workers snapped up pearl necklaces and colorful silk scarves, both said to be favorites of the future princess, and much of the Japanese media worked overtime transforming her from a hardworking, tough-minded career bureaucrat into a flawlessly traditional role model. Other, more hard-boiled types reported the complaints of court officials that Masako was too forward in her comments with the press, too flashy in her appearance, and too careless in her behavior (a creased kimono came in for unfavorable criticism). Masako played along, quitting her job at the Foreign Ministry, toning down her wardrobe, and taking fifty hours of lessons in court etiquette and accomplishments, including the composition of *waka*—a poetry form that has been an imperial tradition for more than a millennium.

Meanwhile, both foreign and Japanese commentators were openly lamenting that Masako was throwing away a brilliant career to play a subservient role in Japan's most rigidly conservative institution. Duke University history professor Andrew Gordon, who had been Masako's academic mentor at Harvard, said "This engagement promotes the idea that the most important thing for women to do is to be married and have a family." Prominent intellectual Shuichi Kato warned that "if [Masako] is not strong, she will be [the Imperial Household Agency's] puppet. They will orchestrate her every move for the rest of her life." *Newsweek* titled its story on Masako "The Reluctant Princess." It aroused a storm of protest in Japan.

Reluctant or not, once Masako accepted Naruhito's hand, she was subjected to the same intensive press scrutiny Michiko had endured three decades earlier. The wedding, on June 9, 1993, was another TV extravaganza, though the excitement didn't reach the fever pitch of 1959. Afterwards, press attention focused on her most important function as an imperial consort—producing an heir. Pregnancy rumors, however, proved unfounded, notching up the media pressure even more.

Meanwhile, Masako remained behind the Chrysanthemum Curtain, answering questions from the media only through a chamberlain and only on her birthday. Her comments were firmly in the imperial tradition; polite, bland, and as uncontroversial as possible. On her thirty-second birthday, in December 1995, she said that the events of the past twelve months, including the Kobe earthquake, "had pained me deeply" and offered her prayer that "the next year be one of peace." No one was about to argue with that.

But speaking at a press conference in December 1996, Princess Masako boldly assured the world that she was "not in a state of depression," presumably over her well-publicized inability to produce an heir. She also criticized the media, especially the foreign press, for exaggerating her difficulties in playing her royal role. She did admit, however, that balancing her public and private life had not been easy. These mild sallies created a large stir in both the domestic and foreign press, even though the Imperial Household Agency had tried to limit the damage by cutting her remarks about her problems from the English-language translation of her press conference.

Masako had another reason to be upset with and wary of the press. In October 1993, following a spate of weekly magazine stories criticizing her as overbearing, Empress Michiko had suffered a breakdown, become mute, and had to withdraw from public life. With the media wolves baying outside the palace gates, the tennis courts of Karuizawa must have seemed far away indeed.

SAKAMOTO, KYU & "SUKIYAKI"

Over the years dozens of Japanese pop singers and groups have recorded, toured, or released records in the United States. Several artists, such as **PINK LADY** and **SEIKO MATSUDA**, have made full-scale assaults on the American market with the backing of major record companies. And several, such as Shonen Knife and Pizzicato Five, have gained a cult following among U.S. music fans. But only one Japanese artist has ever had a number-one record in the United States: Kyu Sakamoto.

The song was "Sukiyaki," which may have been a strange title to give a tune about smiling through your tears, but at least identified it as unmistakably Japanese. Released by Capitol Records in May 1963, "Sukiyaki" shot up to the top of the *Cashbox* magazine chart in its fifth week and held the number-one spot for four straight weeks (*Billboard* magazine listed it at that rank for three weeks on its chart).

Of course, hardly any of his U.S. listeners understood what Sakamoto was singing about, but they didn't need a translation to understand the song's catchy melody, upbeat tempo, and underlying mood of sentimental sadness. (The Japanese title, "Ue o Muite Aruko," means "I'll Walk With My Head Up" and the first two lines of the lyrics translate as "I'll walk with my head up, so as not to let my tears fall. / I'll cry while walking, on this lonely night.") "Sukiyaki" somehow sounded both familiar and different: a rock ballad filtered through a Japanese sensibility.

When Sakamoto arrived in Los Angeles in August he was mobbed at the airport by five thousand fans. Not all were there simply to see their idol, however: as a promo gimmick, the record company had promised a free copy of "Sukiyaki" to anyone who showed up. Though Sakamoto didn't create a Beatles-like sensation, he did appear on the Steve Allen Show, where his sunny personality won him even more fans. Then, in the spring of 1964, he earned what was then the ultimate U.S. music-industry accolade: a Gold Record for selling one million copies.

In Japan, Sakamoto had first risen to prominence in the 1950s as a member of Sons of Drifters, a three-man country-and-western band. Switching to rockabilly, he appeared in the third Western Carnival—a week-long showcase for rockabilly and country-and-western artists—in September 1959 and become known as one of the five top male stars in the genre.

In 1960 he had his first hit with a Japanese-language cover of "Itsy Bitsy Teeny Weeny Yellow Polka Dot Bikini" and in 1961, as the lead singer of a group called Paradise King, released an original Japanese tune called "Kanashiki Rokujusai" (Sad at Sixty). Although not conventionally handsome—his round face was still spotted with adolescent pimples—Sakamoto had a big smile and boyish charm that soon made him a fixture on early Japanese TV music shows.

In October 1961, on one of those shows, NHK's *Yume de Aimasho* (Let's Meet in Our Dreams), he sang a new song titled "Ue o Muite Aruko," with lyrics by Rokusuke Ei and music by Hachidai Nakamura. Because Ei's first name contained the Chinese character for "six," Nakamura's, for "eight" and Sakamoto's, for "nine," they became known at the Six, Eight, and Nine Trio. Two months later, Toshiba Records released "Ue o Muite Aruko" and it became one of year's biggest hits. In the spring of 1962 it was released in Europe, where the title was translated directly into the local languages, with the exception of Holland (Unforgettable Geisha) and England (Sukiyaki). Capitol Records chose the latter title for the U.S. release and Sakamoto began his journey into pop-music history.

Although "Ue o Muite Aruko" was their only international smash, the Six, Eight, and Nine Trio had several more hits in Japan in the mid-1960s. Sakamoto later went on to become a successful television emcee, whose face was still known to millions long after his

The only Japanese artist ever to score a number-one hit on the U.S. record charts: Kyu Sakamoto.

brief tenure as a pop-music idol had faded from mass-audience memory.

On August 7, 1985, Sakamoto attended a concert held by Ei and Nakamura at a Tokyo live house. After the show, he told them that he wanted to work with them again—it would be their first collaboration in nearly two decades. Five days later Sakamoto was aboard a JAL jumbo bound for Osaka that crashed into a mountain, killing five hundred twenty passengers—the biggest disaster in Japan's aviation history. Sakamoto was not one of the four survivors. Nakamura has also since passed on, leaving Ei, who is also known today for his best-selling essay collections, as the only surviving member of the group.

There have been several covers of "Sukiyaki." In 1981 an English-language version by the L.A. disco quartet A Taste of Honey rose to number three on the *Billboard* pop chart and number one on the R & B chart in the United States. In September of 1994 a male vocal group called 4 PM released an a cappella English-language version of the song that reached number eight on the *Billboard* pop chart.

Japanese singers have also rediscovered the song. Sayoko of the rock band Zelda recorded a reggae version in Jamaica for her first solo album, "Me Love You," which was released in February 1995. Also, Shizuro Otaka, who once worked as Sakamoto's back-up singer, included the song in her album "Repeat Performance III," which debuted in May 1995. Asked to comment on the renewed interest in Sakamoto's best-known hit, his widow, Yukiko Kashiwagi, said: "I think both Sakamoto and Hachidai Nakamura are happy in heaven because the song has become popular again with another generation."

Kimpachi Sensei and his charges tackled the Big Issues week after week on *Sannen B Gumi Kimpachi Sensei.*

SANNEN B GUMI KIMPACHI SENSEI

The Japanese educational system resembles nothing so much as a gruelingly hard hurdles race. On reaching the goal—entrance to a good university—the runners usually collapse in exhaustion and relief and spend the next three years avoiding all mental exertion until the next big hurdle—getting a job—looms. Thus the best place to find solitude on a Japanese university campus is often the library, where rows of unread books stand sentinel over empty study tables. The best place to find the students is often on the ski slope, at the beach, behind the counter at McDonald's—anywhere but behind a desk.

But for ninth graders, who are preparing to leap one of the highest hurdles—the entrance exam to high school—the leisured lifestyles of their college-age brothers and sisters are a barely imaginable dream. While they are grinding away at the books, however, they must also deal with all the various difficulties of adolescence, some as universal as raging hormones, others as culturally specific as the peculiarly Japanese insistence on conformity, from teachers and classmates alike, and the harshness of the punishment meted out to those who differ from the norm.

In the late 1970s, student frustration with the educational hurdles race erupted in the form of school violence, bullying, gangs, and the growing number of kids who decided to drop out altogether. High schools and even elementary schools had to contend with this frustration, but the worst affected were the junior high schools, where classrooms often became battle zones and teaching, trench warfare.

In 1979 a drama series debuted on the TBS network that seemed to squarely address the country's education crisis. Titled *Sannen B Gumi Kimpachi Sensei* (Mr. Kimpachi of the Third-Year B Class), the show was set in a junior high school in Tokyo's *shitamachi* (old downtown) section. Played by folk singer Tetsuya Takeda, Kimpachi Sakamoto was a thirtysomething Japanese teacher who looked, with his uncombed shoulder-length hair and wide ties, like an out-of-it aging hippie. Unlike his battle-weary colleagues, who were content to go by the book and collect their paychecks, Sakamoto or, as he was known to his students, Kimpachi Sensei (attaching the honorific *sensei*, or teacher, to a first rather than last name is a sign of familiarity, if not always respect) was a Now Generation ball of fire who may have looked rumpled and unfashionable but was determined to inspire his students and teach them lessons about Life, with a capital L, that they could never get from a textbook.

For Takeda, who had studied to become a teacher at the Fukuoka University of

Education before forming a folk group called Kaientai, Kimpachi Sensei was a dream role. A shameless scenery-chewer whose specialty was salt-of-the-earth characters, Takeda plunged into his on-screen teaching duties with a gusto that went beyond the demands of the part. Lecturing his charges about the Big Issues, he would often get carried away and depart from the script. "If I didn't do it [that way], I couldn't make the students understand," he explained. "Also, I was able to get into it more myself."

As this comment indicated, Takeda may have been a cornball, but he was no fake. In his monologues about the limitless possibilities of youth or the wonderfulness of love, he projected a naked sincerity that reached

directly though the small screen to viewers across the country. At a time when real-life teachers seemed less like dedicated educators and more like bureaucrats obsessed with enforcing petty rules, Takeda's Kimpachi Sensei impressed many viewers as a welcome throwback to a more humanistic age, when life may have been harder but moral values really meant something.

For younger viewers, the attraction was not only Kimpachi Sensei but his class of thirty-two students, which included kids who became, because of their exposure on the show, popular TV idols. Three of the boys—Toshihiko Tahara, Yoshio Nomura, and Masahiko Kondo—formed a singing group called the Tanokin Trio (the name Tanokin was formed by taking one Chinese character from each of their last names) that acquired a huge schoolgirl following.

Most of the show's students were newcomers appearing in their first TV drama and, far from being accomplished actors, behaved much as ordinary ninth graders would in class: rowdy and rude. Takeda later said that "when I was crying as part of my performance, they were yawning in my face." This indifference spurred Takeda on to greater efforts, until his performance seemed so authentic that the kids began to regard him as they would a real teacher. When the kids—not their characters—were getting out of hand, Takeda was often called in by the staff to administer a scolding, though he never sent anyone out into the hall or to the principal's office.

Kimpachi Sensei, however, was more than a platitude-prone role model; he had to deal with contemporary school issues, including teen pregnancy, high school entrance-exam pressures, nit-picking school rules, and the practice of admitting kids to high school based on their athletic ability, not academic performance. The teen-pregnancy story, which depicted its teen mother and father as ordinary kids, not delinquent misfits, so upset the PTA of the junior high school where the show was filming that they withdrew their permission to use the school as a set.

This controversy didn't hurt the show with the people who counted: the viewers. The last program of the first series scored a forty-percent rating. By this time, Kimpachi Sensei had become not only a ratings king but a national byword: Japan's own Mr. Chips. A song titled "Okuru Kotoba" (A Word I Give to You) that Takeda had recorded with Kaientai in 1980 when the show was at the height of its popularity, soared to number one on the *Oricon* singles chart and was often played at school graduation ceremonies, even though it had nothing to do with graduation from anything. It didn't matter: because Kimpachi Sensei sang it, the song was automatically assumed to be "educational."

Although Kimpachi Sensei became a pedagogical hero in the nation's living rooms, in the teachers' rooms he was widely considered a fantasy figure who made the hard job of teaching seem easier than it was. Kimpachi could turn kids around with a few inspiring words; in real life, teachers complained, kids—and their problems—weren't so tractable. TBS, however, was in the business of entertainment, not education, and in Kimpachi Sensei it had found a winner: the network brought him back for two more series and nine special programs in the 1980s. In the fall of 1995, after a hiatus of seven years, Kimpachi Sensei returned to TBS yet again with a new version of the show. By this time Takeda had shorter hair and a more conservative look, but he was still as enthusiastic as ever—and *Sannen B Gumi* was still at the top of the ratings' class.

SANRIO

Japan, as foreign visitors soon discover, is the Country of Cute. Everywhere one looks—on department-store racks, where cuddly creatures cavort on clothing for everyone from tots to teens; on video-store shelves, where saucer-eyed girls with heart-shaped faces simper from porno anime cassettes; and even at home plate, where burly home-run hitters are presented with adorable stuffed animals modeled on the club's logo—one encounters images and objects that ooze cuteness, or *kawairashisa*. These visitors may begin to wonder whether a large part of the population, particularly the female half of it, is suffering from arrested development.

This observation is not totally off the mark, though in the nineties the cute look has largely disappeared from street fashion. It's no longer easy, as it was in the eighties, to find adult women dressing like faux naif grade schoolers, with furry infant animals gamboling on pink sweaters and peeking up from soft cloth handbags. The desired image was eighteen going on twelve, sexy but doesn't know it, i.e., the feminine ideal for legions of Japanese men. By cultivating this image in the early eighties, including the frilly Little Bo Peep costumes she sometimes wore for stage appearances, SEIKO MATSUDA became the most popular female singer of her generation. Inspired by Seiko-chan, legions of *burikko*—girls who acted younger than their age, often to charm the opposite sex—giggled and capered their way across the national landscape.

But a desire to fulfill fantasies of men suffering from what the Japanese call a "Lolita complex" *(roricon)* is not the only reason so many Japanese girls and women (and not a few Japanese men) love the cute. If the meta-message of what many young Western women wear and display is toughness and coolness of stance, in Japan it has long been sweetness and innocence, to better fit into a conservative, groupist society that encourages strictly defined sex roles, with women expected to behave as either virginal maids or pure wives and virtuous mothers.

And what better way to communicate one's sweetness and innocence than by sporting cute stuff made for kids? "She may be a little immature," the little white kitten on the pencil box says of its teenage owner, "but she's really such a nice person." And so charmingly cute, or *kawayui*.

In the Country of Cute the king has long been the manufacturer and retailer Sanrio,

Hello Kitty: the London-born third grader who rules in Sanrio's Kingdom of Cute.

are in the third grade. . . . Her hobbies include music, reading, eating the cookies her sister bakes, and best of all, making new friends") and a lengthy list of video, CD-ROM, and CD credits. She and her friends are even featured in their very own newspaper, the *Ichigo Shimbun* (Strawberry News), which Sanrio has been publishing monthly since 1975. The paper has an Ichigo Mate Club, whose three rules are: (1) Greet everyone in a loud, clear voice; (2) When someone does something for you, say "Thank you"; (3) Try to be kind to others in small ways.

The *Ichigo Shimbun* and the entire world of Sanrio characters—Pochacco the Puppy, Keroppi the Frog, Pippo the Pig, and Pekkle the Duck—are obviously targeted at the very young, but Sanrio has discovered, to the great benefit of its bottom line, that its products appeal to teens and adults as well. Since its founding in 1960 as Yamanashi Silk Center K.K. and its subsequent evolution into a manufacturer and retailer of cheap-but-cute gift items, Sanrio has grown into a multinational company with 1,012 full-time employees, branches in six foreign countries, and sales in fiscal 1995 of 78.5 billion yen.

The core of Sanrio's business is still what it describes as its "social communication gift goods," including all those Hello Kitty memo pads, erasers, and Japanese-style lunch-

which creates cute characters and designs cute character goods that, since 1974, have found their way into the toy box, school bag, and heart of nearly girl in the country—and many of their older sisters.

The first and best-loved of those characters is Hello Kitty, the aforementioned white kitten, whose black-dot eyes, yellow button nose, and off-center red hair ribbon have adorned everything from ballpoint pens to plant-food vials and whose infantile visage has become familiar to every Japanese since her debut in 1974.

But though Hello Kitty may be first and foremost a design motif, she is also a character with an official Sanrio biography ("Hello Kitty was born in London, England, where she lives with her parents and her twin sister, Mimi. Both Hello Kitty and Mimi boxes, which accounted for 87.5 percent of sales in 1995. In Japan Sanrio sells these goods through 127 directly managed stores and nearly 3,000 affiliates.

Since 1990 Sanrio has also been promoting and marketing its character goods through the Sanrio Puroland theme park. Located in Tama City, a Tokyo suburb, Puroland attracts nearly 1.5 million visitors a year. In 1991 Sanrio opened a second park, Harmony Land, in Oita Prefecture as a joint venture with local companies and the prefectural government.

In addition to live performances by Hello Kitty, Keroppi, and the gang at the Fairy Tale theater, visitors to Puroland can enjoy the Monster Planet **GODZILLA** ride, where they can meet the Big G in 3-D, and Discovery Theater, where they can watch famous scientists and inventors at work, in the form of animatronic dolls. Though the inspiration for the park, right down to the soaring fantasy castle that dominates it, is definitely Disney, the execution is pure Sanrio: round, soft shapes, pastel colors, and, everywhere one looks, cute Sanrio characters, including in the inevitable gift shops crowded with souvenir shoppers.

But though Sanrio may be a booming success in Japan—how could it have missed?—its sugary sweet, sub-Disney esthetic was long an object of derision among the resident foreign community in Japan. Sanrio had entered the U.S. market in 1976 and the European market in 1980, but how, foreign skeptics wondered, could they hope to sell their puerile products to hip, street-smart Western kids?

But the skeptics didn't count on the power of reverse chic. In the mid-nineties, having tired of down-and-dirty grunge and rap styles, American teens began discovering the delights of cute. Hard-core rockers like Courtney Love of Hole began sporting pink barrettes in their hair and young women who had been heavily into Harleys and body piercing could be seen carrying Hello Kitty tote bags. Sanrio was suddenly the *dernier cri* of street fashion. In fiscal 1995 U.S. sales grew 14.9 percent to 4.1 billion yen and the number of stores carrying Sanrio goods rose to two thousand.

Of course, American cute wasn't Japanese cute. There was a heavy dose of irony in the American take on Hello Kitty totally absent among Japanese Sanrio fans. Despite the pink barrettes, Courtney Love's punk harlot act hardly radiated sweetness and light. Trampled innocence was more like it. If Hello Kitty could express alarm at the lifestyles of her American cutecore fans— high out of their minds at all-night raves— her little paws would no doubt fly up to her round cheeks and her mouth—often invisible, never larger than a dot—would expand into a big, Munch-like O.

Sazae-san as depicted on the covers of three volumes of the *manga*: forever twenty-three, forever fallibly human, and forever comfortingly sane.

SAZAE-SAN

Japanese television is a cartoon-lover's paradise. Every week, kids living in Tokyo have a choice of more than forty cartoon programs and, during vacation periods, as many as sixty. Usually based on currently popular *manga,* the shows face intense competition for survival. Some try to win viewers by exploiting a fad (soccer this season, basketball the next) and when the fad ends they disappear. Others use ultraviolence or bathroom humor to keep restless fingers off the channel changer. Still others are carefully targeted at a specific sex or age group; the show sister watches with such delight bores brother stiff and vice versa. The most successful, however, tend to be part of a sophisticated media mix campaign that combines manga, TV, film, games, and merchandizing into a powerful money-spinning machine.

But of all the hundreds of TV cartoons to come and go over the years, the most enduringly popular is based on a *manga* series that ended in 1974, whose creator, Machiko Hasegawa, firmly forbade the licensing of dolls, T-shirts, and other spinoffs. Appearing twice a week on Fuji TV, with a new show on Sunday, a rebroadcast on Tuesday, *Sazae-san* is a family show with no sex, no violence (other than an occasional pratfall), and little vulgarity. It is, in fact, a throw-

back to a time when three generations lived under one roof (if not always harmoniously), Mom stayed home all day (though she didn't bake cookies), the neighborhood still felt like a community (though occasionally a nosy one), and the kids played real games with real playmates (instead of spending most of their after-school hours in a cram-school classroom or in front of a TV screen).

Since its start in 1969, *Sazae-san* has evolved with the times—the family TV set is now color instead of black-and-white—but remained firmly behind the curve. Though other shows have temporarily soared past it in the ratings, none have managed to permanently unseat it from its throne as Japan's best-loved TV cartoon program.

Every show presents three segments about the mildly comic misadventures of a middle-class family in suburban Tokyo. The title character, Sazae-san (the "san" is an honorific), is a twenty-three-year-old housewife whose extended family includes husband Masuo, mother Fune, father Namihei, younger brother Katsuo, and younger sister Wakame. Sazae-san and Masuo have a toddler, Tara, who often plays with a little neighbor boy, Ikura.

This, of course, is hardly a typical family in today's urban Japan. For one thing all the family members have sea-related names ("Sazae" means turbo—a kind of marine

snail). For another, three generations are living under one roof—a common arrangement when Hasegawa started the *manga* series in 1946, but increasingly rare today. For still another, Sazae is living with her own parents instead of with her husband's, as has long been more customary.

But though Sazae's family may have its quirks, what Japanese viewers love about it is its comforting normality, by the standards of 1966. Sazae is a full-time housewife, with no discernable career ambitions. Masuo is an ordinary salaryman, who is nowhere near the fast track but safe from the restructuring rubbish heap. Katsuo and Wakame are average kids who have no outstanding talent, save for getting into minor mishaps on a weekly basis, but are spared many of the stresses of modern life, from school bullying to cram-school studying.

The pace of life is relaxed, the mood warm and friendly. Though Sazae may own modern appliances (all drawn to resemble the latest models made by Toshiba, the show's sponsor), she has no satellite dish or cable TV. Freed from these and other electronic distractions, she has oodles of time to chat with Mom, the neighbors, and the local shopkeepers.

And though Masuo puts in the usual long salaryman hours, he is hardly a stressed-out workaholic, tied to his cellular phone or laptop (he has neither). He spends much on-air time at home in kimono, chilling out with a beer and a baseball game. Sazae may boss him around—Masuo is something of a wuss—but they get along with none of the usual prime-time family drama Sturm und Drang.

Though Japan has undergone many

Machiko Hasegawa, with friend: "Society has become so busy and competitive—doesn't everyone long to relax in a warm bath?"

changes and disruptions during the show's long run, *Sazae-san's* mental clock seems permanently stopped in the happy boom days of the 1960s and early 1970s, when Japan was emerging from its postwar poverty into the sunny uplands of prosperity, but had still not lost touch with its traditional customs and mores. The show closely reflects the changes of the seasons—cherry blossoms fall and leaves turn color right on schedule—and carefully marks the arrival of the annual holidays.

On these occasions, Sazae and her kin always do the expected Japanese thing, dressing in kimono for the New Year's shrine visit or in *yukata* (a light cotton robe) for the annual Festival of the Dead dance. In fact everyone behaves so correctly—even the kids speak clearly and politely, in standard Japanese—that the show serves as an excellent language-learning tool and manual of proper Japanese social behavior. The fact

that fewer and fewer people act this way helps give the show its distinctly nostalgic tinge.

The show, however, presents a sanitized version of the *manga* to the world. It uses only half of the 6,400 *manga* stories Hasegawa produced between 1946 and 1974. The *manga*, which accurately reflected the lives and feelings of ordinary Japanese in the harsh early postwar years, showed the characters scouring the countryside for food supplies or scrimping and saving to buy small luxuries. But though they were poor, Sazae-san and her clan had a certain natural ebullience that lifted the spirits of readers—and made *Sazae-san* the most popular *manga* of the day.

Machiko Hasegawa was born in 1920 in Saga Prefecture on the island of Kyushu, which has long been known for producing formidable women (see **OSHIN**). In 1937, following her graduation from Yamawaki Women's High School, she began studying drawing under the cartoonist Suiho Kawachi. Shortly after the end of the war, she drew her first *Sazae-san* four-frame *manga* for a provincial newspaper and, in 1949, moved the strip to *Asahi Shimbun,* a national daily.

Sazae-san made Hasegawa well-off and famous, but she rejected most of the trappings and perks of success. Instead of hobnobbing with the *manga*-world elite, she preferred to spend quiet evenings at home with her elder sister, with whom she lived her entire adult life. She was also an elusive journalistic quarry, though she told one reporter that *Sazae-san* was such a hit because "society has become so busy and competitive—doesn't everyone long to relax in a warm bath?"

Hasegawa, in fact, often got ideas for the *manga* while soaking in the tub, and many came from her own life. (She even gave Sazae her own lumpy hairdo.) But Hasegawa was also far more stressed than her most beloved creation; she was an insomniac, suffered from panic attacks, and underwent surgery for ulcers. Whenever she could, she took a break from the grind and traveled abroad, where she could find blissful anonymity.

Hasegawa was such a private person—she once stated, rather proudly, that she had not a single cartoonist friend—that after she died of heart failure on May 27, 1992, her sister managed to keep her death a secret for three months, at Hasegawa's request. She did not want any obituaries in the paper until her bones were safely at rest in her ancestors' grave.

Sazae-san, however, seems likely to go on indefinitely, forever twenty-three, forever fallibly human, and forever comfortingly sane.

SHONEN JUMP

How big are *manga* in Japan? One frequently used yardstick is *Shukan Shonen Jump* (Boy's Weekly Jump), a weekly comic for boys that is to the rest of the *manga* world what the T Rex was to the other dinosaurs: a beast that dominates, and occasionally devours, its competition. *Jump's* circulation has long surpassed five million and recently reached as high as six million. No other weekly magazine in the Japan, straight or comic—and few in the world—even comes close.

There is, outwardly, little to distinguish this *manga* behemoth from dozens of others that crowd the racks in bookstores, convenience stores, and train-platform kiosks. It has the standard garish color cover, followed by several slick color pages of ads and the lead-in to the week's top *manga*. The bulk of its contents are printed on rough recycled paper, in two colors. Except for the first story, which is in red and black with a white background, all the stories are printed with a distinguishing background tint—orange, yellow, blue, or green—that makes it easy for readers to flip to the one they want (if it's yellow, it must be *Slam Dunk*). At 465 pages, *Jump* is the size of a small city phone book and sells for two hundred yen—a pittance that would seem to barely cover the cost of newsprint.

Shonen Jump: Japan's *manga* behemoth, with weekly sales of between five and six million copies.

both of which debuted in 1959, were the pioneers of and, for a long time, bestsellers among fat, multicolored, weekly *manga* magazines.

When *Jump* began publishing in in 1968, its editors knew that they could not compete head-on with the big boys for the industry's top talent. Instead they decided to cultivate newcomers, signing them to long-term contracts that kept them in the fold even if they later struck *manga* gold.

The editors also conducted a survey that asked readers to respond, in a word, to three basic questions: (1) What warms your heart the most? (2) What is most important to you? (3) What makes you feel the happiest? The answers, they learned, were (1) friendship, (2) effort, and (3) winning. These three keywords have since served as the foundation of *Jump's* editorial policy. In other words, no downer stories about lonely losers. Instead, the magazine has tended to favor sci-fi fantasy (*Dragonball* and its successor, *Dragonball Z*), sci-fi humor (*Dr. Slump),* sports humor (*Kinnikuman,* or Muscle Man) and other action-filled genres. To make sure that readers are getting what they want, *Jump* includes a readers' response card in each issue. If a new series doesn't inspire enough readers to write its

By the standards of Western magazine publishing, Jump is a rather shabby affair. Its audience, however, is not only enormous—each copy, the editors claim, passes through the hands of an average of two or three readers—but extends from boys in elementary school to businessmen in their forties. Among the ads in a recent issue are one for a trade school and another for a scent guaranteed to drive women wild. No, Jump is not just kid's stuff.

Jump was not the first to discover its format. *Shonen Magazine* and *Shonen Sunday,* number in the "three most interesting manga" box, it soon disappears.

While weeding out the dross, this Darwinian system has produced a steady stream of winners. All three of the *manga* series mentioned above generated TV shows, films, and a merchandising bonanza. In addition to running from 1984 to 1995 in *Jump, Dragonball,* and *Dragonball Z*—mildly humorous, wildly violent, incredibly convoluted sagas about the quest of a supernaturally strong boy for five magic "dragonballs"—produced forty-one bestselling-paperback collections, a top-rated animated TV series that ran from 1986 until 1995, and sixteen animated features that consistently ranked in the annual domestic box office top ten. *Jump* can keep its cover price so low because it makes enormous profits selling licensing rights for its hit *manga.*

Unlike American comics for boys, which usually live or die on the popularity of one superhero, *Jump* prefers to spread its bets and keep renewing its talent pool. Though *Dragonball, Dr. Slump,* and *Kinnikuman* were all major franchises in the 1980s, they are gone now, replaced by trendier fare. Among the most popular serials are *Slam Dunk,* a saga about a high-school basketball team that exploits the mid-nineties basketball boom; *Captain Tsubasa* (Captain Wing), a soccer *manga* that soared on the wings of the soccer craze of 1993, but has since returned to earth; and *Dragon Quest,* a long-running serial that has inspired a bestselling Nintendo video game series. The character designer for the games, Akira Toriyama, was also the creator of the *Dragonball, Dragonball Z,* and *Dr. Slump* serials.

Jump, however, is more than the sum of its franchises. Beginning in March of 1995 it ran a ten-part series on the problem of school bullying that featured first-person testimonies from victims, including a twenty-eight-year-old woman who wrote that, as fourth grader, she had been teased by the entire class for her stutter but was able to put a stop to it by breaking her abacus over the ringleader's head. *Jump* editor-in-chief Nobuhiko Horie told the *Shukan Asahi* weekly magazine that, as the nation's biggest medium for children, the magazine had a responsibility to run the series. "The true nature of the problem of bullying will not become clear unless we tackle it," he said.

Jump's publisher, Shueisha, has launched other *Jump* titles, including *Young Jump* for a slightly older male audience, *Business Jump* for salarymen, and *Gekkan Shonen Jump,* a monthly monster of a mag that is to the original *Jump* what Manhattan's phone book is to Trenton's: more, much more. It also publishes a steady stream of special issues, such as *Young Jump for Gals* and *Winter Shonen Jump*. Wherever you look in Japan, there is a *Jump* for you.

SMAP

"Idol" groups and singers once seemed as much a part of the Japanese pop scene as cherry blossoms are a part of the Japanese spring. Every year dozens of new idols debuted on programs like *Star Tanjo* (Birth of a Star), *The Best Ten, Uta no Top Ten* (Song Top Ten), and *Yoru no Hit Studio* (Evening Hit Studio), and many of the older ones, especially women, who were often show-biz veterans by the age of twenty, retired, changed careers, or simply faded away.

"Idol" (*idoru*) was an all-purpose tag for young pop singers who were scouted, trained, and packaged by talent agencies and record companies for mass consumption. The singers didn't necessarily have to be idolized by millions to be considered idols. They didn't even have to sing that well. Although an ability to carry a tune certainly helped, idol handlers often considered looks and personality more important. The preferred image was usually lively, pleasant, and cute, with a soupçon of star quality that set the idol apart from the common herd. The female idols, in particular, were not pre-sented as intimidating musical prodigies or sex symbols but as ideal Miss Averages whom every boy would want for a sister or girlfriend, every girl for a friend, every father for a daughter.

Although the prime venues for idols were the TV pop-music shows that had first emerged in the early 1960s, the agencies also exploited their talents—or exposed their lack thereof—in a wide range of media, including movies, TV dramas, and, most lucratively, TV commercials. The professional ne plus ultra for an idol was to become the face of a TV-ad campaign for chocolate bars, frozen confectionery, curry rice, and other kid-consumer products. The number of such campaign contracts was a frequently mentioned barometer of idol popularity.

The idols were such perfect made-for-TV products themselves that they seemed likely to last as long as kids stayed glued to the tube: in other words, forever. It was not to be, however. In the latter half of the 1980s rock bands like Rebecca, Checkers, Hound Dog, Tube, Anzen Chitai, Bakufu Slump, and Kome Kome Club began to take center stage on the pop scene. Unlike earlier bands, who played Western-style rock for hard-core fans, these groups had a more Japanized sound that ordinary kids could relate to. Also, taking a hint from New Music queen **YUMING**, who mounted spectacular stage shows for her national tours, bands began to put more stress on lights, costumes, and choreography and less on straight musicianship—and their fans loved it. In 1986, when Rebecca, a foursome headed by sultry lead singer Nokko, sold one million copies of its *Rebecca IV* album and surpassed Yuming on the annual sales chart, the music industry realized that rock had arrived as a commercial force.

With the beginning of what came to be called the "band boom," even rockers who had been scuffling for years in smoky basement dives started to fill big clubs and concert halls. One reason was that there were more big clubs and concert halls to fill. Sensing that music consumers were becoming sated with recorded music and more eager to hear the real thing, promoters began building larger, better-appointed venues for live acts, including rock, and fans began crowding into them.

In a replay of the Group Sounds boom of the 1960s (see **ROCKABILLY, GROUP SOUNDS AND THE BIRTH OF JAPANESE ROCK**), amateurs started forming bands of their own. In the latter half of the eighties, sales of electric guitars doubled compared with the previous decade to a half million units a year—the highest total since the Group Sounds era. The Yoyogi Park Sunday pedestrian mall, which had been the scene of the *Takenoku-zoku's* revels in the early 1980s (see **ZOKU**), became a testing ground for amateur bands and several, such

as Jun Sky Walker and The Boom, later went on to successful professional careers.

Television took notice of the band boom. In February 1989 *Heisei Meibutsu TV* (Heisei Famous Product TV), a TBS late-night variety show, began a segment for amateur bands called *Ikasu Band Tengoku* (Groovy Band Heaven) or, as it quickly came to be known, *Ikaten,* that became a nationwide sensation and made several no-name groups famous overnight.

Even young women, who ordinarily would have been prime idol fodder, began to find other avenues to pop fame and fortune. The success of *Yuyake Nyan Nyan* (Meow, Meow at Dusk), a mid-eighties show featuring a group of twenty-four girls called the **ONYANKO CLUB**, challenged the supremacy of the agency idol factories by making instant stars out of ordinary high school girls, while cutting a large and damaging slice out of the music shows' vital teen market.

In the latter half of the decade the growing number of women rockers generated by the band boom posed another kind of challenge. Unlike the idols who were packaged as sugary-sweet ideals by their largely male handlers, "girls' rock" (*gaaruzu rokku*) singers like Nokko of Rebecca and bands like Princess Princess and Show-Ya presented a sassy, sexy image of femininity that was all their own—and made them role models for millions of teenage girls.

The band boom effectively killed the TV music shows that the idols depended on for exposure. Like the New Musicians before them, many bands had no desire to appear on the same TV stage with idol singers and, as they came to dominate the charts, the shows began to seem irrelevant and out of touch. Their ratings plunged, and in the late eighties and early nineties nearly all of them went off air. Idols, with a few hardy exceptions, seemed doomed to extinction.

One idol group, however, not only managed to survive but by mid-decade was ruling the airwaves with a thoroughness that few pop stars had ever equaled.

SMAP may have been a six-man singing and dancing ensemble, but given the frequency of their appearances on not only their own regular programs, but series dramas, radio shows, musicals, concerts, and the inevitable TV commercials, they seemed more like an invading army.

The general of this army—the president of the talent agency that had discovered, groomed, and sold the group—deserved much of the credit. Johnny Kitagawa had launched his career as a manager of young male talent in 1963 with a quartet called, appropriately enough, the Johnnies. He had his first major success with his next foursome, the Four Leaves, one of the decade's most popular male idol groups. After that

there was no stopping Kitagawa and his Johnny's Jimusho (officially known in English as Johnny & Associates) talent agency.

Over the coming decades what came to be known the "Pretty Man Factory" (Bidanshi Fakutorii) churned out group after group of young male idols who won the hearts of generation after generation of Japanese schoolgirls. In the early 1980s—the idol singer's Golden Age—Kitagawa's biggest act was the Tanokin Trio, who shot to fame through their appearances on the SANNEN B GUMI KIMPACHI SENSEI show. Two members of the trio, Toshihiko Tahara and Masahiko Kondo, enjoyed enormous success as solo acts, with Tahara reeling off twelve and Kondo sixteen number-one singles in the first half of the decade.

Another was Shibugakitai (The Cool Kid Gang), a trio that got their start as dancers for the Tanokin Trio. Like their Tanokin seniors, they were soon releasing records, beginning with their 1982 hit debut single, "Nai Nai 16," starring on the big screen in the long-forgotten Headphone Lullaby, and appearing in TV dramas, including a TBS show called Uwasa no Potato Boys (The Much-Talked-About Potato Boys), playing the sons of a Hokkaido potato farmer.

The coolest of the gang turned out to be Masahiro Motoki, nicknamed Mokkun, whose androgynous good looks and bad-boy

The 1995 SMAP lineup: (front to back) Tsuyoshi Kusanagi, Takuya Kimura, Goro Inagaki, Shingo Katori, Masahiro Nagai, and Katsuyuki Mori.

charisma helped propel him to a prosperous career as a model and actor after the group's break-up in 1988. A photo book featuring glimpses of Mokkun's pubic hair made him nationally notorious, but he also won respect from his industry peers for strong performances in such films *Fancy Dance* (1989), *Shiko Funjatta* (Sumo Do, Sumo Don't, 1992), and *Rampo* (Mystery of Rampo, 1995), the last film being distributed in the United States by Samuel Goldwyn Company.

Still another Johnny's Jimusho megagroup was Hikaru Genji, seven guys on roller skates who wowed fans in the late eighties and early nineties with slick, glitzy shows that combined boyishly energetic, if ragged, renditions of their hits with flashy skating routines. In 1988 Hikaru Genji claimed all of the three top-selling singles, the first artists to achieve that feat since **PINK LADY** in 1977. They also became the first group to reel off eight straight number-one hits beginning with their debut single, the August 1987 release "Star Light."

Kitagawa, who had spent his high-school years in Los Angeles, later said that an important inspiration for his style of showmanship was Alice Cooper, the American rock star whose blatantly suggestive lyrics and bizarrely theatrical act earned him lasting notoriety and tons of money in the early seventies. "I was impressed by his ability as an entertainer," said Kitagawa. "Even though he was good enough to appeal to people with his guitar technique alone, he deliberately took to the stage looking like a monster. At first I wondered what was wrong with the guy, but when I thought about it I realized that he was doing it to please the fans. . . . That attitude really impressed me."

Hikaru Genji pleased millions of fans with their sub-Ice-Capades theatrics, but Johnny's Jimusho continued to scout good-looking teen-agers as replacements should they begin to falter. In January 1988, the agency selected twelve boys ranging in age from ten to eighteen as back-up skaters for Hikaru Genji. Shortly afterwards, the agency chose six of these skaters for a new group called SMAP (an acronym meaning "Sports Music Assemble People") whose gimmick would be not skates but skateboards.

The boys proved to be quick studies—they were soon giving workshops on skateboard techniques on national television—and, with constant media exposure as Hikaru Genji's back-ups, they soon became celebrities in their own right and were seen as the rightful heirs to Hikaru Genji's spangled mantles.

But then the band boom began, the music shows died, and idol singers and groups faced hard times. Although SMAP's first single, "Can't Stop!! -Loving-" reached number two in the charts following its release in September 1991, the group did not hit the top until its twelfth single, "Hey Hey Okini Maido Ari" (Hey Hey Thanks Again), which was released in March 1994. A theme song for *Shuuto* (Shoot), a movie starring SMAP that exploited the soccer craze, the record held onto to the number one slot for only one week. Compared with Hikaru Genji, which had cranked out ten number-one singles before breaking up in 1992, SMAP was hardly a hit-making powerhouse.

But though the record-buying public may have become a harder sell for idol groups in the band-boom years, there was still a huge market in a wide range of media for cute guys, and Johnny's Jimusho moved quickly to exploit it. This was not a new strategy—agencies had been turning their idols into stage, screen, and TV "multitalents" (*maru-chitarento*) for decades—but in exploiting SMAP, Johnny's took it to a higher, immensely profitable level.

The beginnings of this strategy were modest enough. Carrying their skateboards, the boys started their nonsinging careers in 1988 with appearances on the *Itsumi, Kato-chan no Waatto Atsmare!!* (Itsumi and Kato's B-i-i-i-g Get-Together!!) variety show and *Abunai Shonen III* (Dangerous Youths III), a series drama in which they played a group of high-school skateboarders who formed a broadcasting club. Their object was to confound the stuck-up girls who ran the school paper, but the boys found more trouble than they had bargained for as they zipped off their boards to cover their next hot story.

Casting SMAP as SMAP was not easy, however, so Johnny's broke up the set, as it were, and marketed the boys as individuals. Starting in October 1988, SMAPper Katsuyuki Mori appeared in a new version of the hit classroom drama **SANNEN B GUMI KIMPACHI SENSEI**, showing off his skateboarding technique every week as the opening titles rolled. In April 1989, another SMAP member, Goro Inagaki, debuted in *Seishun Kazoku* (Youth Family), an NHK morning drama series. Playing a PC-loving, sports-hating nerd, he left his skateboard behind and showed that a SMAPper could do more than grab air. Before long all the boys were displaying their thespian abilities on the tube.

There were, of course, the commercials. SMAP began appearing as TV pitchmen only six months after their formation, for a school-uniform maker. Switching from their usual fashionably casual outfits to high-collared, brass-buttoned Japanese school uniforms, whose design was inspired by the garb of nineteenth-century Prussian schoolboys, may not have done much for their cool-dude image but marked the beginning of a long, lucrative career as ad-campaign faces.

In the 1990s, Johnny's multimedia strategy for SMAP went into high gear. After years of careful nurturing, the group had won a large schoolgirl following and was ready to move from supporting roles to center stage. One indication was the turnout for their first concert, at the Budokan—Japan's Madison Square Garden—on New Year's Day of 1991. Tickets sold out in one day and, to meet the demand, promoters added two more shows, which also quickly sold out. The New Year's Day concert became an annual event, with SMAP putting on five shows to full houses. In 1995, by adding a sixth show to their grueling New Year's celebration, SMAP managed to draw sixty thousand fans, a one-day house record.

In August 1991 the boys starred in their first musical, based on a popular *manga* called *Seinto Seiya* about the struggle of a group of space warriors to save Athena, the goddess of love and peace, from the clutches of an evil king. The show was a smashing success: with 37,200 fans attending its thirty-one-day run. During the miniconcert that ended *Seinto Seiya,* the audience enthusiastically sang along as SMAP performed their soon-to-be-released debut single, "Can't Stop!! - Loving -."

In October, SMAP found further confirmation that they had arrived in the form of a regular program on the TV Tokyo network. Called *I Love SMAP!* (Ai Rabu SMAP or, to translate the pun of the title, Love Love SMAP!) the program became a long-running weekly showcase for the boys' talents, whether singing their latest hit or playing three-on-three basketball.

By the middle of the decade, the members of SMAP were the busiest young men in Japanese show business. In 1995, the boys were appearing, either as a group or individually, on ten regularly scheduled music and variety programs. They were also in demand for TV dramas, playing everything from a nursery-school teacher—Shingo Katori in Fuji TV's *For You*—to samurai warrior—Takuya Kimura in TV Asahi's *Kimi wa Toki no Kanata e* (You Journey Beyond Time). On the radio, they hosted seven regular shows, either together (Bunka Hoso's *Stop the SMAP*) or as individual DJs (Katsuyuki Mori on FM Yokohama's *SMAP In the House!*).

As TV pitchmen, they reigned supreme, selling not only the expected chewing gum, canned drinks, and ice-cream drumsticks but such big-ticket items as cars, PCs, and life insurance. In 1995, they appeared in fourteen commercials—more than any other single artist or group—and the ad industry began to speak of the "SMAP effect" on sales. In February 1996, a steamy TV ad that showed the long-haired, androgynously handsome Takuya Kimura getting his lips and face smeared with a new brand of Kanebo lipstick sent the product's retail sales

soaring to 3.12 million units in the first two months—a company record and well worth the singer's hefty fee, which was estimated as fifty or sixty million yen. The sponsor's only concern was that the campaign's posters, which showed a full-face shot of Kimura, were disappearing from train station walls faster than they could replace them. Not only sexy but, as he proved on countless TV and radio appearances, disarmingly frank and charmingly quick-witted, Kimura had become the favorite boy toy of the 1990s.

Despite their excursions into other forms of popular media, SMAP was still very much involved in the music business. In September 1994, the boys released a single, "Gambarimasho" (Let's Keep Trying) that sold a group record of 910,000 copies and won them new fans with its upbeat lyrics and catchy melody. In 1995 they surpassed that record with "Oretachi ni Ashita wa Aru" (We Have Tomorrow), the theme song of a TV drama starring Kimura, and proved again that their reach now extended beyond their core audience to the pop music mainstream.

It was in concert, however, that the boys demonstrated most vividly the depth and breadth of their appeal. All of their mid-nineties shows were sellouts, just as they had always been, but over the years the composition of the audience had changed. Instead of girls in their early teens, their audiences now included growing numbers of women in their thirties and forties, who screamed and boogied with all the passion of their daughters. "The energy of those six boys is encouraging to me," a forty-one-year-old kindergarten teacher told the *Nikkei Weekly*. "I'm not out to relive my lost youth. I'm still there! I don't feel I've aged; it's natural for me to be interested in young men."

Although not as heavily reported by the media, the boys' androgynous image also won them an enthusiastic following among gay men. That image, according to two tell-all books published in 1996 by former Johnny's talent Jun'ya Hiramoto, reflected the sexual preferences of Johnny Kitagawa himself. Kitagawa, said Hiramoto, seduced the prettier of his charges, while sending the ones who rejected his advances to professional oblivion. Hiramoto even claimed to have seen Kitagawa rape a boy in the dorm where the youngest of the agency's talent slept.

He was not the first former Johnny's talent to have gone public with such revelations. In 1988 a member of the Four Leaves published twelve volumes of a diary that detailed Kitagawa's homosexual activities over a two-year period. And SMAP? According to Hiramoto, Kitagawa's frequent—and painful—attentions to Goro Inagaki caused Inagaki's dancing to become notoriously clumsy. Hiramoto, however, took care to put this and other hearsay, including the story of Kimura's plastic surgery, in a chapter titled "Rumors about Johnny's."

By 1996 the boys of SMAP were growing to adulthood and, after eight years of singing other people's songs, trying to assert themselves as individuals with wills of their own. Also, the popularity of Kimura, known by his fans as simply Kimutaku, was far overshadowing that of the other members. Despite the boys' often-repeated claim that they were as tight as ever, the media began to speak of the group's imminent break up.

Then, early in May 1995, Katsuyuki Mori announced that he was quitting SMAP at the end of the month to pursue a career as a motorbike racer. "Becoming a racer was my dream," he told the press. "But because I don't want my underage fans becoming involved in gambling, I have decided to leave the group." Following Mori's tearful farewell appearance on the highly rated *SMAP X SMAP* show, the remaining members vowed to carry on.

But whatever happens to SMAP, whose success made Johnny's Jimusho Japan's top talent agency in 1995, with earnings of 2.9 billion yen, Johnny Kitagawa and his team are readying other groups of handsome young guys, including Tokio, The Kinki Kids, and V6, to move into the center spotlight. The band boom may have run its course, but idols are forever.

THE SUMO DYNASTY OF
THE HANADAS

Sumo is to Japan what baseball is to the United States: a sport with roots that reach far back into the past (about two thousand years, in sumo's case) and have penetrated deep into the national psyche. Its jargon has entered the language, its heroes have become part of the cultural mythology.

In the postwar era sumo has faced stiff competition from Western sports, most notably baseball and, most recently, professional soccer, but it has held its own quite well; the ratings for NHK's broadcasts of the six annual professional sumo tournaments regularly surpass the thirty-percent mark, while tickets to the tournaments themselves, especially for the first floor-box seats, are scalpers' gold.

Together with the pro-wrestling exploits of **RIKIDOZAN**, sumo was the big draw for the crowds who gathered round the outdoor televisions of the 1950s. And the sumo wrestlers they were watching the most intently were two small (by sumo standards) men with outsized talents: Wakanohana and Tochinishiki. Acclaimed in his younger days for his performances of *shokkiri*, or comic *sumo*, which provided fans at sumo exhibitions not only with pratfalls but a dazzling demonstration of *sumo* rules and techniques, Tochinishiki was a master technician who

earned the nickname "Pit Viper" (*Mamushi*) for his quick and deadly attack that could fell much bigger opponents.

But though Tochinishiki reached the top rank of grand champion, or *yokozuna*, first, in January 1955, he was second in popularity to his archrival, Wakanohana. A brilliant technician in his own right, who was known for slamming opponents flat on their backs in the center of the ring with a spectacular throw called the *yobimodoshi*, Wakanohana was fast, aggressive, and whipcord strong, with an almost uncanny ring sense. A lithe wrestler, who never weighed more than 109 kilograms in his prime, he could nonetheless overpower many of his larger foes and, when on the defensive, seemed to know exactly how to plant himself on the half-buried straw bales that marked the boundary of the round sumo ring. Opponents said he had "eyes in the soles of his feet" and called him the "Devil of the Ring," or *Dohyo no Oni*.

Evenly matched competitors and rivals from early in their careers, Tochinishiki and Wakanohana fought ferocious seesaw battles that made for terrific television. Even fans straining to glimpse blurry black-and-white images from the back of a crowd could feel the excitement as Tochi and Waka contended for yet another championship, or battled to the bitter end simply out of pride.

Wakanohana's life outside of the ring had had plenty of drama as well. Born

Katsuji Hanada in March 1928 to a prosperous young apple grower and his teenage wife, he had a happy, comfortable early childhood in Japan's frigid north country. Then in September 1934 a typhoon devastated the region's orchards, ruining Katsuji's father. Needing to make a new start, he moved his family, including Katsuji and his three younger brothers and older sister, to Muroran, a port city on the northern island of Hokkaido.

While his father was scratching out a living as a coal miner or fighting Japan's wars as a soldier in China, Katsuji was growing up tough on the streets of Muroran. Starting out as a newsboy at the age of six, he held a succession of jobs to help support the growing family. By the age ten he was doing an adult's work as a construction laborer and, by the age of sixteen, was a full-time longshoreman on the Muroran docks.

An outstanding natural athlete with a fine sense of balance and a body hardened by carrying heavy loads up narrow planks to waiting ships, he was already a better worker at sixteen than most adult men— and certainly a better sumo prospect. When a wrestler named Onoumi, who had come to Muroran as a member of a traveling sumo group, invited him to try a career in the ring, Katsuji decided to trade his laborer's headband for a sumo belt and in November 1946 formally joined Onoumi's Nishonoseki sta-

ble under his new sumo name: Wakanohana, or Flower of Youth.

As a new trainee in the Nishonoseki stable, Wakanohana caught the eye of top-division star Rikidozan, who was later to win fame as pro wrestler. Under Riki's strict training regime, the young Wakanohana practiced until he was ready to pass out. Although he rose steadily through the ranks, he once seriously thought about throwing himself into the river to escape Riki's brutal training. In January 1950 he won promotion to the highest of sumo's six divisions—the first wrestler who had entered sumo in the postwar period to reach this exalted status. In May 1951 he fought his first bout against Tochinishiki, then one rung above him at *komusubi,* sumo's fourth-highest rank. After a titantic struggle, Wakanohana forced Tochinishiki to the edge of the ring and, gripping his opponent's sumo belt with his right hand, threw him out for the win. Sumo's most famous rivalry had been born.

By the mid-1950s, this rivalry was riveting millions to radios and TV sets across the country. Wakanohana even starred in his own biopic—*Wakanohana Monogatari: Dohyo no Oni* (The Wakanohana Story: The Devil of the Ring)—which told of his struggles in Muroran, his rise to the top of the sumo world, and his private life, including the tragic loss earlier that year of his four-year-old son, who had died after falling into a pot

Takanohana receives the championship flag from his brother, the former Wakanohana, in January 1975.

of boiling sumo stew. Though Wakanohana was a wooden actor, mouthing his lines with all the enthusiasm of a kid drafted into the sixth-grade class play, the movie was a hit for the Nikkatsu studio.

The peak came in 1959, when Wakanohana and Tochinishiki took five of the year's six tournaments and brought Japan's ancient sport to its postwar height of popularity. In March 1960, they met each other on the fifteenth and final day of the Osaka Tournament with undefeated records—the first such perfect scores by two grand champions in sumo's history. In a hard-fought contest Wakanohana won what the media dubbed "the sumo bout of the century."

It also turned out to be the last meeting between the two rivals; in May, after losing the two first bouts of the Summer Tournament, Tochinishiki suddenly retired. Wakanohana held on for two more years, winning two more tournaments and pushing his total number of tourney victories to ten. In April 1962, after a string of mediocre records, he announced that he was quitting to take the elder name Futagoyama and become the coach of Futagoyama Stable.

Futagoyama was a successful coach, training two *yokozuna* and two *ozeki,* holders of sumo's second-highest rank. One of Futagoyama's *ozeki* was his own brother, Mitsuru Hanada, who rose to heights of popularity that surpassed even his own.

Born in Muroran in 1950, Mitsuru was his mother's tenth and last child. In 1957, after his father's death from cancer, Mitsuru and the rest of the family came to Tokyo to live with Wakanohana. In junior high school, Mitsuru became an outstanding swimmer. After setting a new schoolboy record for the one-hundred-meter butterfly, he was tagged as a hot prospect for the 1968 Olympic Games. But instead of going to Mexico City, Mitsuru decided to enter his older brother's stable. Futagoyama, however, was strongly opposed to the idea. Knowing how tough the sumo world was, and how embarrassing it would be if his brother failed under his tutelage, Futagoyama tried, unsuccessfully, to make Mitsuru change his mind.

Fighting under his surname, Hanada, he shot up through the ranks and won promotion to the top division at the age of eighteen—a sumo record. A lanky, handsome, soft-spoken young man with a steely will to succeed, Hanada was dubbed the "sumo world's prince" by the media. At the age of nineteen he changed his fighting name to Takanohana and, at twenty, secretly married a model and actress several years his senior. He was afraid that his stablemaster brother might oppose the match, but Futagoyama could not protest too loudly; he had kept his own marriage, to the daughter of a relative of a stable assistant, a secret for five years. (He later said he had not told his parents to spare them the expense of traveling from Muroran to Tokyo for the ceremony.)

Like his older brother, Takanohana was lighter than most of his opponents, but instead of relying on technical skills to outfox them, he used a straight-ahead style of sumo, polished in endless practice sessions, to power them out. In September 1972, he earned promotion to *ozeki* and in January 1975 won his first tournament championship in a David-vs.-Goliath play-off with the *yokozuna* Kitanoumi, a beefy, powerful, wrestler who was well-hated by many fans for his arrogant attitude in the ring—and his habit of winning against Takanohana. Fans of the "sumo prince," including nearly all of the women who took any interest in the sport, went wild; Takanohana became the most popular sports figure in the country.

His mediocre record the following tournament, however, kept him from advancing to the *yokozuna* rank. He had another chance after beating Kitanoumi in a play-off for the championship of the September Tournament, but in the November Tournament in Kyushu he finished with only eight wins, not enough for promotion.

After this second disappointment, Takanohana's star faded, but he managed to hold onto his *ozeki* rank for fifty straight tournaments—a sumo record. Finally, after recording only two win in the first six days of the January 1981 Tournament, Takanohana announced his retirement as an active wrestler. In 1982, he assumed the elder name Fujishima and opened Fujishima Stable.

Despite the loss of Takanohana, Futagoyama Stable continued to prosper in the 1980s. Meanwhile, Futagoyama rose to the second highest post in the Japan Sumo Association hierarchy. The only one higher was his old rival, Tochinishiki, who as sumo elder Kasugano had become JSA director in 1974. In 1988, after becoming the longest-serving director in JSA history, Kasugano resigned and was succeeded by Futagoyama. The former Devil of the Dohyo held the sumo world's top job until 1992, when he turned sixty-five and had to retire under Association rules.

By this time, however, public attention had shifted to younger brother Fujishima and his two remarkable sons. Entering sumo in March 1988 under the fighting names Takahanada and Wakahanada, the boys had both shown outstanding promise from the beginning. The younger of the two, Takahanada, shot up through the ranks in record speed, reaching the highest division in May 1990 at the age of seventeen—a postwar record. Wakahanada, who was shorter, smaller, and eighteen months older than his brother, joined him there in September. Third-generation members of the Hanada dynasty, they were sumo royalty whose tickets to the summit seemed already punched.

This pair, collectively known in the press as the "Hanada brothers," or simply "Taka-Waka," became the objects of a media blitz that obliterated their private lives—they could hardly take a step out of their Fujishima Stable quarters without attracting the attention of waiting reporters and fans—and made them the idols of millions of teenage girls, many of whom had never voluntarily watched a sumo match in their lives.

A baby-faced teenager whose public persona was almost robotically remote, if scrupulously polite, Takahanada suffered the brunt of this attention. When he won his first top-division tournament in January 1992 and rode to Fujishima Stable in Tokyo's Nakano Ward in an open car, thousands of fans lined the streets, hung from lampposts, and leaned out of windows to get a glimpse of their hero. The frenzy of the crowds that followed the brothers' every move was, said one Sumo Association official, "a little frightening."

For the Association itself, however, the Taka-Waka boom represented a windfall: fans began camping out in front of the tournament box office days before tickets went on sale. Sumo, which had once been regarded by the trendy young as hopelessly uncool, was suddenly the hottest sport in the country.

Sumo fever rose even higher when newscaster Hiroshi Kume scooped the rest of the media with the announcement, on the October 26, 1992 **NEWS STATION** program, that Takahanada had become engaged to **RIE MIYAZAWA**. An actress, singer, and commercial pitchwoman, the half-Dutch, half-Japanese Miyazawa had become notorious the previous year for appearing in a nude photo album. The media was soon hailing the "wedding of the century," which was scheduled for May 28, 1993, and comparing the couple to Joe Dimaggio and Marilyn Monroe.

The marriage, however, was not to be; Miyazawa's domineering mother and manager, a former dancer, was reportedly opposed to her daughter throwing her brilliant

The second Takanohana, together with his father and mother, greets fans outside Futagoyama Stable.

future away to become a sumo wrestler's wife. Meanwhile, Takahanada's parents insisted that Miyazawa follow sumo tradition and devote herself completely to her husband. Also, they were said to be reluctant to allow Miyazawa's declassé mother to join sumo's royal family. In any case, on January 27, 1993, Takahanada appeared at a press conference to announce that the engagement was off. Miyazawa held her own press conference the same day, at which she revealed that Takahanada had not contacted her since leaving on tour in December and said that they had "grown apart" as a result.

This fiasco damaged the popularity of both Takahanada and Miyazawa and cooled the sumo fever that had been raging since the beginning of the decade. Even so, Takahanada, whose rock-solid lower body and superb belt technique reminded some sumo experts of the great prewar *yokozuna* Futabayama, continued his upward climb through the ranks, winning promotion to *ozeki* in January 1993 and acquiring a new name—Takanohana—from his stablemaster father. At the same time his archrival, a massive wrestler from Hawaii named Akebono, advanced to *yokozuna* rank and commentators hailed the birth of the "Ake-Taka era" in sumo.

Meanwhile, Wakahanada, who had become the sport's finest technician, refused to be forgotten. In March 1993 he won his first tournament and was given the fighting name of his famous uncle, Wakanohana.

Following the merger of Futagoyama and Fujishima stables in February 1992 and the assumption of the Futagoyama name by coach Fujishima, Takanohana and Wakanohana's stable became the strongest in the sumo world. Including the two brothers, the new Futagoyama Stable boasted more top-division wrestlers than any other in the sport. Some commentators argued that the long-standing rule against stablemates fighting each other in regular tournament bouts should be changed to give other wrestlers a fair chance against the Futago-yama juggernaut.

The rule, however, remained and, after winning two consecutive tournaments with a 15-0 mark, Takanohana was promoted to the rank of *yokozuna* in November 1994. At the age of twenty-two years and three months, he was the third-youngest grand champion in sumo history. Takanohana fever resurged, as more than twenty thousand fans turned out to watch his first *yokozuna* ring-entering ceremony—a two-hundred-year-old rite performed to mark the ascension of a new grand champion—at Tokyo's Meiji Shrine.

After his promotion, Takanohana continued to win tournament after tournament. In September 1995 he took his eleventh with a 15-0 record and passed his uncle, the former Wakanohana, on the all-time tournament-win list. Experts said that he had an excellent shot at breaking the record for most tournament victories, thirty-two, held by 1960s grand champion Taiho.

In May 1995 Takanohana married Keiko Konno, a former TV announcer, in a traditional Shinto ceremony at Meiji Shrine. This event, as well as the lavish reception at the Hotel New Otani, was covered by the commercial networks with the same breathless intensity as the marriage of a crown prince. Seventy percent of Japan's population—nearly ninety million people—tuned in.

In March 1996, Takanohana won his twelfth tournament and posed for press photos holding his five-month-old son, Yuichi. The boy was looking intently not at the cameramen or his father but the huge glittering winner's cup. Another generation of Hanada sumo stars may well be in the making.

TAIGA DRAMA

Most Japanese television dramas are what Americans would consider miniseries: they have a limited number of installments, continuing storylines, and a novelistic structure. Others, usually period dramas, have continuing characters but tell one story per episode. Then there is NHK's *taiga* drama (*roman fleuve* or saga drama), which might be described as a year-long maxiseries. Beginning on a Sunday evening in January, viewers tune in for the first of fifty-two one-hour weekly installments whose Tolstoyan story usually centers around famous figures in Japanese history.

Since the first in 1963, *taiga* drama have been prestige productions with big stars and big budgets—the king (or *shogun*) of NHK's drama lineup. Every year NHK mounts a major publicity offensive for its *taiga* drama to hook as many viewers as possible on the first episode. Often it succeeds, but over the years the public broadcaster has had its share of near-misses and embarrassing flops. Hit or miss, the *taiga* drama has become a national institution; even viewers who rarely or never tune in know the latest show's story and stars. It has also become a barometer of the national mood; although the story may be set in the distant past, it frequently (and deliberately) reflects contemporary events and attitudes.

The impetus for making the first *taiga* drama in 1963 was not profits—NHK derives almost all its income from receiver fees—but the desire of NHK Entertainment Department director Taiji Nagasawa to draw the public away from movies to TV dramas and raise the profile of the television medium. In retrospect, it seems strange that he should have bothered; moviegoers were already deserting the theatres for the tube in droves. From a peak of 1.1 billion in 1958, annual movie attendance fell to 373 million by 1965.

Hoping to stem the exodus, the five major studios refused to sell their films to television and instructed their contract stars not to appear in TV dramas. This policy of resistance was proving futile, however; Japanese viewers were tuning in anyway. Eager to clinch victory in the popularity war with his movie-industry rivals, Nagasawa pressed ahead with his plan to produce the TV drama to end all TV dramas. Based on *Hana no Shogai* (The Life of a Flower) by popular historical novelist Shoichi Funabashi, the show was set at the end of the Tokugawa period (1600–1867), when Japan was opening to the West after nearly two hundred fifty years of isolation. In a major coup, NHK signed Shochiku star Keiji Sada to play the lead.

Hana no Shogai, which debuted in April 1963, was a success and Nagasawa embarked on his second *taiga* drama: *Ako Ronin,* based on the classic story about forty-seven masterless samurai, or *ronin,* who sacrifice their lives to avenge the death of their lord. This was the first *taiga* drama to start in January and run for an entire year, setting a pattern that nearly all the others have followed since. Featuring an all-star cast, headed by Kazuo Hasegawa, *Ako Ronin* became a smash hit, with ratings soaring as high as fifty-three percent—a *taiga* drama record that has never been equaled.

The *taiga* drama for 1965, *Taikoki,* was also a ratings winner, further establishing the program as the star of the NHK schedule. But instead of the usual rousing sword fights and melodramatic plot, *Taikoki* producers opted to make a serious historical drama that drew parallels between its seventeenth-century past and the twentieth-century present. The opening shot, of a Bullet Train and Nagoya Station, caused considerable viewer comment, not all favorable, but the show's wealth of historical factoids, including the amount of money in a samurai's pay envelope, and its insistence on depicting its warriors as fallible human beings, instead of Great Stone Faces, won the show a devoted salaryman following.

Despite this fast start, NHK had trouble finding and staying with a winning *taiga* drama formula. Two back-to-back dramas set in the early Meiji period (1868–1912), when Japan was rapidly Westernizing, recorded disappointing ratings—the 1968 *Ryuma ga Yuku* (Ryuma Departs) plunged to an all-time low of 14.5 percent—and led to a policy of alternating eras to avoid boring viewers.

To scotch media rumors of the show's imminent cancellation, producers returned it in 1969 to the popular entertainment fold with *Ten to Chi to* (Heaven and Earth), a stirring drama about Warring States–period (1482–1558) warlords Takeda Shingen and Uesugi Kenshin. Ratings revived and so did the show's fortunes.

Over the next few years, NHK stuck with the period-drama formula and had generally good results, except for dramas set in the *bakumatsu* period—the years leading up to the Meiji Restoration in 1868. *Bakumatsu* history, with its welter of factions and plots, was too dry and complicated for the average viewer. There were too many samurai strategy meetings, too little sword play.

NHK also had its share of bad luck. The leading man for the 1974 *taiga* drama, Tetsuya Watabe, fell ill and had to be replaced by *yakuza* movie star Hiroki Matsukata. Then scriptwriter So Kurimoto fought with the producers and quit in a huff. As if that weren't enough, Matsukata began complaining to reporters about NHK's dictatorial and bureaucratic ways. Somehow, the show survived.

In its fifteenth installment, the *taiga* drama changed course again. Instead of focusing on the usual shoguns and samurai, producer Susumu Kondo decided to try a fresh approach. His 1978 *Ogon Hibi* (Days of Gold) not only had a Warring States–period merchant for its hero but was filmed partly on location in the Philippines—the first time a *taiga* drama had ever gone abroad. The show became a hit.

The 1979 *taiga* drama, *Kusa Moeru* (The Grass Burns), was notable for its focus on the wife of twelfth-century warlord Minamoto no Yoritomo, played by film star Shima Iwashita, the large amount of screen time it devoted to domestic life, and its use of modern Japanese. All marked departures from period-drama convention—and helped make the show a ratings success.

Despite these attempts to stretch the *taiga* drama format, the producers were beginning to run out of premodern history. Japan had been around for nearly two thousand years, but the average viewer was familiar with only a relatively small number of historical figures from the feudal past. It was as

though, having done several shows on George Washington, Thomas Jefferson, and other pre–Civil War presidents, the producers felt they had nowhere else to go but the administration of Millard Fillmore.

The solution, they decided, was the recent past. The *taiga* drama for 1984 focused on World War II, as seen through the eyes of second-generation Japanese-Americans. Called *Sanga Moyu* (Burning Mountains and Rivers), the show depicted its Japanese-American heroes as torn between their mother country and their adopted land. Many Japanese-Americans, however, resented this assumption of divided loyalties and what they perceived as the show's distortions of the historical record. Their protests to the

media proved highly embarrassing to NHK. Also, many older Japanese viewers were unhappy with what they regarded as show's unseemly breast-beating about Japan's deeds during the war. Ratings plunged and, the following year, NHK returned to the safer ground of the Meiji period.

In 1986, the *taiga* drama made a spectacular recovery with *Inochi* (Life), which traced the postwar career of a doctor played by Yoshiko Mita. The story of a woman battling against adversity, including male prejudice, to find success and fulfillment found a large, appreciative female audience.

Not wanting to ignore its male viewers, NHK returned to the traditional period-drama format the following year with

Dokuganryu Masamune (Masamune, The One-Eyed Dragon), the story of a macho warlord in northern Japan. Ratings averaged 39.7 percent—the third-highest in *taiga* drama history. Scriptwriter James Miki tried to depict the late sixteenth and early seventeenth centuries as a modern salaryman might see them, with Masamune's samurai clan as a local company and the chief retainers as middle managers. To hold the interest of female viewers, he included domestic scenes between Masamune and his mother. And to educate younger viewers, for whom the period was as remote and obscure as the French and Indian War is to American teenagers, he tacked two-minute history lessons onto each episode.

With the death of Emperor Showa in 1989 and the end of the Showa era he symbolized, the *taiga* drama reached another turning point. Noticing the winds of change blowing through the world in the new Heisei era, producer Reo Endo decided to make a *taiga* drama on the Northern and Southern Courts period (1336–92). This slice of Japanese history, when the crown was divided between the Nara-based Southern Court of Emperor Go-Daigo and the Kyoto-based Northern Court of the Emperor Komyo, had long been taboo on television because its story of ambition and betrayal showed the Imperial family in a less-than flattering light. But Endo

and his staff pressed on and, when the show finally aired, ratings soared into the thirties and rightist groups, whom they had expected to deluge them with angry protests, remained strangely silent.

In 1990 the appointment of a new NHK president, Keiji Shima, signaled the start of a new era for the *taiga* drama. A business rationalist and broadcasting internationalist, Shima decided to save money by farming out *taiga* drama production to NHK subsidiary NHK Enterprises and design a "media mix" strategy so that NHK could earn extra revenue from *taiga* drama videos, books, and foreign sales.

Shima also broke with the tradition of starting the new *taiga* drama in January and ending it in December. The first series made under the new system, *Ryukyu no Kaze* (The Wind of the Ryukyus), aired from January 1993 to May 1994, while its successor, *Homura Tatsu* (The Fire Burns), was broadcast from May 1994 to March 1995.

The central idea behind the new shows—to view Japanese history and culture from the country's fringes—i.e., the Ryukyu Islands and the far reaches of northern Honshu—was innovative. Also, the determination of the producers to film as much as possible on location, using realistic sets, was admirable. But before the shows could air Shima resigned under a cloud for lying to a Diet subcommittee about his whereabouts during an NHK satellite launch (he was rumored to have been in the room of a female staffer). His successor, Mikio Kawaguchi, pledged to take up where Shima had left off, but the shows failed to attract viewers.

In 1995, with *Hachidai Shogun, Yoshimune* (Yoshimune, the Eighth Shogun), NHK returned the *taiga* drama to its old January starting date and one-year format. The show was a success, recording a peak 31.4 percent rating.

The 1996 *taiga* drama, *Hideyoshi,* which traced the rise of the sixteenth-century warlord Hideyoshi from low-ranking samurai to the most powerful man in Japan, made an even bigger hit with viewers, scoring an average thirty percent rating during its year on the air. One reason was the off-beat but energetic interpretation of the leading role by comic actor Naoto Takenaka. Another was the show's quick tempo, compared with the stately pace of the usual period drama. Still another was a widely reported scene in an early episode that gave viewers an unexpected glimpse inside Takenaka's loincloth.

But though the *taiga* drama may be back on track, it seems likely that its history, like that of the country it portrays, will remain turbulent. And that viewers, fascinated by the twists and turns of its never-ending search for higher ratings, will keep tuning in.

TAKARAZUKA

Foreigners often find the Takarazuka Revue Company—an all-female troupe whose biggest stars play male roles—a bit baffling. Kabuki is somehow easier to understand, partly because the West has a similar gender-bending tradition. In Shakespeare's day boys played the roles of Ophelia and Juliet for much the same reason that, in the Tokugawa era (1600–1867), male actors played flirtatious courtesans and dignified samurai wives: the morality of the day frowned on women taking to the stage. While Western theater has long since abandoned this tradition, Kabuki has embraced it as central to its esthetic.

But what do sophisticated Westerners think when they see young women in men's clothes acting in lavishly staged, unabashedly romantic reworkings of popular *manga*, old Broadway musicals, and, more recently, the Kennedy assassination? A common first reaction is that the women are lesbians camping it up. When the Takarazuka troupe appeared in London in 1994, the gay and lesbian community turned out in force, delighted by what the gay magazine *Phaze* described as "show tunes and sequined frocks on a revolving stage." The article added that lesbians, on seeing the love scenes between the troupe's "men" and women "will not need to do much reading between the lines."

That reading would have deeply shocked troupe founder Ichizo Kobayashi. The president of Hankyu Railways Corporation and an opera buff, Kobayashi noticed that audiences were abandoning classical Japanese drama for Western song-and-dance shows. He thought that, rather than all-male Kabuki, they would enjoy an all-female troupe performing musical dramas that combined elements of Eastern and Western theater.

Although Kobayashi founded his dream troupe in 1914, it was not until 1924 that he built the Takarazuka Grand Theater in the hot springs resort of Takarazuka, the terminus of a Hankyu Railways line that began in Osaka. The Osakans who rode the train to Takarazuka and brought a ticket to the Takarazuka Revue saw leggy girls in splashy tight-fitting costumes prancing and dancing on stage with admirable energy and verve, but nary a hint of sensuality.

No slutty chorines these! They were, as anyone could clearly see, pure flowers of Japanese womanhood, even if they were wearing pants and flourishing pasteboard swords. Kobayashi's object in founding a "girls' opera," he stated, was to offer "clean, proper, and beautiful" entertainment to children of good families. The authorities, particularly the troglodytes who hated the idea of women on stage and feared the baleful influence of Western culture, may have harumphed, but they had to admit that the Takarazuka show hardly represented a threat to public morals. And their own daughters loved it.

This all-female revue eventually found its biggest audience among the younger members of its own sex. Today nearly ninety percent of the 2.5 million fans who attend Takarazuka performances annually are women, most of whom are under the age of twenty-five. Walking through the Hibiya theatrical district of Tokyo on most afternoons, one can see dozens of these young fans outside the theater entrance, waiting patiently to catch a glimpse of their Takarazuka idols.

The war years were tough for the Takarazuka troupe—the authorities frowned on the Western taint in their shows—but it managed to survive and even played before enthusiastic crowds of soldiers on battlefront tours.

After the war, the troupe turned unabashedly to Broadway for material, staging such standards as *Oklahoma*, *West Side Story*, and *South Pacific*. It also found material from such unlikely sources as Puccini (*Madame Butterfly*), David Selznick (*Gone With the Wind*), Shakespeare (*Hamlet*) and the *manga* of Takarazuka city native **OSAMU TEZUKA**, including *Black Jack, Hi no Tori* (The Phoenix), and *Ribbon no Kishi* (Princess Knight).

One American soldier who saw Takarazuka during the Occupation, James Michener, was inspired to write a book that featured a love story between a GI and a Takarazuka actress. In 1957 the book became the movie *Sayonara,* starring Marlon Brando and Miika Taka.

The troupe's most enduringly popular show came not from the West but from a Japanese *manga* by Riyoko Ikeda: **THE ROSE OF VERSAILLES**. The story of a girl who is raised as a boy in an eighteenth-century French noble family, *Beru-Bara,* as it came to be called from its Japanese pronunciation as *Berusai-yau no Bara,* ran from 1974 to 1980 and, in a revival, from 1989 to 1991. The troupe's top stars vied to play the androgynous hero, Oscar.

Over the years the Takarazuka troupe has toured extensively, presenting shows throughout North and South America and Europe. The reception abroad has been mixed; some foreign audiences accept Takarazuka for what it is—a uniquely Japanese phenomenon—while others just don't get it. In addition to adulation from the gay community, during their 1994 U.K. tour the Takarazuka troupe had to endure sniping from male critics that their show wasn't much of a turn-on. "Curiously sexless," griped Michael Billington in *The Guardian.* Sexlessness, however, was the whole point.

Conceived as entertainment for the entire family, the Takarazuka Revue sublimates sex in its shows the way Disney does in its prince-and-princess animated features, showing the audience a chaste kiss or embrace, but no hungry looks. Although Walt himself might have looked askance at the spectacle of a young women in a tuxedo romancing another young woman in a ball dress, in the Japan of 1914, when the troupe first performed, a man and woman kissing, however chastely, on stage would have represented a serious breach of social etiquette. Men and women kissed, of course, but usually in the privacy of their bedrooms, in the course of the sexual act. The stage, obviously, was not the place for it. By keeping the kissers of his troupe all female, Kobayashi was upholding the troupe's image of purity.

He was also following Japanese show-business precedent. Single-sex Kabuki still had a large popular following, though it was under challenge from Westernized drama forms. Even in the imported art of motion pictures, Kabuki actors dominated female roles.

Today, mores and manners have changed, but like so many other Japanese

Ran Otori as Oscar in *The Rose of Versailles.*

cultural institutions, the Takarazuka Revue adheres tenaciously to its artistic traditions. The idea of a male on the Takarazuka stage would be unthinkable, even if the audience demanded it.

But of course the troupe's predominantly young female audience does not demand it. They want the dream of pure romance, not the reality of physical love between the sexes. Also, they can live out their fantasies of power and dominance by identifying with the "men" on the stage—fantasies that they can all-too-seldom realize as women in Japanese society. The *otokoyaku*—the women playing the male roles—have long been Takarazuka's biggest stars.

Attaining that stardom means a long, arduous climb through the Takarazuka hierarchy. Girls between the ages of sixteen and twenty join Takarazuka much as they would an elite high school—through a rigorous competitive audition that selects only forty of nearly sixteen hundred girls who apply each year. The survivors enter the Takarazuka Music School, where they undergo a tough regime of early rising, daily cleaning (no labor-saving electrical appliances allowed), and classes from 9:00 A.M. to 5:00 P.M. To show respect for their seniors, first-year students must walk along the edges of the hallways.

In their first year the students decide whether they want to play male or female roles. Because the competition for the former parts is fierce, however, not all would-be *otokoyaku* are chosen—and only a few finally make it to the top. Starting the second year, the students go their separate ways, with the *otokoyaku* getting masculine hair cuts and learning to carry themselves like future Prince Charmings.

Once they graduate, after two years of training, the budding Takarasiennes—the traditional name for Takazuka performers—enter one of four troupes, with a total of nearly three hundred fifty members: Moon, Flower, Snow, and Star. Each of the troupes puts on a forty-five-day revue twice a year at the Takarazuka Grand Theater (rebuilt in 1993), a thirty-day revue at the Tokyo Takarazuka Theater, and forays to other major cities. To meet the growing demand for their shows, Takarazuka management will launch a fifth troupe when the New Takarazuka Theater, which is being constructed, appropriately, next Tokyo Disneyland, is completed in 1997.

The training for the Takarasiennes is tough, the pay relatively low, and the hours long. Even top stars have little time for lucrative side jobs; they are too busy teaching their juniors and otherwise keeping the organizational gears turning. The Takarazuka Revue doesn't expect its performers to make a lifetime career of it, though. Everyone eventually "graduates," whether to fame in show business or obscurity as an ordinary housewife. But the Takarazuka dream of gloriously zipless romance lives on.

TAKESHI, BEAT

The Japanese, goes the stereotype, are a group-oriented people who avoid standing out or giving offense. The general raucousness of Japanese TV would seem to disprove this stereotype, but the mugging, wisecracking talents on the quiz and variety shows are often working hard to prove that they are just one of a harmless, fun-loving gang. Not stuck-up stars trying to overawe with glamour or impress with talent, but average folks like you and me, or even lovably subnormal. Particularly on the quiz shows, the celebrity contestants often compete to give winsomely knuckle-headed answers that ten-year-olds watching at home can laugh at.

Ironically, the man who has dominated Japanese TV for more than a decade has long worn the label "genius" quite frankly and owned the sharpest tongue in show business. A former strip-joint emcee, Beat Takeshi (or Takeshi Kitano, as he is better known abroad) has taken aim at a long list of targets in the course of his career, including women, gays, and the disabled, in language and actions that are often patently offensive.

This man with the impish eyes, crooked grin, and odd tic of snapping his head to one side, as though trying to crack his neck, would make a good army sergeant (a role he played in Nagisa Oshima's 1983 *Merry Christmas Mr. Lawrence*) or gang boss (as he was in Robert Longo's 1995 *Johnny Mnemonic* and his own 1993 *Sonatine*): he's got the right tough, take-charge persona. But it's more of a stretch for an outsider to imagine him as the best-liked man in Japan in a 1995 *Spa!* magazine poll or the country's favorite TV celebrity every year from 1990 to 1995, according to an annual NHK poll, or the regular host of seven prime time network TV shows in 1996.

What's the secret to Takeshi's appeal? In a comment to the *Spa!* pollsters, a twenty-nine-year-old freelancer explained that he chose Takeshi as his "best liked" because he is "a major presence who transcends genres." A thirty-year-old company employee said simply that Takeshi is "like a god." On a less elevated plane, a twenty-year-old student commented that he "acts really cool in his press conferences," while a twenty-two-year-old student gave him a sympathy vote because "he survived a [nearly fatal] motorbike accident."

Takeshi's astounding success and voracious appetite for work may well seem godlike to ordinary mortals: in addition to being a fixture on prime time, he writes magazine

Beat Takeshi: the genius of Japanese television in a pre-accident role as an inquiring man of science.

columns and books (more than fifty of the latter by the last count), directs and acts in films, makes records, paints, and has even dabbled in the curry-rice restaurant business. But it might be easier to understand Takeshi as a bright, articulate man who has never quite grown up and trades on his naughty Peter Pan appeal—though he frequently crosses the border from naughty to mean (he has often subjected his "army," or *gundan,* of comic disciples to painful, humiliating, and outright dangerous stunts) and nasty (he has a fondness for graphic bathroom humor and raunchy sex jokes).

Among a people who make a clear distinction between public face *(tatemae)* and private feelings *(honne)* and tend to suppress the latter in all but the most relaxed and intimate settings, Takeshi stands out as huge, glaring exception to the norm, exhibiting his inner child—or demons— almost nightly on national television. But instead of being pounded down for his impudence and outrageousness, Takeshi is indulged, petted, and celebrated. One of his most popular programs, which ran from 1985 to 1995 on NTV, was called *Takeshi the Genius's Peppy TV Show!! (Tensai Takeshi no Genki ga Deru Terebi!!).* One explanation for this attitude, among the networks at least, is that when you pull down high ratings on several prime time programs, as Takeshi has done for more than a decade, you become

the bull elephant of the television jungle—a stomper, not a stompee.

But why the high ratings? There has long been a large audience in Japan TV-land for vulgar slapstick humor strongly spiced with cruelty, and Takeshi's brand is among the strongest around. Once, as a gag "punishment" on his *Takeshi Comedy Ultra Quiz* show, he had a busload of losing contestants lowered into the ocean by a large crane. An underwater camera filmed the desperate contestants clawing at the windows, while Takeshi, safe on shore, cackled with roguish delight.

But even viewers who don't see anything amusing in Takeshi's cohorts descending on a unsuspecting elderly man on a deserted street and threatening, with bloodcurdling shouts, to murder him, find themselves tuning in to a Takeshi program. Though he may play the mean-minded prankster one night, the next he is hosting a talk show on the state of the Japanese economy or appearing on an infotainment program to give a lecture on the workings of the solar system. Although his main function is to enliven these shows with his quips, he can also slash into a guest's argument with the skill of a practiced debater or rattle off facts and figures with the ease of a seasoned expert.

Meanwhile, off the tube he is directing critically acclaimed films (his 1993 nihilistic gangster drama *Sonatine* was selected by the BBC as one of one hundred films representing world cinema) or writing, with the aid of an editorial ghost, surprisingly well-informed essays on politics, history, and social issues for national magazines. The man is too protean to easily categorize, too talented to easily dismiss. Like Woody Allen, he has moved to the grown up's table of the nation's cultural life and has every intention of staying.

This is not to say that the entire nation always laughs at Takeshi's excesses or that the media always crawls at his feet. In 1986 the weekly photo magazine *Friday* dared Takeshi's wrath by running pictures of a college student with whom the comedian was reportedly having an affair. When Takeshi and eleven members of his "army" invaded *Friday's* editorial offices on December 19 and attacked five staffers with fists and furled umbrellas, they were arrested on assault charges. Takeshi didn't have to do time—he reached an out-of-court settlement with *Friday's* publisher—but he did have to take a six-month leave from television to demonstrate his contrition. The staff of *Tensai Takeshi Genki ga Deru Terebi!!* put a life-sized Takeshi doll in his place during his absence.

In 1994 an association representing the Ainu—Japan's indigenous people, who have long been subjected to discrimination by the majority Japanese—strenuously protested a segment on *Takeshi's Ultra Quiz* program in which ten comics did an "Ainu dance" wearing nothing but bikini briefs and giant phalluses. They used the latter to spin plates and bat beachballs, to the huge amusement of the studio audience. The NTV network apologized, but Takeshi and his gang remained on the air.

In February 1996, a former Takeshi intimate, *manga* artist Shintaro Koh, published a Takeshi-bashing book in which he argued that Takeshi neglected his old friends and teachers (including Koh), was dictatorial and arrogant towards his subordinates and coworkers, and—the most serious charge of all—was not that funny any more. But he also admitted that Takeshi was a brilliant conversationalist with a wide range of interests and a phenomenal memory, and that no one else had ever made him laugh so hard. He ended the book expressing his admiration for Takeshi's talent and urging him to return to his cabaret roots to renew it.

Takeshi was born Takeshi Kitano in 1947 in Tokyo's Adachi Ward. The youngest of four children, he grew up in the poverty and hardship of the early postwar years. In his autobiography, *Takeshi-kun! Hai!* ("Takeshi!" "Here!"), which NHK latter turned into a serial drama, he described going to a second-hand shop with his older brother to buy a globe that had caught his eye, and returning home in tears because he was one hundred eighty yen short and knew that his parents could not make up the difference. He also wrote that his house painter father drank to drown his shame over his lowly occupation and, when drunk, beat Takeshi's mother.

His mother, however, was a strong-willed woman who was determined to give her children, particularly her studious second son, a good education. When his father complained that the boy's studying was keeping him awake (the family lived in a one-room house), the mother got a flashlight and some rice balls, led the boy outside, and made him read by the light of a street lamp.

Though Takeshi liked dreaming up pranks and gags better than cracking books, he passed the entrance exam to Meiji University's Department of Engineering. His mother firmly believed that engineering was the ticket to a good job and insisted that her sons study it.

Takeshi's older brother listened to his mother and is now a professor of engineering at a prestigious national university. Takeshi, however, had little interest in engineering and dropped out of school at the age of nineteen. Leaving home, he drifted from job to job—jazz coffee-shop waiter, airport baggage handler, taxi driver—before finally becoming an elevator boy at the France-za burlesque theater in the Asakusa entertainment district of Tokyo and finding a vocation. Watching the performances of such comedians as Kiyoshi Atsumi, who later won fame as the star of the **TORA-SAN** series, or Kin'ichi Hagimoto, who later became the biggest comedy star on Japanese television, Takeshi knew that he wanted to do what they were doing, hear the laughter they were hearing. He apprenticed himself to veteran Asakusa comedian Senzaburo Fukami and began learning the craft of comedy.

While continuing to pay the rent with a succession of menial jobs, Takeshi polished his comic skills under Fukami's tutelage, including cracking jokes as a France-za emcee. In 1973 he was asked to substitute for the partner of a comic named Beat Kiyoshi, another of Fukami's disciples. The two men clicked and a new comedy duo was born: Tsuu Biito or Two Beats.

The Two Beats' style of comedy, called *manzai*, had originated in the Kansai (Osaka-Kyoto-Kobe) region and since become a TV programming staple. *Manzai* acts bore a family resemblance to Abbot and

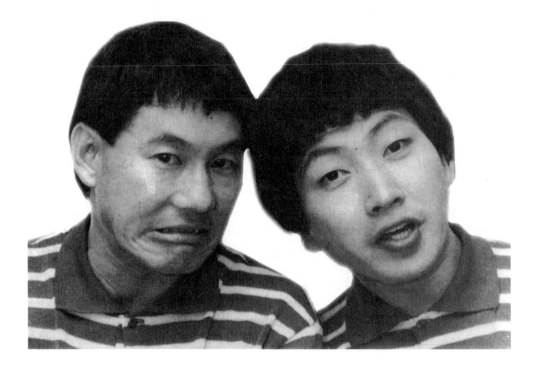

Costello, Martin and Lewis, The Smothers Brothers, and other American comedy duos in which a straight man (called the *tsukkomi* in Japanese) fed gag lines to a scatterbrained partner (the *boke*). One difference was that *manzai* comedians, particularly on television, tended to be more physical than their American counterparts, with the straight man often smacking his partner on the head to display his annoyance—a gesture that never failed to draw a laugh from the studio audience.

The Two Beats' comedy, however, didn't fit the usual *manzai* pattern; Takeshi was too obviously the real brain in the duo to be a good dimwit. But he also happened to be funny, so much so that Two Beats quickly rose to the top rank of the Tokyo *manzai*

world. Television fame and fortune were longer in coming, however; Takeshi's brand of humor was considered too gross and insulting for prime time. In one routine he described a new gourmet delight: "stick a straw up a frog's ass and suck hard." In another he told how the natives of Yamagata, a remote northern prefecture that might described as the Ozarks of Japan, "have just learned how to walk on two feet" and "pray when they see an airplane."

In 1974 the duo made their TV debut on TV Tokyo, but Two Beats remained largely unknown to all but *manzai* cognoscenti until the beginning of the *manzai* boom in 1980. Led by the Fuji TV program *The Manzai*, which hit a ratings peak of 32.6 percent, shows featuring *manzai* acts became the

Beat Takeshi and Beat Kiyoshi: once considered too gross and insulting for primetime, their brand of humor helped ignite the *manzai* boom.

rage among young viewers. Young *manzai* duos like B&B, Za Bonchi, Norio Yoshio, Shinsuke Ryusuke, and All Hanshin Kyojin were suddenly everywhere on the airwaves. Unlike an older generation of *manzai* comedians, these newcomers tended to be casual in dress, wearing stylish sweaters, not stuffy suits and ties, and contemporary in approach: topical gags were in, "classic" routines were out.

Two Beats were among this in-crowd and, in 1980, became regulars on *Waratteru Baai Desu Yo!* (It's Time to Laugh!), a comedy show hosted by Za Bonchi, as well as appearing as guests on other *manzai* programs. After of years of playing dives, they were finally on their way to the big time.

Though the Two Beats' attack style of comedy may have offended *manzai* purists, it was perfect for television, with its short attention span and its large appetite for novelty. When the boom ended in 1982, many of the *manzai* acts retreated to the world of clubs and cabarets from which they had come, but Two Beats, and more particularly, Beat Takeshi remained standouts—and on the air.

The program that made Takeshi a star in his own right was *Oretachi Hyokinzoku* (We Are Wild and Crazy Guys). Launched at the height of the *manzai* boom, in 1981 on Fuji TV, the show took the unbuttoned style of the popular *manzai* acts one step further. Instead of following the usual variety show pattern—regular hosts introducing guests—*Oretachi Hyokinzoku* was an ensemble show, with the members showing up whenever they could fit the program into their schedules.

Pitted against the hottest comedy group on television, the **DRIFTERS**, the producers of *Oretachi Hyokinzoku* studied the competition carefully—and did everything differently. Instead of carefully rehearsed skits that relied on mechanical props for their laughs—the comic formula that had made the Drifters ratings kings—*Oretachi Hyokinzoku* put its emphasis on ad libs, running gags, and free-form parodies of popular songs, TV shows, and commercials. Young viewers loved the show's irreverence and unpredictability and made it a long-running hit. It stayed on the air until 1989—four years after causing the demise of the Drifter's show, *Hachiji Da Yo! Zen'in Shugo*.

Although *Oretachi Hyokinzoku* made stars out of many of its regulars, including Samma Akashiya and Kuniko Yamada, it gave Takeshi the biggest career boost. Takeshi developed several of the show's signature characters, including Take-chan Man, a kind of anti-Superman who crushed the weak and aided the strong. He was also key in defining its over-the-top style, which broke free from *manzai* conventions. The show's chief producer, Takeshi Yokozawa, later admitted that "[Takeshi] was far quicker on the uptake than anyone else. Everyone, including the staff, wanted to make him the center of the show."

Takeshi was also propelled into the national spotlight by *All Night Nippon,* a late-night radio program that aired from 1981 to 1990. Freed to jam on air without looking over his shoulder at TV censors, Takeshi turned *All Night Nippon* into a personal forum for his iconoclastic views and attracted a fanatical following. The show produced some of his best-remembered quips, including "It's not scary to cross at the red light if everyone does it"; "Don't worry . . . old ladies don't have long to live anyway"; and "Remember kids, before you go to bed tonight, be sure to strangle your parents."

As Takeshi's fame and influence grew, he began to acquire the status of a comedy guru and accumulate disciples, or *deshi*— young comics who wanted learn to their craft at the feet of a master. Known as Takeshi's "army," these disciples provided convenient targets for Takeshi's quips and convenient stooges for his pranks and stunts. Life in the Takeshi army was undoubtedly tough: on one *Ultra Quiz* show Takeshi had two army members launched, with glowing sparklers attached to their feet and wearing nothing but their birthday suits, into the ocean in a human fireworks display. But despite the humiliations and dangers, army members have remained fiercely loyal to the man they call *tono* (lord), even risking imprisonment by joining him in his raid on the *Friday* editorial office.

There are, admittedly, compensations. Army members have been featured prominently on several of Takeshi's shows and, because Takeshi is a sports nut, they spend much of their time playing on various army sports teams and appearing on televised games. Several members were elite amateur athletes prior to joining the army and Takeshi's baseball team has a reputation as the strongest in the entertainment world. In 1986 the team took on a team of former professional baseball players and beat them, seven runs to four. Takeshi, the pitcher, snagged two flies hit by SHIGEO NAGASHIMA, the most revered player in the Japanese pros.

The army has even repaid Takeshi in his own pranksterish coin. During a *Genki ga Deru Terebi* show early in 1996, Takeshi, dressed in a wacky costume, was hiding inside a large ball on an amusement park stage, waiting to jump out and surprise the audience. Instead, as a hidden camera watched, smoke started pouring into the ball and sirens sounded outside. Panicked, Takeshi began to claw at the opening and shout for his manager. Then the ball suddenly opened and the audience and army, who were all in on the joke, erupted in

laughter. Takeshi's reaction was to drop his drawers and flash his tormentors.

Having conquered television, Takeshi has branched out into acting, directing, and writing, with varying degrees of success. His first major role, as the brutal POW camp sergeant in Nagisa Oshima's 1983 *Merry Christmas, Mr. Lawrence,* won him both domestic and international acclaim and made him in demand as a dramatic actor. Altogether he has appeared in seventeen films, often as a tough guy capable of explosive violence.

In 1989 he directed his first film, *Sono Otoko, Kyobo ni Tsuki* (Violent Cop), a noirish thriller about a Dirty-Harry-like cop on a mission of personal revenge. Though Takeshi as the cop delivered more slaps, cuffs, kicks, and third-degree grillings than Clint Eastwood did in the entire Dirty Harry series, the film was not a Dirty-Harry-sized box office success. It did, however, win several domestic film prizes, including best director laurels for Takeshi.

His next two films—*3-4 x 10 Gatsu* (Boiling Point), a hyperviolent coming-of-age tale about an innocent's encounter with the underworld, in which Takeshi played a psychotically brutal gang boss, and *Ano Natsu, Ichiban Shizuka na Umi* (A Scene at the Sea), a bleakly sentimental fable about a deaf surfer's fatal search for the perfect wave—did little to broaden his box-office appeal.

When his fourth film, the 1993 *Sonatine,* went far over budget during its location shoot in Okinawa, the film's executive producer, Kazuyoshi Okuyama, accused Takeshi of auteurist ego tripping at the expense of his audience. Okuyama lost his job as Shochiku's head of production when this darkly comic film about a bloody Okinawa gang war failed to recoup at the box office in Japan, but *Sonatine* became a critical favorite and art house hit in England, with U.K. critics hailing Takeshi as Japan's biggest new cinematic talent. Comparisons were made with Ozu, Scorsese, Melville, Tarantino, and Bresson.

Just when Takeshi was receiving wider international recognition as a director and actor, including a leading role as a mysterious *yakuza* boss in Robert Longo's technothriller *Johnny Mnemonic,* he nearly lost it all. Early in the morning of August 2, 1994, after a night of carousing, he rammed his motorscooter into a guard rail in Tokyo's Shinjuku Ward. The crash almost killed him and left the right side of his face partly paralyzed.

In March 1995, after seven months in rehabilitation, he returned to television on the *Heisei Kyoiku Iinkai* (Heisei Education Committee) variety show sporting a rakish eye patch, but the post-crash Takeshi seemed more subdued, less vital than the bad-boy Takeshi of old.

Though Takeshi later admitted that the accident was "a kind of unconscious suicide attempt," he showed no intention of slowing his killing pace. Soon after his return, he was hosting six network programs, writing six regular columns for national magazines and a sports newspaper, and, as though to prove he had not lost his comic touch, releasing his first screen comedy, *Minna Yatteruka?* (Getting Any?). (The movie, however, had been filmed before the accident.) Abandoning Tarantinoesque nihilism—*Sonatine's* last shot showed Takeshi pressing a pistol to his temple and blowing his brains out—he plunged headlong into Jim Carreyian goofiness. *Getting Any?* depicted the lamebrained attempts of a subnormal young man, played by army member Dankan, to get laid by any means necessary. As scriptwriter and director, Takeshi displayed the same unapologetically low sense of humor that had won him so many fans on the tube, but the film also had a surprisingly feminist subtext. Having run through the entire catalogue of male illusions about what women want, while getting no closer to his goal, the hero finally becomes an invisible man—and a happy voyeur.

His 1996 *Kid's Return*, a sharply observed, deeply personal film about two young punks who learn hard lessons about making it in the real world, pleased not only critics but local audiences, who made it his first-ever box-office hit. Just as his TV career was starting to fade—*Tensai Takeshi Genki ga Deru Terebi!!* was canceled in 1996 after more than a decade on the air—his status as a leading Japanese director seemed even more assured.

Which Takeshi will finally win out—the naughty-boy TV comedian or the serious filmmaker? Beat Takeshi or Takeshi Kitano? His manager and long-time intimate, Masayuki Mori, believes that Takeshi intends to keep both sides of his professional personality alive. "He wants to use both to extend the range of his activities," says Mori. "He's very conscious of creating different characters for different audiences. That, I think, is why audiences don't tire of him; he keeps giving them new versions of himself. But essentially he's a very shy man. That's why he gives so few interviews; he believes that his work says all that needs to be said." Given Takeshi's work to date, that's saying quite a lot.

TEZUKA, OSAMU

Japanese *manga* are much more than kid's stuff. From their humble prewar beginnings as mind candy for kids, *manga* have evolved into a major cultural phenomena that encompasses everything from S & M porn to economic history. There are *manga* targeted at nearly every age group, from barely literate preschoolers to middle-aged salarymen. The most popular *manga* magazines, which can be found at nearly every station kiosk and neighborhood bookstore, sell in the millions. Although *manga* still have their detractors—mainly mothers worried that their kids' obsession with comics will ruin their grades and rot their little minds—they account for nearly one-third of all books and magazines published in Japan.

The man most responsible for the rise of *manga* to its dominant role in postwar Japanese pop culture is Osamu Tezuka. An amateur entomologist who, as a boy, wrote and illustrated his own reference books and later used his nickname, Osamushi (a kind of ground beetle), as his *manga* nom de plume, the holder of a medical degree who never practiced medicine, Tezuka had an insatiable intellectual curiosity that encompassed science, history, religion, and space exploration. In his forty-four-year career he tackled everything from a twelve-volume saga of karma and reincarnation (*Hi no Tori,* or The Phoenix) to an examination of the Nazi era through the eyes of a German diplomat and a German Jew living in Japan (*Adolf ni Tsugu,* or The Story of Three Adolfs).

Instead of stainless superheroes, Tezuka depicted fallible individuals who wrestled with issues of guilt and responsibility, doubt and faith, death and rebirth. In the process, he proved that, through the *manga* medium, he could handle weighty themes and create complex characters as well as any novelist.

Almost single-handedly, he made it acceptable for adults to read *manga* and take them seriously as an art form.

Tezuka, however, was not only an uplifter but a popularizer. A fan of Walt Disney animation—he saw *Snow White* fifty times and *Bambi* eighty times, until he had memorized every frame—Tezuka adopted the round, cutesy Disney look for his own creations.

Raised in Takarazuka, the Hyogo Prefecture city where the famed **TAKARAZUKA** Revue Company is headquartered, Tezuka was also inspired by the troupe's gaudy romanticism and spectacular staging. He

later said that his *Ribbon no Kishi* (The Ribbon Knight), a pioneering *manga* for young girls, "describes my whole experience with Takarazuka."

A movie buff, who saw as many as 365 films a year, Tezuka drew his *manga* as though he were shooting a film, often emphasizing action over words and using cinematic techniques to add tension and excitement to his stories. Readers used to the clunky, static gag cartoons that then dominated the *manga* mainstream in the early postwar years were charmed by Tezuka's characters and thrilled by the vitality and freshness of his approach. They had never

Early Tezuka comics: *Chiteikoku no Kaijin* (The Monstrous Fellows of the Country Underground) and *Ribbon no Kishi* (Princess Knight). Disney-style cuteness, cinematic techniques.

read anything like him. Actually, they didn't read his *manga* so much as *watch* them.

Although Tezuka started his first strip, *Ma-chan no Nikki* (Ma-chan's Diary) in 1946 for the *Shokokumin Shimbun* while still a teenage medical student, his first hit *manga* was *Shin Takarajima* (New Treasure Island) in 1947. Even at this early stage in this career, Tezuka was an innovator, using movie-style close-ups and varying the size and shape of the *manga* frame to better dramatize his characters' movements and mental states. In paperback, *Shin Takarajima* sold more than four hundred thousand copies—a huge number for the early postwar years—and launched Tezuka toward superstardom.

Among Japanese baby boomers, his best-known creation is probably *Tetsuwan Atom* (Astro Boy). Running from 1951 to 1969, this *manga* depicted the adventures of a robot boy named Atom in the twenty-first century. Although a robot, Atom had many of the feelings of a human being. At the same time, he had superhuman powers, including the ability to fly (jets were installed in his shoes), see in the dark, and hear at great distances. This fighter for truth and justice, with his ten thousand-horsepower punch and his odd, pointy hair style (based, Tezuka later claimed, on his own unruly hair), starred in Japan's first regularly scheduled TV cartoon show in 1963 and, later, as *Astro Boy,* became

the first *manga* hero to appear in syndication on American television.

During the 1950s and 1960s, when he was at the peak of his popularity and creative powers, Tezuka churned out dozens of *manga* pages a month, slaving into the wee hours of the morning and sleeping only three or four hours a night. Editors for competing publications would camp out at his home, waiting for copy. Sometimes negotiations for first dibs would degenerate into fist fights. Ever the perfectionist, Tezuka would occasionally tear up his completed work in front of his editors' chagrined faces. There was, however, little they could do or say: Tezuka's drawings were *manga* gold.

A confirmed workaholic who could never say no, Tezuka was working himself to a frazzle when, in the 1950s, he began hiring assistants to handle the more mechanical and mundane tasks of *manga* drawing. His mass-production methods allowed him to concentrate more on his creative work and were later adopted by many other *manga* artists. Several of Tezuka's assistants, including Moto Abiko and Shotaro Ishinomori, later went on to successful careers of their own.

When he began making animated cartoons in 1956 in association with Toei, Tezuka's dream was to equal Disney quality. But given the budgetary limitations imposed on Japanese animators at the time, he could

Tetsuwan Atom (Astro Boy) demonstrates his super-powers. In 1962 he starred in Japan's first half-hour TV cartoon show.

not imitate Disney methods. In 1962, when he proposed the idea of making a thirty-minute TV program based on his *Tetsuwan Atom manga*, network execs told him the length would make the cost prohibitive. Tezuka said he could do it for five hundred thousand yen an episode—an unheard-of low sum. The network greenlighted the project and the show became a monster hit.

To make *Tetsuwan Atom* and his other animated series without going broke, Tezuka devised a system of limited animation in which only one part of the image—a character's lips or eyes—moved, saving on cels and costs. He also started an "animation bank" of cels with typical expressions and poses that could be used again and again, further cutting down on the number of cels needed, from six thousand for a half-hour program to as few as three thousand. His innovations became standard practice in the Japanese animation industry, allowing it to make animated entertainment cheaply and quickly for TV and movie audiences.

But even after cutting costs to the bone, Tezuka's animation company, Mushi Puro, could not turn a profit on *Tetsuwan Atom* and other Tezuka *manga* alone. The company began to animate other artists' *manga* to make ends meet. As the workload grew so did the staff, reaching a peak of four hundred. Finally, the burden became too much for Tezuka, who was trying to draw his own

manga while running the company. In 1971, he resigned as Mushi Puro president.

Left without copyright income from Tezuka's works and merchandising royalties from his characters, the company quickly fell into the red and, in 1973, filed for bankruptcy. Tezuka did not return to animation until 1978, with a cartoon for an NTV charity telethon.

Unlike many *manga* artists, who prefer their fantasy worlds to real people, Tezuka loved to meet and mingle with fans and colleagues. His beret, dark-framed glasses, and warm smile were frequent sights at *manga* conventions and events.

But though Tezuka's outgoing, almost childlike disposition was no act, he had a dark side as well. Always a fierce competitor, he found it hard to accept the success of other *manga* artists, even when they had been his trusted assistants. Tezuka once wrote a letter to a fan denouncing a Shotaro Ishinomori *manga* as not being "a legitimate work of *manga* art." Ishinomori, who had loyally served Tezuka for years, later described himself as "terribly hurt" by this slight.

Tezuka was obsessed with his sale figures, following them closely and fretting about any slippage. Though acclaimed the "god of *manga*," he was forever worried about losing his fans to younger, hungrier competitors. He was not above lifting the best ideas from

a newcomer's work and incorporating them into his own. Given Tezuka's power and status in the industry, the newcomer had no choice but to regard the master's borrowings as a compliment.

In the late 1960s, Tezuka moved from such popular fare as *Tetsuwan Atom* to works with heavier, more complex themes. When his mass audience refused to wade through multivolumed *sagas* about the life of Buddha or the political struggles of Japan's feudal clans, Tezuka plunged into depression, feeling that he had lost his touch. But though his sales fell, he retained his godly status in the industry he had done so much to build.

In the last decade of his life Tezuka was plagued by ill health but kept working at a superhuman pace and dreaming up new projects, including a biography of Beethoven and a retelling of the Faust story with a female Mephistopheles. When he died on February 9, 1989 at the age of sixty, he left as his legacy five hundred *manga* volumes, each from two hundred to four hundred pages in length, and more than one thousand *manga* characters.

In the years since his death, Tezuka's reputation in Japan has, if anything, grown. In 1990 the National Museum of Modern Art mounted a major exhibition of his work—an unprecedented honor for a *manga* artist. In 1994 the Osamu Tezuka Museum opened in

Takarazuka, where Tezuka lived for twenty years before moving to Tokyo at the age of twenty-four. The opening day attracted forty thousand visitors, who viewed the one thousand Tezuka publications on display and attended screenings of his animated films.

The museum, however, was just the beginning. In February 1996 Tezuka Production, Tezuka's old production company, announced plans to build a theme park based on Tezuka's works. Called Tezuka World, the park was to be sited near a Bullet Train stop within one hundred kilometers of Tokyo and have an area twice the size of Tokyo Disneyland. Tezuka Production estimated that, with the support of thirty construction companies, banks, and other corporate partners, construction of the park would cost one hundred billion yen and be completed in 2003. The company forecast annual admissions of ten million a year.

But the most striking posthumous tribute to Tezuka's work was probably the letter signed in August 1994 by 158 prominent Japanese, including many well-known *manga* artists, protesting the resemblance of Disney's *Lion King* to Tezuka's *Jungle Taitei* (The Jungle Emperor). A popular *manga* in the 1950s that became the basis for the first color TV cartoon show in Japan, *Jungle Taitei* told the story of a young lion named Kimba who goes into exile after the murder of his father and later returns to overthrow the usurper, his uncle. Disney, however, denied ripping off the *manga* and the TV show, which was broadcast in the United States in 1966. The protesters, pointing out the many similarities between the Tezuka *manga* and the Disney movie, were not satisfied. Tezuka, however, might well have felt honored—and seen the irony. After all those hours of watching and stealing from *Bambi,* now, finally, it was pay-back time.

TORA-SAN

Tora-san has long been a peculiarly Japanese national icon. For nearly three decades local audiences loved this wandering peddler from Tokyo's *shitamachi* (old downtown) section, while foreigners never quite got the point. The clearest sign of that love was Tora's box-office longevity: the series of films featuring Kiyoshi Atsumi as Tora, which went under the collective title *Otoko wa Tsurai Yo* (It's Tough Being a Man), ran to forty-eight installments—a Guinness Book record. Though the basic story line—Tora-san is a fool for love, but never gets the girl—never changed since the series' start in 1969, the Japanese audience kept coming back for more. The films, which Shochiku at first released twice a year, but later reserved exclusively for the peak New Year's season, regularly finished in the Japanese box office top ten, often beating out heavy Hollywood competition.

Abroad, however, the Tora-san films never made much of a stir outside the Japanese expatriate community. Foreigners living in Japan also failed to see the point. The series, they often said, was formulaic, sentimental, not all that funny, little more than a cinematic soap opera with an unusually long run.

There is no denying the series' sameness. In every installment Tora visits his half-sister and her family in the Shibamata section of Tokyo, falls in love with a "madonna" (series' jargon for Tora's leading lady), and travels to a picturesque corner of Japan (provincial cities and towns competed for the honor of the being chosen as a series locale). Inevitably, by the final frame, Tora is once again free of romantic entanglements, sometimes by choice, sometimes not, and selling trinkets or telling fortunes to the passing holiday crowd.

But for Tora's Japanese audience, this very sameness was a major attraction. They went to the films knowing that they would get certain pleasures, if few surprises. And Tora seldom disappointed, serving up the same brand of folksy comedy time and time again.

Series director and scriptwriter Yoji Yamada often compared himself to a ramen chef who makes bowls of good noodle soup the same way every time. Furthermore, far from despising his repetitious labors or regarding them as a cash cow for his other, more artistic projects—Yamada directed several nonseries films that won major Japanese film awards—he insisted that the series was his true life work. "I guess I am unique in making only Tora-san movies," he once said. "It takes a lot of effort, but I'm glad I can do it."

Is the series really "good soup"? The Japanese film industry seems to think so. In 1977 Yamada won the Japan Academy Award for Best Director for a Tora-san film. Also, Kiyoshi Atsumi, who played Tora-san in every episode, was given a Special Prize for his series work at the Fourth Japan Academy Awards ceremony in 1980.

The soup's main ingredient, Atsumi, was born and raised in the same *shitamachi* milieu as Tora and played the character since Tora's first appearance in 1968 on a TV series. Although he once had a thriving career in nonseries comedies, for nearly three decades, until his death of lung cancer on August 4, 1996, Atsumi appeared principally in Tora-san movies and even dressed in his Tora getup—beige check suit, belly band and wooden clogs—for his infrequent public appearances.

Tora, whose full name is Torajiro Kuruma, hails from Shibamata, a *shitamachi*

Yuko Tanaka and Kiyoshi Atsumi in the thirtieth installment of the Tora-san series, *Otoko wa Tsurai Yo: Hana mo Arashi mo Torajiro* (Tora-san the Expert), released in December 1982.

neighborhood that preserves the traditional values of the common folk of Edo (premodern Tokyo). Tora exemplifies those values. He may be hot-tempered, shortsighted, and hopelessly unlucky in love, but he also goes out of his way to do right by those to whom he feels obliged, especially if they happen to be young, pretty, and female. The opposite of the work-obsessed, upwardly mobile, elite salaryman, he has plenty of time, little money, and gives of both freely. He is, said Yamada, "a member of a vanishing species in modern Japan."

Yamada said that audiences watch Tora-san the way they would a period drama. "They feel a nostalgia for a world that no longer exists," he explained. Did it exist even in 1969? That year, *Midnight Cowboy* won the Best Picture Oscar and the big surprise hit was *Easy Rider*. In Japan, students were rioting in the streets and youth culture was worshiping the same Dionysian gods as its Western counterparts. Today the turf of Colombian streetwalkers and Taiwanese gangbangers, Tokyo's Shinjuku district was a hotbed of coffee-house radicalism and a hideout for American deserters from the Vietnam War.

But across town in the Shibamata heartland, the good folks at the Toraya, the dumpling shop that served as Tora's home base, were a close-knit if sometimes contentious family within in a close-knit if somewhat wacky community. Though Tora was a bastard son without a proper education or job, who picked most of the quarrels and got into one idiotic mess after another, he was also an integral member of that family and community.

In the course of the series, Tora became not just another cinematic franchise, but a national hero. Comparisons were often made with Chaplin's *Tramp*. Both Tora and the Tramp are free spirits living precarious existences on the fringes of society and both are instantly recognizable figures who always wear the same clothes (Tora's suit was long cut from a pattern no longer made; Shochiku kept a bolt of cloth that had to last the life of the series) and never age or change (though Atsumi was in his mid-sixties by the series' last episodes, Tora was forever in his early forties and forever on the lookout for love).

The differences between the two are also striking. Chaplin's comedy is primarily physical and deliberately universal; Atsumi's verbal and intensely local. Though he may act the uneducated dimwit, Tora is a born salesman and raconteur whose funniest moments are often his (untranslatable) monologues. And though he may wander to the far corners of Japan (by the end of the series he had been to every prefecture, several more than once), he always returns to Shibamata to regale his family and friends at the Toraya dumpling shop with the stories of his travels and exasperate them with his fecklessness. The most long-suffering is his sister Sakura, played in all installments by Chieko Baisho, who has spent her adult life waiting, fruitlessly, for her older brother to settle down.

In the last few episodes, however, the emphasis shifted from Tora to Sakura's son Mitsuo (Hidetaka Yoshioka), a nice, normal kid who went from being a middling student at a middling college to working as a middling salaryman for a middling shoe company. His romantic misadventures, with Uncle Tora at his side giving him dubious advice, had their charms, but as a comic presence, Mitsuo was no match for Tora. He could no more have replaced his uncle than Zeppo could have replaced Groucho. Now that Atsumi is gone, so is the series.

But though Atsumi never made it to episode forty-nine, which was scheduled to start shooting in the fall of 1996, *Otoko wa Tsurai Yo* will probably have a permanent lock not only on its Guinness Book record as the longest movie series ever—**GODZILLA** and James Bond don't even begin to come close—but the affections of Japanese movie-goers. And foreigners who still don't have a clue? Try one bowl of Toraya soup—you may find yourself coming back for more.

THE TRENDY DRAMA

Prime-time Japanese TV dramas would seem to resemble American soaps in their continuing characters and plot lines that tangle and spread like kudzu weed. There is a difference, however; Japanese TV dramas have a beginning, middle, and, usually after twelve weeks, end, no matter how high their ratings. Reruns are uncommon, though some dramas find second lives on video shelves.

But though their on-air lives may be relatively short, popular TV dramas have a way of reproducing themselves. The writers, producers, and actors often go on to make other dramas that resemble the hit show that rocketed them all to fame, and other networks, not surprisingly, follow the leader.

One advantage of the twelve-week format is that the show's producers can respond quickly to trends in society at large. Instead of trying to flog a tired format for yet another season, they can make programs that really reflect what is going on in their viewers' lives.

In the 1980s, the main social change affecting drama programs was the splintering of the mass audience that had fueled the TV boom of the past two decades. Instead of one TV set in the living room, around which the whole family gathered—two- and even three-set households became the norm. As the audience dispersed, tastes diversified.

Young single women no longer wanted to watch their mother's beloved "home dramas," with their weepy tales of family misfortune, or the youth-targeted dramas featuring the latest teen idols that riveted their younger sisters.

In the boom years of Japan's bubble economy, a growing number of these women were making good money at *katakana* jobs, so called because the job titles were written in the *katakana* syllabary usually reserved for transcribing foreign words, such as *dezainaa* (designer) and *jaanarisuto* (journalist). They were using their fat bonus checks to enjoy lifestyles that their mothers and older sisters could only imagine, buying designer clothes, traveling abroad, and living independent lives in their own condos. Even those who were still commuting from home and spending the New Year's holiday standing in an hour-long lift line at a Nagano ski resort could dream. But the networks, who had found the old formulas successful so long, were slow to make shows that reflected those dreams.

Then in 1988, at the height of the bubble economy, a drama called *Dakishimetai!* (I Want to Hug You!) debuted on the Fuji Television network. It told the story of nineteen-year-old stylist Asako (Atsuko Asano) and her childhood friend Natsuko (Yuko Asano), a housewife who seeks refuge at Asako's apartment after leaving her husband.

Instead of revolving around domestic troubles, in the classic home-drama mold, *Dakishimetai* focused on the renewed friendship of the two women, with Natsuko, a spoiled, calculating type, getting the good-natured Asako into jam after jam.

For much of their on-air time, though, Natsuko and Asako just talked, rating the men in their lives, calculating their prospects for marriage, and, in Asako's case, complaining about her job. They said what many of their young female viewers were really thinking and feeling, with an honesty that many found refreshing. Also, instead of passively submitting to social pressures and norms, they tried to make their own way in the world, on a basis of equality with the men around them.

The show, however, was not just in touch but relentlessly trendy, showing off its heroines in the latest fashions, decorating their new condo in the latest interior styles, and sending them off to Tokyo's waterfront hot spots in snazzy sports cars. The characters, including Asako, had groovy *katakana* jobs. No dull, conventional, tea-pouring, secretary's existence for them!

Though the show's love-comedy story line was hardly original, its attitude and approach struck viewers as fresh and new. In a carryover from Japan's filmmaking tradition, TV dramas had long been vehicles for their creators' sometimes ponderous messages. *Dakishimetai,* however, was made from its target viewers' point of view and expressed their fantasies. This new packaging propelled the show up the ratings chart and the two Asanos, who were not related, to stardom. Other actors on the show, including Jun'ichi Ishida and Masatoshi Motoki, also later made the TV big time.

Dakishimetai gave birth to a new genre: the "trendy drama" (*torendii dorama*). Show producer Yoshiaki Yamada and director Shunsaku Kawake went on to make other trendy dramas with exclamation marks in their titles, including *Kimi no Hitomi ni Aishiteru!* (I'm in Love with Your Eyes!) and *Ashiatteru Kai!* (Do We Love Each Other!). Rival networks soon weighed in with trendy dramas of their own.

Like *Dakishimetai,* these shows were usually light-hearted looks at the love troubles of fashionable young urbanites living affluent bubble-era lives. They generated big rating numbers for Fuji TV and other networks in the late 1980s and early 1990s. Not everyone was enthralled with the new genre's success, however. Critics trashed the trendy dramas for being air-headed exercises that bore only the faintest relationship to reality. "A lot of older producers consider me an outlaw, but I don't care what they think," said Fuji TV trendy drama producer Toru Ota. "Unlike a lot of producers, I have the mentality of a salaryman, not an artist. . . . I want to make dramas that everyone can watch, not necessarily ones that I want to watch."

For a time, it seemed that viewers wanted to watch nearly anything with the trendy drama label. But with the end of the bubble economy and beginning of Japan's long recession, the trend was no longer conspicuous consumption but bargain hunting, not frothy romantic comedies but achingly sincere dramas about storm-tossed-but-steadfast pure love or *junsui ai*. Following the flop of *Ai no Paradise* (Paradise of Love), a 1990 trendy drama starring Yuko Asano, Ota quickly reversed tack and made *Tokyo Love Story,* a "pure love" drama that recorded a 37.4 rating in its final episode in 1991. The show's theme song "Love Story wa Totsuzen" (Love Comes Suddenly) sold a whopping 2.8 million copies. Ota was still the hottest young producer on Japanese television—and the trendy drama boom was history.

This is not to say that characters in today's dramas are shaving their heads, donning monk's robes, and heading off to the mountains to drown their various love troubles under a waterfall. Many TV dramas are still as trendy as ever, with hot young talents in starring roles (even though they have never acted in anything longer than a TV commercial), who wear the latest fashions (whether their characters can afford them or not), live in stylishly furnished apartments on pieces of prime real estate (with no mention of how the rent gets paid) and work at jobs that most young people would kill to get (and, given the grim employment situation of the mid-nineties, might have to). The trendy drama legacy still lives, in other words, even though the bubble-economy culture that nurtured it is as passé as gold-flake saké.

TRANS-AMERICA ULTRA QUIZ

No pain, no gain. That thought is hardly new or uniquely Japanese, but the Japanese have taken it to extremes and made it an integral part of their culture. From the pro baseball players who undergo the notorious "one thousand *fungo*" drill, in which they field one thousand straight hits (unless they drop from exhaustion first), to the salarymen who ride hours on packed rush-hour trains to get to the office and the schoolboys who wear shorts and T-shirts outside in the dead of winter, the Japanese tough it out, or *gaman suru,* day after day, in a myriad of ways.

But perhaps the ultimate expression of *gaman* on television was *Trans-America Ultra Quiz,* a quiz program which, during its six-teen-year run, required an intestinal fortitude of its contestants seldom seen outside Olympic training camps or Arctic expeditions or, detractors might add, a masochism seldom witnessed outside the wilder S & M clubs.

Conceived when foreign travel was still a luxury for the few and the United States was still the glamour destination—the wealth! the freedom! the wide open spaces! everything that the poor, crowded, rule-bound Japan was not!—*Trans-America Ultra Quiz* offered a few lucky contestants a free, all-expenses-paid foreign trip, with plenty of stops on the way. But to reach their final destination, New York, those contestants had to endure trials and tortures that made a month at a Parris Island boot camp seem like a Club Med vacation.

Though the show struck foreign observers as quintessentially Japanese—an extension of the self-sacrificial kamikaze ethic—it marked a dramatic departure from local quiz-show convention when it debuted on NTV in 1977. First of all, *Ultra Quiz* was not studio bound—the contestants spent most of their air-time in the great outdoors, getting plenty of (often involuntary) exercise. Second, the contest was not limited to a single time slot, but continued over a period of weeks, like a serial drama with an ever-dwindling cast. Finally, instead of focusing solely on the winners, the program gave equal time to the losers, although many of them would no doubt have preferred a quick exit and a painless plane ride back to obscurity.

The first *Trans-America Ultra Quiz* began in Tokyo's Korakuen Stadium with 404 contestants and consisted of two hour-and-a-half installments. As the show's popularity grew—it regularly scored ratings in the thirties—it stretched to as many as five installments and, in 1991, attracted a record 28,523 contestants. But the long and winding road to the Big Apple took its toll. During the show's sixteen-year run, only thirty-one of the 213,430 contestants made it to the final quiz, at the foot of the Statue of Liberty. *Ultra Quiz* might be described as the ultimate Japanese entrance exam, far tougher to pass than the exam for elite Tokyo University or even Japan's notorious law boards, with their three-percent success rate.

The quiz began simply enough, with stadium players answering true and false questions, until all but a few dozen remained. Then came the first leg of the overseas journey, to Guam. But there were, alas, never enough seats on the airplane, so the contestants played a game of scissors-paper-stone to see who would board. The losers had little choice but to wave good-bye to the winners and haul their brand-new luggage, packed with clothes for a tropical holiday, back to the train for the trip home.

In some ways, however, these early losers were the lucky ones. The contestants who fell by the wayside on the show's ever-changing foreign stopovers, including Hawaii, Europe, and South America, had to endure a "punishment game," or *batsu geemu*. Sometimes the punishment was instantaneous. On Guam, contestants answered true or false questions by running and leaping through one of two curtains. A wrong guess and the contestant landed in pool of mud.

Other punishments for losers were more elaborate. After being dragged out of bed at two in the morning and forced to answer questions until dawn, one loser had to paint a one-kilometer-long line on the airport tarmac on a blisteringly hot Hawaiian day, while his agonies were being recorded for the folks back home.

Some punishments were downright dangerous. In Mexico a losing female contestant was thrust into in a bull ring with a full-grown bull. She ran for her life and managed to escape unscathed, crying tears of hysterical relief for the camera. The show's emcee, Norio Fukudome, later explained that the producers had intended to put a calf in the ring, but someone had screwed up. "I couldn't help crying a bit myself," he said.

In the United States such a slip might have resulted in a law suit. But despite the show's cruel and unusual punishments, contestants never called their lawyers, digging instead into their apparently limitless reserves of *gaman*. And there was a seemingly limitless supply of contestants. As the show became a TV institution in the 1980s, college students across the country formed quiz clubs where they spent hours practicing trivia questions, especially the current events questions that the show favored. If nothing else, *Ultra Quiz* increased the percentage of the population who could name the current U.S. trade representative, not to mention the amount of the current trade deficit.

But though the contestants kept coming, in the 1990s the show's ratings started slipping. Vicarious overseas trips packed less of a thrill for *Ultra Quiz's* young core audience, many of whom were flying to foreign destinations as casually as they would drive to Izu for the weekend, without the inconvenience of being turned back at the boarding gate. Also, the production costs—at one hundred million yen per installment nearly three times higher than those of conventional quiz shows—were not getting any cheaper.

A final blow came when emcee Fukudome, whose rapid-fire quips and older brotherly words of encouragement had added greatly to the show's ratings appeal, decided to call it quits at the fifteenth *Ultra Quiz,* handing over his mike to his successor before a packed crowd at Tokyo Dome.

But though NTV pulled the plug on the show after the 1992 edition, the *gaman* genre that *Ultra Quiz* spawned lives on. One popular example is *TV Champion,* a TV Tokyo game show that, since its debut in April 1992, has found champions in a variety of off-the-wall competitions, including most capacious sushi swallower, spiciest food eater, sweetest sweet tooth, and sweatiest body. For the last, contestants wearing sweatsuits were made to gorge on spicy food, then work out on a raised platform that funneled their sweat into a bottle placed strategically underneath.

The show has sent its champions on overseas tours, where they take on local challengers. But be it devouring piles of beefsteaks or downing boxes of macadamia-nut candies, the champions nearly always win. When it comes to *gaman,* the Japanese are still tough to beat.

ULTRAMAN

Godzilla director Ishiro Honda often maintained that his most famous creation was inspired by the U.S. hydrogen bomb test at Bikini Atoll and was intended as a protest against nuclear weapons. But what was the inspiration for Ultraman? Debuting on TBS in 1966 with a show called *Ultra Q,* the

Ultraman series was a good-superhero-versus-bad-space-monster show, a TV ancestor of the **POWER RANGERS**. Taking a hint from Honda, director Akio Jissoji said he regarded his monsters as "symbols of nature": "[In the 1960s] the pace of suburban development was accelerating and mountains and fields were quickly disappearing. The monsters were victims of human selfishness, with whom we could sympathize as weaker beings."

In other words, not such bad guys after all. Watching the show's skyscraper-sized monsters smashing urban landscapes to kindling while battling Ultraman, casual viewers may find it hard to agree. The monsters can't really help themselves, however. Poor Pestar was driven around the bend by drinking crude oil, Jiras by swallowing tainted fishing bait, and Jamila by having a close encounter with an orbiting satellite. This was relevant stuff for the 1960s, when Japan was destroying its environment and afflicting its citizens with pollution-related diseases in the process of boosting its GNP.

The Ultraman series' similarity to Godzilla extended beyond its sympathy for its monsters. Its creator, Eiji Tsuburaya, was also responsible for the special effects on the 1954 film, including the big guy's latex suit. A co-production of Tsuburaya's production company and the TBS network, the series was filmed in a ramshackle wooden warehouse in Tokyo's Setagaya Ward that was the Tsuburaya studio.

The series' premise bears a family resemblance to that of Superman and other U.S. superhero comics. Ultraman has come from the M-78 nebula to help the Earth in its never-ending battle with space monsters. To avoid frightening earthlings, he assumes human form as Hayata, a member of the Science Special Search Party (SSSP). When the SSSP encounters space monsters and its human members can no longer cope with their massive foes, Hayata morphs into Ultraman, a forty-meter-tall hero in a skintight red-and-silver suit who battles the monsters with his spacium beam, as well as an array of martial-arts kicks and throws.

Compared with today's sci-fi extravaganzas, the early Ultraman shows look clunky and crude, with their latex-suited monsters clumsily flailing about in miniature pasteboard sets. There are no computer graphics and the only special effect is the light of Ultraman's beam. But the shows' first viewers—mostly boys under the age of ten—loved the goofy grotesquery of the monsters and Ultraman's Kabuki-esque heroics. The ratings climbed as high as thirty-nine percent and the series became a national phenomenon. Unfortunately, the special effects staff couldn't make the monsters fast enough; they needed one month to complete each one, but Ultraman dispatched one a

Ultraman: a lean, mean, forty-meter-tall fighting machine.

week. Finally, when he had wiped out Tsuburaya's stock of space meanies, he had to fly back to his home nebula and the show had to go temporarily off the air.

Ultra Q ran from January to July 1966, then morphed into *Ultraman,* which aired from July 1966 to April 1967. After a six-month break, *Ultraman Seven* brought a new Ultra hero to the small screen from October 1967 to September 1968.

The show then left the air until 1971, when it reappeared as—what else?—*Ultraman Returns (Kaette Kita Urutoraman).* There was also a half-hour cartoon show, *The Ultraman,* which debuted in 1979 and a live-action series, *Ultraman 80,* which aired in 1980. In September 1996, Tsuburaya launched its latest live-action show. Altogether Tsuburaya has made ten live-action and two animated Ultraman series.

Each new show retained the basic story line but introduced new characters and situations. The hero of *Ultra Seven* is another native of the M-78 nebula who, taking the human name Dan Moroboshi, joins the Ultra Squad of the Terrestrial Defense Force to—what else?—protect the earth from space aliens. Unlike the original Ultraman, Ultra Seven battles the baddies with not only his trusty beam weapons, but with Capsule Monsters—creature companions from the home nebula.

Eventually, an entire family of Ultra beings took their places in the Ultraman pantheon, including Ultraman Leo, Ultraman Jack, Ultraman Ace, and Yullian—an Ultra woman who was the fighting companion of Ultraman 80. Naturally, these characters spawned the usual merchandising spin-offs, including enough plastic Ultramen and space monsters to fill the toy box of every kid in Japan. In the mid-nineties, nearly two thousand licensed products were generating eighty to one hundred billion yen annually in revenue.

Ultraman also went international, appearing in the United States, France, Spain, Thailand, and, in 1993, China. The series made an especially big hit with Chinese kids. In May 1994 one hundred thousand fans jammed into a park in Shanghai to catch an Ultraman stage show. When the crowd rushed the stage after the first of five scheduled performances, sponsors decided to cancel the remaining four. Ultraman and his allies may have conquered space monsters, but they couldn't stop a mob of excited seven-year-old Shanghaiese.

Tsuburaya has made seven Ultraman movies, including the animated features *Ultraman: The Adventure Begins* and *Ultraman Kids.* In 1993, in partnership with Harvey Comics, it launched an English-language Ultraman comic and, in 1994, made a thirteen-part video series in the United States together with Major Havoc Entertainment.

Titled *Ultraman: The Ultimate Hero,* the series featured American actors and English dialogue. Instead of coming from outer space, the monsters were mutants created by industrial pollution, and the old shows' chopsocky violence was toned down to please American parental sensibilities.

In March 1996 Shochiku released *The Wonderful World of Ultraman,* a three-part omnibus that included a live-action short, *Ultraman Forever,* an animated short, *Ultraman Company,* and the main feature, *Ultraman Zearth.* In line with the contemporary preference for heroes who are not so heroic, Zearth in his human form is a klutz who is forever goofing up and getting scolded by his seniors in the Mysterious Yonder Defense Organization (MYDO). He even has a cleanliness obsession: a hero, in other words, who hates to get his hands dirty. Even after morphing into Ultraman Zearth, he doesn't fit the flawless superhero mold. When he deploys his ultimate weapon—the Supeshushula Beam—he hits himself instead of his target. But though Zearth may have been a goof, the movie was a hit.

Then, in September Tsuburaya debuted its twenty-third Ultraman character and its first new one in sixteen years in a new series on the TBS network. Called Ultraman Tiga, the latest savior of the Earth stands fifty-three meters tall, weighs forty-four thousand tons and, when battling space monsters, morphs into three different forms: Multi Type, Sky Type, and Power Type. Though of the same superheroic line as the original Ultraman and his family, he is not an Ultra blood relation. Also, he came to Earth thirty million years ago, almost long enough to make him a native. A new Ultraman indeed.

When Tsuburaya held a meeting to explain marketing opportunities for this addition to its lineup, nearly five hundred representatives from fifty companies showed up, demonstrating yet again that the years had not dimmed the power of the Ultraman franchise.

Despite its attempts to internationalize and modernize, Tsuburaya has not lost touch with its corporate roots and superhero tradition. As a tribute to the work of his father and company founder, second-generation former Tsuburaya president Noboru Tsuburaya built an Ultramanland theme park in Kumamoto Prefecture, on the island of Kyushu. Constructed at a cost of one billion yen on a 8,200 square-meter site, the park opened in March 1995. Greeting visitors is a ten-meter tall statue of the original Ultraman—only one-quarter the size of the real thing, but still an impressive specimen of alien manhood in his silver-and-red suit, still bravely protecting us all from the dangers lurking in the stars.

WAKA DAISHO

The Japanese 1960s were marked by many of same political and social upheavals that characterized the decade in the United States and Europe. The timing, however, was somewhat different. In 1960, when American students were still basking in the somnolent glow of the Eisenhower years and the war in Vietnam was not even a glimmer in Lyndon Johnson's eye, the streets of Tokyo were erupting in massive protests against the signing of the revised U.S.–Japan security treaty by prime minister Nobusuke Kishi. In the forefront of the anti-treaty movement was the radical student group Zengakuren, many of whose members attended elite universities.

A recent graduate of one of those universities, Yuzo Kayama, was not on the streets, however, but in the studio, acting in movies for Toho. The son of popular 1930s leading man Ken Uehara and actress Yoko Kozakura, Kayama was a good-looking, athletic kid with a pleasant singing voice and winningly crooked grin. There was nothing in his acting that indicated greatness, but Toho saw a likability of star caliber in this former Keio University student. In 1961, only a year after he had finished hitting the books for real, Kayama went back to school in a college movie titled *Daigaku*

no Waka Daisho (The Young Captain of the University).

Intended as a B programmer for the bottom half of a double bill, *Daigaku no Waka Daisho* featured Kayama as a big man on the campus of Kyonan Daigaku, a private university in Tokyo. The captain of the swimming team, the leader of a Hawaiian music band, and popular with the ladies, Kayama eminently deserves his Waka Daisho nickname.

There is, however, nothing big headed about this BMOC; the son of a poor-but-proud sukiyaki-shop owner, Kayama cheerfully works at various part-time jobs to earn his college keep. He is respectful to his elders, friendly to his inferiors, and always ready to do a good turn for those in need. He is not, however, a goody two-shoes; he covers for his absent teammates when the English

teacher calls roll and, when forced, can be quick with his fists.

The plot exists only to display these and other sterling qualities of Waka Daisho. He has a rival in Kunie Tanaka's Ao Daisho (one reading of "Ao Daisho" is "Green Captain; another is *Elaphe climacophora*—a kind of large green snake. In this case, both seem appropriate), a spoiled rich kid who leads a gang of like-minded slackers and envies Waka Daisho's status and success. But Waka Daisho is too big a man to become really angry at Ao Daisho's schemes aimed at stealing his thunder.

The only exception is when Ao Daisho becomes interested in a pretty working girl named Sumiko (Yuriko Hoshi) who has a crush on Waka Daisho. The cad takes her for a sail on Lake Ashinoko in the fashionable resort of Hakone and, after his cronies dive off the boat at a prearranged signal and swim for shore, he tries to molest her. Working as beach lifeguard, Waka Daisho spots Sumiko's struggles through his binoculars, rides to the rescue on his motorboat, and promptly knocks Ao Daisho into the water.

But, clean-living youth that he is, Waka Daisho has little time or inclination for romance. Instead he is busy practicing for a big swimming meet, selling tickets for his club's dance party, and dreaming up ways to make his dad's business prosper (his big idea: install barbecue grills).

He is also busy promoting the romances of others. When his father and grandmother persuade him to go to an *omiai* (an arranged meeting for the purpose of marriage) with the beautiful daughter of a rich business-man—he saved the businessman's life at Lake Ashinoko and the *omiai* is his reward—he reluctantly agrees, but following the stan-dard introductory chitchat, he bluntly tells the young lady that he is not interested in her. He then produces the blushing swim-team manager, who is desperately in love with the lady in question, and announces that the manager will take his place. Without further ado, he exits in a cloud of selfless glory.

Daigaku no Waka Daisho, of course, had nothing to do with real campus life in 1961 or any other known era or universe. With its grab bag of songs, gags, romance, and sports heroics—in the climax Waka Daisho comes from behind to win the big swimming relay race—the movie was intended as feel-good entertainment, not serious social com-mentary. In the entire picture there was no indication that, in the recent past, campuses very much like Waka Daisho's had been seething with anti-treaty activity: speeches, marches, and riots. It was as though Hollywood were to make, in 1971, a film about modern-day college students without a single reference to the Vietnam War.

But as out-of-it as the movie may sound in retrospect, it became a box office winner, spawning a total of seventeen sequels. Kayama played Waka Daisho until 1971, when he was advancing into middle age and the campus life of the early series entries looked as dated as a Meiji-era woodblock print. (By the latter installments, however, Kayama was playing a young salaryman).

The sequels repeated the formula of the original movie: Waka Daisho showed his mettle at sports, worked diligently at a part-time job, wowed the party crowd with his singing and guitar playing, and displayed his Mr. Nice Guy-ness on every possible occa-sion. Though every film in the series featured a different love interest and sport, Waka Daisho himself remained the same—and his fans loved him for it. Once, in the 1965 *Umi no Waka Daisho* (The Young Captain at the Ocean), the scriptwriter varied the formula by writing in a bed scene for Waka Daisho, but Toho studio execs didn't go for it; they were worried about spoiling their star's clean-cut image. The series never departed from the straight-and-narrow again.

Over the years, however, the series de-voted an increasing amount of screen time to Kayama's musical talents. The second

1965 series entry, *Ereki no Waka Daisho* (The Young Captain of the Electric Guitar), was essentially a pop musical. A song Kayama composed for the film, *Kimi to Itsumademo* (Always Together With You), sold three million copies and propelled the movie into the box-office stratosphere. After that, Kayama the singer-songwriter started to outstrip Kayama the nice-guy personality as a factor in the series' popularity (see **ROCKABILLY, GROUP SOUNDS AND THE BIRTH OF JAPANESE ROCK**).

Another reason for the series success is that it tapped into its audience's longings for a richer, freer, more Westernized lifestyle. After sixteen years of postwar recovery, the Japanese economy was poised to take off, but the living conditions of most Japanese were still spartan, their working conditions harsh. The sight of Waka Daisho driving a speedboat, eating beef with his buddies, and leisurely practicing his guitar in his dorm was like a dream to many moviegoers, including Kayama's contemporaries. He was living out their consumerist fantasies on screen.

The series capitalized on this audience fascination with Waka Daisho's glamorous life, sending him to exotic foreign climes (Hawaii, Tahiti, Rio, New Zealand) and giving him expensive toys to play with (skis, cars, sailboats). "Waka Daisho was three decades ahead of his time," Kayama later told an interviewer. "The series was depicting . . . an ideal life of thirty years in the future. All of the things that appear in it are now a matter of course, but through [the series] moviegoers could dream about things that were then economically out of reach."

The series made Kayama a generational hero, but it also hopelessly typecast him. Though he acquitted himself well in non-series films, including Akira Kurosawa's 1965 *Akahige* (Red Beard), he could never break free of the Waka Daisho image. After the series ended in 1971, he appeared sporadically in films but his career seemed to be going nowhere. Then, as he entered middle age, nostalgia for the Waka Daisho series led to revival screenings and a comeback for its star in TV dramas, music programs, and quiz shows. In 1981, Kayama appeared in one more Waka Daisho film—*Kaette Kita Waka Daisho* (Waka Daisho Returns)—but the old magic was gone. Young moviegoers were jetting off to Hawaii themselves—and leaving the innocent salad days of Waka Daisho far, far behind.

YAKUZA MOVIES

Like Hollywood gangster movies, films about Japan's indigenous gangsters, the *yakuza*, have long constituted a distinct film genre. And just as gangster movies have evolved, over the years, from the crudely powerful drama of *Little Caesar*, to the more sophisticated villainies of the Godfather trilogy, *yakuza* movies have also undergone changes in accordance with audience tastes, market pressures, and directorial ambition. The 1960s films of Ken Takakura and Koji Tsuruta, which contrasted the nobility of the good-gangster hero to the black-heartedness of his bad-gangster rivals, have since given way to the violently nihilistic dramas of Takeshi Kitano, whose heroes also have bloody hands. The genre still thrives on video and cable television (Nikkatsu's NECO channel devotes large chunks of its schedule to the studio's *yakuza* movie output), but has slowly faded from the theatre screen. One reason is the general exodus from the movie theatre to the small screen—theatre admissions have fallen to one-tenth of their 1958 peak. Another is that many of the stars who carried the genre to its heights of popularity in the 1960s and 1970s have retired, died, or gone on to better things and the studios have not been able to find suitable replacements. "The young actors we have today are no good," explained Tan Takaiwa, the president of Toei Company, Limited, the studio that created and nurtured the *yakuza* genre. "People see them acting on TV in all sorts of roles and can no longer believe in them as *yakuza* tough guys." Still another is that the *yakuza* themselves have retreated from the national consciousness. "The police have been cracking down on them, using the new anti-gang law," said Takaiwa. "As result *yakuza* movies have come to seem like fantasies."

To outsiders, *yakuza* may seem to be living in a feudalistic world, under a code of conduct derived from samurai ideals of unwavering fealty to emperor, lord, and clan, and an absolute willingness to sacrifice one's life and limb rather than endure dishonor or disgrace. The realities of modern gang life, however, have often made that code a mere facade, masking the gangs' economic raison d'être and nasty deeds. From their Edo-era beginnings as bands of outcast brothers who lived by gambling, street peddling, and other disreputable means (*yakuza* literally means "good for nothing"), the biggest of the *yakuza* gangs have since become multitiered, highly structured organizations involved in everything from prostitution and drug running to real estate speculation and corporate extortion.

The classic *yakuza* film or *ninkyo eiga* (literally, "chivalry film") explores this tension between the ideal and the real, but with a stylization that borders on fantasy. Though the hero may engage in moneymaking gang activities (nothing too dirty, however), he is in fact a throwback to an earlier, purer time, before the corruption of Westernization had set in. He lives by the code, and quite often dies by it. Finding such a spotless hero among the *yakuza* of the 1960s, however, would have been easy as finding a John Wayne lawman among the cops of the Fort Apache precinct in the Bronx. Consequently, *ninkyo eiga* were set in the approximately seventy-year period from the beginning of the Meiji era (1868–1912) to the early years of the Showa era (1926– 89), when traditional values were struggling against the tide of modernization but still very much alive. Even so, the intent was usually to create not a realistic backdrop but a mythological universe.

The first *ninkyo eiga* is considered to be Tadashi Sawashima's *Jinsei Gekijo: Hishakaku* (The Theater of Life: Hishakaku), a 1963 Toei release. Koji Tsuruta plays Hishakaku, a gangster who is on the run with Otoyo (Ryoko Sakauma), a Yokohama courtesan. With the help of a Tokyo gang boss, played by Ryunosuke Tsukigata, they hole up in Fukagawa, a Tokyo amusement quarter, but Hishakaku finally turns himself in to pay off an old debt. While he is in prison, Otoyo takes up with another man.

Although there had been gang films before, *Jinsei Gekijo: Hishakaku* established the genre formula of the good-gangster hero who wears Japanese-style clothes (as a way of underlining that goodness) and upholds the traditional ethic of *giri-ninjo* (i.e., fulfilling one's obligations and acting according to one's human feelings rather than cold, selfish pragmatism) against the backdrop of

early modern Japan. The theme of the hero sacrificing love for the sake of duty was a familiar one from the samurai period dramas that Toei and other studios had been making for years.

Soon afterwards, the Nikkatsu studio made its own contribution to the genre with Akinori Matsuo's *Otoko no Monsho* (Emblem of Manhood), a film about the son of a gang boss who wants to become a doctor but is forced to take over the gang when his father is rubbed out by a rival mob. Starring Hideki Takahashi as the son, *Otoko no Monsho* became a hit and launched a ten-part series that ran until 1966.

Although other studios made *ninkyo eiga,* the two most closely associated with the genre were the ones who first defined it: Toei and Nikkatsu. It was Toei, however, that nurtured the biggest stars, had the biggest hits, and created the greatest impact during the genre's peak years, from the mid-1960s to the mid-1970s.

Following the success of *Jinsei Gekijo: Hishakaku* and other early Toei *yakuza* movies, including the top-four box-office earners among the fifty-eight nonanimated feature films it released in 1964, the studio quickly converted the bulk of its production schedule to gang epics. In 1967 the genre accounted for thirty-seven of the studio's fifty-five feature films. Toei was able to crank up production so quickly because it already

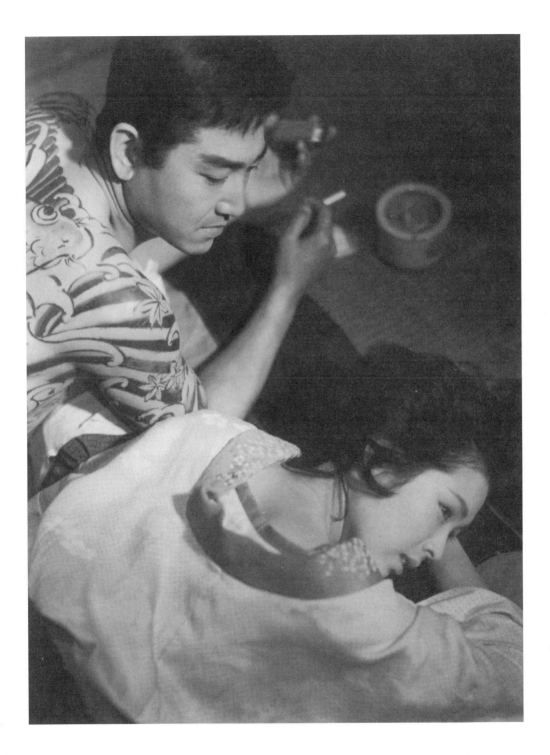

had the staff, cast, and facilities. Many of these human and material resources had been devoted to the production of samurai dramas—Toei had made seventy in the peak year of 1955—but when *yakuza* movies came in, starting in 1963, samurai dramas began to die at the box office and Toei had their actors exchange their samurai skirts for a gangster belly bands. By 1966 Toei had stopped making samurai dramas altogether and the genre's stars shifted their field of action to televison.

The studio assembly line needed hits to keep running, however. Fortunately, Toei was able to quickly cultivate *ninkyo eiga* stars—Ken Takakura, Koji Tsuruta, and, beginning in the mid-1960s, Fuji Junko— and build enduringly popular series around them, including *Jinsei Gekijo: Hishakaku* (1963–64, three entries), *Abashiri Bangaichi* (Abashiri Prison, 1965–73, eighteen entries), *Nihon Kyokakuden* (Tales of Japanese Chivalry, 1964–71, eleven entries), and *Hibotan Bakuto* (Red Peony, 1968–72, eight entries). These and other series became "brand names" that enabled Toei to attract a large and loyal following for its films and build an insurmountable box office advantage over its rivals.

Nikkatsu did not become seriously committed to the *ninkyo eiga* genre until Toei had already established a clear lead. Instead it kept churning out its "borderless action" (*mukokuseki akushon*) films, in which a lone, guitar-strumming hero wanders into town, finds bad gangsters harassing innocent folk, defeats them single-handedly, and leaves town, after winning and finally spurning the love of a pure-hearted maiden.

Although Nikkatsu began making actioners with a loner hero played by YUJIRO ISHIHARA in the mid-1950s, the purest examples of *mukokuseki* action could be found in the *Wataridori* (Bird of Passage) series starring Akira Kobayashi, which ran for nine installments from 1959 to 1962. Modeled on *Shane*—a well-remembered box-office hit in Japan—the series featured Kobayashi wearing buckskins and fringes and singing in a tenor voice, though "Home On the Range" was not in his repertoire. Keiichiro Akagi and Koji Wada were other *mukokuseki* action stars who emerged about the same time and, together with Ishihara and Kobayashi, constituted the Big Four of the Nikkatsu action-star line-up.

The *mukokuseki* action films, which borrowed heavily from Hollywood for their storylines and style, reached their peak in the late 1950s and early 1960s. But when Toei's *ninkyo eiga* started to surpass them at the box office in the mid-1960s, Nikkatsu had to play catchup. By 1969, it had expanded production of *yakuza* films to twenty-eight—or the majority of the fifty feature films in its lineup. That same year, twenty-four of Toei's fifty-one features for the year fell into the *yakuza* genre.

But though Nikkatsu briefly surpassed Toei in quantity, for aficionados Toei's films were the real thing and Nikkatsu's but a pale imitation (in some cases, they were literal remakes of Toei hits). Also, even Nikkatsu's better *mukokuseki* action pictures didn't fit the mood of the times as well as the Toei *yakuza* films.

In the boom days of the 1960s, when Japan's corporations were recruiting all able-bodied males in the fight for a bigger market share and a higher GNP, thousands of willing volunteers poured in from the countryside to study and work in the big cities—and often found themselves lost and alone, without the social networks of their rural towns and villages. To these young students and workers, the Toei *ninkyo eiga* were comforting and inspiring throwbacks to earlier, better times. Unlike the Nikkatsu *mukokuseki* action hero, who emerged from nowhere and owed nothing to no one, the typical Toei *ninkyo eiga* hero operated within the context of the gang society and the gang code. Though a lonelier figure than the typical period-drama samurai, he stood foursquare for the old ways, right down to his belly band and his Japanese-style sword.

One classic example of this hero, though in a modern setting, can be found in Teruo Ishii's *Abashiri Bangaichi: Bokyohen* (Abashiri Prison: Longing for Home). The third installment in the *Abashiri Bangaichi* series, this film became a big hit for Toei in 1965 and helped propel the series to a total of eighteen installments.

Escaped convict Ken Takakura arrives in Nagasaki to pay his respects to a friend in the Asahi gang to whom he owes a debt of gratitude. Learning that the gang is involved in a turf war over the Nagasaki waterfront with a ruthless rival, the Yasui, Takakura decides to help out, though some of the gang members distrust him as an outsider. At first, he tries a nonviolent approach to bring peace, but despite temporary victories, the Yasui gangsters remains determined to rule by any means necessary.

When Yasui thugs kill Takakura's prison buddy, who has joined the struggle out of friendship, and when the Yasui gang boss knifes the feeble old Asahi boss, who has come to the docks to investigate the murder, Takakura explodes in righteous indignation. Telling the other gang members to wait at headquarters—he doesn't want them to do time in prison—he walks into the night to fight the rival gang alone, a single sword tucked in his belly band.

Storming into a nest of Yasui gangsters, all armed with swords and knives, he heads straight for the boss and, after dispatching several of his underlings, slices and dices him. Then he faces the gang's hit man

(Naoki Sugiura)—a cool dude wearing a white trenchcoat and shades—and delivers a fatal cut, but not before being wounded himself. In the final scene, we see him leaning against a lamppost and gazing reflectively at the harbor, bloodied but unbowed.

Although there are modern elements in this story, included a half-black, half-Japanese street boy whom Takakura befriends, the hero is old-fashioned nobility personified. He follows the *yakuza* code of chivalry to the letter, even though he risks recapture, injury, and death by doing so. That code, we see, is not only uprightly self-denying but flamboyantly masochistic. Attacked by Yasui punks on his first day on the job as a dockside foreman, Takakura allows one after another to take a clear shot at his jaw, brushing off the blows with an expression of mild annoyance, as though they were the buzzing of insects. At first contemptuous of Takakura's nonresistance, the punks are finally overawed by his superhuman toughness—and scatter like frightened children.

Soon after, the gang's hit man ambles over with several henchmen, sneering and coughing tubercular blood, Doc-Holliday-style, into a handkerchief. He challenges Takakura's claim to being straight by pointing to the tattoo—a *yakuza* trademark—on Takakura's bicep. Takakura offers to remove it and, taking out a lighter, begins to burn it

off, whistling nonchalantly. His face twitching, his nostrils recoiling at the smell of charred flesh, the hit man finally turns away, defeated.

Takakura's self-immolating machismo may have seemed a pole apart from the hyper-violent brand Clint Eastwood had defined the year before as the Man With No Name in Sergio Leone's *Fistful of Dollars* (a spaghetti-Western remake of Akira Kurosawa's *Yojimbo*) but both men, with their strong-but-silent charisma, struck audiences as the epitome of cool. They shot to superstardom less as actors playing roles than as iconographic figures, repeating the same gestures and attitudes in film after film. But whereas Eastwood's specialty was killing stylishly, Takakura's was dying beautifully.

Born in Fukuoka in 1931, Takakura had lived through the darkness of the war years and the chaos of the early postwar years as an impressionable teenager. After graduating from Meiji University, he passed an audition to become one of Toei's "new face" contract players and made his film debut in 1956 in *Denko Karate Uchi* (Lightning Karate Blow). After that he was cast in gang and salaryman pictures, but as a salaryman he was a flop. It wasn't until he appeared as the loner hero in the *Abashiri Bangaichi* series that he became a star.

Takakura, of course, was not the only big name in Toei's *yakuza* film lineup. Koji

Ken Takakura: despite his appearance of stoic dignity, he could suddenly erupt in displays of edgy, kinetic violence.

Tsuruta had been a major star for more than a decade before appearing in *Jinsei Gekijo: Hishakaku*. After winning popularity among female moviegoers as a romantic leading man in the early 1950s, Tsuruta had broadened his range, appearing in war movies, period action films, and gang pictures for every major studio but Nikkatsu. He also started his own short-lived production company whose first release, Masahiro Makino's period gangster film *Yataro Gasa* (Yataro's Bamboo Hat), became a hit in 1952.

Born in 1924 and raised by his grandmother after his parent's divorce, Tsuruta was a feisty-but-affection-starved kid who roamed the streets of Osaka with a gang and once fought a rumble single-handedly against more than a dozen opponents. (He lost and was beaten with his own wooden clogs, an indignity that he never suffered in the movies.) Trained as an imperial navy pilot during World War II, he watched many of his comrades fly off to their deaths in the last desperate days of the war and, long afterward, suffered from survivor's guilt. He also carried psychic scars from a torrid love affair with actress Keiko Kishi, his costar in the 1953 *Hawaii no Yoru* (Hawaiian Nights), that his studio, Shochiku, had forced him to end. In short, his romantic-gangster credentials were in order in a way that the younger, college-educated Takakura's were not.

Takakura, in fact, freely admitted that he was anything but a *yakuza* type: off-screen he was a straight arrow who didn't smoke, drink, or gamble. On-screen, however, he exuded a youthful macho charisma that was confident rather than cocky, bold rather than blustering. Despite his appearance of stoic dignity, he could suddenly erupt in displays of edgy, kinetic violence.

Tsuruta, by contrast, often portrayed an older, wearier, more tragic figure in his *yakuza* films, who was somehow too good to live in this corrupt modern world. Tough, yes, but with a streak of loneliness and vulnerability. If Takakura was a Mitchum-like natural, Tsuruta was a Bogart-like man-of-the-world who had somehow managed to keep his soul clean in a dirty business.

Though these two were the main pillars of Toei's early *yakuza* films, the studio soon added a third: Junko Fuji. The daughter of a Toei producer, Koji Toshifuji, Fuji had ambitions to join the **TAKARAZUKA** theater troupe

while a girl growing up in Osaka. After moving to Kyoto at the age of seventeen, she was scouted by Toei director Masahiro Makino and cast in Makino's 1958 *Otoko no Sakazuki* (A Man's Saké Cup) as a *yakuza*'s flighty lover. She made an impression and was soon a rising young star on the Toei lot, appearing in as many as ten pictures a year.

In the mid-1960s, she became a favorite of *yakuza* movie fans, appearing opposite Ken Takakura and Koji Tsuruta in the *Nihon Kyokakuden* series, in which she often played a beautiful-but-strong-spirited woman of the people who falls in love with a pure-hearted gangster. From supporting roles, Fuji quickly rose to *yakuza* movie superstardom and, in 1968, launched a series of her own with *Hibotan Bakuto*, playing a wandering gambler who seeks revenge for the murder of her gang-leader father. In the series' eight installments, Fuji displayed her skills

at not only cards, but martial arts, flattening her loutish male foes with superbly timed throws or, when the situation demanded, deftly carving them up with her short sword.

Though she claimed that her tough-as-nails characters were nothing like her real-life self, Fuji was convincing on the screen playing a woman who was the equal, mentally and physically, of any *yakuza* tough guy. A willowy beauty, she had a steely glare, a thrillingly husky voice, and, dressed in a dark, elegant kimono, a dignified, masterful, but undeniably feminine presence. Whether facing down a roomful of armed men or crying on cue at the deathbed of a *yakuza* boss, her performance was all of a piece, her on-screen embodiment of gang code as powerful as that of her male costars.

Her biggest fans were male, who may have been hard-core chauvinists at home and in the office but admired the gutsy Fuji. (For many she was, depending on taste, either the ideal mother figure or the dream dominatrix.) Though other actresses before and after her portrayed female *yakuza* on the screen, she was unmatched in her popularity and impact.

In 1972, she made her last film, Masahiro Makino's *Kanto Hizakura Ikka* (The Red Cherry Blossom Family of the Kanto), and retired to marry Kabuki actor Kikunosuke Onoe. Toei tried hard to find a replacement, but failed. Fuji's loss was so great that Japanese film critics commonly date the decline of the *ninkyo eiga* genre from her screen retirement.

In the late 1960s directors such as Kinji Fukasaku, Kosaku Yamashita, and Jun'ya Sato began making *yakuza* movies that more closely reflected contemporary realities, with a gritty violence and brutality that had little to do with *giri-ninjo* ideals and everything to do with life and death on Japan's mean streets. These "line of realism," or *jitsuroku rosen* films generated major hits, including Fukasaku's nine-part *Jingi Naki Tatakai* (Fight Without Honor, 1973–79) series about gang warfare in postwar Hiroshima, and began to displace the classic *yakuza* movies, with their romantic fantasies of days gone by.

In 1971 Nikkatsu went out of the action movie business altogether and began making softcore porno. Toei continued to make *yakuza* movies, but despite the popularity of *Jingi Naki Tatakai* star Bunta Sugawara, who injected a wild, explosive energy into many of the *jitsuroku rosen* pictures, they began to decline at the box office in the mid-1970s, never to regain the heights of their heyday.

The death blow to the *yakuza* movie came in the 1980s, with the arrival of VCR. Now able to enjoy their favorite violent fantasies in the privacy of their six-mat rooms for less than half the price of a movie ticket, the single males who had always been the genre's biggest audience stayed away from the theatres in droves.

An exception to this downward trend was the *Gokudo no Onnatachi* (Gang Wives) series, which debuted in 1986 and has been the only *yakuza* series in recent years to enjoy theatrical box-office success, with the first eight entries earning eleven billion yen in theatrical rental and video revenues. Based on a nonfiction book about the wives of *yakuza* by freelance journalist Shoko Ieda, who lived with her subjects for more than a year and had close brushes with an ongoing gang war, the series features Shima Iwashita as a strong-willed gangster-wife-turned-boss and depicts the feminine side of gang life in an often lurid and melodramatic light. The ninth and latest entry, *Kiken na Kake* (Dangerous Gamble) appeared in the theaters in June 1996.

Toei, however, did not consider the *Gokudo* films as really belonging to the *yakuza* genre ("It's all a fantasy," said Toei president Tan Takaiwa. "There are no real women *yakuza*.") Finally, in 1994, Toei announced that it was making its "last *yakuza* movie": *Don o Totta Otoko* (The Man Who Killed the Don), starring Hiroki Matsukata. Actually, the announcement was a PR ploy; if the movie made more than four hundred million yen, Toei execs said, they would reconsider their decision.

Unfortunately, few fans turned out for

this pallid reworking of genre cliches and Toei announced, this time for real, that it was closing its *yakuza* shop. This did not mean, however, that *yakuza* movies would no longer be made. Toei was still churning them out for the video shelves, where they enjoyed great success. But Toei's and other "new *yakuza*" made-for-video movies were, in their fast-paced, hard-edged mix of sex and violence, closer to the mass-market action films of modern Hollywood than the classic *ninkyo eiga*.

Meanwhile, independent directors such as Takashi Ishii and Takeshi Kitano (see **BEAT TAKESHI**) were trying to redefine the genre for the 1990s. But though Kitano impressed foreign critics in 1993 with *Sonatine*, a black-comic take on gang warfare in Okinawa

whose gangsters killed and died with a robotic impassivity, Japanese audiences stayed away. Ishii's 1995 *Gonin*, a dark, turbulent drama of murder and revenge, pushed the genre envelope much the way Quentin Tarantino's 1994 *Pulp Fiction* did; its violence hit audiences where they weren't, with surrealistically shocking imagery. But though Ishii journeyed to the end of the underworld night with considerable style and boldness, his film's bleak, nihilistic message did not attract enough paying travelers to become a hit.

In 1996, Atsushi Muroga tried a direct ripoff of Tarantino in *Score*, a low-budget movie about thieves on the lam that shamelessly copied *Reservoir Dogs*, right down to the funny nicknames for the Japanese

Bunta Sugawara injected a wild, explosive energy into many of his *jitsuroku rosen* pictures.

heroes—Chance, Tequila, Right, Peking Duck—and the scenes of gruesome violence in an abandoned concrete plant, but local moviegoers, having already seen the real thing, didn't bite.

Whatever the genre's future may be, don't look for the old stars to brighten it. Koji Tsuruta died of cancer in 1987 at the age of sixty-two, Junko Fuji is still in semiretirement, and though Ken Takakura is still making movies—his latest was Kon Ichikawa's 1994 period drama *Shiju Shichinin no Shikaku* (Forty-seven Ronin) he has not played a gangster in many years. International audiences may remember him as the fatherly foil to Michael Douglas's Ugly American cop in Ridley Scott's 1989 *Black Rain* or Tom Selleck's bemused manager in Fred Schepisi's 1992 *Mr. Baseball*. Older and wiser, perhaps, but not nearly as cool as when he was searing off his skin or slicing up baddies with a sword. More than any of his present-day successors, he gave us a glimpse into the romantic soul of a Japanese stoic.

YAMAGUCHI, MOMOE

Some stars rise to greater heights of fan adulation after leaving the stage for good; we miss them more than we thought we would. In addition to the dead legends—James Dean, Marilyn Monroe, Elvis Presley—there are the singers who took early retirement, the groups that split up while still in their musical prime. If the Beatles had stayed together instead of disbanding in 1970, would the world have awaited their latest album with bated breath or with yawns that this collection of rock fossils was still making music together?

In Japan, the still-living star whose absence has been most lamented by her fans is Momoe Yamaguchi. Even though she hasn't sung in concert, cut a record, or made a movie since 1980, this former queen of Japanese pop music has been a mainstay of the weekly gossip magazines for the past decade and a half. In the early years after her retirement at the age of twenty, few details of her daily existence as wife of actor Tomokazu Miura were too mundane for the mags' Momoe watchers to miss. Her son's postpartum homecoming, nursery school graduation ceremony, and first day at elementary school rated cover headlines—simply because Mom happened to be in the picture.

In recent years, the media harassment has eased, but rumors that Momoe might appear in the 1994 KOHAKU UTA GASSEN (Red-and-White Song Contest) stirred up a fresh storm of tabloid speculation. There was no truth to the rumors; Momoe had no intention of breaking her silence, but they demonstrated the still-intense public interest in this woman, who has now been a suburban housewife twice as long as she was a teenage "idol" singer.

Momoe became a legend not so much for her talent, though she displayed a three-octave range, as for her public persona, the perfect arc of her career, and her manner of leaving it.

Momoe and her younger sister were raised in a tiny apartment by their chronically ill mother in the seaport of Yokosuka, the site of a big U.S. Navy base. Her family was so poor that Momoe had to deliver newspapers to a pay for a study desk. Then, in the summer of 1972, CBS Sony record producer Masatoshi Sakai spotted her photo on the desk of the director of *Star Tanjo!* (Birth of a Star!), a talent-scout show on the NTV network. As Sakai later reminisced, the photo showed a thirteen-year-old girl wearing a white blouse and a miniskirt. Her legs, he thought, "were thick and misshapen," but there was also a "refreshing purity and firmly rooted boldness" that struck him as unusual—and potentially profitable. Against opposition at CBS Sony—many of his fellow talent spotters thought her "gloomy-looking" and "dull"—he persuaded the company to sign her and began grooming her for stardom.

In 1972 Momoe made her debut on *Star Tanjo!*, which not only discovered beginners but launched a lucky few on their way to stardom with repeated TV appearances. NTV had developed *Star Tanjo!* as a counter to Watanabe Production, a talent agency whose large stable of groomed-for-TV pop stars enabled it to dominate the airwaves. Watanabe wielded its formidable power like a bludgeon; in 1973 it started its own talent show on rival network NET and announced that its singers would no longer appear on a music show that NTV was broadcasting in the same time slot. When NTV complained, Watanabe bluntly told the net to change the show's scheduling.

From that moment on, it was all-out war between Watanabe and NTV. Working together with a rising new agency, Hori Production, NTV was determined to create its own stars. Momoe thus became more than just another kid singer, but a vital counter in a bitterly contested power struggle; she *had* to succeed.

Since its start in 1971, *Star Tanjo!* had already nurtured one star—the thirteen-year-old Masako Mori—and in 1972 was looking for others. The auditions, held on Sunday from ten in the morning until six in the evening, processed as many as 120 young hopefuls an hour—thirty seconds for each. Momoe passed and, together with Mori and fellow newcomer Junko Sakarada, soon became known as the Hana no Chusan Trio (The Three Flowers Trio).

Of the three flowers, however, Momoe

Momoe Yamaguchi: what becomes a Japanese pop legend most?

seemed the least likely to bloom. She didn't have Mori's big, melodious voice or Sakarada's bouncy, vibrant personality. Her 1973 debut single, "Toshigoro" (Adolescence) sold seventy thousand copies—not bad for a beginner, but hardly indicative of a superstar future. Also, her fellow trio members were scoring much bigger numbers for their single releases.

But Momoe's second record, "Aoi Kajitsu" (Green Fruit), rocketed up the charts, as did her third, "Hito Natsu no Taiken" (One Summer's Experience), and her fourth, "Chippoke na Kansho" (A Little Senti-mental). One reason was that for a thirteen-year-old kid Momoe was singing some pretty hot lyrics. In "Aoi Kajitsu" she told an unnamed lover that "if you want, I'll let you do anything to me" and in "Hito Natsu no Taiken" announced to that same certain someone that she would "give you a girl's most important thing."

Some called these lyrics exploitation, but they sold records for the young singer, who had showed up for her first recording session in her sailor-suit school uniform. In the latter half of her career Momoe rarely performed her early songs—she wrote in her bestselling 1980 autobiography, *Aoi Toki* (Green Time), that "in my heart I completely rejected them."

Though not conventionally cute or sexy, Momoe had a quietly sultry presence that seemed to belie her years. With her sloe eyes, dusky complexion, direct gaze, and low, husky voice, she came across as a touch exotic, although she had never ventured farther from Japan than the Yokosuka bar district catering to U.S. sailors. Without really trying, she was soon melting hearts of teenage boys from Hokkaido to Kyushu.

But what really launched Momoe to stardom and signaled the second stage of her career were the songs written for her by husand-wife team of lyricist Yoko Agi and composer Ryudo Usaki. These so-called "punk" (*tsuppari*) songs, including "Yoko-suka Story" and "Playback Part 2," proclaimed that Momoe was no longer a girl who could be used by men but a woman ready to stand on her own two feet and take charge of her own life. Initially Momoe's agency and record company had opposed using this pair, saying that their music didn't

fit her image, but she had insisted—and changed her image instead.

At the same time, at the urging of Sony Records, she pleased the fans who had liked her softer side with such sentimental ballads as "Ii Hi Tabidachi" (Leaving on a Good Day) and "Aki Zakura" (Fall Cherry Blossoms). These and other tunes reached the top of the charts, but earned her relatively little critical or industry recognition; Momoe never won an industry record award in her entire eight-year career. Even so, she never threw a public snit fit over this snub or conducted a Paul McCartney-like campaign for honors. In this and other ways, she was, from beginning to end, a class act.

Momoe's movie career began only a year after her recording debut, in 1974 with the release of *Izu no Odoriko* (The Izu Dancer) Her costar was a baby-faced unknown named Tomokazu Miura. The movie was the sixth based on the classic Yasunari Kawabata story about an ill-starred romance between a young dancer and a high-school student. *Izu no Odoriko* was an unimaginative attempt to capitalize on Momoe's popularity as a singing idol, but the two young stars clicked—and soon the public was demanding more of what came to be know as the "golden combination." Momoe and Tomokazu made eleven more pictures together, all of them moneymakers.

Momoe and Tomokazu: a match made in box-office heaven.

Not surprisingly, given all the time they spent playing on-screen lovers, their romance began to bloom off the set as well as on it. Though Tomokazu was already twenty-two when he was first paired with the fifteen year-old Momoe, no eyebrows were raised. As far as their handlers and the public were considered, theirs was a match made in box-office heaven.

But though their pairing may have had its start as commerce, Momoe fell hard. For this teenager, whose parents had never married and whose father had performed an early disappearing act, the older Tomokazu represented a firm anchor in a turbulent world. She paid him her greatest compliment when she told record producer Sakai that "he's not like someone from the entertainment business."

As she grew to maturity, the idea of becoming Mrs. Miura and getting out of the pop-music rat race altogether become more attractive. She had always been in the entertainment world, but not of it—a distance that had been part of her appeal. In her autobiography she wrote that "I didn't like this job. . . . My singing was turned into work, without any regard for my own wishes. Forced to sing the same song over and over everyday, I came to hate singing."

Then in 1978, a popular pop trio called The Candies suddenly announced that they were quitting "to become ordinary girls again." Although Momoe was skeptical about their chances of returning to blissful anonymity, their example planted the idea of retirement more firmly in her mind.

In 1980, she finally announced her decision to marry Tomokazu and quit show business. The news hit many of her fans hard. Though they may have applauded her marriage, they regretted her retirement. It meant no more music from Momoe. Why, not a few of them wondered, did it have to be both? Why couldn't she keep singing, as so many other married pop stars had? Momoe, however, had made up her mind to get out, and nothing could change it.

Though to the less understanding her decision may have seemed regrettably old-fashioned—feminists complained that she was setting the women's movement in Japan back by ten years—to millions of her more traditionally minded fans there was something splendidly self-sacrificial about her exit, like Ingrid Bergman getting on the plane with the good-but-dull Paul Henried instead of hanging around Casablanca with the cynical-but-exciting Humphrey Bogart.

The more perceptive of those fans knew that without Momoe, Tomokazu was just a journeyman pretty-boy actor, whose career would never rise above the middling (they were right—it hasn't). But for the majority, she was doing the pure thing, the right thing, the romantic thing by giving it all up for her man. Her last recording, "Watashi wa Onna" (I Am a Woman), seemed to express this attitude. Momoe sang about wanting to give her love "with both hands." The song shot to number one on the charts.

Momoe went out in a blaze of glory, with her popularity and her reputation still intact. In a society that celebrated (and still celebrates) the average and conventional, in which women were (and still are) often expected to quit their jobs when they marry or give birth, the decision of this wealthy, famous, and powerful star to join the ranks of the buggy-pushing, grocery-shopping masses underlined, more than any song lyric ever could, her Ms. Averageness. Despite all the perks and temptations of stardom, her fans could say, she was always one of us, will always be one of us. They could conceive of no greater compliment. Her life story was also theirs—forever.

YMO

Over the years many Japanese singers and groups have tried to acquire international cachet by recording, performing, or releasing records abroad. In 1963 KYU SAKAMOTO reigned briefly at the top of the U.S. and European charts with "Sukiyaki," but he ended as a one-hit wonder. The first Japanese group to make a deep and lasting impact on the world pop-music scene and attain international pop stardom was Yellow Magic Orchestra, or as the group soon became acronymically known, YMO.

A trio of veteran studio musicians—Ryuichi Sakamoto, Haruomi Hosono, and Yukihiro Takahashi—YMO was the first Japanese pop group to use electronic sounds to produce a new kind of music called techno-pop. Influenced by such electronic music pioneers as Tangerine Dream, Giorgio Moroder, and Kraftwerk, YMO's debut album, the 1978 *Yellow Magic Orchestra* contained a complex-but-catchy blend of sing-songy melodies that sounded vaguely like Chinese restaurant music, together with electronic beeps and squawks that reminded not a few Japanese fans of the then-popular Space Invaders arcade game.

While self-consciously creating music that was neither "white" nor "black," but "yellow," YMO wanted to undermine stereotypes of what such a "yellow" music should sound like. "We were making fun of the cliched image of Oriental music that some people had gotten through music and TV," Sakamoto later told an interviewer for *Pulse* magazine. "We were, in a sense, commenting on this misunderstanding."

The parodistic intent, however, was often

lost on early audiences and critics. Disco fans liked the danceable hooks in "Firecracker" and other first-album tunes, while techno nerds were wowed by YMO's heavy use of synthesizers and other esoteric gear. Meanwhile, rock purists bemoaned the coldness and impersonality of YMO's music and the eerie detachment of their stage performances. Instead of playing and singing their guts out in approved rock-star style, YMO appeared on stage with herky-jerky gestures, like cyborgs whose emotional response programs had crashed. Even their clothes, with their coyly austere Red Guard look, underscored their affectless act. After attending a 1979 YMO concert, a reviewer for *The Washington Post* called their music "Transitorized Tchaikovsky, Diode Disco, Robot Rock" and described their performance as "dreary musical mush." "[YMO] preferred to let their gadgets do their work for them," the reviewer complained, "and, at times, it wasn't clear whether the men were playing the machines or vice versa."

Despite such critical lambastings, YMO prospered in purveying their tongue-in-cheek brand of electronic Orientalisme. Raised on pop music that had been heavily influenced by Western models, enamored of everything electronic, and eager to latch onto new trends, Japanese kids found YMO exotically different and definitively hip. But though YMO quickly conquered the Japanese market, their real target was the West. In the spring of 1979 they released their first album in the United States and, six months later, became the first Japanese pop band to set out on a world tour.

Considered a big gamble at the time, the tour made YMO worldwide techno-pop stars. Although the music itself certainly made an impact, the group's hipper-than-thou fashions (drummer Yukihiro Takahashi was a fashion designer and boutique owner) and the delicate, dusky handsomeness of keyboardist Ryuichi Sakamoto (whom the overseas press dubbed "the most beautiful man in the world") helped YMO win over Western audiences. Their second world tour, in 1980, was another smashing success, attracting nearly one hundred thousand fans.

But while selling their records in thirty-three foreign countries and playing gigs at the Venue in London, the Greek Theater in Los Angeles, and the Bottom Line in New York, Hosono, Takahashi, and Sakamoto were beginning to feel the pressures of stardom and the tensions from being chained together in an entity called YMO. "We had such strong egos," Sakamoto later reminisced. "We were so independent of each other. We were not like regular musicians: 'Hey, let's jam.'. . . I always joke about it: we were like three novelists writing one novel in a small room."

The "novelists" already had flourishing careers prior to producing their musical magnum opus in YMO. A classically trained pianist, Sakamoto received an MFA in composition from Tokyo University of Arts and, after graduating, became an in-demand session musician. In 1978, just prior to joining YMO, he released his first solo album, *The Thousand Knives of Ryuichi Sakamoto*.

Drummer Yukihiro Takahashi had been in bands since his high-school days, when his older brother was a member of Fingers, a popular Group Sounds ensemble. He later became part of the folk and rock scene, playing for the folk group Garo and, in 1973, joining The Sadistic Mika Band, who made a hit in the U.K. as Japanese glam rockers. In 1975, after touring the U.K. for one month with Roxy Music, The Sadistic Mika Band broke up and Takahashi, together with other former members, formed The Sadistics, a soul fusion ensemble. He released his first solo album, *Saraba!*, in 1977.

Though Sakamoto and Takahashi were already accomplished veteran musicians when they joined YMO, the guiding light of the group was Haruomi Hosono. After beginning his career in the Group Sounds band April Fool, he joined Happy End, a seminal early 1970s group acclaimed for being the first to successfully adapt Japanese-language lyrics to the rock idiom. Following Happy End's break up in 1972 he released the solo album *Hosono House* and formed the band Caramel Mama. In 1974 the group changed its name to Tin Pan Alley and shifted the focus of its activities from stage to studio, serving as back-up musicians for primarily New Music artists, including Yumi Arai (later Yumi Matsutoya, see YUMING AND THE BIRTH OF NEW MUSIC), Akiko Yano, Taeko Onuki, Tatsuro Yamashita, and Eiichi Otaki, although Hosono, working as a producer, arranger, and musician, ranged as far afield as *enka* ballads and pop tunes for "idol" singers.

Hosono's invitation to Takahashi and Sakamoto to appear on his 1978 solo album *Haraiso* marked the real beginning of YMO. During the recording sessions, Hosono talked about his idea for a group that would produce world-class music with an Eastern flavor. Music that, as he later explained, "would sound 'Oriental' to Westerners and 'Oriental' to Japanese." On the album Hosono billed himself as "Harry Hosono" and Takahashi and Sakamoto as members of the "Yellow Magic Band." Not long after, the three musicians returned to the studio to record *Yellow Magic Orchestra*.

But after rocketing from relative obscurity to worldwide fame, Sakamoto, Takahashi, and Hosono had little interest in playing the role of rock star, even though, as Sakamoto noted in a 1984 interview, some their fans were as fervent as believers in one of Japan's so-called New Religions. "If they look at

YMO with a rapturous gleam in their eyes, like true believers, that's up to them," he said. "But we who are doing the performing couldn't care less about that kind of thing. Every fan has the right to misunderstand us in his or her own way, so our feeling is, 'go ahead and enjoy yourselves.'"

Finally, after five years and eleven albums, Sakamoto, Takahashi, and Hosono decided they had nothing more musically to say together and announced that they were "putting a seal" on YMO. They were, they explained, "extending" (*sankai*) their activi-

ties, not "disbanding" (*kaisan*), a play on words—or rather Chinese characters—that left them the option of reviving the band at a later date. YMO held its last concert at the Budokan arena in December 1983.

Although all three members pursued solo careers after the end of YMO, Sakamoto had by far the most international success. He earned critical praise for his portrayal of the sexually ambiguous prison commandant in Nagisa Oshima's 1983 *Merry Christmas Mr. Lawrence* and won an Oscar for scoring Bernardo Bertolucci' s 1987 *The Last Emperor*.

After the latter triumph, he became the hottest film composer in the business, with a credit list that included Bertolucci's *The Sheltering Sky* and *Little Buddha,* Volker Schlondorff's *The Handmaid's Tale,* Pedro Almodovar's *High Heels,* and Peter Kosminsky's *Wuthering Heights.* He further expanded his resume by writing the theme music to the opening ceremony of the 1992 Barcelona Olympics and a symphonic score for a CD-ROM game.

While working on these and other commissions, he continued to pursue his personal music interests, releasing the solo albums *Beauty* (1990), *Heartbeat* (1992), and *Sweet Revenge* (1995). But compared with his YMO albums, they stirred nary a sales ripple. That didn't seem to bother the retiring Sakamoto. "I know that there are people who like my music," he told an interviewer for *Urb* magazine in 1995, "but I don't want to be Michael Jackson."

In 1993 YMO united briefly to record an album, *Technodon,* and hold two concerts at Tokyo Dome. In the interim, the techno-pop they had pioneered had inspired countless bands and spawned myriads of digitalized genres. Realizing that their early YMO hits now sounded as dated as, well, a Space Invaders game, the trio juiced up *Technodon* with vocal samplings from such certifiably hip celebrities as William Burroughs, William Gibson, and John C. Lilly, and made heavy use of the latest studio gear, including samplers and sequencers, to revamp their sound for the 1990s.

At their sellout concerts in the fifty-two-thousand-seat Dome, YMO put on a spectacular show that filled three enormous screens with state-of-the-art graphics, montages and lighting effects. Though most of the fans were on the far side of thirty and had come to relive the days of their youth, the band spent most of the evening playing cuts from their latest album, whose trendy ambient grooves were more sophisticated and subtle, but not as much fun to dance to as the old YMO sound.

The crowds dispersed, the album disappeared from the charts, and YMO put another seal on the band, probably for the last time.

Somehow, the magic was gone.

YOSHINAGA, SAYURI

There may have been better actresses in Japanese films, but few have ever been more enduringly popular than Sayuri Yoshinaga. Her fans, called *Sayurisuto* ("Sayurists"), have kept a warm spot in their hearts for their idol in the decades since her 1959 screen debut, despite the indifferent quality of many of her more than one hundred films. One way to explain this phenomenon, to Americans at least, is to say that Sayuri is the closest the Japanese entertainment industry of the time ever came to Annette Funicello.

Like Annette, Sayuri ripened from button-cute girlhood to vibrant womanhood on the screen, just as the Baby Boom generation was growing to maturity. And like Annette, Sayuri had a squeaky-clean image—a girl you could take home to Mom. Modest, sensitive, considerate, and eternally pure—Sayuri portrayed the typical male ideal of Japanese femininity in film after film.

But whereas, in the late 1960s, Annette's career crashed as the innocent delights of beach-blanket bingo and wild bikini stuffing gave way to the more dubious pleasures of the Now Generation, Sayuri successfully negotiated the difficult transition to adult roles. Though critics have derided the limits of her range, she has managed to remain an eminently bankable star throughout the four decades of her career, while many of her contemporaries have either retired or resigned themselves to playing aging housewives on TV soaps.

In her roles, as opposed to her career as a teenage phenomenon, Sayuri also differed significantly from Annette. Though playing typical teenagers, she did not spend much time hanging out at the beach or at the soda shop. Instead her specialty was suffering nobly and dying beautifully.

Born in March 1945, in Tokyo's Shibuya district, Sayuri was the second of three sisters. Following the failure of her father's publishing business, her family struggled to survive in the harsh poverty of early postwar Japan. But while fending off bill collectors, her parents exposed her to music and drama from an early age. As a sixth grader, she beat out seven hundred fifty other hopefuls for the role of the heroine on *Akado Susunosuke,* a children's period drama on Radio Tokyo (today's TBS network). Her character was also named Sayuri, a coincidence that may well have helped her win the part.

The program, which was a based on a popular comic about a fatherless boy who becomes the best swordsman in Japan, was a long-running hit. Sayuri, as one of the leads, found herself in the national spotlight for the first time.

In 1959, Sayuri made her screen debut in *Asa o Yobu Kuchibue* (The Whistle That Calls the Morning), a teenage drama about a hard-working paper boy. In 1960, shortly after graduating from junior high school, she agreed to become a contract player with the Nikkatsu studio, on the condition that she make only two films a year. After working so hard in junior high school and missing one-third of her classes, she wanted to experience life as a normal teenager. Her first Nikkatsu film was *Denko Sekka no Otoko*

(The Man Like a Flash of Lightning) in which she played a waitress. Her salary of ten thousand yen a month, with an added twenty thousand yen for every film appearance, was then the monthly wage of an average salaryman.

In 1961, Sayuri made an impression in her first starring role as a girl who commits suicide with her teenage boyfriend in *Garasu no Naka no Shojo* (The Girl In the Glass). The following year she appeared in sixteen movies, most of them instantly forgettable. Sayuri developed ulcers from the stress of her schedule, but kept running on what she later described in her autobiography as the "Nikkatsu conveyer belt."

In 1962, her performance as the spunky, pure-hearted daughter of a poor working-class family in Kiriro Urayama's *Kyupora no Aru Machi* (A Street of Cupolas) won her the prestigious Blue Ribbon acting award, making her the youngest actress to be so honored. Also, a duet record she cut with Yukio Hashi, *Itsudemo Yume o* (Always Keep Dreaming), became a smash hit and earned her an invitation to appear on the NHK year-end special **KOHAKU UTA GASSEN** (Red-and-White Song Contest).

Now the studio's biggest asset, she began grinding out nearly a movie a month, usually opposite her *Garasu no Naka no Shojo* costar, the boyishly handsome Mitsuo Harada. Her dream of living like an ordinary teenager was gone for good—she had to drop out of the public high school was attending—even as she was playing a succession of schoolgirl roles in front of the cameras.

Most of her films were a variation on the theme of star-crossed love, with Sayuri often expiring by the final frame. Audiences wept hot tears watching her love suicide in the snow in *Doro Darake no Junjo* (Mud-Spattered True Love) and her death by a wasting disease in *Ai to Shi o Mitsumete* (Looking At Love and Death).

Not all her films were simple boy-meets-girl, boy-loses-girl stories, however. In *Ai to Shi no Kiroku* (A Record of Love and Death) she fell in love with a boy who was dying of radiation sickness from the Hiroshima atomic blast. And in *A A Himeyuri no To* (Ah! Ah! The Tower of Lilies) she portrayed a student teacher who nursed wounded soldiers during the Battle of Okinawa. But whatever the theme, the object was usually to get the audience to wring out their hankies.

While making bundles of yen for Nikkatsu, Sayuri passed a high-school equivalency exam and, in 1965, entered the Literature Department of Waseda University. Despite her killing schedule at the studio, she faithfully attended night classes and, in 1969, graduated as class salutatorian. The topic of her graduation essay was Greek drama.

Sayuri in a poster for *Cupola no Aru Machi* (A Street of Cupolas). Her specialty was suffering nobly and dying beautifully.

By the time she finished college, Sayuri was tiring of her all-work-no-play lifestyle. Instead of reading Aristophanes, she began to go drinking in Shinjuku with friends and live it up a bit. She was also fed up with the sameness of her roles. In 1968 she established her own production company, Yoshinaga Jimusho, and in 1969 planned to produce and star in *Nomugi Toge* (Nomugi Pass), a film about the harsh lives of women silk factory workers in the Meiji period (1868–1912) that she hoped would change her image.

But her father, who was president of the company, didn't care for the ensemble-piece scenario, which did not have a big part for Sayuri. He fired the scriptwriter and hired another, but the result was still unsatisfactory. The film was never made. In her autobiography, Sayuri blamed herself for not expressing her own doubts about the script, which she felt "did not have the lyrical flavor that I wanted," until the project was well under way.

In 1972 she blew another chance to change the direction of her career when she turned down the starring role in Kei Kumai's *Shinobugawa* (The Shinobu River). Kumai demanded that the film, which was based on a prize-winning novel about a man who falls in love with a teahouse geisha, be made in black and white and that Sayuri do a nude scene. Her father vetoed both ideas,

particularly the latter, and the part went to Komaki Kurihara. The movie became a critical and popular success and made Kurihara a star.

About this time career-related stress, which had been building for years, caused Sayuri to lose her voice. At this low point in her life, she found support in Taro Okada, a TV director whom she had known since she was a teenager. Her fans were shocked when, in 1973, Sayuri married this middle-aged man, instead of Harada or another of the clean-cut youths with whom she had so

Youth), in which she played a young widow who is tortured by sexual desire. But even the sight of Sayuri in the throes of passion did not destroy her "pure" image for her fans. Like American Boomers who still nostalgically tuned into Annette in reruns of the old Mickey Mouse Club show, Sayurists wanted to keep her forever frozen in a certain attitude, at a certain moment of time.

In the 1990s, Sayuri made new attempts to broaden her range and establish herself as a serious actress. In Nobuyoshi Obayashi's 1994 *Onna Zakari* (A Woman's Prime) she played an editorial writer on a major newspaper who is not above engaging in political blackmail and using her sexual wiles to baffle her enemies and keep her job. Though her character is smart, tough, and determined, she is also, inevitably, Sayuri. In 1996 she appeared with Shima Iwashita in Masanobu Deme's *Kiri no Shigosen* (The Meridian In the Mist)—her one hundred sixth screen appearance. Paired together for the first time in their long careers, these two veterans played middle-aged friends who found a second chance at love while pursuing fulfilling careers and living amidst surroundings that seem taken directly from the pages of a glossy interior decorating magazine.

In many ways a traditional Japanese women's picture, *Kiri no Shigosen* presented elegantly dressed and perfectly coifed stars suffering in lovely settings, with the object of

often been paired on the screen. Her parents resented Okada for loosening their hold over their daughter and did not even attend the wedding.

After her marriage, Sayuri began living the kind of ordinary life she had always dreamed of. Instead of emoting for the cameras, she spent her days like any other housewife, doing the grocery shopping and chopping up white radishes for her husband's dinner. She found contentment—and regained her voice.

But she also discovered she still wanted to act. In 1975, at the age of thirty, Sayuri finally made the leap to on-screen adulthood in Kiriro Urayama's *Seishun no Mon* (Gate of winning audience admiration for the stars' wounded nobility and wringing audience tears from the beautiful sadness of it all.

And once again Sayuri died in style, collapsing in her friend's arms before the altar of an old Scandinavian church, as the afternoon light streamed through the stained glass windows and the violins on the soundtrack soared. Sayurists could hardly ask for more.

YUMING & THE BIRTH OF NEW MUSIC

In June 1975 four Japanese folk musicians formed a small record company, with twenty-three employees and thirty million yen in capital. Though For Life Records hardly represented a threat to Polydor, Crown, King, and other industry giants, the Japanese music world regarded its launch as an epoch-making event. This was the first company in Japan started by musicians for the express purpose of making the kind of music they, not a label's A&R man, wanted to make.

Also, the four musicians—Takuro Yoshida, Yosui Inoue, Hitoshi Komuro, and Shigeru Izumiya—were big names in a hot genre: folk music. Folk had started in Japan in the early 1960s much the way rock had started the decade before, with Japanese

musicians latching onto an American trend and copying American sounds, in this case the music of the Kingston Trio, the Brothers Four, Pete Seeger, and Peter, Paul, and Mary. All toured Japan in the first half of the decade and made a big impression on Japanese folk fans.

Most early folkies were college kids who took up the music as a hobby, with no intention of turning professional. The first to discover that folk music could be the route to worldly fame and fortune was Mike Maki, whose "Bara ga Saita" (The Rose Has Bloomed), a heartfelt ditty on a home-sweet-home theme, sold seven hundred thousand copies in 1965 and launched Maki on a long, if erratic, musical career.

While the Tokyo-based college folk (*karejji fooku*) singers were crooning about their individual joys and sorrows, in 1967 folkies in Osaka began singing angry protest songs about the social issues of the day, including the growing opposition to the war in Vietnam and the renewal of Japan's Mutual Security Treaty with the United States. The leader of this underground folk (*angura fooku*) movement was the bearded, husky-voiced Nobuyasu Okabayshi, whose 1968 debut "San'ya Blues," told of the down-and-out in the San'ya area of Tokyo.

But it was For Life founder Takuro Yoshida who brought folk music into the mainstream with his 1972 hit "Kekkon Shiyo yo" (Let's Get Married), an upbeat number that changed the popular image of folk as dark music for troubled souls. With message music sounding increasing irrelevant in the Me Decade, more folk singers followed Yoshida with songs that expressed personal feelings, not political statements. Among the most successful was another For Life founder, Yosui Inoue, who followed his smash 1972 debut, "Kasa ga Nai" (I Don't Have an Umbrella), with a string of hits that made him a nationally known star. His 1973 debut album *Kori no Sekai* (World of Ice) sold one million copies—a pop-music record.

Based on the chord progression of Grand Funk Railroad's "Heart Breaker," "Kasa ga Nai" was a dryly ironic song confessing that the singer's only concern is not having an umbrella for a rainy-day date, even though the newspapers and TV newscasts are full of doom and gloom. The song perfectly expressed the exhaustion many Japanese Baby Boomers felt after nearly a decade of marches and protests and became an anthem for an inward-turning decade.

But though Inoue and Yoshida made folk a major music-industry genre, they refused to appear on television, the industry's biggest marketplace for its products. In the early 1970s, when the TV pop-music shows were in their ratings heyday, with the power to launch a teen idol singer to stardom virtual-ly overnight, Inoue and Yoshida's anti-TV stand struck many as a noble demonstration of personal integrity, if not good business sense. Yoshida explained that he didn't want to sing shortened-for-TV versions of his songs or "be judged as a human being on the basis of a song that happens to become a hit." A more practical reason, however, was that Yoshida, Inoue, and other folk singers were already getting enough exposure from con-certs, records, and radio. They needed to appear on a TV pop music show with Hiromi Go, Hideki Saijo, and other pretty-boy teen stars as much as Bob Dylan needed to share a Las Vegas stage with Donny Osmond.

Ironically, the singer who recorded For Life's biggest sales in its first year was not one of the founders but a twenty-one-year-old singer-songwriter named Yumi Arai, whose 1975 For Life singles—"Rouge no Dengon" (Rouge Message) and "Ano Hi ni Kaeritai" (I Want to Go Back to That Day)—and album—*Cobalt Hour*—all became big hits. Even more ironically, it was Arai, not her male mentors, who was to bring about a marriage of folk music and mainstream Japanese pop, creating a hugely popular new genre.

Born in the Tokyo suburb of Hachioji in 1954, the second daughter of a kimono store owner, Arai received an upbringing suitable for a proper young lady of Japan's rising

middle class, complete with piano lessons, starting at the age of six, and membership in a choral group.

But after Arai entered a private junior high school, she spent less time practicing Bach and Handel and more time hanging around Roppongi discos. During her night-time wanderings, she became acquainted with many of the area's musicians and furthered her pop-musical education.

In 1969 she shot to fame when Katsumi Kahashi, a former member of the Spiders who was then appearing in the rock musical *Hair*, received a new song from a friend called "Ai wa Totsuzen" (Love, Suddenly) and decided to record it, not knowing that the songwriter was a fifteen-year-old school-girl. When her identity was discovered, Arai found herself feted as the child prodigy of the pop world. In 1972 Arai entered Tama University of Arts, near her parent's home, and began her songwriting career in earnest. In July of that year, she released her first single, "Henji wa Iranai" (I Don't Need an Answer); it sold all of 300 copies.

The following year, she made her real debut with the single "Kitto Ieru/Hikoki Gumo" (I Can Definitely Say/Airplane Clouds) and her first album *Hikoki Gumo* (Airplane Clouds). The latter record, especially, challenged then-current conceptions of what folk music was supposed to be. This was still the age of the flannel-shirted, blue-denimed folk singer who portrayed himself (or herself) as the poor-but-honest salt of the earthy earth, and, on television, of the teen-idol singer who tried to appeal to fans with a reassuringly conventional, endearingly non-threatening Mr. (or Miss) Average image.

Arai would have none of that. Her influences were the arty progressive rock of Procol Harum and the sophisticated Europop of Michel Polnareff, not scratchy old records by obscure Mississippi bluesmen or vacuous teenage ear candy by Japanese record-company hacks. Her music expressed the upscale sensibilities and tastes of a young adult woman living an unfettered, prosperous existence in the world's second-largest economy. Arai told an interviewer that, not long ago, people had been yearning for the simple life in a four-and-a-half-mat flat, (as expressed by "Kandagawa," the 1973 folk hit by Kosetsu Minami and Kaguya Hime) but that she wanted to "create a rich, fashionable world." Arai frankly described her music as a "middle-class sound" for fellow Baby Boomers whose standards of living were rising together with Japan's GNP. When that didn't seem to ring a bell, she started calling it "New Music" (*nyuu myuujikku*).

Though *Hikoki Gumo* marked a departure, *Cobalt Hour*—her third album but her first for For Life—was a breakthrough; critics praised it as fusing the essence of contemporary American and European pop music, together with echoes of American sixties pop, into an integrated whole that was unmistakably Arai. That same year her single "Ano Hi ni Kaeritai" became the theme song for a TBS drama and rocketed to the top of the charts. Having won critical esteem and popular acclaim, Arai quickly became the single biggest earner in Japanese pop music. In 1976 sales from her records and tape amounted to 3.17 billion yen—a fabulous amount for a Japanese pop singer.

That same year Arai married Masataka Matsutoya, who had been her keyboardist since *Hikoki Gumo* three years earlier, and changed her stage name to Yumi Matsutoya or simply "Yuming." But though Matsutoya far outdistanced her husband professionally, the media sympathetically presented her as a woman who skillfully balanced the demands of being a good housewife and mother while managing a high-powered career. In other words, despite her wealth and fame, Matsutoya was still trying to lead a normal middle-class existence, a stance that endeared to her millions of female fans.

Record-company execs loved her because in New Music Matsutoya had created a conveniently vague label that had none of the still negative connotations of rock and folk and could be applied to virtually any singer-songwriter, from hard rockers to crooners of Western-influenced mainstream Japanese pop music. In the mid-1970s, many of those singer-songwriters happened to be women, including Akiko Yano, a pianist who had recorded on Little Feat's debut album in Los Angeles and made her own acclaimed first album *Japanese Girl* in 1976; Ami Osaki, a sweet-sounding vocalist whom Matsutoya had helped launch that same year with the single "Meiso" (Meditation); and Anri, who debuted in

Yumi Masutoya (née Arai): the queen of a New Music that refuses to grow old.

1978 with the Ami Osaki song "Olivia o Kikinagara" (While Listening to Olivia) and later rose to prominence with a sound strongly influenced by U.S. black music.

Among early male stars of the New Music boom was former Happy End (see **ROCKABILLY, GROUP SOUNDS, AND THE BIRTH OF JAPANESE ROCK**) member Eiichi Otaki, who started the Niagara label in 1975 to showcase his work and that of other New Music artists, including Tatsu Yamashita, Taeko Onuki, and Ginji Ito. Otaki's 1981 solo album *A Long Vacation* was hailed by critics as a pop masterpiece that translated American and British rock sounds into a distinctly Japanese idiom.

Another male artist who made a big impact on the New Music scene was Motoharu Sano, a singer-songwriter with a background in advertising and radio whose 1980 debut album *Back to the Street* had a pure rock'n'roll flavor while speaking directly to teens in the streets in their own language. Critics praised the record as marking a new era in Japanese rock and pop and dozens of imitators tried to copy the Sano style. Sano went on to success after recording success and started his own label, M's Factory, in 1986.

As Sano, Otaki, and other New Music artists moved into the mainstream of the industry—in 1978 New Music records outsold both *enka* and Japanese "idol" pop and

by 1980 were accounting for more than half of all records sold—their work began to change the Japanese pop scene that dominated the TV airwaves. Although still largely easy-to-digest ear candy for mass consumption, Japanese pop began to expand from its narrow confines of lyrical content and musical style, incorporating more difficult chords, different musical genres, and diverse emotional tones, from straight descriptiveness to free form fantasy. Suddenly it was all right for idol singers to express more of their real personalities and not fit themselves into a mold of "proper" pop-idol behavior. Japanese pop, which had so long been unabashed entertainment, with hardly a thought in its head beyond boy-meets-girl, acquired a new self-awareness and sophistication. Though there was still a lot of lighter-than-air music floating through the TV ether, the enormous success of New Music made it okay to be more grown-up as well.

One exemplar of this trend was "idol" star **MOMOE YAMAGUCHI**, who used songs by the husband-and-wife songwriting team of Yoko Agi and Ryudo Usaki—both members of the Downtown Boogie Woogie Band—to successfully project a more assertive, independent image in the latter half of her career.

This cross-genre fertilization resulted in a blurring of the previously clear distinctions between rock, folk, and Japanese pop. Groups like Alice, Tulip, Alfee, Monta & Brothers, and Anzen Chitai ("Safety Zone") attracted large followings without falling neatly into any of the usual categories. They could rock, but in a way unmistakably Japanese. They could entertain, but tried to say something more than the usual teeny-bopper tune.

Although it's hard to credit all this to Matsutoya—she happened to be riding the crest of a wave that had been building since the early 1970s—she continued to lead the New Music genre into the 1980s and 1990s, selling two million or more albums per outing while staying one step ahead of the decade's trends: the queen of a New Music that refuses to grow old.

ZOKU

Since the end of World War II, Japan has witnessed the rise (and often rapid disappearance) of a succession of subcultures, some imported, some homegrown, that the local media often referred to as "tribes," or *zoku*, though there may be little tribal about them beyond a common preference for a certain style, attitude, or behavior that happens, for the moment, to mark the *zoku* as different from the crowd. Some *zoku* have contributed little more than a catchphrase, while others have had a large and lasting impact on the culture at large. Here is a *zoku* chronology, with comments:

1948. *Shayo-zoku* (Setting Sun Tribe). Named for a 1947 Osamu Dazai novel, *Shayo* (The Setting Sun), this tribe included former military officers, members of the nobility, and others who were ruined by Japan's defeat in the war and the radical changes in postwar Japanese society. The sons of generals who worked as sandwich men and impoverished counts who committed suicide out of despair were some of the *Shayo-zoku*'s typical representatives. Dazai himself was from a aristocratic family that shared in the postwar decline, though when he jumped into the Tama Reservoir and drowned in June 1948 he was a celebrated author whose personal troubles had started long before the end of the war.

1951. *Shayo-zoku* (Company Business Tribe). A pun on the earlier Setting Sun Tribe, this tribe consisted of the growing number of businessmen who were enjoying expense-account wining and dining in the economic boom generated by the Korean War. Objects of envy among those still struggling to emerge from early postwar poverty, this *zoku* continued to flourish, with occasional recessionary dips, until the bursting of the bubble economy in the early 1990s and the consequent reaction against the lavish entertaining of important clients and patrons, often in expensive clubs and teahouses, or *ryotei*. With corporate cost-cutting and downsizing, the *shayo-zoku* has become a dwindling, if not endangered, tribe.

1956. *Taiyo-zoku* (Sun Tribe). Members of this tribe, which took its name from *Taiyo no Kisetsu* (Season of the Sun), the 1956 best-seller by Shintaro Ishihara, were rudderless youths who had grown up in the chaos of the early postwar years and were contemptuous of prewar values, but had only American-style hedonism to put in their place. Instead of dying for the emperor or slaving for the company, like their fathers and older brothers, they preferred to cruise the Ginza looking for girls, in imitation of the novel's boxer hero, or head off to the beach, in imitation of YUJIRO ISHIHARA, Shintaro's handsome younger brother, who shot to fame in a movie version of the novel and was reputed to spend much of his off-camera time sailing, swimming, and otherwise having fashionable fun in the warm Kamakura sun. The male members of the tribe wore Yujiro-style aloha shirts and crew-cuts. Many also belonged to the so-called *gekko-zoku* (moonlight tribe), kids who cruised popular beach resorts at night, or *gurentai*, gangs of young urban hoodlums that were breeding grounds for the *yakuza*.

1958. *Danchi-zoku* (Public Housing Development Tribe). A catchphrase first coined in a *Shukan Asahi* (Weekly Asahi) special feature, *danchi-zoku* referred to the residents of the public housing developments that were springing up in urban areas. Though freed from the traditional constraints of life in rural villages or close-knit urban neighborhoods, public housing dwellers often suffered from the impersonality and anonymity of their new lifestyles. The largest of the *danchi*, Takashimadaira in northwestern Tokyo, became notorious as a favorite place for suicides, who climbed to the roof, carefully removed their shoes, and leapt to their deaths.

1958. *Nagara-zoku* (While Tribe). A catch-phrase coined by Nippon Medical School professor Fumio Kita to describe people who could no longer concentrate on one thing at a time, but had to always be doing two or more things at once. Television was a major cause of what Kita came to call the "while neurosis," or *nagara shinkeisho.*

1959. *Kaminari-zoku* (Thunder Tribe). Japan's first bikers, the *kaminari-zoku* greased their hair, took the mufflers off their motorbikes, rode like maniacs, and otherwise styled themselves after Marlon Brando and his buddies in *The Wild Ones* (see **ROCKABILLY, GROUP SOUNDS, AND THE BIRTH OF JAPANESE ROCK**). But like the rockabilly boom they seemed to symbolize, the *kaminari-zoku*'s moment in the media spotlight was a short one.

In the mid-1970s Japan's bikers re-emerged in force as *boso-zoku* or the Wild Speed Tribe. At one time there were as many as thirty thousand *boso-zoku* blasting around the streets in the wee hours of the morning, shattering sleep with the roar of their engines and the blare of their claxons, until even the most peace-loving law-abiding citizens were plotting murder and destruction in their futons. Some *boso-zoku* haters tried to carry out their plans, throwing a railway tie in the path of a speeding bike or wreaking havoc on an engine while its owner was reveling with his comrades in a biker bar.

Cordially detested by straight society, the bikers developed a subculture with its own fashions, symbols, and rituals. The gangs spray painted the gang name—Black Emperor, Minagoroshi (Massacre), Spector, Jokers, Alley Cats—on walls and underpasses and carried flags with the gang emblem, deathheads and scorpions beings favorite motifs. Many wore Brillo-pad hairstyles called "punch perms" to underline their tough-guy stance, headbands to advertise their gang affiliation, and surgical masks to hide their identities from inquisitive cops.

But though they often traveled in procession, flags waving, like a conquering army, the *boso-zoku* were harmless compared with their American counterparts. They may have ingested illegal substances (paint thinner and speed being among the favorites) and intimidated the occasional square but they seldom became involved in Hell's-Angel-style rape and pillage. One favorite biker technique was to surround a prosperous-looking square and his trophy girlfriend in a restaurant parking lot from all four sides, trapping him in his fancy sports car. They would then smoke, drink and otherwise take their ease, while the square steamed inside his metal and glass prison.

The bikers who aspired to serious careers as professional criminals usually joined the *yakuza.* The bike gangs themselves were mainly for play, display, and petty mischief making. When the cops began to crack down with a new traffic law in 1979, many gangs decided to quit rather than fight. Today the hard-core remnants of the *boso-zoku* have faded from the popular imagination, if not from the urban night.

1964. *Miyuki-zoku* (Miyuki Tribe). Named for Miyuki Street in the Ginza, where they often hung out on the weekend, this mainly college-kid tribe was deep into fashion as defined by Van, a Japanese garment maker that specialized in the American casual look. Though Miyuki tribesmen, with their Van windbreakers, button-down madras shirts, white socks and penny loafers looked about as threatening as models in a J. C. Penney's catalogue ad to Western eyes, to older Japanese, especially, whose concept of Western-style clothing for men ran the gamut from gray suits to blue suits, the *Miyuki-zoku* were aliens from another planet. Real Japanese men certainly didn't, like the *Miyuki-zoku* swells, wear shirts and jackets of the same fashionable pattern, use blow dryers to give their short hair the neat-but-casual Ivy look, and anoint their bodies with M5 cologne.

Many Miyuki tribesmen were rebels of a laid-back kind, listening to the Kingston Trio and other folkies, both Japanese and American. A favorite *Miyuki-zoku* accessory was a guitar case with a Van sticker pasted on the side. When they weren't crooning "Where Have All the Flowers Gone," the *Miyuki-zoku* liked to hop in their Skyline GT for a drive to Komazawa Park or drive over to Roppongi for a burger and shake at the Hamburger Inn.

At their principal hangout, the Ginza, the *Miyuki-zoku* began to attract the attention of the cops, who didn't care for their look, their attitude, or their loitering on some of Japan's most expensive real estate. In September 1964 the police began a crackdown and, though their Ivy look lived to triumph in the years and decades to come, the *Miyuki-zoku* disappeared, never to return.

1965. *Ereki-zoku.* (Electric Guitar Tribe). This tribe was devoted to the electric sounds of the Ventures, the Beatles, and the dozens of Japanese groups that emerged in the mid-sixties electric guitar boom, or *ereki buumu* (see **ROCKABILLY, GROUP SOUNDS AND THE BIRTH OF JAPANESE ROCK**). Adults condemned the music as "unJapanese" and the longhaired Beatles look as "unclean." The kids didn't care—and made the electric sound a permanent part of the Japan's musical landscape.

1967. *Hippie-zoku* (Hippie Tribe). This is one American import that never really took root. Japanese hippies had the tie-dyed t-shirts, jeans, and long hair, but few tuned in, turned on, and dropped out. No dope, for one thing. In Japan, the street drug of choice was speed and the druggies were mainly hard-bitten underworld types, not laid-back long hairs. No Haight-Ashbury, for another, though Tokyo's Shinjuku amusement district served as a substitute for many. Be that as it may, a lot of college kids in the late 1960s wanted to freak out, even if it only meant sitting in a Shinjuku coffee shop listening to imported Jimi Hendrix sides.

Seeing another youth fad to exploit, Seibu Department Store in Shibuya—a Tokyo subcenter that was, and is, a major under-twenty-five hangout zone—launched a hippie fashion corner called Be-In. Hippie wanna-bes crowded in to buy freaky clothes and accessories, including dashikis and peace pendants. Other department stores rushed to cash in on the hippie boom. Few of the customers seemed to mind that they were being coopted and ripped off by the capitalist pigs who owned and ran these giant retail operations. In this respect many *hippie-zoku* members were like their *Miyuki-zoku* elders: fashion trendies who wanted to be in with the in crowd. They quickly moved on to the next new thing when flower power faded.

1977. *Annon-zoku* (Annon Tribe). Members of this tribe were young women who slavishly followed the dictates of *an•an* and *non•no*, two women's magazines that ruled the fashion roost in the late 1970s. When these mag-azines recommended a funky little folk village or other off-the-beaten-path tourist spot, so many readers descended on it—all wearing fashions from photos in the travel piece—that the disapproving begin to speak of "*annon* pollution" (*annon kogai*).

1977. *Madogiwa-zoku* (Window-Side Tribe). First coined by the *Hokkaido Shimbun* newspaper, *madogiwa-zoku* referred to the men who had been hired in large numbers during the boom days of the 1960s but were rapidly becoming redundant in the tougher economic climate of the late 1970s. *Madogiwa* referred to the practice of giving surplus employees desks by the window, so they could at least have a pleasant view while idling away the hours and not be a distraction to the company's more productive workers.

Madogiwa-zoku has since became a part of the language, though in the 1990s companies have developed more efficient ways of dealing with their excess workers, including shipping them off to subsidiaries and offering them early retirement. Allowing middle-aged employees to study cloud formations while drawing full salary is a luxury that fewer companies can afford.

1979. *Yugure-zoku* (Dusk Tribe). Their name taken from *Yugure Made* (Until Dusk), the title of a best-selling novel by Junnosuke Yoshi-yuki, members of this tribe were men and women who cheated on their spouses. In the anything-goes eighties, as traditional moral strictures continued to erode, cheating, or furin, became a buzzword and the subject of countless novels, magazine articles, and TV dramas. The sex industry was quick to pick up on this trend; today dozens of call-girl agencies run ads in weekly magazines and daily tabloids offering the services of "gentle wives" (yasashi hitozuma), "part-timer wives" (arubaito okusama), and "garter-belt married ladies" (gaataa beruto kifujin).

1980. Takenoko-zoku (Bamboo Shoot Tribe). In the summer of 1979 a small boutique called Takenoko opened in Harajuku, a fashion center for the young in west central Tokyo. It featured freaky unisex clothing, including billowing pantaloons and baggy coats that came down to the ankles, in a range of bright colors such as Flamingo Pink and Halloween Pumpkin Orange. By the fall kids wearing Takenoko fashions began dancing on Omotesando, a tree-lined shopping street with wide sidewalks, just a stone's throw away from the boutique. Their clothes inspired them to loosen their inhibitions and frolic in a childishly carefree way that stood in stark contrast to the stylized macho posturings of the greaser dancers who then dominated the Omotesando scene.

After Angle magazine ran a story on the dancers, they became the media darlings of 1980, with reporters and cameramen from dozens of TV stations, newspapers, and magazines descending on the Sunday pedestrian mall near Yoyogi Park, where they had moved after the cops had chased them from Omotesando. With the media hordes came crowds of onlookers, including nearly every foreign tourist in town who happened to have a camera.

Encouraged by this attention, the takenoko-zoku grew quickly, until there were as many as thirty subtribes, with ten to thirty members each. Although the tribesmen were, underneath their Takenoko clothes, ordinary-enough teenagers and danced to ordinary-enough pop sounds—favorites included YMO, ELO, Olivia Newton-John, and The Nolans—there was also something creepy about the takenoko-zoku as they romped with such calculated glee, like members of a religious cult bent on demonstrating their spiritual liberation to an unbelieving world.

The fin de siécle charm of the takenoko-zoku attracted the attention of Talking Heads lead singer David Byrne, who included a clip of the dancers in the video for the group's "Once in a Lifetime" single. Also, one dancer, Hiroyuki Okita, aka Hiro, rose to brief fame as a magazine cover boy and teenage heartthrob. But as the takenoko-zoku act grew mannered and stale, media interest began to wane and tribesmen began to drift away. Today, the *takenoko-zoku* exists only as a memory and in images preserved in thousands of photo albums around the world: symbols of contemporary Japanese youth who did their own thing in perfect conformity with every other member of their candy-colored tribe.

1980. *Crystal-zoku* (Crystal Tribe). This tribe was named after *Nantonaku Crystal* (Somehow, Crystal), a best-selling novel by Yasuo Tanaka. Like the novel's heroine, a college girl who lives in a condo in a fashionable Tokyo neighborhood, works part-time as a fashion model, and spends outrageous sums on designer clothes, the members of the Crystal Tribe were flagrant materialists, hedonists, and trendies who worshiped Pierre Cardin and Courreges, bought *Popeye* magazine to follow all the West Coast fads and fashions, and watched *Best Hits USA,* a weekly late-night TV program hosted by bilingual DJ Katsuya Takahashi, playing video clips from the U.S. top twenty and featuring interviews with visiting foreign pop stars.

Crystal tribesmen loved to flavor their conversation with words borrowed from English and other foreign languages and converted into the *katakana* syllabary. Tanaka's novel became known for its 442 footnotes explaining the *katakana* words in the text, including brand names, restaurant names, and trendy jargon words like *aidentii* (identity) and *puressha* (pressure).

The novel puzzled and annoyed many members of the older generation, who had no idea what the characters were talking about and found their Westernized lifestyles profoundly strange. Even kids from the Crystal tribesmen's generation thought the *Nantonaku Crystal* phenomenon more hype than substance. One member of that generation, Yuji Kotari, published a parody novel, *Yappari, Futsu no Garasu* (Nope, Just Plain Glass), whose heroine prepares for the day not by tuning in the groovy rock sounds of the U.S. military's Far East Network, like her *Nantonaku Crystal* counterpart, but by splashing her face with water heated in a humble brass kettle.

1981. *Sango-zoku* (Three Words Tribe). Members of this tribe were teenaged girls whose entire conversation seemed to consist of three words: *uso* (no kidding!), *honto* (really?), and *kawaii* (Oh, cute!). Uttered with drawling intonations and expressions of exaggerated disbelief *(uso!)*, skepticism *(honto?)*, and delight *(kawaii!)*, they served approximately the same purposes as "like," "y'know," and "awesome" in Valley Girl talk. As linguistic filler they still survive, but as generational signifiers they have become passé. In the nineties, the trend among teenage girls is to talk rough and tough, using language previously reserved exclusively for males.

1984. *Kurenai-zoku* (Won't-Do-It-for-Me Tribe). Made popular by the TBS serial drama *Kurenai-zoku no Hanran* (The Rebellion of the Won't-Do-It-for-Me Tribe), *kurenai-zoku* originally referred to selfish, pampered kids who were constantly complaining that Mom and Dad and other people in their life wouldn't do things for them (in Japanese, *nani mo shite kurenai*). After the drama became a hit, however, this catchphrase came to refer to whining housewives who, like the drama's heroine, were dissatisfied with their significant others.

After the mid-eighties, the *zoku* tag fell out of media fashion, though *zoku*-like phenomena continued to emerge and flourish. Among the most prominent:

1986. *Ojo-sama* (Young Ladies). *Ojo-sama* were young women who came from the best homes and had been schooled in the most refined of the traditional arts, including tea ceremony, flower arranging, and Japanese calligraphy. As a consequence they were well-mannered, well-groomed, and well-sheltered from life's more unpleasant realities, though in postwar Japan it was acceptable and even desirable for the *ojo-sama* to have carefully controlled exposure to foreign languages and cultures. A stay at a Swiss girls' boarding school to polish one's French was okay, living in sin with a Swiss boyfriend was not.

The *ojo-sama* type had been around for generations, but in the mid-eighties, as the media focused on the Crown Prince Akihito's long and fruitless search for a bride (see **ROYAL WEDDINGS**), young women who were not from an upper-crust background began to aspire to *ojo-sama* status, mainly by buying the *ojo-sama* look, including conservative designer suits that a Western twenty-year-old would consider more appropriate for her mother, and taking up *ojo-sama* pursuits. A popular game of the time was distinguishing between real and fake *ojo-sama*; it was not enough to play a few tunes on a *koto* in a kimono; one to had to be to the manner born.

If the aspiring *ojo-sama*, both real and fake, were hoping to catch the eye of the Crown Prince, they were sorely disappointed. Masako Owada, who finally became the Crown Princess, may have come from the right background—her father was an elite diplomat and she had studied at Harvard and Oxford—but she preferred playing softball to plucking the *koto*, was criticized by the media for wearing a creased kimono and, most un-*ojo-sama*-like of all, had been a hard-working career woman on the fast track in the Ministry of Foreign Affairs.

But by the time of the imperial wedding, in June 1993, the *ojo-sama* boom was a long-forgotten relic of the bubble economy years. In the midst of Japan's longest postwar recession, young women were more interested in landing a job, any job, after graduation, not learning the fine points of tea-ceremony etiquette.

And their older sister's koto was, if not in the pawn shop, usually in the closet.

1988. *Nyuu Haafu* (New Half). In May 1988 a popular noontime program called *Waratte Ii to mo* (It's All Right to Laugh) started a new segment or *koona* ("corner"). Every Monday, host Tamori—a comedian whose dark glasses and slicked-back hair had been among the most familiar sights on TV since the early 1980s—introduced young women who, on first glance, seemed to be charming embodiments of Japanese femininity. But the perfectly coifed hair, the designer dresses, girlish giggles, and slender-but-curvy bodies could not quite disguise the fact that, as Tamori discovered to his amazement and delight week after week, these women were, or had been . . . men! They were transsexuals or, in Japanese media-speak, "New Half" or "Mister Lady." (Several, as they were happy to explain in graphic detail, really

were "half," or still in the midst of the transition from male to female.)

Waratte Ii to mo was not the first show to feature the New Half. In the early 1980s transsexual singer Rumiko Matsubara had made frequent appearances on late-night TV and helped start a New Half boom, but Tamori's program, as a daytime show that had a large, devoted housewife following, brought New Half into the mainstream, so to speak. Over the course of the segment's life, Tamori and his comic cohorts interviewed twenty-five New Half. Although many were working in the various branches of the sex industry, several had serious show-business aspirations. One, who called herself Hikari, became a regular on the *All-Night Fuji* discussion program and even released a CD with Columbia Records.

Soon dozens of magazines for both men and women were running winkingly racy stories on the New Half, including interviews with New Half talking about their operations, love lives, and techniques for pleasing men. Late-night programs featured New Half talents who sang, danced, and displayed what made them "half" to their shocked hosts (though not, with the exception of the occasional flashed tit, to the audience).

The craze for the New Half coincided with renewed media interest in homosexuality the late 1980s and early 1990s. The two, after all, were inextricably linked in the public mind, despite the frequent public protestations by the New Half themselves that they were essentially female, not gay. Magazines that printed before and after pictures of New Half were soon taking readers on guided tours of the Shinjuku Nichome district—Tokyo's Greenwich Village or Castro. The late-night shows, with on-the-scene camera crews and leering reporters, were not far behind.

Not all of this interest was shallow and prurient, however. *Crea,* a monthly woman's magazine, devoted most of its February 1991 issue to an in-depth exploration of homosexuality in Japan, including an interview with cross-dressing gay singer Ken'ichi Mikawa and a roundtable discussion with three gays hosted by Erika Sakurazawa, a *manga* artist whose work often featured gay characters and was popular with young women.

It was in fact those same women, including W*aratte Ii to mo*'s housewives, who largely supported the gay boom, just as they supported **TAKARAZUKA,** the **ROSE OF VERSAILLES,** and other pop-cultural blurrings of the sexual boundaries. They not only eagerly watched the TV shows with gay themes or guests (including a TV drama, *Dosokai,* or "Alumni Reunion," whose male leads turned out to be homosexual) and read the *manga* with gay stories or characters, but explored the Nichome bars and other gay hangouts. In Takejiro Nakajima's 1992 *Okoge* (Fag

Hag), Misa Shimizu plays one such woman, who befriends a gay couple and lends them her apartment for their lovemaking. The film became a long-running art-house hit and helped, through mass-media coverage of its unusual theme, bring awareness of gay life further into the mainstream.

But the gay boom, as all booms, came to an end. Though careers of individual gay talents, notably that of the elegant and unflappable Mikawa, continued to flourish, by the middle of the decade TV-drama heroes were no longer working as hostesses in transvestite bars and hardly a media word was heard about the now vanished New Half. And real gays? In Japan's conservative male-dominated society, many remained firmly closeted, while the few who came out faced blatant discrimination.

1989. *Otaku.* It is tempting to translate *otaku* as "nerd," but though both are often thought of, humorously, as socially inept loners, *otaku* are also fanatically knowledgeable in one abstruse field, be it **GODZILLA** movies or the history of sumo wrestling. *Otaku* got their name from their habit of addressing others as *otaku,* a form of the second-person singular and plural that is polite, impersonal, and, in certain social contexts, bizarrely off-putting, like calling a classmate "sir." Foreign fans of Japanese *manga* and animation who can recite **HAYAO**

MIYAZAKI's entire filmography proudly refer to themselves as *otaku,* though in Japan it is a label that also carries implications of serious strangeness.

Exactly how strange became apparent in 1989 when a printer's assistant in Itsukaichi, Tokyo was arrested for the abduction and murder of four young girls. He had not only dismembered and cremated the corpses but videotaped them and sent the remains to the girls' families. He was a *manga* and porno video *otaku,* with a collection of 5,700 tapes, including many S & M and child porno titles. It was his case, if fact, that brought the *otaku* phenomenon to widespread public attention.

Not all *otaku* were murderous creeps, though. In 1992, an action-comedy called *Shichinin no Otaku* (Cult Seven) featured seven *otaku* heroes who used their expertise to rescue a baby from a nefarious gang boss and return it to his Filipino ex-wife. The *otaku* were mostly the expected assortment of misfits, including a martial artist who dressed up in superhero costumes, a survival-game buff who spent his Sundays tromping through the woods in camouflage get-up, and an idol fanzine publisher who cruised the streets in his "idol hunter" van. Two of the *otaku,* however, didn't fit the profile: a shy young woman who communicated with the world via her ham-radio gear and a handsome computer expert who

brought his leggy non-*otaku* girlfriend along on the rescue mission.

Though *Cult Seven* had its moments, including a comically staged raid on the gang boss's island hideout, it did not make the hoped-for splash at the box office. The *otaku* boom was already ending, though the *otaku* themselves had become a permanent part of the cultural landscape.

1992. *Chiimaa* (Teamers). Shibuya has long been a hang-out zone for the young, but in the flush days of the bubble economy, it began to attract rich kids from nearby Setagaya Ward who cruised the night streets in their Jeep Cherokees, Pajeros, and other pricey recreational vehicles or, as they soon came to be known, RVs. Though the original object may have been simply to pick up girls or show off their wheels, the RV crowd began to form gangs whose members were called *chiimaa* or "teamers."

Before long even the RV-less were running in their own *chiimaa,* particularly on and around the main shopping street called "Center Gai" (Center Street). Trouble soon followed as *chiimaa* began ripping off local merchants, harassing passersby, or battling other *chiimaa* for turf.

As the *chiimaa* phenomenon attracted media attention, Shibuya became a late-night mecca for teenagers from all over the city and even neighboring prefectures. It also drew drug dealers, who did a brisk business in uppers, downers, marijuana, and other illegal substances.

But just when it seemed that Shibuya was on its way to becoming Sodom East, the cops began to crack down and, as the crowds grew, being a *chiimaa* lost its cachet and the boom started to fade. The decisive factor in the demise of the *chiimaa* was reportedly muscle from the local *yakuza,* who viewed the *chiimaa* as threats to the businesses they ran and serviced (although they also recruited the more promising *chiimaa* as junior gangsters). Today throngs of high-school kids still crowd Center Gai at all hours of the day and night, but *chiimaa* are nowhere to be found. 1996. *Amuraa* (Amur-ers). Following the spectacular rise to stardom in late 1995 and early 1996 of Okinawan-born singer Namie Amuro (see **TETSUYA KOMURO**), millions of teenage girls all over Japan began to imitate her boldly sexy look, which might be described by shocked fathers as Seventies Hooker Redux. Girls who wore prim sailor suits to school on the weekdays turned up at Shibuya and other urban hot spots on the weekends in figure-revealing tops that stopped at the belly-button, microminis or hot pants, and knee-high boots with platform heels. The basic look also included layer-cut long hair dyed various shades of brown, pierced ears displaying small silver earrings, eyebrows shaped into pencil-thin arches, eyes mascaraed for that exotic touch, and lips painted a pearly white.

All aspects of this look were not unique to Amuro—the silver earrings, for example, had been a staple of *chiimaa* fashion—but she defined it in its totality. The girls who adopted it in all or part were known as *Amuraa* (Amur-ers).

There was, however, more to being an *Amuraa* than style. *Amuraa* also admired Amuro's slender-but-healthy looks, her dynamic sense of rhythm, soulful vocals, disarmingly sweet smile, and the frank way she answered interviewers' questions, which they attributed to her more "liberated" Okinawan upbringing. She was, said the teenage consensus, both *chokawaii* (super cute) and *chokakkoii* (super cool)—a combination that was their highest form of approbation.

But *Amuraa* who could not aspire to equaling their idol in the looks and singing department, could at least acquire the attitude and accessories that solidified their *Amuraa* identity. A pocket pager was one, a cellular phone, another—both were handy for fielding calls from their many admirers. Although boys could not, properly, be *Amuraa,* not a few were fans happy to get next to the next-best to the real thing. Fathers of *Amuraa,* meanwhile, were no doubt hoping for the next new idol to come along—and praying that, at the very least, her top would cover her belly button.

BIBLIOGRAPHY

Aidoru Sutaa Daihyakka, Tokyo: Jigyoshi Nihonsha, 1983.

Amano, Yumiko, and Kumiko Ariki, eds. *SMAP Year Book 1994–1995 Revival & Evolution*. Wani Books, 1995.

Amura Tettei Kenkyukai, comp. *Kogaru no Hoshi: Amuro Namie no Kenkyu*. Tokyo: Ariakedo, 1996.

Chiba, Tetsuya, and Asao Takamori. *Ashita no Joe 16*. Tokyo: Shueisha, 1995.

Chusonji, Yutsuko. *Ojyodan*. Tokyo: Futabasha, 1994.

Cortazzi, Hugh. *The Japanese Achievement*. London: Sidgwick & Jackson Ltd.; New York: St. Martin's Press, Inc., 1990.

Doraemon Kenkyukai, comp. *Doraemon no Himitsu*. Tokyo: Data House, 1993.

Editorial Work, comp. and ed. *Yomigaere! Tantei Monogatari*. Tokyo: Nippon Television Network Corporation, 1994.

Fujibayashi, Hitoshi, ed. *1970 Ongakujin Hyakka*. Tokyo: Gakushu Kenkyusha, 1994.

Fukuma, Kenji, and Mikio Yamazaki, eds. *Dai Yakuza Eiga Yomihon*. Tokyo: Yosensha, 1993.

Go, Tomohide, ed. *Manga Hanseiki: Kakareta Nihon no Shakai*. Tokyo: Tokyo Shimbun, 1995.

Hasegawa, Machiko. *Sazae-san*. Tokyo: Asahi Shimbunsha, 1994–95.

Hiramoto, Jun'ya. *Johnny's no Subete: Shonen Ai no Kan*. Tokyo: Rokusaisha, 1996.

————. *Johnny's no Subete 2: Hanran no Ashiato*. Tokyo: Rokusaisha, 1996.

Iizuka, Tetsuo, ed. *Hochi Graph Natsu Kigo, Takarazuka Kigeki Part 3: Otori Ran*. Tokyo: Hochi Shimbunsha, 1976.

Inoue, Hiromu, ed. *Sei Media no Gojunen*. Tokyo: Takarajimasha, 1995.

————. *Ura Tokyo no Kanko*. Tokyo: Takarajimasha, 1996.

Inoue, Kozo. *Kagami no Naka no Seiko*. Tokyo: Asuka Shinsha, 1996.

Inomata, Katsuhiko, and Rikiya Tayama. *Nihon Eiga Haiyu Zenshi (Danyu Hen)*. Tokyo: Shakai Shisosha, 1977.

————. *Nihon Eiga Haiyu Zenshi (Joyu Hen)*. Tokyo: Shakai Shisosha, 1977.

Ishii, Shinji, ed. *Gei no Okurimono*. Tokyo: JICC Shuppankyoku, 1992.

Itami, Yu, ed. *Nihon no Rokku 50's — '90s*. Tokyo: Heibonsha, 1993.

Kaburagi, Kazuo. *Saredo Kohaku Uta Gassen*. Tokyo: Bureen Shuppan, 1995.

Kanazawa, Nobuyuki, ed. *Pia Cinema Club 1993 (Hoga Hen)*. Tokyo: Pia, 1993.

Kano, Masanao, ed. *Nihon Bunka no Rekishi*, Vol. 13. Tokyo: Shogakkan, 1981.

Kitanaka, Masakazu. *Nihon no Sengo Kayoshi*. Tokyo: Shinchosha, 1995.

Ko, Shintaro. *Beat Takeshi no Somi Kigen*. Tokyo: Tsunetomo Shuppan, 1996.

Koike, Satoyuki, ed. *Orikon No. 1 Hits 500 1968–1985*. Tokyo: Club House Co., Ltd., 1994.

———. *Orikon No. 1 Hits 500 1986– 1994*. Tokyo: Club House Co., Ltd., 1994.

Kurosawa, Susumu. *Nihon Rokku Ki GS Hen* Tokyo: Shinko Mujikku, 1994.

Kuroyanagi, Tetsuko. *Madogiwa no Totto-chan*. Tokyo: Kodansha, 1981.

Marrero, Robert. *Godzilla, King of the Movie Monsters*. Key West: Fantasma Books, 1996.

Matsumoto, Hitoshi. *Isho*. Tokyo: Toppan Insatsu, 1994.

McKeldin, Caroline. *Japanese Jive: Wacky and Wonderful Products from Japan*. New York: Weatherhill, 1993.

Miyamoto, Haruo. *Sengo Hiiroo Hiroin*. Tokyo: Asahi Shimbunsha, 1995.

Miyamoto, Susumu, ed. *Sengo 50 Nen 1945–1994*. Tokyo: Sashi Shimbun, 1994.

Mori, Takuya, ed. *Nippon Eiga Sengo 50 Nen 1945–1995*. Tokyo: Asahi Sonorama,1995.

Murakami Noboru. *Onyanko Panic!* Tokyo: Fuji Terebi Shuppan, 1986.

Nishii, Kazuo. *Sengo 50 Nen Post War 50 Years*. Tokyo: Mainichi Shimbunsha, 1996.

Okano, Satoshi, ed. *Sengo 50 Nen Nippon no Kiseki Shita*. Tokyo: Yomiuri Shimbunsha, 1995.

Ono, Hironobu, and Watanabe, Tsutomu, *Sengo Umare no Hiirootachi*. Tokyo: Earth Shuppankyoku, 1995.

Osaka Downtown Kenkyukai, comp. and ed. *Matsumoto & Hamada DX Hyakka*. Nishinomiya: Rokusaisha, 1996.

Oshita, Eiji. *Japaniizu Hiiroo wa Sekai o Seisu*. Tokyo: Kadokawa Shoten, 1995.

Powers, Richard Gid and Hidetoshi Kato. *The Handbook of Japanese Popular Culture*. Westport, Connecticut: Greenwood Press, 1989.

Ren'ai Kajin Kenkyukai, comp. *Yuming: Matsutoya Yumi no Nazo*. Aoyasha, Tokyo: 1996.

Sakai, Masatoshi. *Shinwa o Kizuita Sutaa no Sugao*. Tokyo: Bungei Shunju, 1995.

Sato, Tadao. *Currents In Japanese Cinema*. Tokyo: Kodansha International, Ltd., 1982.

———. *Nihon Eigashi Dai-ni Kan*. Tokyo: Iwanami Shoten, 1995.

———. *Nihon Eigashi Dai-san Kan*. Tokyo: Iwanami Shoten, 1995.

Schodt, Fredrik L. *Dreamland Japan: Writings on Modern Manga*. Berkeley: Stone Bridge Press, 1996.

Seidensticker, Edward. *Tokyo Rising: The City Since the Great Earthquake*. Rutland, Vermont, and Tokyo: Tuttle, 1991.

Sekikawa, Makoto, ed. *1980 Nen Daihyakka*. Takarajimasha, 1990.

Shinoyama, Kishin. *Santa Fe*. Tokyo: Asahi Shuppansha, 1991.

Showa Day by Day [Showa Niman Nichi no Zenkiroku]. Tokyo: Kodansha, 1991.

SMAP Oendan. *SMAP Mitsuketa!* Tokyo: Roku-saisha, 1996.

Suei, Akira. *Pachinko Dorubako Tengoku*. Tokyo: Fuga Shobo, 1995.

Suzuki, Atsushi, ed. *Waka Daisho Graffiti*. Tokyo: Kadokawa Shoten, 1995.

Takamizawa, Jun. *Miyazawa Rie Kyoshokusho Nikki*. Tokyo: Datahouse, 1995.

Takeshi, Beat. *Dakara Watashi wa Kirawareru*. Tokyo: Shinchosha, 1991.

———. *Takeshi Memo*. Tokyo: Nippon Television Corporation, 1995.

———. *Takeshi no 20 Seiki Nihonshi*. Tokyo: Shinchosha, 1996.

TK Project, comp. and ed. *Komuro Tetsuya Eiko to Satetsu*. Nishinomiya: Rokusaisha, 1996.

Tobin, Joseph J., ed. *Re-made In Japan: Everyday Life and Consumer Taste In a Changing Society*. New Haven and London: Yale University Press, 1992.

Tomita, Takeshi. *Yuming Ai no Shinso*. Tokyo: Bookmansha, 1992.

Ueda, Atsushi, ed. *The Electric Geisha: Exploring Japan's Popular Culture*. Tokyo: Kodansha International, 1994.

Usami, Tadashi. *Takarazuka Yomihon*. Osaka: Osaka Shoseki, 1987.

Yaegashi, Ken'ichi. *1970 Nen Daihyakka*. Tokyo: Takarajimasha, 1990.

————. *1960 Nen Daihyakka*. Tokyo: Takarajimasha, 1991.

Yamada, Masami. *Gojira Hon no Saishu Heiki!!* Tokyo: Kadokawa Shoten, 1995.

Yamaguchi, Takeshi. *Matsuda Yusaku Hono Shizuka ni*. Tokyo: Shakai Shisosha, 1994.

Yamazaki, Kazuo. *Gindama Oyakata no CR Ki Pachinko ga Mikka de Kateru Hon*. Tokyo: Byakusha Shobo, 1996.

Yomiuri Shimbun Gakugeibu, ed. *Terebi Bangumi no 40 Nen*. Tokyo: NHK, 1994.

SUBJECT GUIDE

ANIME

COMICS AND COMEDY

FADS, TRENDS & OBSESSIONS

FOOD

GAMES, TOYS & TECHNOLOGY

SCANDAL & CONTROVERSEY

SPORTS & MARTIAL ARTS

TELEVISION & TELEVISION SHOWS

INDEX

ILLUSTRATION CREDITS

Page 23. *Namennayo!* cat, reprinted from *Sengo 50 Nen Post War 50 Years.*

Page 26. Ashita no Joe, reprinted from *Ashita no Joe,* No. 16, published by Shueisha.

Page 28. Condoms, reprinted from *Japanese Jive.*

Page 31. Chibi Maruko-chan, reproduced with the permission of Nippon Animation.

Page 33. The Three Sacred Treasures of early postwar consumerism, reprinted from *Manga Hanseiki.*

Page 35. Early outdoor televsion broadcast, reproduced with the permission of Japan Actor's Association and Nippon Hoso Kyokai.

Page 40. Doraemon and Nobita, reproduced with the permission of Fujiko Production / Shogakkan / TV Asahi.

Page 43. Doraemon, reproduced with the permission of Fujiko Production / Shogakkan / TV Asahi.

Page 46. Hitoshi Matsumoto and Masatoshi Hamada, reproduced with the permission of Kyodo Tsushin.

Page 53. The Drifters, reprinted from a promotional photograph.

Page 56. Kyosen Ohashi, reproduced with the permission of Kyodo Tsushin.

Page 66. Cover of a 1964 *Heibon Punch.*

Page 69. Instant ramen, photo courtesy of Nissin Food Products Co. Ltd.

Page 72. Poster of *Arashi o Yobu Otoko,* starring Yujiro Ishihara.

Page 77. Platform fan dancers at Juliana's, reprinted from *Sengo 50 Nen Post War 50 Years.*

Page 82. Hiroko Yakushimaru in a still from *Sailor Fuku to Kikanju.*

Page 97. A still from *Kohaku Uta Gassen,* reproduced with the permission of Nippon Hoso Kyokai.

Page 107. Covers of the Japanese and English editions of *Totto-chan,* reproduced with the permission of Kodansha.

Page 112. Mario © 1997 Nintendo. Image courtesy of Nintendo America, Inc.

Page 117. Seiko Matsuda, reprinted from a publicity still for *Karibu Ai no Symphony* (Carib, Symphony of Love).

Page 119. Seiko Matsuda, reprinted from a publicity still for *Karibu Ai no Symphony* (Carib, Symphony of Love).

Page 126. The cover of a 1994 book about the series *Tantei Monogatari,* reproduced with the permission of Nippon Television Network.

Page 131. Hibari Misora, reproduced with the permission of Hibari Productions.

Page 136. Still from *Mito Komon*, reproduced with the permission of Tokyo Broadcasting System, Inc.

Page 139. *Majo no Takkyubin* (Kiki's Delivery Service), © 1989 Eiko Kadono / Nibariki / Tokuma Shoten Publishing Co., Ltd, reproduced with the permission of Studio Ghibli.

Page 142. *Tonari no Totoro* (My Neighbor Totoro), © 1988 Nibariki / Tokuma Shoten Publishing Co., Ltd, reproduced with the permission of Studio Ghibli.

Page 145. *Pom Poko*, © Hatake Jimusyo • TNHG / 1994, reproduced with the permission of Studio Ghibli.

Page 148. Rie Miyazawa in the cover shot from *Santa Fe*, photograph by Kishin Shinoyama, reproduced with the permission of Asahi Shuppansha.

Page 152. Hitoshi Ueki with the Crazy Cats and cast members of *Nippon Musekinin Jidai,* reproduced from publicity stills.

Page 158. *Naruhodo the World*, reprinted from a Fuji TV publicity still.

Page 161. *News Station*, reprinted from a TV Asahi publicity still.

Page 165. Still from *Nodo Jiman*, reproduced with the permission of Nippon Hoso Kyokai.

Page 167. Onyanko Club, reprinted from *Onyanko Panic!*

Page 170. Ayako Kobayashi as Oshin, reproduced with the permission of Nippon Hoso Kyokai.

Page 173. *Akira*, by Otomo Katsuhiro. Copyright © 1984 Mash.Room Co., Ltd. All rights reserved.

Page 185. *Pachinko,* photograph by Tomoyuki Furuichi.

Page 188. Pink Lady, reproduced from *Myojo* magazine with the permission of Mitsuyo Nemoto, Keiko Matsuda, *Myojo,* and Victor Records.

Page 191. The Power Rangers, reproduced with the permission of Toei Co., Ltd.

Page 195. Rikidozan, reprinted from *Manga Hanseiki.*

Page 203. The Tigers, reprinted from *Nihon no Rokku 50's–90's.*

Page 207. *The Rose of Versailles*, reproduced with the permission of Riyoko Ikeda and Shueisha Bunko.

Page 211. Crown Prince Akihito and Princess Michiko's wedding procession, reproduced with the permission of Kyodo Tsushin.

Page 217. Kyu Sakamoto, reprinted from *Nihon no Rokku 50's–90's.*

Page 219. Still from *Sannen B Gumi Kimpachi Sensei*, reproduced with the permission of Tokyo Broadcasting System, Inc.

Page 222. Hello Kitty, reproduced with the permission of Sanrio.

Page 225. Covers of three volumes of the *Sazaesan manga* series.

Page 226. Machiko Hasegawa, reprinted from *Sengo 50 Nen Post War 50 Years.*

Page 228. Cover of *Shonen Jump.*

Page 233. The 1995 SMAP line-up, reprinted from *SMAP Year Book 1994–1995 Revival & Evolution.*

Page 240. Takanohana receives the championship flag from his brother, the former Wakanohana, reproduced with the permission of *Sumo World.*

Page 243. The second Takanohana, together with his father and mother, greet fans outside Futagoyama Stable, reproduced with the permission of *Sumo World.*

Page 247. Onoe Kikugoro and Ken Ogata in a still from *Minamoto Yoshitsune,* reproduced with the permission of Japan Actor's Association and Nippon Hoso Kyokai.

Page 252. Ran Otori, reprinted from *Hochi Graph,* reproduced with the permission of Takarazuka.

Page 255. Beat Takeshi, reprinted from *Sengo 50 Nen Post War 50 Years.*

Page 258. Beat Takeshi and Beat Kiyoshi, reprinted from *Sengo 50 Nen Post War 50 Years.*

Page 261. Beat Takeshi in a still from *Sonatine,* reproduced with the permission of Office Takano and Shochiku Co., Ltd.

Page 264. Early Tekuza comics, reproduced with the permission of Tezuka Productions.

Page 267. Tetsuwan Atom (Astro Boy), reproduced with the permission of Tezuka Productions.

Page 270. Yuko Tanaka and Kiyoshi Atsumi in a still from *Otoko was Tsurai yo: Hana mo Arashi mo Torajiro* (Tora-san, The Expert), reproduced with the permission of Shochiku Co., Ltd.

Page 279. Ultraman, reproduced with the permission of Tsuburaya Productions Co., Ltd. Ultra-man is a registered trademark of Tsuburaya Productions Co., Ltd. © 1997 Tsuburaya Productions.

Page 282. Waka Daisho, reprinted from a publicity still.

Page 287. Koji Tsuruta and Ryoko Sakauma in a still from *Jinsei Gekijo: Hishakaku* (The Theater of Life: Hishakaku), reproduced with the permission of Toei Co., Ltd.

Page 291. Ken Takakura in a still from *Nihon Yakuza Den: Socho e no Michi,* reproduced with the permission of Toei Co., Ltd.

Page 292. Junko Fuji in a still from *Hibotan Bakuto: Tekkaba Retsuden,* reproduced with the permission of Toei Co., Ltd.

Page 294. Bunta Sugawara in a still from *Jingi Naki Tatakai,* reproduced with the permission of Toei Co., Ltd.

Page 297. Momoe Yamaguchi, reprinted from a publicity still for *Kiri no Hata* (The Banner of Mist).

Page 298. Momoe Yamaguchi and Tomokazu Miura, reprinted from a publicity still for *Kiri no Hata* (The Banner of Mist).

Page 302. YMO, reproduced with the permission of Alpha Records.

Page 307. Sayuri Yoshinaga in a poster for *Cupola no Aru Machi* (A Street of Cupolas).

Page 308. Sayuri Yoshinaga, reprinted from a publicity still.

Page 311. Yosui Inoue, reprinted from *Nihon no Rokku 50's–90's.*

Page 313. Yumi Matsutoya (née Arai), reprinted from *Nihon no Rokku 50's–90's.*

The "weathermark" identifies this book as a production of Weatherhill, publishers of fine books on Asia and the Pacific. Editorial supervision: Jeffrey Hunter. Book and cover design: David S. Noble. Production supervision: Bill Rose. Printing and binding: Quebecor Printing Company, Fairfield, Pennsylvania. The typefaces used are Stone Informal and Stone Sans, with Bauhaus for display.